Forensic Linguistics

Forensic Linguistics

Advances in Forensic Stylistics

Gerald R. McMenamin

with contributions by

Dongdoo Choi
Forensic Linguistics Institute
California State University, Fresno
Fresno, California

P.J. Mistry
Department of Linguistics
California State University, Fresno
Fresno, California

Susan Morton
Criminalistics Laboratory
San Francisco Police Department
San Francisco, California

Wakako Yasuda
Forensic Linguistics Institute
California State University, Fresno
Fresno, California

CRC PRESS

Boca Raton   London   New York   Washington, D.C.

Library of Congress Cataloging-in-Publication Data

Forensic linguistics : advances in forensic stylistics / by Gerald R. McMenamin.
   p. cm.
Includes bibliographical references and index.
ISBN 0-8493-0966-2 (alk. paper)
   1. Forensic linguistics. 2. Language and languages--Style. I. McMenamin, Gerald R.

K5485 . F674 2002
410--dc21

2002017447

Visit the CRC Press Web site at www.crcpress.com

© 2002 by CRC Press LLC

No claim to original U.S. Government works
International Standard Book Number 0-8493-0966-2
Library of Congress Card Number 2002017447
Printed in the United States of America 1 2 3 4 5 6 7 8 9 0
Printed on acid-free paper

For Marguerite,

¡me regalas las flores de la esperanza!

The Author

Gerald McMenamin lives with his wife, Marguerite, on a small Tivy Valley citrus ranch near Sanger, CA. He benefited from an intense elementary and secondary education at Salesian schools in California and New Jersey. In 1968, he received a B.A. in philosophy, with minors in classical languages and English, from the University of California at Irvine, and in 1972 an M.A. in linguistics from California State University, Fresno. In 1978, he received his doctorate in Spanish linguistics from El Colegio de México. Part of his doctoral program was 2 years study of linguistic variation at the University of Pennsylvania. His other study and research venues include the University of California at Santa Cruz, the UCLA Medical Center, and Oxford University.

Dr. McMenamin has taught a variety of courses in English and Spanish linguistics in positions at the Universidad Autónoma de Guadalajara, the University of Delaware, and UCLA. Since 1980 he has been a Professor of Linguistics at California State University, Fresno, and is a former chair of the CSUF linguistics department. His interest in linguistic stylistics began in 1976 with an authorship study of the picaresque novel, *Lazarillo de Tormes*; this experience quickly extended to forensic applications. Since that time, Dr. McMenamin has taught various courses and special training seminars in linguistic stylistics and has worked on more than 250 civil and criminal cases of questioned authorship. He is the author of several publications in forensic linguistics, including the 1993 book *Forensic Stylistics*.

Contributors

Dongdoo Choi
Forensic Linguistics Institute
California State University, Fresno
Fresno, California

P.J. Mistry
Department of Linguistics
California State University, Fresno
Fresno, California

Susan Morton
Criminalistics Laboratory, San Francisco
  Police Department
San Francisco, California

Wakako Yasuda
Forensic Linguistics Institute
California State University, Fresno
Fresno, California

Introduction

The first questions I am presented with on direct examination are always to describe and explain what I do. This requires a series of brief and clear responses defining the theory and the nested array of analytical tools used in cases of questioned authorship: language, linguistics, linguistic variation, forensic linguistics, style, stylistics, and forensic stylistics.

Consequently, I have used these questions to define the aims and structure of this book: to provide an introduction to *language, linguistics,* and *linguistic variation* for nonlinguists (e.g., attorneys) who need to understand what linguist-witnesses do; to introduce the discipline of *forensic linguistics;* and to situate *forensic stylistics* as a field of language study and forensic analysis within the discipline of forensic linguistics. Chapters 1 through 6 will approximate this sequence.

Although the linguistic study of language is well established, linguistics is something new for many jurors, judges, attorneys, and other forensic specialists. In addition, many linguists must learn how to talk about what they do in nontechnical terms, something accomplished to some degree here, I hope.

Forensic linguistics is not a new field, but over the past few years it has become more structured and better defined within the academic and forensic communities. Is it the accused killer's voice on the 911 recording reporting the crime? What exactly does it mean to die by accident, e.g., is sudden infant death an accident? Is it a request for drugs if a kid asks an undercover police officer, "What's chillin?" Does it make any sense to say that someone did not commit genocide, just acts of genocide (*The New York Times,* August 26, 2001)? Who did, or did not, write that ransom note found in the JonBenét Ramsey home? If a detective asks a suspect, "… do you want to speak with us about why you were arrested?" is the suspect waiving his right not to speak by answering, "Yes, I would like to know why I was arrested"? Does McDonald's own the *Mc* at the beginning of my last name (Liptak, 2001:10)?

These examples illustrate a few of the questions for forensic linguistics: *phonetics* (911 call), *semantics* (meaning of *accident*), *pragmatics* (intended meanings of "What's chillin'?" and *genocide*), *stylistics* (authorship of the ransom note), *discourse analysis* (suspect waiver of rights), and *trademarks* (McDonald's *Mc*).

An understanding of language, linguistics, and the field of forensic linguistics will enable the reader to develop a more informed understanding of recent advances in the theory and method of forensic stylistics for authorship identification. Style is a reflection of individual and group variation in written language. Linguistic stylistics is the scientific study of individual style-markers as described for the idiolect of a single writer and of class style-markers identified for language and dialect groups. Forensic stylistics is the application of the science of linguistic stylistics to forensic contexts and purposes.

"Advances" in forensic stylistics refers to the progressive development of a deeper understanding of why and how present approaches work, as well as changes being made in the application of style analysis to cases of questioned authorship. Such advances have several sources: recent casework, new federal requirements for scientific evidence in the U.S., reexamination of the theory of style and its application to the forensic context, and critical response to documented approaches such as those presented in *Forensic Stylistics* (McMenamin, 1993). Advances in forensic stylistics are the matter of Chapters 7 to 11. Chapters 12 to 15 reflect new work in the stylistics of languages other than English.

Clarification of the theoretical underpinnings of stylistic analysis is an important step forward because, first, it helps explain and reduce differences between practitioners (linguists) in the forensic application of stylistics, and second, it provides a stronger theoretical foundation for the actual forensic application of stylistics to authorship questions.

Although linguists will not need the chapters of this book that outline the basics of language and linguistics, the chapters on forensic linguistics, authorship identification, and forensic practice are meant for linguists, as well as others. One goal of this book is to convince more linguists to "come in from the outside," i.e., become involved in the actual casework of forensic linguistics, or what Roger Shuy (2000:1) refers to as "insider linguists":

> ... I will divide this work that forensic linguists do into two types: work that is done without becoming involved in specific litigation, which I will call outsider work, and work that is carried out within individual law cases, which I refer to as insider work.

The discipline and science of forensic linguistics will not develop the way it should from "outside" study, commentary, and observation. Linguists must take some of Shuy's hints about how to immerse themselves in the problems presented by actual cases, then develop their linguistic and forensic perspectives based on that work.

Many colleagues have helped me during the preparation of this book. While any and all deficiencies in my work are my sole responsibility, I would like to acknowledge and thank those who have worked through this project with me. First and foremost, my wife Marguerite, is a safe harbor of constancy and encouragement. She says that she missed me during this project but seems to have enjoyed single handedly finding a diesel-powered lift and painting our big barn under the wide-eyed and very solicitous supervision of half a dozen neighboring farmers. Karen Mistry read the typescript, combining the mind of a perceptive linguist with the eye of a meticulous reader and editor. Ray Weitzman prepared the phonetics demonstrations in Figures 4.1 and 4.2. Cecilia Shore sent me references on individualization in the acquisition of writing. A Forsyth and Holmes (1996) article directed me to the 1817 words of Coleridge: "Every man's language has, first, it individualities; second, the common properties of the class to which he belongs; and third, words and phrases of universal use." Roger Gong, Merlyn Price, Kerala Serio, Alan Shows, and, especially, John Telles joined their skilled forces to keep me alive and well, at work, and (almost) on time. Zachary Scheufele and Chasse Byrd frequently reminded me of other things in life. Deans Luis Costa and Vida Samiian of the California State University (CSU) Fresno School of Arts and Humanities provided periodic financial assistance for research.

Roger Shuy evaluated my initial prospectus and also provided me with the written version of his Georgetown University Round Table in Linguistics (GURT) 2000 keynote address so that I would not have to depend on my notes for reference. Fred Brengelman, Duane Dillon, and Roy Huber also took the time to comment on the initial plan of this book. Kristina Perez did the identification of variables from the as yet undigitized corpus of written American English, reflected in Chapter 10. Shannon Bills classified and counted the variables from the 80 authorship cases reviewed in Chapter 11. Alejandra Herrera analyzed the Spanish language data from student e-mails reported on in Chapter 12. Rekha Dayalu did the research necessary for me to understand the field of software forensics outlined in Chapter 4. CSU Fresno Librarian Jan Byrd patiently and efficiently ordered and returned books in the continuous year-long flow of interlibrary loan materials needed to complete this project. Lynnette Zelezny provided a critical review of Chapter 8, and Phyllis Kuehn a statistical perspective on parts of Chapter 10.

All my associates in the Southwestern Association of Forensic Document Examiners, especially the late professor Dean Ray, have provided me with nearly 20 years of training in forensic science, and individual document examiners have provided help with cases and issues reported on here, namely Martha Blake, Lloyd Cunningham, Bill Flynn, Sandy Homewood, Dave Moore, Janet Masson, Sue Morton, Dave Oleksow, Howard Rile, and Peter Tytell.

I am particularly indebted to the contributors of this volume who generously provided reports of their own research in the style analysis of languages other than English and Spanish: P. J. Mistry for Gujarati, from Northern India (Chapter 13), Dongdoo Choi for Korean (Chapter 14), and Wakako Yasuda for Japanese (Chapter 15). Another contribution is the insightful essay found in Appendix 2, *Expert Testimony*, by Susan Morton of the San Francisco Police Criminalistics Laboratory, wherein she shares with forensic specialists what she has tried to make me understand for years.

References

Forsyth, R. S. and Holmes, D. I., Feature-finding for text classification, *Lit. Linguistic Comput.*, 11:4:163–174, 1996.

Lewis, N. A., Did machete-wielding Hutus commit genocide or just "acts of genocide," *The New York Times*, August 26, 2001, Sec. 4, p. 7.

Liptak, A. Legally, the alphabet isn't as simple as A, B, C, *The New York Times*, September 2, 2001, Sec. 4, p. 10.

McMenamin, G., *Forensic Stylistics*, Elsevier Science Publishers, Amsterdam, 1993.

Shuy, R., Breaking into language and law: the trials of the insider-linguist, paper presented at *Georgetown University Round Table in Linguistics (GURT): Languages of the Professions*, May 4, 2000.

Table of Contents

4   Forensic Linguistics   67

Gerald R. McMenamin

13   Stylistic Features of Gujarati Letter Writing: A Note   269

P. J. Mistry

Language

GERALD R. McMENAMIN

1

1.1 Overview

The purpose of this chapter is to present an introduction to language for the nonlinguist. Perhaps the most difficult task for specialists in any field is to provide a brief, but clear and simple, description of the object of their scientific study. Expert witnesses, including linguists, are asked to do this almost every time they testify. Linguists must be able to successfully answer the question, "What is language?" for everyone in the courtroom, i.e., judges and juries (triers of fact) and all attorneys involved in a case, as well as observers. This is no small task, given the usual time constraints, varying individual levels of prior knowledge about language, and the expert's need to avoid technical descriptions that may be incomprehensible to everyone else.

The ability of speakers and writers to use language does not usually correspond to much of an understanding of the inner workings of the linguistic system that they possess and so easily apply. The use of language, driven as it is by unconscious knowledge, is analogous to how one does many things, such as driving a car without understanding its internal electromechanical systems. Yet, someone needs to understand them: a mechanic must know, evaluate, and maintain the car's under-the-hood systems to keep it running; a doctor knows enough about under-the-skin systems to keep one alive and well.

The goal of the linguist is to understand units of language, their possible rule-governed combinations, and the conditions for how language is used, as well as the norms of correct and appropriate language for a given speech community. The objective of the forensic linguist is to do the same within the narrower context of the court, i.e., to examine what language users know and do, and make everyone in the courtroom a good "backyard mechanic" of language for the duration of a case.

Therefore, another more practical purpose of this chapter is to ask and answer the questions on language asked at trial, usually during direct examination: What is grammar? What is language? How is language acquired? Are there individual differences in language acquisition? What is linguistic variation? What is written language? How is written language acquired? Are there individual differences in the acquisition of written language? The focus on written language surfaces in questioned-authorship cases. What follows reflects this series of typical questions and provides responses that will hopefully become the basis for understanding the goals, methods, and outcomes of forensic linguistics and forensic stylistics.

1.2   Grammar

Linguists recognize that the word "grammar" is used in different ways, and they purposely use its multiple meanings to identify three objects of scientific inquiry. Grammar$_1$ cannot be found in a book because it refers to the internal system of language that every native speaker acquires and uses. Grammar$_2$ is the systematic study and description of that internal system of language, a "descriptive grammar" that is documented in a book. Grammar$_3$ is a set of rules and examples of the do's and don't's of a language and is the type of prescriptive grammar reflected in library reference works and school texts directed to prescribing the correct and appropriate use of language, i.e., speaking and writing well.

The purpose for explaining the three uses of grammar is to specify that asking and answering the question, "What is language?" takes place mostly within the context of grammar$_1$, the internal system of language that allows speakers and writers to automatically use language. See Figure 1.1 for a summary of the meanings of grammar in the outline of "What is language?"

1.3   Language

Language is a system of communication. In this broad sense, human language is a code that communicates meaning, as do other types of communication systems such as animal sounds and movements, Morse code dots and dashes, traffic control signs and lights, human gestures and body language, and even computer source code.

More precisely, human language is a system of communication that combines sounds with meanings to produce what people know and use as natural language. This narrower definition of natural language distinguishes human language from other communication systems such as those mentioned above. The speaker of a language acquires the ability to combine one or more sounds into words, and words into larger structures, which the speaker and listener then mutually associate with meanings specific to that particular language and social context.

Furthermore, language can be studied on the two complementary and inseparable planes of form and function. Form corresponds to the structure of language, defined as a linguistic system. Function relates to a focus on language use, defined as an integral part of human social interaction. The

Grammar and Language

THREE MEANINGS OF "GRAMMAR"

1. *The internal system* of language that every native speaker acquires
2. The *systematic study and description of that internal system* of language: descriptive
3. *A set of rules and examples* for correct and appropriate use of a language: prescriptive

LANGUAGE FORM

Phonetics is the study of speech sounds:
segmental sounds: consonants and vowels; *suprasegmental* sounds: stress, intonation, tone, intensity, speed

Phonology is the study of how a language arranges sounds in predictable patterns:
inventory of sounds: "phonemes"; *distribution* of sounds: word position, syllable structure, consonant clusters, processes of sound change; *spelling*: sounds and letters

Morphology is the study of word formation:
morphemes: building blocks of meaning; *analytic* vis-à-vis *synthetic* languages; *roots* and *affixes*; *allomorphs* of roots and affixes; *word-formation processes*; *function* words: articles, conjunctions, etc., vis-à-vis *content* words: nouns, verbs, adjectives, adverbs

The Lexicon is the collection of word-parts and words that combine into larger units: word-parts into words, and words into utterances

Syntax is the study of how words are combined into longer sequences:
phrase and sentence structure; basic sentences vis-à-vis transformed sentences; grammatical categories: 1. relate language to situation of utterance (person, number, case, tense, mood), 2. parts of speech (noun, verb, adjective, adverb, article, conjunction, preposition, pronoun, interjection), 3. elements of sentence-function (subject, predicate, complement, adverbial, (in)transitive, auxiliary verb, active/passive)

Semantics is the study of meaning in words and sentences:
meaning in words: *sense* (words vis-a-vis other words, e.g., synonyms, antonyms, etc.), *reference* (words vis-à-vis things/situations/action in the world; meaning in sentences: the sum of parts vis-à-vis the arrangement of parts

LANGUAGE FUNCTION

Discourse Analysis is the study of language units beyond the sentence:
units of speech and writing as they relate to communicative events; as they relate to their cultural and social contexts of use; *conversation*; *narratives*

Pragmatics is the study of intended meaning:
intended meaning; *speech acts* and *performative verbs*; how to do things with language; *(in)directness*

Figure 1.1 What is language?

functions of language relate to how language is used in the contexts of speaking and getting things done through communication.

Note that linguists routinely break language up into the various components laid out in Figure 1.1. Such compartmentalization makes language easier to study and describe, and it is often useful to separate the components of language study to better understand language. On the other hand, language itself simultaneously incorporates all these components together in speakers and writers.

1.3.1 Language Form

Phonetics is the study of speech sounds. Human speech sounds are studied in three ways: articulatory phonetics focuses on how sounds are physically formed in the human vocal tract; acoustic phonetics studies the physical characteristics of the sounds as they are transmitted from the speaker; and auditory phonetics studies sound characteristics as they are received and perceived by the hearer. For practical purposes, such as describing language sounds, articulatory descriptions are often the most useful, but acoustic means are frequently used to study units of sound and how they are produced, perceived, described, and analyzed in forensic contexts.

Languages have two types of sounds: the segmental sounds of every language are its consonants and vowels, and the suprasegmental sounds of a language are phonetic elements that occur on and around vowels and consonants, such as stress on vowels, intonation on sentences, tone on words, intensity (loudness), and speed of speech.

Consonants are described in terms of three articulatory variables: point of articulation, manner of articulation (e.g., air flow and relative mouth opening), and voicing (vibration of the vocal folds). The consonants of English can be described this way (see Figure 1.2).

Note that English sometimes has more than one spelling for a single consonant sound, e.g., /k/ in *cake* and *kick*, or more than one sound represented by a single consonant spelling, e.g., /s/ and /z/ in *gas* and *was*. (Symbols like /k/ inside diagonal bars refer to the sounds of language, not their spellings.) Figure 1.3 relates sounds to spellings for English consonants.

The vowels of English are described in terms of the vertical and horizontal position of the tongue in the mouth. The tongue is simultaneously in one of the vertical positions (high, mid, or low), and in one of the horizontal positions (front, central, or back), as may be seen in Figure 1.4.

Note also that English sometimes has more than one spelling (letter) for a single vowel sound (e.g., $/i_1/$ in *beet* and *beat*), or more than one sound represented by a single vowel spelling (e.g., $/i_1/$ and $/e_1/$ in *meat* and *great*). Other sounds vis-à-vis spellings of English vowels are listed in Figure 1.5.

Point of Articulation

Manner of Articulation		BILABIAL	LABIODENTAL	INTERDENTAL	ALVEOLAR	PALATAL	VELAR	GLOTTAL
STOPS	Voiceless →	/p/ pear			/t/ tear		/k/ care	/ʔ/ uh-oh
	Voiced →	/b/ bear			/d/ dare		/g/ gap	
FRICATIVES	Voiceless →		/f/ fair	/th/₁ theory	/s/ Sarah	/sh/ share		/h/ hair
	Voiced →		/v/ very	/th/₂ there	/z/ zoo	/zh/ leisure		
AFFRICATES	Voiceless →					/tsh/ chair		
	Voiced →					/dzh/ jar		
NASALS	Voiceless →							
	Voiced →	/m/ mare			/n/ near		/ng/ ring	
LIQUIDS	Voiceless →							
	Voiced →				/l/ lair /r/ rare			
GLIDES	Voiceless →							
	Voiced →	/w/ wear				/y/ year		

Figure 1.2 The consonant sounds of English.

CONSONANTS	Single-Letter Regular-Spellings[1]	Double-Letter Regular-Spellings[2]	Exceptional Spellings[3]
STOPS			
/p/	pear	apple	hiccough
/b/	bear	cobble	
/t/	tear	tattle	kissed, doubt, debt, ptomaine, yacht
/d/	dare	ladder	raised
/k/	care, act, chic, comic, kitten, make, tank	kicker, kick	character, boutique, /ks/: excellent, /kw/: quick
/g/	gap	giggle	ghost, ghoul, burgh
FRICATIVES			
/f/	fair	coffee, puff	photograph, philosophy, laugh, cough
/v/	very, ever, move, stove		of
/th/₁	theory, think, ether, bath, wreath		
/th/₂	there, the, either, bathe		
/s/	cinder, cellar, sister, ice, cast, case	kissing, miss	psychology, science
/z/	zoo, rose, advise, incise	fuzzy, buzz	kisses, scissors, Xerox, is, was
/sh/	share, ashen, wish, nation, racial, mission		sure, ocean, chagrin, mustache, schnitzel
/zh/	leisure, vision, decision		genre, azure, fission, garage,
/h/	hair		who, jalapeño
AFFRICATES			
/tsh/	chair, teacher, beach	pitcher, catch	future, righteous
/dzh/	jar, gem, raging, page	judging, judge	residual

Adapted from Brengelman (1970), *The English Language: An Introduction for Teachers,* Prentice-Hall, Englewood Cliffs, NJ. With permission.

Notes:

[1] Single-Letter Regular-Spellings = morpheme initial and other environments

[2] Double-Letter Regular-Spellings = between Vs after short/stressed V, and word-final after short V for fricatives

[3] Exceptional Spellings = common as well as uncommon exceptions to the regular spellings.

Figure 1.3 Variable spellings for English consonants.

CONSONANTS	Single-Letter Regular-Spellings[1]	Double-Letter Regular-Spellings[2]	Exceptional Spellings[3]
NASALS			
/m/	mare, steaming, steam, swim	mammal, swimming	autumn, comb
/n/	near, planer, tan, pain	planner	gnome, gnat, know, knife, mnemonic, pneumonia
/ng/	think, ring, ringer		
LIQUIDS			
/l/	let, inlet, tail, tailor, tangle	tall, taller, telling	kiln
/r/	rare, bury, bearing, bar	berry, barring	write, rhyme
GLIDES			
/w/	wear, twin		quick, where
/y/	year		unit, few, fuel, feud, mute, view

Adapted from Brengelman (1970), *The English Language*: *An Introduction for Teachers*, Prentice-Hall, Englewood Cliffs, NJ. With permission.

Notes:
[1] Single-Letter Regular-Spellings = morpheme initial and other environments
[2] Double-Letter Regular-Spellings = between Vs after short/stressed V, and word-final after short V for fricatives
[3] Exceptional Spellings = common as well as uncommon exceptions to the regular spellings.

Figure 1.3 (Continued) Variable spellings for English consonants.

Vertical Tongue Position	Horizontal Tongue Position		
	FRONT	**CENTRAL**	**BACK**
HIGH	/i/₁ beet /i/₂ bit		/u/₁ boot /u/₂ put
MID	/e/₁ bait /e/₂ bet	/u/₃ cut	/o/₁ boat /o/₂ bought
LOW	/a/₁ bat	/a/₂ pot	

Diphthongs (two vowels combined into one)

/a/ + /i/ = **/ay/** bite
/a/ + /u/ = **/aw/** bout
/o/ + /i/ = **/oy/** boy

Notes: Shaded vowels / **V** / = "long" vowels.

Unshaded vowels / **V** / = "short" vowels.

Figure 1.4 The vowel sounds of English.

VOWELS	LENGTH	Usual Regular-Spellings[1]	Other Regular-Spellings[2]	Exceptional Spellings[3]
HIGH				
/i/₁	Long	beet, beat, impede	be, thief, receive, yield	ski, seize, key, people
/i/₂	Short	bit	myth, nymph	build, been[4]
/u/₁	Long	tune, moot, too	due, dew, group	shoe, who, do, you, flu, through, two, to
/u/₂	Short	put, foot		would, should, could
MID				
/e/₁	Long	bate, bait, say	vein, sleigh	great, break, they, where
/e/₂	Short	bet, dead, ebb		said
/u/₃	Short	up, cut[5]	sir, burn, word, tough, young, country	blood, were, was, learn, does, some, ton, love, one
/o/₁	Long	vote, boat, bow, own	bore, boar, oat, open, toe, so, bow, dough, most, old	sew
/o/₂	Short	log	bought, caught, balk	broad
LOW				
/a/₁	Short	at, bat		plaid, laugh, bawl, pawn
/a/₂	Short	pot	far, on, ha ha, wad, calm	heart, are

DIPHTHONGS				
/ay/	Long	bite	fire, idle, die, by, bye, cycle find, mild, light, sign	guy, buy, aisle height
/aw/	Long	bow, our, hour, trout	hour, out, cow, plough	sauerkraut
/oy/	Long	oil, boil, boys, boy		buoyed

Notes:

[1] Usual Regular-Spellings = spellings found in most words.
[2] Other Regular-Spellings = spellings found in special environments, like before -r, word-initial/-final, etc.
[3] Exceptional Spellings = common exceptions to the regular spellings.
[4] Vowel sounds may not match all English dialects, e.g., been may rhyme with "tin" or "ten."
[5] Vowels for cut and sir will have different sounds in the so-called r-less dialects of English.

Source: Adapted from Brengelman (1970), *The English Language: An Introduction for Teachers*, Prentice Hall, Englewood Cliffs, NJ. With permission.

Figure 1.5 Variable spellings for English vowels.

Phonology is the study of how a language arranges sounds in predictable patterns. Such patterns include the actual inventory of sounds (phonemes) for a given language, as well as the distribution of the sounds in that language. The inventory of sounds is the specific and relatively small set of sounds used by a language, taken from the large set of all possible human language sounds. For example, English has the j-sound in "**judge**," but most varieties of Spanish do not have this sound.

The distribution of sounds refers to four ways that sounds are positioned. First, the phonology specifies possible initial, medial, or final word positions of sounds, i.e., where in a word of the language (beginning, middle, or end) a particular sound can occur. For example, English has many words that end in -*b* and -*g* sounds, but words in Spanish do not end in -*b* or -*g*. In English, all vowels and consonants except /h/ appear in word-medial and -final positions, and all except /ng/ and /zh/ occur in word-initial position. In contrast, word-final consonant sounds in Spanish are only -*r, -d, -l, -s, -n* (with some exceptions occurring in borrowed words).

Second, vowels form the nucleus of the syllable, and the phonology specifies how and which consonants may group around a vowel to make a syllable. Syllables are divided into two parts, onset and rhyme. The onset consists of any consonants that precede the vowel. The rhyme consists of the vowel nucleus and the coda, i.e., any consonants following the vowel, ranging from none to three. English has 16 possible syllable structures, although some of these do not occur very often. Other languages have very different syllable structures. For example, most varieties of Hmong, a language spoken in the highlands of Laos and now in parts of the U.S., have just two syllable types: CV and CCV. The syllable types of English are listed in Figure 1.6.

Third, only certain consonants will group together into those clusters that occur before and after vowels, and the phonology of a language tells which ones can cluster, in what order, and where the clusters can appear in the word. For example, English allows many words to end in one, two, and three consonants (e.g., *an, ant, ants*), but the consonant limit at the end of a word in Spanish is one. Word-initial sound clusters in English are /pl- pr- py- pw- tr- tw- kl- kr- ky- kw- bl- br- by- dr- dw- gl- gr- gy- fl- fr- fy- th$_1$r- th$_1$w- hy- hw- vy- my- ny- sl- sw- sp- st- sk- sf- sv- sm- sn- sl- sr- sw- sn- spl- spr- spy- str- skl- skr- skw-/, etc. Word-final sound clusters in English are /-ps -ts -ks -fs -th$_1$s -bz -dz -gz -vz -dz -mz -nz -nzh -lz -rz -ns -ls -rs -mp -nt -nd -nk -mps -nts -ndz -nks -nth$_1$ -mf -ntsh -ns -lp -lt -lk -lps -rst -tsht -sht -pt -sp -st -sk -skt/, etc.

Last, consonants combine with other sounds in and around them, and the phonology of a language describes and predicts the slight changes each sound might undergo in certain predictable contexts. For example, say the words *lip* and *pill*, and notice that the *ls* are slightly different sounds, what

SYLLABLE				EXAMPLES
↓				
ONSET +		RHYME		O | V | C
		↓		N | O | O
				S | W | D
				E | E | A
		Vowel + Coda		T | L |
1.		V		| *a* |
2.	C	V		*n* | *o* |
3.	CC	V		*fl* | *ow* |
4.	CCC	V		*spr* | *ay* |
5.		V	C	| *i* | *n*
6.	C	V	C	*t* | *i* | *n*
7.	CC	V	C	*sp* | *i* | *n*
8.	CCC	V	C	*spl* | *i* | *t*
9.		V	CC	| *a* | *sk*
10.	C	V	CC	*t* | *a* | *sk*
11.	CC	V	CC	*fl* | *a* | *sk*
12.	CCC	V	CC	*str* | *i* | *pped*
13.		V	CCC	| *a* | *sked*
14.	C	V	CCC	*m* | *a* | *sked*
15.	CC	V	CCC	*pr* | *a* | *nks*
16.	CCC	V	CCC	*str* | *a* | *nds*

Notes:

1. Syllable structure is based on *sounds*, not spelling, e.g., "brought" has a CCVC structure: **/brɑt/**.
2. Parts of the syllable are these:

    Syllable = two parts: onset + rhyme
    Onset   = consonants that appear before the vowel
    Rhyme = two parts: nucleus + coda
    Nucleus = the vowel
    Coda   = consonants that appear after the vowel

Figure 1.6 The structure of English syllables.

the dictionary calls the word-initial *light l* of *lip* and the word-final *dark l* of *pill*. In *vowel reduction,* all English vowels sound something like the vowel in *cut* when they are not stressed, e.g., the different pronunciation of *man-* in *mánly* vs. *-man* in *fíreman.* In *syllabication,* these same vowels tend to be lost when they occur before vowel-like consonants such as /-l, -r, -m, -n, -ng/, e.g., *fireman* sounds like *firemn.* In *flapping,* consonants /t/ and /d/ are just a quick d-like flap of the tongue tip in words like *otter* ands *spider.* In *aspiration,* the consonants /p, t, k/ expel a slight puff of air when they are word-initial before a vowel, e.g., note the slightly plosive pronunciation of /p/ in *pin* but not in *spin.*

Writers, especially those challenged by spelling, sometimes console themselves by recalling comments about the randomness and irregularity of English spelling. There are certainly irregularities and exceptions to rules, but English spelling follows some general principles of sound–letter correspondence. Most consonant sounds have predictable spellings, and vowels are generally predictable in stressed syllables. Writers, however, often encounter problems for a number of reasons. First, there are many more sounds and sound combinations in English, especially vowel sounds, than letters in the alphabet or possible letter combinations to represent them. One recent study (Paulesu et al., 2001) counts 1120 different possible combinations of letters to represent the 40+ basic sounds of English, in contrast to Italian, which uses just 33 letter combinations to represent its 25 sounds. Second, English consonant sounds are spelled differently in word-initial, -medial, and -final positions. Third, unstressed vowels are difficult to spell and, fourth, some writers have simply not internalized the underlying rules of sound–letter correspondences. In other words, they just did not learn how to spell.

The scope of this chapter does not allow a detailed treatment of the English spelling system, but a few examples of the underlying principles of sound–letter correspondence can be given to demonstrate, especially to the spelling-challenged writer, that a system is successfully acquired by children and adults. A good source for understanding the English spelling system, and the source for this summary, is Brengelman (1970).

Some of the systematic spellings for English consonants are as follows:

1. Consonant sounds /v, h, w, y/ do not double and are spelled with one letter: ne**v**er, **h**eaven, **w**in, **y**et.
2. Consonants /th$_1$, th$_2$/ do not double but are spelled with two letters: e**th**er, ei**th**er.
3. Consonants /sh, zh/ do not double and are spelled with one or two letters: **s**ure, wi**sh**, mi**ss**ion, deri**s**ion.
4. Consonants /p, t, k, b, d, g, f, s, z, tsh, dzh, m, n, l, r/ are single or double. They are spelled with one letter in word-initial and -final positions; they are spelled with two letters only if they follow a stressed short vowel within the word, e.g., **p**a**p**er, pe**p**, pa**p**er, pe**pp**er.
5. Consonants /f, l, k, s, z, dzh/ are spelled with one letter in word-initial position and after long vowels in word-final position; they are spelled with two letters only if they follow a stressed short vowel within or at the end of the word, e.g., **f**air, li**f**e, o**ff**er, o**ff**; **j**udge, ma**j**or, ju**dg**e; ea**ch**, it**ch**. /f/ is spelled *ph* and *gh* in a few words: gra**ph**, cou**gh**. /k/ is spelled *k* before *i* and *e* (**k**itten, **k**eg), and *c* before letters *a*, *o*, and *u*: **c**at, **c**oat, **c**oot. /ks/ is spelled *x* in root words: bo**x**. /kw/ is spelled *qu*: **qu**ick.

6. A single consonant will double if a suffix beginning with a vowel is added, thereby satisfying the conditions for doubling after short vowels, e.g., sit, sitter; cab, cabbie; tug, tugging.

Some systematic spellings for English vowels are as follows:

1. Short vowels /i/$_2$ bit, /e/$_2$ bet, /a/$_1$ bat, /a/$_2$ pot, /u/$_3$ putt, /u/$_2$ put are usually spelled with one letter.
2. Long vowels /i/$_1$ beet, /e/$_1$ bait, /u/$_1$ boot, /o/$_1$ boat, /ay/ buy, /aw/ bow, /oy/ boy are usually spelled with a sequence of two letters.
3. Word-final e serves one of two purposes: first, when a word ends in a consonant sound, the final e signals the preceding vowel is long; the e is just the second part of the vowel's multiletter spelling: fate, stove, use, rose, kite, mouse, voice. Second, it can make a word-final consonant like the /g/ of hug sound like the g-sound /dzh/ in huge, and the c with a k sound softens to /s/, e.g., picnic vs. nice.

Some vowels are just hard to spell. Recall that the nucleus of every syllable is a vowel. When English vowels appear in polysyllabic words, the vowels in stressed syllables are clearly pronounced and usually easily spelled, but vowels in the nonstressed syllables end up sounding like a nondescript uh sound as in /u/$_3$ putt. Deemphasizing unstressed vowels is a common process in English called *vowel reduction*. Consider the four syllables in the word *catastrophe*: CA TA STRO PHE. The second and fourth vowels are stressed; the first and third vowels are reduced to the uh, a vowel sound not so easily perceived or spelled as one of the five available vowel letters.

Why is a discussion of English spelling more appropriate to phonology than phonetics? While sound–letter correspondences in an alphabetic language are, in greater or lesser measure, phonetic, recall that phonology is the study of units of sound and the patterned variation of their perception and production in the context of other sounds. Such spoken variation is perceived by speakers and is then very often reflected as repeated and patterned spellings or misspellings in their writing. Thus, at one level, spelling is a matching of phonetic sound to alphabetic letter, but at another level, spelling is a system that reflects some of the intricately patterned rules of the phonology of the language. The writer will produce systematically correct spellings if he or she is able to match the graphic system to the sound system according to both phonetic and phonological rules. The writer may also produce systematically incorrect spellings (misspellings) as a result of mismatching the systems.

Here is an example of how a writer's accurate perception of a voiceless consonant turned into a systematic misspelling. A voiced sound is one with vibration of the vocal cords, and a voiceless sound is one without vocal cord vibration. A voiced /g/ sound appears in the word *gusto*, but the same /g/ may easily be perceived and produced as a voiceless /k/ in the word *disgust* because the /g/ takes on (assimilates to) the voiceless quality of the preceding /s/. Say the word and notice that the /g/ sound does indeed change to a /k/ sound in this context (after voiceless /s/). The writer in this case repeatedly and consistently spelled *disgust* with a *q*: d-i-s-**q**-u-s-t. This writer's accurate hearing and perception of the /g/ sound as a /k/ probably caused her to spell the *g* as *q* (a letter that only relates to the /k/ sound), thereby replacing any other possible, but apparently unavailable, strategies for correctly spelling the word d-i-s-**g**-u-s-t.

Here is another example that incorporates acoustic information about sounds. The sounds /p/, /t/, and /k/ all share two important phonetic characteristics: they each stop the flow of air for some milliseconds and each is made without voicing, i.e., without vibration of the vocal cords. Thus, they are called voiceless stops. The differences that allow speakers and hearers to discriminate them are their respective points of articulation in the vocal tract: bilabial, alveolar, and velar. However, the /p/ and /k/ sounds are easily perceived to be similar because their respective positions at the front and back of the mouth actually give them a certain acoustic similarity. So, in some varieties of Spanish, for example, speakers will pronounce "Pepsi" as /pepsi/ or /peksi/. This pronunciation variant appeared as a systematic variable (class feature) in the written Spanish of one suspect-author.

Morphology is the study of word formation. The building blocks of words are meaningful segments called *morphemes*. A morpheme is the smallest unit of language that carries meaning. Note that "meaning" here indicates a word or word-part with referential meaning, e.g., *book, run, happy*, etc., or one with grammatical meaning, e.g., *the, in,* ac*tive*, etc. Content morphemes are those with referential meaning; function morphemes and words have grammatical meaning. For example, at the word level, nouns, verbs, adjectives, and adverbs are content words, but articles, prepositions, and conjunctions are function words.

In the languages of the world, words are formed in many ways, and specific languages are characterized according to how they form words. English is a synthetic language, meaning that it makes words by combining morphemes; in addition to words with just one root morpheme, like *tract*, other words can be formed by combining various other morphemes, like *tract+or, tract+or+s, con+tract+or+s*, and *sub+con+tract+or+s*. Other examples of synthetic languages are Spanish, Japanese, Korean, Punjabi, and Tagalog. On the other hand, languages like Cantonese, Mandarin, Khmer, Hmong, Lao, and Vietnamese are analytic languages. Their words are formed without combining morphemes; each word has just one morpheme.

The morphemes of English are roots and affixes. As a practical matter, a root may be identified as the morpheme that gives a word its basic meaning. Affixes are prefixes and suffixes that attach to the root. For example, the word *proposal* has three morphemes, pro + pose + al (prefix + root + suffix). Derivational affixes make it possible to derive many different words by attaching to roots. Here are some examples of one root *mit/mis* ("send") with various affixes (in bold): **per**mit, **per**miss**ion**, **per**miss**ive**, **ad**mit, **re**mit, **com**mit, **sub**mit, emit, **inter**mittent, **trans**mit, **dis**miss, **re**miss**ion**, **ad**miss**ion**, and **un-sub**-miss-**ive-ly**. Some of the most common derivational affixes of English, both prefixes and suffixes, are listed in Figure 1.7.

The understanding of English morphology also involves the concept of the allomorph. Morphemes are often spoken and written in somewhat different forms. A variant form of a base morpheme is called an allomorph, a "mixture" of forms. Some root morphemes have various allomorphs, depending on their source and history. Figure 1.8 demonstrates examples of some common English roots with their respective allomorphs. In addition to the allomorphic forms of root morphemes, some frequently occurring Latinate prefixes in English have various allomorphs; some are described in Figure 1.9.

Synthetic languages like English form new words by combining morphemes in various ways. New-word derivation (see above) is common. New words created by compounding are also frequent. A compound word combines two roots into one and can be heard as one word because the new word will have only one primary stress instead of two, e.g., *basketball* or *door stop*. Note that compound words are not always spelled as one word. They can be spelled in various ways, e.g., as one word, hyphenated, or with space between the words, e.g., raincoat, White House, school-bus. In addition to compounding and derivation, other important word formation processes are outlined in Figure 1.10: blending, borrowing from another language (e.g., *espionage* from French), clipping and back formation, acronym and abbreviation, coinage, functional shift, proper naming, and morphological misanalysis.

English also has eight inflectional morphemes, all appearing as single suffixes with grammatical meaning at the end of a word: -s (book**s**), -s (he walk**s**), -'s (Pete**'s**), -ed (he walk**ed**), -ing (he is walk**ing**), -en (he has eat**en**), -er (tall**er**), -est (tall**est**). Of these, the three **-s** morphemes and the *-ed*, also have allomorphs. The *-s* morphemes will sound like [-s], [-z], [-iz], depending on whether the base word ends in a voiceless, voiced, or s-like sound, e.g., [-s] in cat+**s**, [-z] in dog+**s**, [-iz] in kiss+**es**. The *-ed* morpheme will sound like [-t], [-d], [-id], depending on whether the base word ends in a voiceless, voiced, or a /t/ or /d/ sound, e.g., [-t] in wi**sh+ed**, [-d] in roam+**ed**, and [-id] in wait+**ed**.

Morphology is also related to English spelling in other more general and important ways. First, recognizing the morphemes in a word helps a writer

PREFIXES

Place/Direction:	ab- ad- con- de- ex- in- en- intro- inter- intra- contra- ob- per- pro- sub- trans- ultra- retro-
Time:	ante- pre- re- post-
Negation:	anti- in- un- dis- mis- a- non-
Descriptive:	ambi- ana- mini-
Numerals:	mon- uni- bi- duo- tri- quad- tetra- quin- penta- sex- hex- sept- hept- oct- nov- deca- semi-

SUFFIXES

Verb to Noun:	-ion -ure -ence -ency -ance -ment (e.g., persuade → persuasion)
Noun to Adjective:	-(i)ar -ate -ic -id -ish -less -like -ly -ful -ite -ous -al -some (e.g., child → childish)
Verb to Adjective:	-able -ible -ile -er -or (e.g., like → likable)
Adjective to Noun:	-ity -ness -hood -(i)an -ism -ist -ite -ship (e.g., happy → happiness)
Adjective to Verb:	-ate -ize -(i)fy (e.g., rational → rationalize)
Adjective to Adverb:	-ly -wise (e.g., sad → sadly)
Combinations:	-ate+ion (mutation); -ate+ure (literature); -ify+ic (terrific); -al+ly (finally); -ent+ial (sequential); -a/ence+y (vacancy); -ate+ory (purgatory); -ar+ity (circularity); -ate+ion (termination); -ite+ize (sanitize)

Figure 1.7 Some common affixes of English.

ROOT	MEANING	ALLOMORPHS	EXAMPLES
MIT	"send"	MIT, MISS	per**mit**, ad**miss**ion
CORD	"heart"	CORD, CARD, COEUR	dis**cord**, **card**iac, **Coeur** d'Alene
DICT	"say"	DICT, DIT	ver**dict**, **dict**ionary, e**dit**, ad**dit**ion
FECT	"make"	FECT, FACT, FAC, FIC	in**fect**, **fact**or, sur**fac**e, **fic**tion
PROB	"test"	PROB, PROV	**prob**ation, **prob**e, ap**prov**e, **prov**e
CLUD	"close"	CLUD, CLUS, CLOS	in**clud**e, ex**clus**ion, **clos**ure, **clos**e
REG	"straight"	REG, RIG, RECT	**reg**ulate, **rig**orous, **rect**itude
DOG	"teach"	DOX, DOC, DOCT	**dog**ma, ortho**dox**, **doc**ent, **doct**or
PED	"foot"	PED, POD, PUS	**ped**al, **pod**iatrist, octo**pus**
VERT	"turn"	VERT, VERS, VERG	re**vert**, re**vers**e, in**vers**ion, con**verg**e
FORT	"strong"	FORT, FORCE	com**fort**, **fort**itude, **force**
GRAPH	"write"	GRAPH, GRAM, GRAV	**graph**ite, tele**gram**, en**grav**e

Figure 1.8 Some frequent Latinate roots and allomorphs of English.

decide between two phonetically good spellings: *tax* is a singular noun, but its homonym *tacks* is a plural noun. In other words, spelling different morphemes that sound alike requires recognition of each word and its context, e.g., the *play's* the thing; the play's second act, the plays were interesting, she plays a lot (Bryant, Nunes, and Aidinis, 1999:114).

Second, when there is not a discernable sound–letter correspondence, a morpheme is often spelled the same. For example, whatever the pronunciations of the inflectional [-s] or [-ed] endings, their respective spellings are just *-s* or *-es*, and *-ed*. Perhaps the most important example of using morpheme recognition to correctly spell phonetically unpredictable words relates to vowel sounds that are weakened in the unstressed syllables of polysyllabic words like *catastrophe*. Writers often have trouble spelling such words according to how they sound. At this point, the writer's knowledge of English morphology compensates because morphemes tend to be spelled consistently. "… most polysyllables are made up of more than one morpheme, and in English a given morpheme tends to retain the same or nearly the same spelling regardless of changes in its sound," (Brengelman, 1970:91). For example, notice that the vowels in the morpheme *photo-* (meaning "light") are pronounced differently but spelled the same in each of these related words: ph**o**to, ph**o**tograph, ph**o**tography.

The lexicon is the collection of word parts and words that combine into larger units, word parts (morphemes) into words, and words into utterances; it is the part of grammar that contains all the different words of the language. Each lexical entry contains details of a word's pronunciation, spelling, meaning, referents, and functions. The lexicon of a language is represented by its

PREFIX	MEANING	ALLOMORPHS	EXAMPLES
AD-	to/toward	AD- AS- AG- AF- AT- AR- AP-	admit, assert, aggress, affect, attend, arrive, appoint
OB-	in front of	OB- OF- OP- OC- O-	obstruct, offer, oppose, occlude, omit
SUB-	under	SUB- SUF- SUP- SUG- SUC-	submit, suffer, support, suggest, succeed
CON-	with	CON- COL- COM- COR- CO-	contain, collate, commit, correct, co-op
EX-	from/out of	EX- EC- EF- E-	exhume, eccentric, effect, egregious or emit
IN-	not	IN- IL- IM- IR-	inoperable, illicit, impossible, irregular

Figure 1.9 Allomorphs of prefixes.

PROCESS	DESCRIPTION	EXAMPLES
DERIVATION	add derivation to root	conference
COMPOUNDING	combine two roots	overcoat, byline
BLENDING	fuse two words	motel, brunch, skorts
BORROWING	from another language	espionage, burrito
INITIALISM	say first letters of word	UCLA
ACRONYM	make word w/ first letters	NAFTA
CLIPPING	cut off word "anywhere"	lab (laboratory)
BACK FORMATION	cut off at morpheme break	dorm (dormitory)
COINAGE	create a new word	jello, kleenex, google
FUNCTIONAL SHIFT	make word another part of speech	impact (n.), impact (v.)
PROPER NAMING	make a word with a name	levis, leotard, herz
MORPHOLOGICAL MISANALYSIS	make new word w/ a clipped word	pre+quel, toy+brary, her+story

Figure 1.10 Word formation processes of English.

dictionary. The lexicon of a particular person refers to the set of words and morphemes that that particular speaker and writer knows and uses.

Syntax is the study of how words are combined into longer sequences, such as phrases, clauses, and sentences. The technical focus of syntax is on the internal grammatical structure of sentences. A sentence is a linear string of constituent words that can be isolated and described, one by one, from left to right in English. However, the hearer or reader is immediately drawn to do more than interpret each word of the string as a separate unit. In addition to sizing up the sentence as a linear string, the listener or reader subconsciously decodes it, or the linguist consciously describes it, by identifying clumps of words that naturally group together as phrases, forming nested subparts of the whole sentence. For example, units like subject noun phrase and verb phrase are universal. In the sentence "John kissed the frog," two high-level constituents can be identified: the subject noun phrase "John" and the verb phrase "kissed the frog."

It is important to note that speakers and writers do what comes naturally: they quickly acquire the ability to construct grammatical and acceptable syntactic structures, then they produce utterances which are more or less elaborate sentences. Linguists find ways to observe and understand how language is acquired, analyze what speakers and writers do, and then account for how and why.

The key to meaningful description and understanding of grammatical structure is the analysis of sentence levels and their embedded structures. For example, "John kissed the frog" is the highest sentence level; "John" + "kissed the frog" is the next noun phrase + verb phrase level, and dividing the object noun phrase into its parts of "the" + "frog" is the lowest level of article + noun. Of course, the length and underlying intricacy of a sentence can make it challenging to establish the sequence and hierarchy of all elements in the sentence that correspond to its speaker's or writer's intended meaning. The basic phrase structure of the English sentence contains a noun phrase, auxiliary verb, and verb phrase; some examples are presented in Figure 1.11.

Most linguistic approaches to sentence structure revolve around a two-level description of the sentence. The first is a focus on the basic phrase structure of the language (discussed above), and the second is a study of various ways in which speakers or writers manipulate these basic phrase structures to create an increasing variety of structures, as well as more complex sentences. The speaker's or writer's "manipulation" of basic structures is accomplished by taking the first-generated structures and effecting various transformations on them, i.e., adding, deleting, or moving elements. Linguists model this process by first specifying the basic phrase structures, then defining the various transformations in utterances that result in sentences. Examples of a few commonly used transformations appear in Figure 1.12.

NOUN PHRASE	AUXILIARY VERB			VERB PHRASE		
(ART) (ADJ) NOUN SENT	MODAL	PERF	PROGRESSIVE	MAIN VERB	COMPLEMENT	ADVERBIALS
John				snores.		
Mary				slept		there.
The man	might			stop		here.
A tall student			is	studying	math	in the classroom.
His sons	may	have		driven	the car	carefully.
A good teacher	should		be	thinking		clearly every day.
These two noisy birds	could	have	been	looking for	other birds	all night long.
Many students	will			seem	quiet	at first.
Mom's car			was	rolling		down the street.
Her sister				rolled down	the shade	quietly last night.
The player who got hit	must	have	been	hoping	to draw a foul	during the game.

Figure 1.11 Some basic phrase structures of English.

TRANSFORMATION	TYPE	BASIC PHRASE STRUCTURE	CHANGE TO NEW STRUCTURE
Negation	Addition	John may go.	John may <u>not</u> go.
Yes/No Question	Movement	John will go.	<u>Will</u> John go?
Contraction	Deletion	John should not go.	John shoul<u>dn't</u> go.
Do **insertion**	Addition	John loves Mary.	John <u>does</u> love Mary.
Negation	2 additions	John loves Mary.	John <u>does</u> <u>not</u> love Mary.
Wh- Questions	All 3	John will leave now.	<u>When</u> <u>will</u> John leave [___].
Passive	All 3	John saw Mary.	<u>Mary</u> <u>was</u> seen.

Figure 1.12   Some commonly used transformations of English.

Sentences are made up of words and phrases that, from the earliest grammarians, have been placed into various grammatical categories. Categories of words that relate the language to the situation, time, and place of an utterance are as follows:

Person — first (I/we), second (you), third (he, she, it, they)
Number — singular and plural of nouns and pronouns
Gender — he or she
Case — subject (I, he, she, we, they) or object (me, him, her, us, them)
Tense — past, present, and future grammatical forms that relate the time
  of the action referred to in the sentence to the time of the utterance
  of the sentence
Mood — the expression in the sentence of the attitude of the speaker
  toward the facts of what is said, marking with modal verbs (may,
  might, can, could, will, would, shall, should, and must) the speaker's
  wish, intention, necessity, obligation, certainty, and possibility (Mood
  is not so clearly marked in declarative, imperative, and interrogative
  sentences.)
Aspect — in English verbs relating to perfect (completed) actions or
  events (e.g., "I left."), progressive (not completed) actions (e.g., "I was
  leaving."), and the so-called "stative" verbs (e.g., know, understand,
  hate, love) that already contain the notion of duration and therefore
  do not occur in the progressive

The most well known grammatical categories are the parts of speech. Just as with content and functional morphemes, there are the lexical parts of speech, i.e., nouns, verbs, adjectives, and adverbs. Then, there are the grammatical words used to bind together the content words: prepositions, conjunctions, pronouns, and interjections. These word classes are very useful, but they seldom catch nuances or account for the variety of each class. For example, there are many kinds of verbs, starting with main verb and auxiliary verbs, and proceeding to various subclasses of verbs.

A third kind of grammatical category includes grammatical elements that relate to their function in the sentence: subjects, predicates, complements; adverbials of time, place, and manner; transitive, intransitive, and reflexive verbs; uses of the verb *to be* (existential, possessive, locative), auxiliary verbs; and the active and passive voice of sentences.

Semantics is the study of meaning in words and sentences. Word meaning relates to the sense of a word vis-à-vis other words in the language, e.g., synonymy (words with the same meaning, like synonyms *little* and *small*); antonymy (words with opposite meanings, like antonyms *good* and *bad*); homonymy (words with the same sound or form but different meanings, like homonyms *mail* and *male*); hyponymy (words included within the class of another word, like hyponyms *apple* and *orange* vis-à-vis *fruit*, or hyponyms *fruit* vis-à-vis *plant*); and polysemy (single words with more than one meaning, like the polysemous word *watch* (i.e., see, wristwatch, vigil). Word meaning relates as well to a word's reference to things, actions, and situations in the world, such as *horse, run,* and *happy.* However, understanding a word and its referent is sometimes difficult to do for two reasons: it is not always possible to relate some words like verbs or function words to something in the world, and one cannot always agree on the relationship between a word and its referent. For example, is the White House a house or is the tomato a fruit?

Sentence meaning relates to the interpretation of the whole sentence as a unit of meaning. For example, even though "John kissed Mary" and "Mary kissed John" are two sentences that contain the same words, their meanings are different. Each sentence conveys its respective meaning as not only the sum of its parts but also their arrangement within the sentence.

1.3.2   Language Function

Discourse analysis is the study of language units beyond the sentence. These units of discourse in speech and writing are studied by relating them as communicative events to their cultural and social contexts of use. Such contexts include forms and purposes of talk associated with interviews, negotiations, debates, greetings, narratives of personal experience, and other types of natural conversations. Discourse is studied by observing large samples of natural language used in specific contexts, then describing the language and intended meaning of participants, their resultant success or failure to communicate or comprehend the meaning of what was said, the organization and rules of conversational interaction, and the social and cultural constraints on speech and writing.

An important focus of discourse analysis is on the organization and situational constraints of *conversations*, i.e., characteristics such as openings, closings, feedback, turn-taking, side information, nonparticipants, interruptions, and hearable messages from outside the immediate conversation.

One of the best communicative contexts for observing natural language discourse is within narratives of personal experience, wherein speakers and writers structure their personal experiences in stories that have an overall structure of up to six parts: abstract, orientation, complicating action, evaluation of events, result or resolution, and coda.

Pragmatics is the study of intended meaning. This is distinct from semantics (the study of linguistic meaning) insofar as a given utterance is interpreted based on the intention of the speaker or writer, which may or may not be the same as the overt linguistic meaning of the sentence. For example, "Please open the window," and "It sure is hot in here," may both be requests to open the window, but the latter will be interpreted as such by the listener only within the situational context of the statement.

This example makes it clear that the successful communication of intended meanings (i.e., pragmatic uses of language) depends on reference to nonlinguistic information such as the identity and social relationships of speaker or writer and listener or reader; the place, time, and topic of conversation; the purpose of the communication; the language used, etc. Without this contextual information, the intended meaning of a sentence like "It sure is hot in here" may be misinterpreted or remain unknown.

Speakers' and writers' uses of language to "do things with words" are speech acts. Some of the clearest examples of speech acts are the so-called performative verbs, e.g., assert, ask, order, request, threaten, warn, bet, advise, promise, pronounce, etc. These are verbs whose use in given contexts goes beyond being a mere linguistic event but becomes the act itself. Note the difference between "He pronounced them husband and wife" and "I pronounce you husband and wife." The former use of "pronounce" reports on the event, but the latter actually makes the couple husband and wife, producing situational conditions allow (e.g., desire to get married, the power to marry someone, etc.).

Pragmatics is, therefore, very much the study of how to do things with language. Think of how many ways one might communicate any of the following in a variety of social contexts: accusing, addressing, advising, announcing, apologizing, asking, asserting, blaming, boasting, claiming, complaining, commanding, congratulating, condoling, convincing, demanding, disapproving, greeting, instructing, introducing, inviting, offering, ordering, pardoning, parting, persuading, praising, promising, recommending, refusing, reporting, reprimanding, requesting, stating, suggesting, telephone talking, thanking, threatening, vowing, etc.

Directness is another important result of the contrast of literal vs. intended meanings. Linguists study the ability of the speaker or writer to fit the message on a continuum between the two, communicating literal meaning with very direct statements and intended meaning with more indirect language. Although it is not always easy to locate various statements at an exact place on the direct–indirect continuum, speakers and writers do use and recognize degrees of directness. Consider these requests to open a window:

1. Open the window.
2. Please open the window.
3. Will you please open the window?
4. Would you please open the window?
5. Would you mind opening the window?
6. The window is shut.
7. Are the windows locked?
8. Is anyone else hot?
9. I must be having a hot flash.

1.3.3 Language Acquisition

Children take in the sounds, words, phrases, and sentences of spoken language and use this input to build an internal grammar of the language. Their grammatical knowledge is implicit, complex, and so quickly and unconsciously acquired that one is led to say that children are innately prewired for language in a way unique to the species. The study of language acquisition examines children's language development in relation to the input they receive, to when and how specific structures and functions of language are acquired, and to how this all jibes with their capacity for so successfully sifting out their own language from their linguistic and social environment.

Understanding language acquisition and use relies on an important distinction that is made in the context of asking what it means to acquire and know a language: competence vis-à-vis performance. *Competence* is the speaker's or writer's implicit knowledge and ability to create, use, and understand grammatical, meaningful, and appropriate utterances in his or her language. "Appropriate utterances" refers to Hymes' (1971) important expansion of linguistic competence to include *communicative competence,* thereby including a speaker's knowledge of the social and cultural constraints on appropriate use of language.

Performance, on the other hand, is a reflection of competence in the speaker's or writer's actual use of language. Since performance is affected by external factors and the variable conditions experienced by the speaker or writer, it is rarely a perfect reflection of competence. In this model, errors and linguistic variation are sometimes mistakenly explained as "accidental" characteristics of language that are related to external performance factors, not as "essential" characteristics that are related to linguistic competence in a rule-governed, systematic way.

Individual differences in language acquisition: There is significant evidence that individual children acquire language at different rates and in different ways (Nelson, 1981; Shore, 1995). Individual differences are described in four general ways (Shore, 1995:15): referential vs. expressive (child's grasp of language functions); nominal vs. pronominal (child's preference for nouns or pronouns); analytic vs. holistic (child's interpretation and use of words or whole utterances); and risk-taking vs. conservative (child's loose or careful approach to acquisition).

More specifically, in vocabulary children demonstrate differences in acquisition and use of personal social words, content words (like nouns) vs. function words, object naming with nouns, formulaic utterances, and nouns vs. pronouns. In phonology, individual differences arise in order of phoneme acquisition, focus on individual sounds vs. whole prosodic utterances, and willingness to add items to the phonological system. Individual differences in morphology are found in the acquisition of grammatical morphemes such as function words and inflections. The acquisition of syntax demonstrates variability in word-order rules. The acquisition of language functions demonstrates individual preference for information functions or interpersonal functions of language, and variability in the coherence and conversational relevance of utterances (Shore, 1995:17).

1.3.4 Linguistic Variation

Language changes. By its very nature, language is not a static system; this dynamic is first reflected as variation in the spoken and written language of groups and individuals. The most convincing modern-day argument for this theoretical position was articulated by Weinreich, Labov, and Herzog (1968:188) more than 30 years ago: "... all change [in language structure] involves variability and heterogeneity." Since then, this understanding of linguistic variability has been confirmed again and again by hundreds of studies of the analysis of linguistic variation.

This position is in contrast to traditional views of variation, and it is this very difference in theoretical orientation that accounts for differences in approach and methodology in stylistics and authorship identification. Recall the account of variation in Section 1.3.3 as a kind of accidental byproduct of performance factors experienced by the speaker or writer. In this scheme of things, variation is not part of the language user's underlying rule-governed competence. However, the competence–performance distinction makes more sense if a speaker's or writer's competence is understood to include orderly heterogeneity, and most variation is recognized to be too systematic to be explained away as performance.

All languages, then, demonstrate internal variation caused by internal and external factors. Internal factors include structural and functional effects on linguistic change (Labov, 1994:1). External factors relate to variables that cause relative isolation of groups of speakers and writers, or of individual language users, i.e., their distance from one another caused by separation in time (generation), geography, social class (sex, age, race, ethnicity, education, occupation, income level), and the immediate social context of language use (topic, intended listener or reader, communicative purpose, place, and time).

The linguistic variation that results from such internal and external catalysts for change is usually described in terms of dialects and styles of speaking and writing. A dialect is a form of a language that develops differently due to the geographic or social separation, partial or total, of one group of speakers from another. Geographic dialects are due to physical separation and social dialects are due to social distance. A style is a form of language defined by its context of use. A written-language style is also defined by the individual writer's range of variation, i.e., the aggregate set of variable forms and uses of language, conditioned separately and together as a set by the conscious and unconscious choices the writer makes during the writing process.

The linguistic distance between two dialects or styles of a language is described in terms of their variable differences in pronunciation (and spelling), word formation, sentence structure, word and sentence meaning, larger discourse units, and ways of doing things with language. Linguistic distance is usually most obvious when a given dialect or style is described vis-à-vis the standard variety of the language; for convenience, linguists often describe dialects and styles in terms of the standard. The standard variety is not usually viewed as a regional or social dialect, although there are different regional standards in countries like the U.S. Linguists often use the term *variety* to refer neutrally to a dialect of a language, even though some speakers see dialects as less formal, less correct, or less prestigious forms of a standard variety.

1.3.5 Written Language

Writing systems: The approximately 6000 languages of the world are grouped into about 20 major families, the largest in terms of number of speakers belonging to the Indo–European family. English is part of the Indo–European group. Scholars use internal (linguistic) criteria as well as external (historical, social, cultural, and geographical) criteria for grouping languages into their respective families. The linguistic characteristics used to establish family relationships among languages are their sounds, ways of forming words, and sentence structures.

The writing systems of so many different languages represent considerable diversity. They vary according to whether their graphic segments represent meaningful content or linguistic forms. In pictographic writing systems, recognizable symbols of shapes and markings represent things, situations, and actions, although languages are no longer written in pictographic writing because it is limiting and inefficient. In logographic writing, each graph represents a unit of linguistic meaning, i.e., a morpheme or a word. Chinese and languages that borrow Chinese characters (Japanese and Korean) are now the only languages that use logographic writing. Various languages use syllabic writing, in which each graph represents a syllable. Japanese, for example, has two syllable collections, or "syllabaries": *hiragana* are used to write Japanese function words and inflections, and *katagana* represent syllables used to write foreign words. In alphabetic writing, vowel and consonant sounds are associated with individual alphabetic symbols (letters); English has an alphabetic system. While many other languages share the Roman alphabet with English, many languages use alphabets different from the Roman alphabet. In alphabetic systems, the fit between sound and letter may be nearly perfect as in Spanish, or far from perfect as in English.

Many languages use some combination of writing systems. Japanese orthography combines Chinese logographs to represent content words, the Chinese *kanji* characters, with Japanese syllable symbols, and the two *kana* syllabaries (Akita and Hatano, 1999:214). Korean writing uses an interesting combination of alphabetic and syllabic. Each written segment contains discrete letter symbols compactly arranged into a syllable, thereby making written segments simultaneously alphabetic and syllabic (Lyovin, 1997:34). Even languages like English, deemed to be completely alphabetic, use iconic symbols like those found at the top of the keyboard: @, #, $, %, &, * .

This very brief treatment of writing systems is perhaps sufficient to give the uninitiated lay-linguist a background in orthography; however, it does not allow for discussion of many of the most interesting and important historical or linguistic aspects. For further study, consult basic works such as Coulmas (1989), Daniels and Bright (1995), and Lyovin (1997, Chapter 2).

Writing: Writing is defined variably in historical, linguistic, developmental, and cognitive terms. All the varied definitions are accurate and useful, at least in part. Writing is a graphic system for representing and communicating information; visual symbols like road signs are nonlinguistic graphic systems, but symbols like letters, syllables, and characters are linguistic. Writing is the process of making visible marks (symbols) on a physical surface like wax, clay, papyrus, paper, or a computer monitor. Writing directly represents information about things and events and what is said about those events, i.e., utterances made up of sounds, words, and sentences. Therefore, writing is a linguistic-based script systematically segmented into graphs representing things, words, syllables, or sounds of a language. Writing also refers to hand printing or handwriting.

The definition of writing historically most prevalent is that writing is an explicit representation of spoken language, or that writing derives from speech. This view goes at least as far back as Aristotle, extending later into the development of European and American linguistics of the early 20th century. Presently, however, general agreement is that the properties, acquisition, and acts of writing and speaking are different in so many ways that writing is considered to be related to but not derivative of speech (e.g., Chafe, 1986:12; Garton and Pratt, 1998:4; Olson, 1997:4; Wolf Nelson, 1988a:21). In spite of these many observations and research findings, it is not uncommon to see the traditional view of the primacy of spoken language articulated today without qualification. For example, Lyovin (1997:29) says, "Writing is only a secondary aspect of language, that is, it is only a means of symbolizing spoken languages, often a very imperfect means at that."

Composing a coherent text is also writing, as is discourse, first with respect to its objectives, i.e., the purposes and functions of writing, then with respect to its features, i.e., the elements, devices, and mechanisms used (Lloyd–Jones, 1977:33). Writing is creating a product such as a poem, business letter, report, etc. Writing is also a process of producing written text: planning, starting, making continuous decisions about language and meaning, reviewing, revising, etc. Writers determine what they want to say and how they wish to say it, given the broad array of available choices for the elaboration of both.

Differences between written and spoken language: The differences between written and spoken language are well documented and important to understand. In physical form, speech is ephemeral (temporary), occurs in real time, aural (requires listening), quick, social, and fragmentary. Writing is durable, occurs in space, visual (requires seeing), slow, often solitary, deliberate, and allows editing during and after. In function, as determined by social and situational factors, speech is conversation, more informal in style, more varied. In manner of presentation, speech has many nonlinguistic and paralinguistic discourse markers for linking ideas, and is subject to more dialect, accent, and slang variability. Writing must use forms of emphasis like the exclamation mark, underlining, capital letters, and italics; it is subject to less variability, and its conventions are more widespread (Garton and Pratt, 1998:4).

Additionally, in spoken language lots of meaning is contextualized, i.e., related to nonverbal context, and is usually face to face in the here and now. In writing, all meaning must be encoded in words or punctuation — not contextualized — and there is usually a greater distance between the writer and reader, with resulting adjustments in vocabulary and sentence structure (Wolf Nelson, 1988a:21).

In addition to the studies cited already, other good sources characterizing the distinctions between spoken and written language are Chafe (1985 and 1986) and Robbins (1989:114). The breadth of research on speech vis-à-vis writing is documented in McMenamin (1993:124).

Acquisition of written language: Writing requires the progressive development of two kinds of skills: graphic and linguistic. "Handwriting is a mechanical performance skill whose only role is to make writing decipherable. Learning how to handwrite does *not* teach the child how to write, compose language and express ideas, or master writing-as-conceptual-act," (Klein, 1985:33). Garton and Pratt (1998:188) focus on the combined skills in similar fashion: "Learning to write involves mastering a diverse range of skills and understandings ... grouped under four headings — early distinctions; letter formation and printing skills; the functions of the written word; putting the message in writing."

Acquisition of the mechanical skills requires small muscle development (fine motor skill), eye–hand coordination, holding a writing tool, basic strokes, letter perception, and orientation to printed language (Lamme, 1979), as well as differentiating between drawing and writing, development of letters and letter-like shapes, and concepts of linearity, uniformity, inner complexity, symmetry, placement, and left-to-right and top-to-bottom motion (DeFord, 1980). Writers of the signs and symbols of various scripts throughout the world and over time, including present-day logographs, syllabaries, and alphabets, demonstrate these same skills for graphic representation (Wann, Wing, and Sõvik, 1991).

Acquisition of writing-as-conceptual-act requires combinations of letters and spaces indicating understanding of units (letters, words, sentences), recognition of isolated words, sound–letter correspondences, writing simple sentences with invented spelling, sentence combinations, and control of punctuation and capitalization, as well as the understanding and use of various forms of discourse (DeFord, 1980).

Children learn to produce language as speaking and writing and, in conjunction with the allied receptive language counterparts of listening and reading, they bring together these skills to create and communicate meaning. Thus, writing acquisition is a process of development in which the child actively constructs the capacity to write by writing, i.e., by becoming progressively involved with the writing process and system, and by understanding the situational purpose of writing, i.e., interacting with the physical, social, and cultural context of writing.

The acquisition process usually requires formal instruction involving basic skills in reading (the alphabetic principle of letter–sound correspondences), then copying letters, spelling difficult words, and then forms of writing like stories and diary entries (Garton and Pratt, 1998:183). Children's success depends on many factors:

- Their active involvement (writing because they want to) in the learning process
- Knowledge that they have before they start school
- Opportunities and encouragement for writing
- Writing what they say (vs. what others like the teacher say)
- Their grasp of the alphabet, i.e., letters represent sounds, and these are used to form words
- Exposure to print in an environment that results in stimulation of interest in writing
- Opportunities for contact with others whom they can watch writing (Garton and Pratt, 1998:188).

One often thinks of writing development taking place in the young child, yet older youth in the 9 to 19-year-old age range continue to develop their ability to write with "… the gradual acquisition of low-frequency structures and the ability to form unique combinations of structures" (Scott, 1988:50). Such structures include longer sentences and an increase in the type and number of subordinate clauses used. Older youth also begin to expand writing contexts to the setting and occasion, as well as to distinct discourse genres (Scott, 1988:51).

Although sentence length can vary dramatically within the same individual as a function of context and discourse type, sentence length increases in preadolescent and adolescent years. Clause length (mean number of words per clause) also increases with age. Degree of subordination (average number of clauses per terminable (T)-unit, and main + subordinate clauses per T-unit) increases over time and is expressed as the subordination index, the ratio of the number of clauses over total T-units (Scott, 1988:55).

Note that the unit of analysis of written syntax traditionally was the sentence. However, because of difficulties in determining just what a sentence is, the terminable unit or *T-unit* has long been taken to be a more precise measure and is used now to segment discourse in many studies: "… the T-unit consists of a main clause with all subordinate clauses or nonclausal structures attached to or embedded within. All main clauses that begin with coordinating conjunctions (*and, but, or*) initiate a new T-unit unless there is co-referential subject deletion in the second clause" (Scott, 1988:55).

Individual differences in the acquisition of written language: There are significant individual differences in the acquisition of writing. One of the reasons for cataloging skills involved in the acquisition of writing was to demonstrate the many variables that can result in individuation.

Given that all language processes are interrelated, especially the expressive and productive skills of speaking and writing, individual differences in the acquisition of oral language will result in differences in written-language acquisition (Dyson, 1983 and 1985; Klein, 1985; Macintosh, 1964; Moffett, 1973; Possien, 1969; Russell, 1953). For example, Dyson (1985:59) comments that "... the nature of the individual child, the nature of the situational context, and the complex nature of the writing system itself all interact in written language growth, just as they do in oral language growth.... The interplay of these factors suggests that individual differences are to be expected in writing development."

A child's acquisition of writing becomes more and more individualized because the language itself, its expressed and intended meanings, the person of the writer, and the intended reader "become increasingly differentiated, or distanced from one another, and also linked or integrated in news ways," (Dyson, 1985:62). Resulting individual differences in writing are demonstrated by beginning writers and also by youth at later developmental levels (Wolf Nelson, 1988b).

While case studies reviewed by Dyson (1985:118) demonstrate many similarities in children's acquisition of writing, she concludes that "the differences between children were more striking than the similarities." Differences centered on their intentions for writing and ways of approaching writing. Research on individual differences related to memory, fluency, coherence, and revising of writing include Robinson (1984), McCutchen et al. (1994), McCutchen (1996), Swanson and Berninger (1996a and 1996b), Zellermayer and Cohen (1996), and Torrance, Glyn, and Robinson (1999).

Group-specific differences in writing acquisition are also useful in determining "class features" of writers. Recent neurological research focuses on countries that have more people with symptoms of dyslexia than others (Paulesu et al., 2001). PET scans were used to observe brain activity in English-, French-, and Italian-speaking adults to determine language-specific differences in readers while they were connecting language sounds with the letters that spell each sound. Results indicated less neural activity for Italian readers than for the French or English speakers, meaning that certain written languages, like English and French, make the dyslexic condition worse because their spelling is often so different from how words sound. This stands to reason, given that written language is neurologically a relatively new human activity. Matching sounds in a word to the symbols that represent them on the page is more difficult for some readers and writers than for others. For example, the $/i_1/$ sound can be written ten ways in English (b**ee**t, b**ea**t, b**e**, k**ey**, bab**y**, p**eo**ple, rel**ie**ve, dec**ei**ve, sal**i**ne, kero**se**ne), but only one way in Italian or Spanish. Just the English vowel in the "-ough" letter combination can be pronounced at least five ways: $/o/_1$: th**ough**, /aw/: b**ough**, $/u/_1$: thr**ough**, /a/: c**ough**, and $/u/_3$: t**ough**.

References

Akita, K. and Hatano, G., Learning to read and write in Japanese, in Harris, M. and Hatano, G., Eds., *Learning to Read and Write: a Cross-Linguistic Perspective*, Cambridge University Press, New York, 1999, 214–234.

Brengelman, F., *The English Language: an Introduction for Teachers*, Prentice Hall, Engelwood Cliffs, NJ, 1970.

Bryant, P., Nunes, T., and Aidinis, A., Different morphemes, same spelling problems: cross-linguistic developmental studies, in Harris, M. and Hatano, G., Eds., *Learning to Read and Write: A Cross-Linguistic Perspective*, Cambridge University Press, Cambirdge, 1999, 112–133.

Chafe, W. L., Linguistic differences produced by differences between speaking and writing, in Olson, D. R., Torrance, N., and Hildyard, A., Eds., *Literacy, Language and Learning: the Nature and Consequences of Reading and Writing*, Cambridge University Press, Cambridge, 1985.

Chafe, W. L., Writing in the perspective of speaking, in Cooper, C. R. and Greenbaum, S., Eds., *Studying Writing: Linguistic Approaches*, Sage, Beverly Hills, 1986, 12.

Coulmas, F., *The Writing Systems of the World*, Blackwell, Oxford, 1989.

Daniels, P. T. and Bright, W., Eds., *The World's Writing Systems*, Oxford University Press, New York, 1995.

DeFord, D., Young children and their writing, in DeFord, D., Ed., *Learning to Write: an Expression of Language*, The Ohio State University, Columbus, 1980, 157–162.

Dyson, A. H., Individual differences in emerging writing, in Farr, M., Ed., *Advances in Writing Research: Children's Early Writing Development*, Ablex, Norwood, 1985, 59–125.

Dyson, A. H. The role of oral language in the early writing process, *Res. Teaching English*, 17:1–30, 1983.

Garton, A. and Pratt, C., *Learning to Be Literate: the Development of Spoken and Written Language*, 2nd ed., Blackwell, Oxford, 1998.

Hymes, D., Competence and performance in linguistic theory, in Huxley, R. and Ingram, E., Eds., *Language Acquisition: Models and Methods*, Academic Press, London, 1971.

Klein, M. L., *The Development of Writing in Children: Pre-K through Grade 8*, Prentice Hall, Engelwood Cliffs, NJ, 1985.

Labov, W., *Principles of Linguistic Change, Vol. 1: Internal Factors*, Blackwell, Oxford, 1994.

Lamme, L., Handwriting in an early childhood curriculum, *Young Children*, 35:20–27, 1979.

Lloyd–Jones, R., Primary trait scoring, in Cooper, C. R. and Odell, L., Eds., *Evaluating Writing: Describing, Measuring, Judging*, NCTE, Urbana, 1977.

Lyovin, A. V., *An Introduction to the Languages of the World*, Oxford University Press, New York, 1997.

Macintosh, H. K., Ed., *Children and Oral Language*, Association of Childhood Education International, Washington, D.C., 1964.

McCutchen, D., A capacity theory of writing: working memory in composition, *Educ. Psychol. Rev.*, 8:3:299–325, 1996.

McCutchen, D. et al., Individual differences in writing: implications of translating fluency, *J. Educ. Psychol.*, 86:2:256–266, 1994.

McMenamin, G. R., *Forensic Stylistics*, Elsevier, Amsterdam, 1993, 124.

Moffett, J., *A Student-Centered Language Arts Curriculum, Grades K–6: A Handbook for Teachers*, Houghton Mifflin, Boston, 1973.

Nelson, K., Individual differences in language development: implications for development and language, *Develop. Psychol.*, 17:170–187, 1981.

Olson, D. R., On the relation between speech and writing, in Pontecorvo, C., Ed., *Writing Development: an Interdisciplinary View*, John Benjamins, Amsterdam, 1997, 4.

Paulesu, E. et al., Dyslexia: cultural diversity and biological unity, *Science*, 291: 2165–2167, 2001.

Possien, W. M., Ed., *They All Need to Talk*, Appleton Century Crofts, New York, 1969.

Robbins, R. H., *General Linguistics*, 4th ed., Longman, London, 1989, 114.

Robinson, S. F., Coherence in student writing, *Diss. Abs. Int.*, 45:6–A:1671, 1984.

Russell, D. H., Ed., *Child Development and the Language Arts*, NCTE, Champaign, IL, 1953.

Scott, C. M., Spoken and written syntax, in *Later Language Development: Ages Nine through Nineteen*, Nippold, M. A., Ed., College-Hill, Boston, 1988, 49–95.

Shore, C. M., *Individual Differences in Language Development*, Sage, Thousand Oaks, CA, 1995.

Swanson, H. L. and Berninger, V. W., Individual differences in children's working memory and writing skill, *J. Exp. Child Psychol.*, 63:2:358–385, 1996a.

Swanson, H. L. and Berninger, V. W., Individual differences in children's writing: a function of working memory or reading or both processes? *Reading Writing*, 8:4:357–383, 1996b.

Torrance, M. T., Glyn, V., and Robinson, E. J., Individual differences in the writing behaviour of undergraduate students, *Br. J. Educ. Psychol.*, 69:2:189–199, 1999.

Wann, J., Wing, A. M., and Sōvik, N., *Development of Graphic Skills: Research Perspectives and Educational Implications*, Academic Press, London, 1991.

Weinreich, U., Labov, W., and Herzog, M. I., Empirical foundations for a theory of language change, in Lehmann, W. and Malkiel, Y., Eds., *Directions for Historical Linguistics: a Symposium*, University of Texas Press, Austin, 1968, 95–195.

Wolf-Nelson, N., The nature of literacy, in Nippold, M. A., Ed., *Later Language Development: Ages Nine through Nineteen*, College–Hill, Boston, 1988a, 11–28.

Wolf-Nelson, N., Reading and writing, in Nippold, M. A., Ed., *Later Language Development: Ages Nine through Nineteen*, College–Hill, Boston, 1988b, 97–125.

Zellermayer, M. and Cohen, J., Varying paths for learning to revise, *Instructional Sci.*, 24:3:177–195, 1996.

Linguistics

GERALD R. McMENAMIN

2

2.1 Linguistics

Linguistics is the scientific study of language. Language is the association of the combination of sounds, words, and sentences to conventional meanings used and understood by a community of speakers. Scientific means the "investigation [of language] by means of controlled and empirically verifiable observations and with reference to some general theory of language structure" (Lyons, 1968:1). Linguistics is a social science because its primary focus is on language as a human behavior, although some of its descriptive and analytical methods reflect those of mathematics and the natural sciences.

2.1.1 The History of Linguistics

The earliest known study of language dates back to around 400 BC in India, when Panini began a grammatical tradition based on the linguistic observation and description of Sanskrit in the sacred Indian texts known as the *Vedas*. The Greeks developed a grammar based on the language of their literature. The Romans adapted the Greek grammar to Latin, which in turn was used, through the Middle Ages and the Renaissance, as the paradigm to account for the languages of Europe.

By the 17th century, European scholars realized that fitting languages into the structure of Greek and Latin made it difficult to capture accurately the characteristics of their own languages as well as of languages discovered in explorations of the New World. This brought them back to Panini. Their new contact with non-European languages and their rediscovery of Sanskrit and the Indic tradition of grammatical description made them see the grammars of Greek and Latin as inadequate for their new descriptive needs. The resulting freedom from the limitations of language-specific grammatical categories opened the door for the development of present-day scientific linguistics.

During the 18th and 19th centuries, scholars focused on the Indo–European languages as well as on other language families. Their discoveries led essentially to the development of four principles: 1. language changes over time, 2. the changes are slow but systematic, 3. the regularity of changes within a language can be described, and 4. interlanguage comparison of changes will indicate the origin of a language and its relationship to other languages. Due to this initial focus on the evolution of language, linguistic science can be said to have started as an historical endeavor.

In the late 19th and early to mid 20th centuries, scholars from Germany, France, Holland, Denmark, Russia, Japan, and China saw the need to examine the system of a language at a given point in time as a contextual reference point for understanding change. This provided a new descriptive and theoretical basis for comparative studies, thus expanding the scope of linguistic inquiry and motivating the study of other languages and dialects of Europe and the languages of Asia. At the same time, American anthropologists *qua* linguists began to focus their attention, first, on American Indian languages, then on Sanskrit, African, other Indo–European, Semitic, and English languages.

2.1.2 Language and Linguistics

Linguistics is about understanding the system of language. The aims of linguistic science are theoretical insofar as linguists discover the underlying rules and patterns of language and then describe them in the languages of the world. Linguists look for language characteristics that are present in all languages (universals), as well as features found only in certain language families or individual languages. The universal and distinctive features of the languages of the world are described in work such as that of Lyovin (1997).

The goals of linguistics are also practical insofar as linguists attempt to use this knowledge for the good of speakers and languages, e.g., language teaching, forensic applications, etc. It is also important to point out that linguistics is descriptive not prescriptive, i.e., its goal is to understand and describe language and languages, not prescribe rules for correct and appropriate usage.

The focus of linguistic study is on what a person internalizes during the relatively short period of time it takes to acquire a first language. Speakers simultaneously acquire the forms of a language (its structures) along with the uses for the language (its functions). While this division between form and function is made for convenience of analysis, the two cannot be separated, and together they constitute the language that is acquired. In the process of second-language acquisition, one is sometimes able to see the consequence of learning forms alone in students who learn the sounds, words, and sentences of a language without really acquiring the ability to use that language in a context outside the classroom. After finishing high school foreign language classes, can one actually speak the language?

Language users have four channels for language available to them. Two of these are productive abilities of expression: speaking and writing. The other two are receptive capacities of comprehension: listening and reading. All speaking and hearing language users have the two channels of spoken

Linguistic Level	Spoken Language	Written Language
LANGUAGE FORM		
PHONETICS	Sounds (*phonemes*)	Letters (*graphemes*)
PHONOLOGY	Sound patterns + blends	Letters + digraphs
MORPHOLOGY	Word formation (*morphemes*)	Word parts: (*roots + affixes*)
LEXICON	Words	Vocabulary (*dictionary*)
SYNTAX	Sentence formation	Written sentences (*grammar*)
SEMANTICS	Expressed meaning	Meaning of words + sentences
LANGUAGE FUNCTION		
DISCOURSE	Conversations + narratives	Written equivalents (*stories*)
PRAGMATICS	Doing things with words	Written equivalents

Figure 2.1 Linguistic levels in spoken and written language.

language, i.e., listening and speaking; literate language users possess the skills of written language, i.e., reading and writing.

In addition, language skills are described by linguistic levels: sounds, words, sentences, meaning, discourse, and language use. Figure 2.1 is a paradigm of the layered linguistic levels of spoken and written language, including the technical names linguists or educators give them. See also Chapter 1, and compendia such as McArthur and McArthur (1992) for greater detail.

2.1.3   The Meaning of Grammar

The forms and uses of language are usually detailed and explained in a grammar, which usually takes the form of a book. There are two kinds of grammars: descriptive and prescriptive. A descriptive grammar provides an objective and accurate picture of the total language system; it is not evaluative. A prescriptive grammar states rules for how language should and should not be used. Therefore, it is evaluative, based as it is on conventional norms of linguistically correct and socially acceptable language use.

Language is also studied in somewhat different ways within each of these traditions. A descriptive grammar can be constructed based on careful observation of speakers' actual use of the language, or it can be shaped based on an explicit representation of what an ideal speaker must know in order to use the language. While most prescriptive grammars focus on how language should be used, some grammars are proscriptive, i.e., designed to help speakers and writers avoid mistakes by focusing on how language should *not* be used. While some works of grammar combine these elements, most will have a specific purpose: linguistic grammars attempt to be completely descriptive, and school grammars will weigh in heavily on prescription.

The distinction between description and prescription is especially important in the study of writing style. In general terms, linguistic stylistics, which
is the basis of forensic stylistics, is descriptive. It is literary stylistics which,
in various ways, is evaluative or prescriptive. For a complete discussion of
this distinction as it applies to stylistics, see McMenamin (1993:161).

2.1.4 Linguistics as a Science

Total agreement does not exist on exactly what constitutes science and the
methods of science, probably due to the diversity of activities and disciplines
that involve systematic and objective (i.e., scientific) observation. Science is
an inductive way to reason within a theoretical framework, starting from
facts experienced and observed and continuing on to testable explanations
of those facts. Most elements of modern science are included in definitions
such as this one: "Science is, first, a body of tested facts and concepts that
satisfactorily interpret natural phenomena and disclose causal relationships,
and, second, a means for discovering such facts and principles and for applying them in the solution of problems (Benton, 1966).

While there is no universally accepted scientific method, scientific study
usually involves most of these elements:

- Systematic and unbiased observation of facts
- The classification of these observations
- The observation of interactions among actions and events
- The formulation of principles related to organized observations
- Generalizations resulting from combining various principles
- The construction of a theory based on relationships among principles
- The communication of results to other scientists to achieve a level of
  intersubjective agreement on all of the steps
- Inference, taking what is known to form hypotheses that predict new
  outcomes
- The application of the theory to further observations and to human
  endeavors

Figure 2.2 is a summary of these elements, containing examples of linguistic variation in English.

2.2 Applied Linguistics

Applied linguistics is broadly defined as the application of linguistic knowledge and principles to human needs. The British Association for Applied
Linguistics defines it this way:

Applied linguistics is both an approach to understanding language issues in the real world, drawing on theory and empirical analysis, [and] an interdisciplinary area of study, in which linguistics is combined with issues, methods and perspectives drawn from other disciplines (BAAL, 2000: Website).

The relationship between general linguistics and applied linguistics and between scientific theory and practice, is not always easy to understand. On the one hand, theorists see their work as unfettered by practical application, and therefore objective, unbiased, and adequate. Applied linguists, on the other hand, consider more the reasons for observing language, gathering and analyzing linguistic data, synthesizing findings, drawing conclusions, and finally offering opinions. Of course, theory development is an important objective of linguistic analysis, but linguistic theory, data, and facts can also be used to understand real world issues and solve puzzles associated with human behaviors like language. This is a productive way to view the close relationship between linguistics and applied linguistics, and it provides a sound scientific basis for the development of both theory and practice in disciplines such as forensic linguistics. These comments are based on an interpretation of Labov's (1988:159) insightful explication of the theory and practice issue relative to forensic applications.

2.2.1 Areas of Applied Linguistics

Although applied linguistics first related only to the study of how languages were taught and acquired, the field has broadened to include many endeavors outside education. No fewer than 25 scientific commissions are supported by the Association Internationale de Linguistique Appliquée (IALA Website):

Adult language learning
Child language
Communications in the professions
Contrastive linguistics and error analysis
Discourse analysis
Educational technology and language learning
Foreign language teaching methodology and teacher education
Forensic linguistics
Immersion education
Interpreting and translating
Language and ecology
Language education in multilingual settings
Language and gender
Sociolinguistics
Language and the media

ELEMENTS OF SCIENCE USED IN LINGUISTICS	EXAMPLES FROM DIALECT VARIATION IN ENGLISH
1. Linguistic *facts* are observations of human language behavior.	A variety of English spoken by many African Americans demonstrates the forms in (1) to (4): (1) I **am** goin'. (2) I**'m** goin'. (3) I goin'. (4) I **be** goin'.
2. *Classification* of facts results from ordering and grouping them.	First, sentences (1) to (4) fall into two groups, based on meaning. Second, sentences (1) to (3) are ordered "all to nothing": full verb, partial contracted verb, no verb. "I am going now." "I usually go." (1) I **am** goin'. (4) I **be** goin'. (2) I**'m** goin'. (3) I goin'.
3. *Relationships* are found based on the interaction of observed phenomena.	These facts interact with another set of facts (* sentences are ungrammatical): (5) I know where I **am**. (6) * I know where I**'m**. (7) * I know where I.
4. *Principles* result from observing relationships among facts.	Two principles result from the facts observed in this variety of English. Principle #1: the verb *am* (*be*) can be contracted or lost before *goin'*. Principle #2: the verb *am* (*be*) cannot be contracted or lost at sentence end.
5. *Generalizations* result from combining various principles.	Principles #1 and #2 allow the generalization that deletion of the verb *am* (*be*) is related to contraction in this way: in this variety of English, *am* (*be*) is deleted only where it can be contracted in standard English.
6. *Theory* is based on the interrelatedness of generalizations.	This generalization and others like it allow hypotheses such as, African American English is rule governed, and it is related to other varieties of English in regular ways.
7. *Communication* and peer review of results occur in exchanges of information and views:	Steps 1 to 6 have been followed and reported on for this and many other varieties of English and other languages.

Figure 2.2 The science of linguistics.

ELEMENTS OF SCIENCE USED IN LINGUISTICS	EXAMPLES FROM DIALECT VARIATION IN ENGLISH
8. *Inference* takes what we know, allowing us to form hypotheses that predict new outcomes.	One possible inference is that speakers of this variety will use sentences like, "I be goin'," with different meaning and in very different contexts than (1) to (3).
9. *Applications* of science are to continue theory building or to use it for human purposes.	Primary application of this insight into English dialects is to education. Forensic applications rely on variation analysis in voice and authorship identification.

Figure 2.2 (Continued) The science of linguistics.

Language for special purposes
Language planning
Language autonomy in language learning
Lexicography and lexicology
Literacy
Mother tongue education
Psycholinguistics
Rhetoric and *stylistics*
Second language acquisition
Sign language

Emphasis is added to indicate the presence of commissions on *forensic linguistics* and *stylistics*. See also the website of the AAAL (the American Association of Applied Linguistics).

2.2.2   Forensic Linguistics

The field of applied linguistics that is the focal point of this book is forensic linguistics, one of many developing disciplines in applied linguistics, which draws on the scientific study of language to solve forensic problems. Applications of forensic linguistics include voice identification, interpretation of expressed meaning in laws and legal writings, analysis of discourse in legal settings, interpretation of intended meaning in oral and written statements (e.g., confessions), authorship identification, the language of the law (e.g., plain language), analysis of courtroom language used by trial participants (i.e., judges, lawyers, and witnesses), trademark law, and interpretation and translation when more than one language must be used in a legal context. (See Chapter 4 for greater detail.)

All areas of linguistics are used in forensic applications: phonetics and phonology (including spelling), morphology, syntax, semantics, discourse analysis, pragmatics, stylistics, and interpretation and translation:

Auditory phonetics makes use of auditory methods of analysis for the discrimination and identification of speakers by victims and witnesses.

Acoustic phonetics analyzes speech using acoustic methods for speaker discrimination and identification by instrumental means.

Semantics focuses on the comprehensibility and interpretation of written and spoken language that is difficult to understand, e.g., consumer product warnings, jury instructions, trademarks, etc.

Discourse analysis is the study of extended utterances, such as narratives and conversations of the type that take place within the judicial process.

Pragmatics is the analysis of a speaker's intended meaning in contexts of actual language use. Forensic linguists use the theoretical tools provided by discourse analysis and pragmatics to analyze the function of language used in specific contexts, such as dictation, conversations, hearings, questioning, and the language of specific speech acts, e.g., threats, promises, warnings, etc.

Stylistics examines cases of questioned authorship. Forensic applications of methods for determining authorship are related to cases requiring the linguist to determine (1) if all the writings in a questioned set were authored by one person, (2) if a questioned writing was written by one of a number of possible authors, or (3) if a questioned writing was or was not authored by one writer who is proposed as the suspect-author based on external nonlinguistic evidence. All levels of language (sounds as represented by spelling, words, meaning, sentence grammar, and language use) are possible markers of writing style.

Language of the law is concerned with assuring that the legal language of statutes and of legal and consumer writings be clear, brief, and simple, i.e., plain language.

Language of the courtroom studies courtroom discourse, including analyses of the language of witnesses, lawyers, and judges.

Interpretation of one spoken language into another is the object of studies on interpretation tasks specific to legal venues, e.g., questions and answers in testimony, pretrial interpretation, the role and task of the interpreter, etc.

Translation work relates to providing reliable translations of written material needed in legal proceedings.

References

American Association of Applied Linguistics (AAAL): *http://www.aaal.org/*

Association Internationale de Linguistique Appliquée (IALA): *http://www.brad.ac.uk.acad/aila/*

Benton, W., publisher, *Encyclopaedia Britannica*, v. 20, University of Chicago, Chicago, 1966.

British Association for Applied Linguistics (BAAL): *http://www.baal.org.uk/*

Labov, W., The judicial testing of linguistic theory, in Tannen, D., Ed., *Linguistics in Context: Connecting Observation and Understanding*, Ablex, Norwood, 159–182, 1988.

Lyons, J., *Introduction to Theoretical Linguistics*, Cambridge University Press, Cambridge, 1968.

Lyovin, A. V., *An Introduction to the Languages of the World*, Oxford University Press, Oxford, 1997.

McArthur, T. and McArthur, F., Eds., *The Oxford Companion to the English Language*, Oxford University Press, Oxford, 1992.

McMenamin, G. R., *Forensic Stylistics*, Elsevier Science Publishers, Amsterdam, 1993.

Linguistic Variation

3

GERALD R. McMENAMIN

3.1 Variation

All of us make sense of experience by placing the objects and actions we observe into categories according to shared properties. Science does this systematically and explicitly. The members of a category have one or more characteristics in common. For example, consider the letter *x* in ten different font styles: x, x, **x, x,** x, x, *x, x, **x, x.*** In addition to the font style, other variation could be added, e.g., size differences. All ten xs share the stable properties needed for each to be recognized as x, but they vary enough in style for a layperson to discriminate them or for an expert, like a typesetter or document examiner, to identify each font and size.

Forensic scientists look past the usually stable and constant similarities that serve to categorize objects like bullets and cartridges (or tires, shoes, fingers, genes, etc.) toward the variation that makes it possible to discriminate one fired bullet from another. The analysis of variation is important in the forensic sciences because the variation left in trace evidence can be associated with the individual or class characteristics of the instruments or persons involved in a crime. The language left by a speaker in a recorded message or by a writer in an anonymous letter can likewise be associated with the language known to be used by groups and individuals.

3.2 Variation in Language

Everyone is familiar with language variation — the I-say-*tomehto*-you-say-*tomahto* experience. For example, on HGTV's Emeril Lagassi program, at least three variants of the *r*-sound in the chef's spoken English can be heard: 1. a clearly pronounced /r/ in words like *red, rim, green, orange, first,* and *butter,* 2. omission of the /r/ in the words like *sharp, hearts (of palm), parsley,* etc., and 3. insertion of an "intrusive" /r/ at the ends of words like *raw* and *saw.* For these variants, see Figure 3.1. Most U.S. West Coast viewers will notice this variation because their /r/ is always pronounced, and they do not end *raw* and *saw* with an /r/. (Note that this observation of such variation is merely descriptive and not intended to be evaluative.)

This variation is part of Emeril's internalized system of language. Language (*langue*) is the internal communication system of a community of

Pronounced /r/	Absent /r/		Intrusive /r/	
r-word	r-word	sounds like	r-word	sounds like
red	sharp	"sháhp"	raw	"rar egg"
rim	hearts	"háhts"	saw	"sar it"
green	parsley	"páhsley"		
first	garnish	"gáhnish		
butter	artichoke	"áhtichoke"		
	garlic	"gáhlic"		
	barbara	"báhbara"		
	air	"aih"		

Figure 3.1 Some examples of /r/ variation in one speaker.

speakers and is sometimes referred to as the speaker's or writer's competence. Speech (*parole*) is the individual use of that underlying communal system by a member of the group, often now called the speaker's or writer's performance. Language and speech also vary within the individual, as well as within and across communities.

Two kinds of variation are commonly observed within a single community of speakers and writers: intraspeaker variation within one person and interspeaker variation among all language users of the speech community. These two principles of linguistic variation have been developed and established since the onset of variation studies. Many observers have articulated them; one of the most succinct statements is that of Frank Anshen: "Not only do any two members of what should reasonably be the same speech community use different variants of the same linguistic form, but so does each individual member" (Anshen, 1978:1).

The question that often goes unidentified or unsettled relates to the role of variation in linguistic competence and performance. Traditionally, the ever-present variation in language is considered to be simply free variation, i.e., an accident contingent on a single speaker's performance. In this view, thought and language are abstract, thereby transcending actual instances of language use by speakers and writers. The analysis of language takes place outside the "messy" context of its use and without regard for the constraints of performance. So, stylistic variation is merely a nonsystematic optional ingredient in the language recipe of individual speakers and is analyzed only outside the realm of competence.

A new approach, proposed in the late 1960s and developed during the past 30 years, is that variation in language is systematically conditioned by actual speakers and writers in authentic real world communication. In this view, access to the underlying system of language is provided by observation of language use. Careful observation and analysis of natural language show that linguistic variation can be described and measured insofar as it is systematically conditioned by linguistic (internal) and nonlinguistic (external) factors. Thus, variation is no longer seen as an ornament of performance appended to the abstract system of linguistic competence. Stylistic variation in language is now understood to be a systematic property of the language, analyzed within the realm of competence. Competence is thereby reflected in large-scale observations of the variable performance of speakers and writers.

The way that analysts see variation fitting in, however, determines their theoretical approach to stylistic analysis. Some traditionalists see the homogeneity of the forest, never taking seriously the variation represented by the trees. Such a limited view of the role of variation causes them to ignore rich sources of variation such as spelling, vocabulary variation, or grammatical variation; they claim that these may not be reliable indicators of an author's writing style.

Most modern linguists find a way to incorporate linguistic variation into their theory of language because they see the complementary roles of the two approaches: natural language cannot be successfully observed outside a theoretical paradigm, but the paradigm cannot be constructed without the observation of language as it is used. This is not a new thought, e.g., Dwight Bolinger's comment of over 40 years ago: "[I want to illustrate] a certain proneness to skimp the specimen-gathering phase of our science and to base generalizations on insufficient data ..." (Bolinger, 1960:366). Variation in language form and function is inherent in the notion of the speaker's or writer's competence and, as a result, "specimen-gathering" observations can be used to identify individual (idiolectal) or group (dialectal) characteristics of speakers and writers.

The first step toward accounting for variation is to observe it, then see that it is systematic, and finally discover the relative significance of each variant as, for example, one of a set of features that mark a writer's style. Even in the previous examples of TV chef Emeril's spoken language (Figure 3.1), one can observe the beginnings of a systematic distribution of /r/. For example, /r/ at the beginning of a word and /r/ in a cluster like *gr-* are pronounced, while /r/ at the end of a syllable containing a stressed /á/ is absent and /r/ is inserted at the ends of monosyllables like *raw* and *saw*.

For an example of written variation, consider in Figure 3.2 how some central California berry growers spell the words *strawberry* and *strawberries* on their roadside signs. Pictures of the actual signs are included because a simple printed list might have been beyond belief for some readers. The variation falls into four broad categories: spelling, plural marking, compound-word formation, and position of word parts or use of words vis-à-vis images. Types of variation within those categories are outlined in Figure 3.3.

Figure 3.2 Roadside signs in Central California for "strawberry" and "straw-berries."

For purposes of easy illustration, a single word used by many writers was chosen. The signs contain what might be referred to as extreme variation because about half of them were produced by semiliterate writers who speak English as a second language. Also note that sign pairs 14a/14b, 17a/17b, and 18a/18b appear to be the same or similar, but the *a* sign in each pair is distinct from the *b* sign, i.e., one sign for each traffic direction. Both signs are included in Figure 3.2 to anticipate the suggestion that the variation merely represents a sign painter's error or a performance mistake of the writer. On the contrary, the variation is repeated (at no small effort) on the second sign in each case.

No.	"Strawberry/ Strawberries"	VARIATION
		A. Variation in Spelling:
	Singular	1. <u>STRAW</u>
		STARW- (14a, 14b)
1	STRAWBERRIE	STRAM- (13)
2	STRAWBERRI	**S** + [Image] (21)
3	STRWBERI	
		2. <u>BERRY: final -Y in forms intended to be singular</u>
	Plural	BERRIE (1)
		BERRI (2, 3)
4	<u>STRAWBERRIES</u>	
5	STRAWBERRYS	3. <u>BERRY/BERRIES: double RR</u>
6	STRAWBERRIE'S	-BERI (3)
7	STRAWBERRIS	-BERIES (11, 13)
8	STRAW BERRYS	-BREEIE (12)
9	STRAW-BERRIES	
10	BoysenBerries	4. <u>BERRIES: BERR- sequence</u>
11	STRAWBERIES	**BRR**Y
12	STRAWBREEIE	**BREEI**E
13	STRAMBERIES	
14a	STARWBERRY	**B. Word Formation — marked and unmarked plural forms:**
14b	STARWBERRY	1. <u>BERRIES: final –IES in forms intended to be plural</u>
15	STRAWBRRY	a. Various spellings with plural marker
16	STRAWBERRV	-BERRIES (9, 10, 13, 18a, 18b)
17a	STRAWBERR	BERRIE'S (6)
17b	STRAWBERR	BERRYS (5, 8, 20)
18a	STRAWBERRIE- S	BERRIS (7)
18b	STRAWBERRIE- S	b. Various spellings without plural marker
19	STRAWBERR- IES	BERRY (14a, 14b, 15)
		BERRV (16)
20	STRAW- BERRYS	BERR _ (17a, 17b)
		C. Word Formation — compound-word forms:
	Iconic	1. No separation: STRAWBERRIES (1-7, 11-19)
		2. Space: STRAW BERRYS (8)
		3. Hyphen: STRAW-BERRYS (9)
21	FRESH + S + [Image]	4. Capital B: BoysenBerries (10)
22	FRESH + [Images]	5. Alphabetic + Iconic (21)
23	[Image]	6. Iconic with other words (22)
		7. Iconic only (23)
		D. Variation in Positioning of Word Elements
		1. –S on next line just under word-ending: STRAWBERRIE- S (18a, 18b)
		2. –IES on next line just under word ending: STRAWBERR- IES (19)
		3. BERRYS on next line under whole word: STRAW- BERRYS (20)

Figure 3.3 Types of variation present in 26 signs for "strawberry" and "strawberries."

The key to understanding linguistic variation is to know how language changes. Language is traditionally observed at a single point in time, resulting in what is called a synchronic description. Given that language changes very slowly, stability or change in language is observed and described by comparing two synchronic descriptions from widely separate points in real time, resulting in what is called a diachronic description. It is now known, however, that language change is always present, that speakers are often conscious of it, and that it can be observed over shorter periods of time in the form of linguistic variation.

One of the newer ways of observing linguistic change in progress is the analysis of differences in apparent time. Studies on the analysis of variation, e.g., Bailey et al. (1991), will examine differences among living generations, assuming that each generation of speakers reflects the language of the time it was acquired. Findings from apparent-time studies indicate that generational differences in language reflect processes of diachronic change as described in real-time studies. Sometimes, like the diverse effects of a gene, some variation dominates and becomes an actual change in progress, while another variation recedes or remains stable.

3.3   Variation as Ordered Heterogeneity

Since a good understanding of linguistic variation is very important to the theory and practice of stylistics and authorship identification, it is important to examine the basis of current variation theory. From this perspective, the grammar of the speaker or writer demonstrates internal, nonrandom orderly differentiation. Language is an object possessing orderly heterogeneity. Language does not have to be without variation (polymorphisms) to be structured. It does not have to be a homogeneous system to be regular, i.e., rule-governed (Weinreich, Labov, and Herzog, 1968:187). Further, variation does not mean just switching back and forth between two nonvariable systems available to the speaker or writer, given that, "nativelike command of heterogeneous structures is not a matter of multidialectalism or 'mere' performance but is a part of unilingual linguistic competence [of the speaker]"(Weinreich, Labov, and Herzog, 1968:101).

3.4   Group vis-à-vis Individual Variation

3.4.1   Class vs. Individual Markers in the Forensic Sciences

This section is a synthesis of Inman and Rudin's lucid chapter on the nature of physical evidence, but adapted here to stylistics. They outline the task of forensic science and the types of evidence leading to individuation: *associations, identification of class features,* and finally *individuation* (Inman and Rudin, (1997:3).

The task of forensic science is to describe and measure evidential traits left in a crime and compare them to traits found in known reference materials. If the traits are found to be similar, then an association is created between the evidence and the reference item. The value of such evidence lies in comparing both identifying and individualizing traits between two objects and rendering a conclusion regarding the strength of an association between the two.

Forensic science, then, first establishes associations: bullet + weapon, fingerprint + finger of person, shoeprint + shoe of person, handwriting + writer, language + author, blood + DNA. By its nature, physical evidence (e.g., writing or blood) is circumstantial. It does not directly facilitate an association but instead provides information that allows a deductive inference (indirect evidence) about a possible association.

Second, systematic specification of class characteristics serves to narrow the field by eliminating many writers not associated with the class features of a particular writing. Class characteristics are those imposed on the individual by outside influences on the language of his or her specific speech community, e.g., geography, social class, communication contexts, etc. The individual is thus identified (i.e., grouped) by his or her class features.

Stylistics examines linguistic traits (grammatical minutiae) so rare, either alone or in combination with other traits, that they could not be duplicated by chance alone in the language of more than one individual, thus individuating the language of a writer. Individuating traits are reflected in variables acquired during language development and re-occuring in language use. By analogy, the tracks made by a tire reflect the class features of its design and manufacture, but the individual patterns of characteristic use of its car and driver.

Linguistic individuation is virtually always established as a combination of traits rather than a single trait, because singular unique language forms are rare. Consider the form of the envelope address in Figure 3.4. Each line is indented five spaces, a class characteristic of older American writers. However, in two places the writer follows the current advice of the U.S. Postal Service, using the modern abbreviation and punctuation of California as CA without a period. Note also the *U.* abbreviation for *University,* as well as the very modern use of the nine-number (zip + 4) postal zip code. (The writer of this address is not, in fact, a senior citizen.)

To say that individuation is related to a constellation of variable forms is not to say that unique forms do not appear. An example of a unique form that has not (to date) been found anywhere else is the misspelling of the

Figure 3.4 Multiple variables in individual writing.

QUESTIONED WRITING	KNOWN WRITINGS
diffulgties	**diffulgities**
	difulgity
	Difulgity

Figure 3.5 A possibly unique marker of writing style.

word *difficulties* from a case of questioned authorship: *diffulgties* or *diffulgities* (see Figure 3.5).

3.4.2 Language and Dialect

In 1817, Coleridge described what are now referred to as *idiolect*, *dialect*, and *language*: "Every man's language has, first, its *individualities*; second, the common properties of the *class* to which he belongs; and third, words and phrases of *universal* use" (Coleridge, 1817:53).

Language and dialect are both group phenomena. A language is defined by its group of speakers. A dialect is a variety of the language used by a subgroup of speakers who are more or less separated from other speakers of the group by geography or social factors. Geographical isolation of groups is the result of separation by long distances, barriers (oceans, rivers, roads, mountains, etc.), or otherwise spatially restricted communication. Social distance also causes linguistic variation between groups and is related to differences in social class (education, occupation, income), race, ethnicity, age, sex, and social context (style). Since all speakers belong to various subgroups,

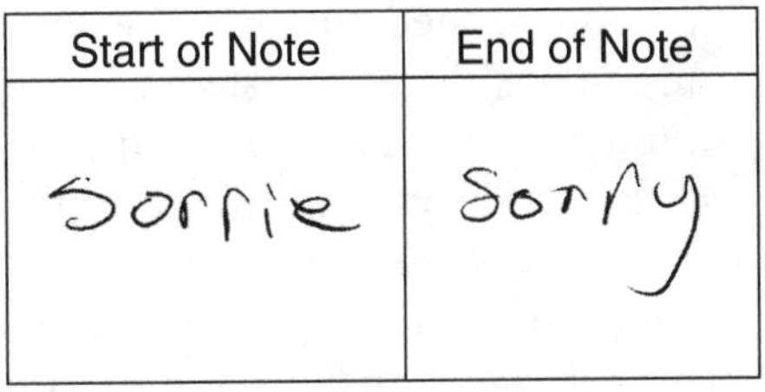

Figure 3.6 Individual variation in a short written note.

especially in highly urbanized communities, variation is always present in language. Variation is a defining characteristic of a dialect community. If one group's variant is used more frequently and distributed more widely across groups, it may represent a change in the language.

3.4.3 Idiolect

The idiolect has been referred to as a personal dialect. No two individuals use and perceive language in exactly the same way, so there will always be at least small differences in the grammar each person has internalized to speak, write, and respond to other speakers and writers. The idiolect is the individual's unconscious and unique combination of linguistic knowledge, cognitive associations, and extra-linguistic influences.

Language can only be observed in individuals, whose idiolectal features are very important for applications related to authorship identification. However, such individual characteristics become unimportant for the description of the speaker's dialect or language (the usual goal of linguistic analysis), wherein the focus is on group characteristics shared by all speakers or writers of the speech community. Dialects are not simply large collections of individual idiolects but are a synthesis of shared elements. Since language variation and change within a dialect or language are group phenomena, the idiolect is less the source of variation and more its reflection in the individual.

When language changes over time, there are periods when "competing" new and old forms exist side by side in the whole speech community. Multiple forms will also be found in the language of an individual speaker, i.e., in his or her idiolect. Such individual variation is due to changes going on in the speech community, as well as to changes occurring in the person's own process of language acquisition and use. Consider a student who recently left a brief (53-word) note explaining why she would not be in my class. To start the note, she said, "*Sorrie* can't make it today," and at the end of the note she repeated the thought, "*Sorry* can't make it," but with the different spelling the second time, as can be seen in Figure 3.6.

The idiolect and its importance for stylistics and forensic stylistics are reviewed in McMenamin (1993:52). A good historical overview of the

19th-century linguistic roots of the idiolect, one with a view to placing the locus of language change in the linguistic system of the group, may be found in Weinreich, Labov, and Herzog (1968:104). There is now also renewed interest in stressing the role of the individual as the initial locus of variation and change, e.g., Johnstone (1996 and 2000). In this view, language creates and reflects human individuality: "Through talk and other aspects of behavior, individuals display their individuality. In other words, people express their individuality with everything they do ..." (Johnstone, 2000:407).

3.5   The Analysis of Variation

3.5.1   Hierarchical Models for the Study of Variation

Differences in method for studying variation are often explained by reference to what constitutes a hierarchical orientation to language study: the bottom-up model (e.g., Labov, 1972; Schiffrin, 1994) vis-à-vis a top-down approach (e.g., Sinclair and Coulthard, 1975; Edmonson, 1981). The bottom-up model searches for recurrent patterns, distributions, and forms of organization in the writing in order to come up with evidence for the presence of units, existence of patterns, and formulation of rules related to a writer's style (adapted from Schiffrin, 1994). A top-down model of style analysis refers to the search for a predetermined taxonomy of stylistic items which would allow for the discrimination of writers within a certain speech community.

Given these two very different theoretical starting points, it is not difficult to understand how questions have come up on both sides regarding specific differences in the practice of stylistic analysis, i.e.: the basis for establishing criteria for identification (style-markers), the purpose of a corpus, database, and statistical analysis of data mined from them, and the meaning of *impression, description*, and *analysis* as applied to style data.

Part of the focus of later chapters will be to 1. examine the outcomes of the bottom-up model for analysis of variation in writing style, 2. determine the weight of seemingly serious theoretical differences that result from using different but complementary models of analysis, and 3. respond to specific issues raised in relation to three issues in the analysis of variation in written language: the identification of style-markers, the statistical analysis of corpus data, and the way one talks about variation analysis within the context of science.

3.5.2   Linguistic Variables

Linguistic variation refers to the presence of more than one way to say or write the same thing in the language of a community or individual. Such multiple forms are variants available to the speaker or writer. A community

Five Variables with Two Variants Each	Known Letters		Questioned Letter	
	n	%	n	%
1. Verb *to be*				
PRESENT: I know you **are** a good man.	54/69	78%	3/12	25%
ABSENT: Know you good man	15/69	22%	9/12	75%
2. Auxiliary Verb *do*				
PRESENT: But **do** not think he will take	17/17	100%	3/13	23%
ABSENT: He say he not want my money.	0/17	0%	10/13	77%
3. Other Auxiliary Verbs				
PRESENT: I **was** losing hope then they come	42/50	84%	11/28	39%
ABSENT: You tell me I taking to much dope.	8/50	16%	17/28	61%
4. Article *a*				
PRESENT: So I know you are **a** good man.	19/58	33%	0/34	0%
ABSENT: Know you good man and will do....	39/58	67%	34/34	100%
5. Past Tense Marker				
PRESENT: The nurse **told** me that Ed asked	188/209	90%	21/95	22%
ABSENT: Nurse **tell** me to put	21/209	10%	74/95	78%

Figure 3.7 Relative proportions of variants for each of five variables.

or individual may always or never use a particular variant, in which case the variation is categorically present or absent. However, the more typical case is the relative use of two or more variants, in which case a linguistic variable is constructed to quantify the relative presence or absence of each variant vis-à-vis all possible occurrences of the variable, and thereby reflect the proportionate degree and type of variation for a particular segment of the speech community, or for a given speaker or writer. A writer, for example, may have the three variants *can not*, *cannot*, and *can't* available, but reserve one or another for certain writing contexts, alternate forms with seeming abandon, or simply use one form all the time.

Consider the case of a letter written to change the beneficiaries specified in the will of a large estate (*Estate of Violet Houssien*). The decedent was a speaker of Hawaiian Creole English, but her written language demonstrated relatively low frequencies of five Creole features. The writers of the letter were acquainted with the decedent and were well aware of the Creole influence on her English. However, in their clumsy effort at disguise, they exaggerated the Creole markers to stereotypical proportions by increasing the frequency and consistency of the Creole variants. Figure 3.7 shows the respective differences in the questioned vs. known variation for each of the five variables.

Such attempts at disguise are not the exclusive work of openly accused perpetrators but have on occasion been attempted by would-be experts and their unscrupulous client attorneys. Another case (*Oregon v. Crescenzi*) presented a questioned letter describing a woman's death and the known reference writings of her suspect husband. After all prosecution discovery and authorship analysis had been done and disclosed to opposing counsel, the defense proffered two "mystery letters" and asked the district attorney to have his expert linguist determine their authorship. The covert intent of the defense was to impeach the incriminating testimony of the prosecution by leading its expert to mistakenly identify the defendant as the author of the new letters, which had been created by the defense's expert, a University of California, Berkeley, English professor. The ethics of such a stunt aside, the mystery letters were quite different from the questioned letter and the known writings of the defendant. Previously identified style-markers, their frequencies measured by instances per text line in all writings, were found to occur in the mystery letters at a rate double (200%) that of the known and questioned writings.

3.6   Language as a Discrete Combinatorial System

Language is what is known as a discrete combinatorial system (Pinker, 1994:84). This means three things: 1. language units are separate from one another; 2. language combines small units into larger ones to create meaning, and 3. and the combinations start with the smallest units of language (sounds) and become progressively larger — sounds grouping into words, words into sentences, and sentences into discourse. All combinations are rule-governed and systematic, i.e., realized according to the rules of the language.

It is in this sense that Wilhelm von Humbolt (1836) observed that language "makes infinite use of finite media," a concept explained by Studdert–Kennedy (1990:758) in this way:

> This is the principle by which a limited set of discrete elements (gestures, phonemes, morphemes) is repeatedly sampled, combined, and permuted to yield larger elements (phonemes, morphemes, phrases) having properties quite different, in structure and functional scope, from those of their constitutive elements. ... Each language is thus one of an uncountable set of solutions to the problem of selecting from the available variants a finite set will afford ....

Pinker (1994:84) points out that this principle underlying grammar is unusual in the natural world:

> A grammar is an example of a 'discrete combinatorial system.' ... In a discrete combinatorial system like language, there can be an unlimited number of completely distinct combinations with an infinite range of properties. ... Most

of the complicated systems we see in the world, in contrast, are *blending systems*, like geology, paint mixing, cooking, sound, light, and weather. In a blending system the properties of the combination lie *between* the properties of its elements, and the properties of the elements are lost in the average or mixture.

Studdert–Kennedy (1990:758) also comments on the paucity of systems other than language that make infinite use of finite media:

> The principle ... is quite rare in the natural world. Abler (1989), terming it "the particulate principle of self-diversifying system," has shown that it is shared by two other systems: chemical interaction, for which the particulate units are atoms, and biological inheritance, for which the particulate units are genes.

The theory and practice of linguistic stylistics depends on the discrete nature of language units in two important ways. First, it is written language that best demonstrates the discrete nature of language elements:

> The acoustic parameters that can be attached to the flow of speech ... are continuous with respect to time. From the psychological point of view, however, it is clear that speech is discrete in some sense; it is composed of discontinuous elements ... [which] recur constantly. One of the best proofs for the discrete nature of language is that alphabetic writing is possible. Alphabetic writing, in fact, indicates two types of segmentation into discrete units. On the one hand, sentences can be considered as sequences of letters (or phonemes); on the other, they can be analyzed as sequences of words (Gross, 1972:19).

Second, seeing even a relatively small number of the possible combinations of discrete elements in a sentence provides a notion of the vast magnitude of choices every speaker or writer has and makes. Knowing how quickly a writer's choices can multiply is the theoretical lynchpin of variation analysis in stylistics, since style in writing is reflected in the constant and multiple choices made by a writer during the writing process. The set of all sounds and letters in a language is finite; the morphemes and words are also limited in number and in length (though they are numerous enough to allow multiple lexical choices). However, in spoken and written discourse, there is no upper bound in number or length to the sentences a writer can piece together. Consider the sentence in Figure 3.8 (adapted from Gross, 1972:21) in which the speaker or writer is presented with seven opportunities for choice in a string of seven word sets. At just the word level, i.e., moving along the sequence of the string from one decision point to the next, it is possible for

1	2	3	4	5	6	7
This The That Our	pitcher goalie flautist contestant survivor captain	is was	probably certainly surely I think I believe we think we believe one hopes	a another	gorgeous pretty smart lovely beautiful ravishing wonderful striking	one. girl. woman. lady. female. player.

Figure 3.8 A sentence string with seven opportunities for word choice.

Sentence #1:

The	pitcher	is	probably	a	gorgeous	one.

....

Sentence #36,864:

Our	captain	was	one hopes	another	striking	player.

Figure 3.9 Two of the 36,864 possible choices from a seven-state string.

the speaker or writer to construct $4 \times 6 \times 2 \times 8 \times 2 \times 8 \times 6 = 36,864$ sentences from the 36 words available (counting two-word clauses like *I think*, etc. as one word). Figure 3.9 contains two illustrative possibilities.

In addition, if one factors in the speaker's or writer's choices of linguistic units at levels higher than contiguous single words, possible outcomes begin to multiply without end. There is a hint of this in the sentences embedded as options in word-set #4 in Figure 3.8: *I think, I believe, we think, we believe, and one hopes.*

Note that emphasis on stylistic variation in written language has led to a focus almost exclusively in this section on the principal source of that variation: the combinatorial possibilities of finite sets of discrete linguistic units. It is, however, important to understand that these finite sets can be very large and varied, within a language or across languages, and the individual units of a set are also significant sources for linguistic variation. This is demonstrated in the detailed guides to linguistic description that provide frameworks for linguistic field workers. These contain very long and intricate lists of the kinds of units that can occur in the languages of the world. See, for example, Comrie and Smith (1977).

3.7 Another Discrete Combinatorial System: DNA

3.7.1 Analogy in the Forensic Sciences

Analogies aid understanding. For example, the linguistic analysis of language style has often been compared, casually and seriously, to fingerprint analysis. This analogy is accurate in some important ways, but it simultaneously overstates the consistency and understates the potential of stylistic analysis. Good fingerprints will yield constant and reliable results because the identifying points are few, focused, finite in number, and idiosyncratic. On the other hand, the best of language samples vary in analytical outcome because the identifying points can be few or many (potentially infinite in number), spread throughout all language levels, and representative of the combined class and individual features uniquely synthesized by each writer. Therefore, continued caution in using the fingerprint analogy is advised (see McMenamin, 1993:157).

With the increased application of DNA analysis for individuation, it is now quite common to hear or read that forensic stylistic analysis has the identifying power of DNA. Although they rarely appear in writing, comments such as the following are not uncommon: "The scientific analysis of a text … can reveal features as sharp and telling as anything this side of fingerprints and DNA. … After the crime, the words remain. Like fingerprints and DNA" (Foster, 2000:4).

A good analogy signals some similarity of how two elements work within their respective contexts. The analogy between DNA and stylistics can be stated in this fashion: as DNA analysis is to genetic individuation, so stylistics is to linguistic individuation. Language makes infinite use of finite media as does DNA, and language and DNA are both discrete combinatorial systems (vs. blended systems). However, differences between the systems lie in the nature of the elements of the respective systems and in the methods of analysis, description, and measurement of variation. DNA is a chemical and biological system, described in a natural science paradigm; however, written language is a neurological, psychological, and sociocultural system, described principally within a social-science framework.

An historical precedent for caution in the matter of analogy is the failure of spectographic analysis for voice identification to measure up to the fingerprint comparison:

> Spurious argument, and false analogy with fingerprint analysis …, almost sealed the fate of forensic phonetics forever. The basic fallacy of "voiceprint-ing" (still practiced in some parts of the world) lies in a failure to appreciate the great variability of speech within a single speaker, and the overlap of speech characteristics by different speakers sharing common physiological, sociological, dialectal or other characteristics. (Howard et al., 1995:35).

Careless comparison of the identifying power of DNA and stylistics could lead stylistics down the path of the voiceprint because it creates expectations that can only sometimes be met. Therefore, it makes sense to analyze closely the analogy between stylistics and DNA. After all, if it is a good analogy in any respect, it will be of great help to triers of fact in their effort to understand linguistic evidence and assess its weight as evidence of authorship.

3.7.2   The Analogy between DNA and Language

Is DNA a valid analogy for individuation in language? The analogy is valid and helpful, but significant differences between their analytical methods and outcomes remain. Judges, juries, and attorneys are often relatively familiar with forensic DNA analysis. In the course of court testimony related to linguistic variation, the intent of certain questions is to elicit an evaluative comparison of the conclusions and opinions resulting from style analysis to those from DNA analysis. Such questions are directed toward the respective types of systematic variation found in both DNA and written language, then toward the relative individuating power of their scientific analysis, description, and measurement.

Informed answers to questions related to the language and DNA analogy are useful ways to make stylistics understandable. However, it is important to understand the details of such a comparison so that the analogy is valid and not overstated. The analogy between DNA and language is not new; they are compared in two principal ways. First is the language used to describe the respective systems. Explicit comparisons have long been made between DNA as the recipe for life, and grammar the recipe for language. Second is the comparison of the elements and organization of the respective systems, i.e., ways in which DNA demonstrates internal variation similar to that found in language variation.

3.7.3   The Language of DNA and Linguistics

The parallels between language and DNA have prompted genetic scientists to borrow the language of linguistic description to talk about DNA. The first appears to be Niels Jerne, who early in the study of DNA proposed the comparison:

> ... if we consider the variable region that characterizes an antibody molecule ... we may find a more reasonable analogy between language and the immune system, namely by regarding the variable region of a given antibody molecule not as a *word* but as a *sentence* or a phrase. The immense repertoire of the immune system then becomes not a vocabulary of words, but a lexicon of sentences which is capable of responding to any sentence expressed by the multitude of antigens which the immune system may encounter (Jerne, 1985:737).

a.	CELL	The human body contains about 100 trillion *cells*, each 1/10 mm thick.
b.	NUCLEUS	Each cell contains a *nucleus*.
c.	GENOME	Each nucleus contains two sets (mom's + dad's) of the *human genome*.
d.	CHROMOSOME	Each human genome contains *23 chromosomes*.
e.	GENE	Each set of the 23 chromosomes includes 30,000-80,000 *genes*.
f.	LOCUS	In DNA, a molecular location is called a *locus*.
g.	ALLELES	Different forms of the same gene or marker at a locus are *alleles*.
h.	BASES	Genes have are four chemical building blocks called *bases*: A T G C, Adenine, Thymine, Guanine, Cytosine, aligned like beads on a string.

Figure 3.10 Parts of the human genome.

And most recently, Pinker draws attention to the parallel between language and DNA:

> Another noteworthy discrete combinatorial system in the natural world is the genetic code in DNA, where four kinds of nucleotides are combined into 64 kinds of condons, and the condons can be strung into an unlimited number of different genes (Pinker, 1994:84–85).

Grammar has been metaphorically considered the recipe for language and DNA is likewise seen as the recipe for life. To set up the recipe-for-life metaphor, Ridley (1999:7) lays out the parts of the human genome (put together in Figure 3.10 on something like a card from God's recipe box in the kitchen of creation). At this point, Ridley proceeds to the language vis-à-vis DNA analogy:

> Imagine that the genome is a book. There are 23 chapters, called CHRO-MOSOMES. Each chapter contains several thousand stories, called GENES. Each story is made up of paragraphs, called EXONS, which are interrupted by advertisements called INTRONS. Each paragraph is made up of words, called CONDONS. Each word is written in letters called BASES. ... There are one billion words in the book .... (Ridley, 1999:7).

Ridley explains the bases or "letters" in the following way:

> The filament of DNA is information, a message written in a code of chemicals, one chemical for each letter. It is almost too good to be true, but the code turns out to be written in a way that we can understand. Just like written English, the genetic code is a linear language, written in a straight line. Just like written English, it is digital, in that every letter bears the same importance. Moreover, the language of DNA is considerably simpler than English, since it has an alphabet of only four letters, conventionally known as A, C, G, T (Ridley, 1999:7).

3.7.4   The Systems of DNA and Language

DNA was first studied as the vehicle of generational transference of heritable traits, specifically, disease markers. Then personal identification was discovered to be another application of DNA technology. Language has always been studied as a group phenomenon, with very little attention given to the so-called idiolect. Stylistics started out as a study of genre, then progressed to authorship identification.

Variation in DNA and language: If one considers that only 2% of human DNA is different from that of the chimpanzee, and only 0.5% differentiates human individuals, it is easy to see that it is only the smallest of DNA variations that differentiate people. Languages likewise demonstrate significant interlanguage universals and intralanguage similarity among speakers. Only the very little that is left over from the common pool of language acquired and used by all speakers of a language will reflect the idiolect of a single speaker or writer.

The existence of multiple DNA alleles of a marker at a single locus is called *polymorphism* (i.e., variation). There are two types of polymorphisms in DNA: sequence polymorphisms and length polymorphisms. The sequence of bases at a particular locus, sequence polymorphisms, are like different (acceptable or deviant) spellings for the same four-letter word. The length of a DNA fragment between two defined endpoints, length polymorphisms, is a tandem repeat of the same DNA "word" sequence (Inman and Rudin, 1997:34).

Scientists are beginning to understand a third type of polymorphism in the form of the unique tangles and knots of the DNA strand. The narrow DNA double helix is only molecules in width, but its length can be measured in centimeters. The long DNA strand is tightly tangled and knotted inside the cell nucleus. Cell division and replication require the double DNA strands to separate, but they are so compactly knotted up that untangling them requires a kind of chemical scissors in the form of enzymes that cut the tangles to straighten out the strands, then reattach the ends. Genetics has borrowed concepts of knot theory from mathematics to understand variations in DNA structure related to how DNA strands are tangled and then untangled due to the action of "cutting-enzymes." For an introduction to knot theory and how it relates to DNA, see *http://www.freelearning.com/knots/today.htm*.

There are hundreds of possible variables in spoken and written language, including thousands of variants in format, spelling, word formation, syntax, expressed meaning, discourse, and intended meaning. Although the types of variation may be fewer in the three types of DNA polymorphisms than in language sequences, the number of variants for the three DNA variables combined would be far greater than the total number of actual linguistic variants for a given language.

Describing and measuring variation in DNA and language: Research has established standard locations where the DNA sequence varies more than usual between people. DNA has 20 to 80 marker-types present at any one locus, and each type occurs with a fairly low frequency. A genetic type determined by several loci in combination, each with many possible types, will be rare. So, very few individuals in any population will have the types detected in an item of evidence.

Standard grammatical points of variation have not been identified for spoken or written language. In fact, it is impossible to establish universal points of individuating variation across language groups, and probably impossible to do the same within a language group. However, within a same-language, and especially a same-dialect community of speaker or writers, empirical identification of least and most frequently occurring variation in written language is possible, though difficult, and may allow a set of identifying (class) stylistic variables to be defined. The set of most-individuating (individual) markers is still only definable as the unique combination of class characteristics that can occur, plus the rare unique feature of language that could occur.

The identification of a set of style-markers that would discriminate all writers in a given speech community would of necessity be a top-down undertaking, i.e., style-markers would be predetermined *a priori* in other than an empirical way. Such an approach does not allow the data of each language sample to drive its analysis. If and when sufficient research on each speech community is done, a set of class characteristics of writing may, under certain conditions, be predetermined as discriminating for that group of language users. The conditions for accomplishing this, though, are formidable:

1. The corpus of writing used for reference must be representative (i.e., large) and contain authentic, natural, nonrequest writing.
2. The vast array of possible variation from all types of individual speakers and writers must be described.
3. The large number and complex combinations of extralinguistic contexts that affect language use must be controlled or accounted for in some other way.
4. This research must be repeated from time to time due to language change over time.

The method of measurement is similar for DNA and language, which are both studied in terms of sequences or strings of characters, e.g., Khmelev and Tweedie (2001), and Benedetto et al. (2002). In language, a corpus of writing is collected, and a database of style-markers is established according to identified variation. Then each marker can be established to occur with a base-rate frequency in specific contexts of writing within the population of the speech community. Each marker is also analyzed to determine its relative independence or interdependence vis-à-vis other markers.

When questioned and known reference writings are presented, their similarities and differences are described. Suspect writers whose similarities and differences do not match the respective types and frequencies of those class features of the speech community are excluded. Other suspect writers whose similarities and differences match the presence and frequency of respective class features of the speech community are included as possible writers. Individuation of the writer is then accomplished by examining more than one marker, thereby reducing the known occurrence of a combined set of two or more markers to the lowest frequency possible in the population of writers. Since the respective frequency of each marker in the set is known for a particular speech community, the findings may be expressed as the frequency of Marker 1 in the speech community multiplied by (or added to) the frequency of Marker 2, etc. As more markers are considered, the percentage of the population included as possible writers becomes smaller and smaller, until only one writer remains.

References

Abler, W. L., On the particulate principle of self-diversifying systems, *J. Soc. Biological Structures*, 12:1–13, 1989.

Anshen, F., *Statistics for Linguists*, Newbury House, Rowley, MA, 1978.

Bailey, G. et al., The apparent time construct, *Language Variation Change*, 3:241–264, 1991.

Benedetto, D., Caglioti, E., and Loreto, V. "Language trees and zipping," *Physical Review Letters*, 88:4:1–4, Jan. 28, 2002.

Bolinger, D. W., Syntactic blends and other matters, *Language*, 36:207–221, 1960.

Coleridge, S. T., *Biographia Literaria; or Biographical Sketches of my Literary Life and Opinions*, Vol. II, Fenner, London, 1817.

Comrie, B. and Smith, N., Lingua descriptive studies: questionnaire, *Lingua*, 42:1–72, 1977.

Edmonson, W., *Spoken Discourse: a Model for Analysis*, Longman, London, 1981.

Foster, D., *Author Unknown: on the Trail of the Anonymous*, Holt, New York, 2000.

Gross, M., *Mathematical Models in Linguistics*, Prentice Hall, Englewood Cliffs, NJ, 1972.

Howard, D. M. et al., Spectography of disputed speech samples by peripheral human hearing modelling, *Foren. Linguis.*, 2:1:28–38, 1995.

Inman, K. and Rudin, N., *An Introduction to Forensic DNA Analysis*, CRC Press, Boca Raton, FL, 1997.

Jerne, N. K., The generative grammar of the immune system, Nobel lecture, in I. Lefkovits (Ed.), *A Portrait of the Immune System: Scientific Publications of N. K. Jerne*, v. 2, World Scientific Series in 20th Century Biology, Singapore, 1985.

Johnstone, B., The individual voice in language, Durham, W. H., Daniel, E. V., and Schieffelin, B., Eds., *Ann. Rev. Anthropol.*, 29:405–446, Annual Reviews, Palo Alto, 2000.

Johnstone, B., *The Linguistic Individual: Self-Expression in Language and Linguistics*, Oxford University Press, New York, 1996.

Khmelev, D. V. and Tweedie, F. J., "Using Markov chains for identification of writers," *Literary & Linguistic Computing*, 16:3:299–308, 2001.

Labov, W., Some principles of linguistic methodology, *Language Soc.*, 1:97–120, 1972.

McMenamin, G. R., *Forensic Stylistics*, Elsevier, Amsterdam, 1993.

Pinker, S., *Language Instinct*, William Morrow, New York, 1994.

Ridley, M., *Genome: the Autobiography of a Species in 23 Chapters*, Harper Collins, New York, 1999.

Schiffrin, D., *Approaches to Discourse*, Blackwell, Cambridge, 1994.

Sinclair, J. and Coulthard, M., *Towards an Analysis of Discourse*, Oxford University Press, London, 1975.

Studdert–Kennedy, M. This view of language: commentary on Pinker and Bloom, in Pinker, S. and Bloom, P., Natural language and natural selection, *Behav. Brain Sci.*, 13:707–784, 1990.

von Humbolt, W., *Linguistic Variability and Intellectual Development*, Trans. G. C. Buck and F. Raven, University of Pennsylvania Press, Philadelphia, (1836) 1972.

Weinreich, U., Labov, W., and Herzog, M. I., Empirical foundations for a theory of language change, in Lehmann, W. and Malkiel, Y., Eds., *Directions for Historical Linguistics: a Symposium*, University of Texas Press, Austin, 1968, 95–195.

Cases Cited

Estate of Violet Houssien, Superior Court for the State of Alaska, Third Judicial District at Anchorage, Case No. 3AN-98-59 P/R.

Oregon v. Crescenzi, CA A90559, Court of Appeals, Oregon, 152 Ore. App. 567.

Forensic Linguistics

4

GERALD R. McMENAMIN

4.1 Forensic Linguistics

Forensic linguistics is the scientific study of language as applied to forensic purposes and contexts. It is a very new area of linguistics vis-à-vis its 2400-year history and is a recent and rapidly growing area of modern applied linguistics.

Linguists who did much of the ground-breaking work in forensic linguistics are often heard to say that what they do is linguistics that happens to be in a forensic context, and that a forensic linguist must first be a good linguist. Such observations are not meant to minimize the task of learning how to function within the judicial system, but they do signal the primary importance of the connection forensic linguistics has as a discipline to the scientific theories and methods developed over time within general and applied linguistics. The purpose of this chapter is to trace the foundations of forensic linguistics and to outline specific areas of current research and practice within the field.

Early work on language and the law is significant. One of the first and most interesting works is Bryant's (1930) compendium on function words in legal language. The work of Wetter (1960) on the style of written appellate decisions elaborates an early discussion of writing style in a legal context and presents many example opinions. Melinkoff (1963) began his influential plain language campaign, which was carried on by him and others through the next three decades. The relatively early article by Danet (1980) on the language of fact-oriented disputes is formidable for its breadth, depth, and attention to topics (e.g., pragmatics) that were not seriously studied until much later. Levi (1982) prepared the first comprehensive bibliography in the field. Systematic study of courtroom language was begun by O'Barr (1982) and his colleagues, and linguistic applications, especially in the areas of discourse and pragmatics, were developed by Shuy (1984, 1986). Robin Lakoff's earlier courses and lectures on language and the law are also significant, especially her observations about courtroom language, i.e., the formality of the courtroom, and the nonreciprocity and public nature of courtroom discourse (Lakoff, 1990, Chapters 5 and 6).

More recent research demonstrates a rapid, large-scale surge of interest and basic scientific work in forensic linguistics. Overviews of language, law, and the legal process have been done by Gibbons (1990), Kniffka (1990),

Tiersma (1993), Eades (1994), Levi (1994b), Murphy, (1998) and Butters (2001). O'Barr has continued work on the language of the courtroom (Conley and O'Barr, 1998), and Shuy on analysis of discourse in the language used in legal settings (Shuy, 1993, 1998). Specific studies and collections relating to various linguistic applications to the law have been written or edited by Levi and Walker (1990), Rieber and Stewart (1990), Gibbons (1994), Eades (1995), and Kniffka et al. (1996). In addition, Levi (1994a) has expanded her bibliographic work by continuing to identify and document advances in forensic linguistics.

A complete compilation of all the milestones and international developments in forensic linguistics is not within the reach of this chapter, but some of the most important will be identified. Levi and Walker organized and coordinated the 1985 Georgetown University conference on *language in the judicial process* and published their eponymous volume of work on language and law (Levi and Walker, 1990). In 1995 Dumas started *Language in the Judicial Process*, an electronic newsletter aimed at disseminating information on bibliography, organizations, courses and programs, and legal cases.

During and after this time, courses were developed and presented around the world. For example, Dumas' course on language and law at the University of Tennessee focused on legal language, interpretation, courtroom language, plain English, pragmatics, jury instructions, language in legal settings and proceedings, and the language of consumer product warnings. Similar courses have been developed at various universities such as University of Wales (Bangor), University of Birmingham, Cambridge University, University of New South Wales, University of Melbourne, Georgetown University, Montclair State, University of California (San Diego), San Diego State, California State University (Fresno), and many others.

Perhaps the single most effective advance in the study of forensic linguistics during the past decade was the 1994 initiation at the University of Birmingham of *Forensic Linguistics: The International Journal of Speech, Language and the Law*, and the founding of the International Association of Forensic Linguistics. This journal, edited by Malcolm Coulthard and Peter French, and the IAFL (website in reference section) have since provided serious venues for the presentation of research that is more regular, unified, and formal than ever before.

The above-cited works demonstrate that forensic linguistics is a well established area of applied linguistics. However, when a field such as forensic linguistics goes through the process of defining itself, there are certain to be instances of ambiguity related to what is or is not part of the discipline. Psycholinguistics has been represented (in Section 4.4.1) as an example of an effort considered misnamed and best left to another specialty. The psycholinguistics practiced in American forensic contexts contrasts to the field of psycholinguistics (as studied in linguistics and psychology) in much the same way astrology does to astronomy, i.e., both astrology and "psycholinguistics" are interesting and may be useful, but are of questionable scientific consequence.

Another type of ambiguity is created when a single area of forensic linguistics is defined as the field itself. For example, the entry on forensic linguistics in *The Cambridge Encyclopedia of Language* (Crystal, 1987:69) includes only a discussion of stylistics. A later entry called "(forensic) stylometry" in *The Cambridge Encyclopedia of the English Language* (Crystal, 1995:423) claims that "this application [of stylometry] has generated yet another name for the subject: forensic linguistics." The field cannot be accurately understood when defined by synecdochic descriptions of this type.

The description of forensic linguistics that follows categorizes areas within the field and cites related bibliographies. While differences in categorization paradigms are to be expected (e.g., compare that on the bibliography website of the University of Birmingham), it is not possible to avoid overlap in the multifaceted research areas of forensic linguistics. In addition, the scope of this chapter does not allow exhaustive bibliographic citation. Instead, every effort has been made to include representative works in every category of forensic linguistic study and application. Note also that a list of selected electronic sources for forensic linguistics is included in the reference section.

4.2   Areas of Forensic Linguistics

The classification of areas in forensic linguistics evolves as the field develops. It usually follows existing classifications in the structure and function of language (see Chapter 1) as a basis for cataloging actual and potential subject areas. In some cases, however, even narrower specification is needed. For example, studies in forensic phonetics apply, separately or simultaneously, three distinct modes of phonetic description: acoustic, auditory and articulatory. In some instances, forensic studies make use of a broad array of analytical tools from overlapping subfields of linguistics, making tidy classification decisions difficult. For example, a comprehensibility study will first be related to spoken or written language, and may then be simultaneously founded in one or more other areas, such as morphology, syntax, semantics, discourse, or pragmatics.

A solution to the classification problem is to allow the research and casework of forensic linguists to define the field and thereby develop its taxonomy. When there is overlap in subfields, one should attempt to duplicate the inclusion of the study in the other appropriate categories. Therefore, the organization of forensic linguistics outlined here reflects actual research and practice. The range, number, and quality of studies in forensic linguistics, especially those of the last 8 to 10 years, demonstrate strong interest and increasing activity in the field and make a bibliography-based definition of linguistics *qua* forensic science a practical possibility.

4.2.1 Auditory Phonetics

Auditory phonetics is the study of language sounds based on what is heard and interpreted by the human listener, i.e., the aural–perceptual character-istics of speech. Although auditory studies are isolated here for convenience, studies in forensic phonetics often use both auditory and acoustic methods of analysis. A good overview of the auditory approach to forensic examina-tions is given by French (1994:174). The primary areas of auditory research in forensic phonetics are speaker discrimination and identification by victims and witnesses, voice perception, discrimination, imitation, and disguise, and identification of class characteristics of speakers, including first-language interference, regional or social accent and dialect, and speaker age:

1. *Speaker identification by victims and witnesses, sometimes called "ear-witnesses"*: Hecker, 1971; Lloyd–Bostock and Clifford, 1983; Nolan, 1991; Künzel, 1994; Braun and Köster, 1995; Künzel, 1996; Schiller and Köster, 1998, Köster et al., 1998; Hollien and Schwartz, 2000
2. *Earwitness line-ups, also called voice line-ups or voice parades*: Clifford, 1980; Lloyd–Bostock and Clifford, 1983; Deffenbacher et al., 1989; Hollien et al., 1995; Broeders, 1996; Hollien, 1996; Nolan and Grabe, 1996; Schiller et al., 1997; Stuart Laubstein, 1997; Hollien and Schwartz, 2000; Yarmay, 2001.
3. *Voice perception and discrimination*: Rose and Duncan, 1995
4. *Voice imitation or disguise*: Hollien et al., 1982; Masthoff, 1996; Schli-chting and Sullivan, 1997
5. *Effects of listener's first language on speaker identification*: Schiller and Köster, 1996; Schiller et al., 1997; Köster and Schiller, 1997; Sullivan and Schlichting, 2000
6. *Effect of style-shifting on voice identification*: Huntley Bahr and Pass, 1996
7. *Identification of social or regional accent or dialect*: Ellis, 1994; McClel-land, 1994; Bobda et al., 1999
8. *Listener perception of speaker age*: Braun, 1996; Sullivan and Kügler, 2001.
9. *Reverse speech*: Newbrook and Curtain, 1998
10. *Telephone speaker recognition*: Kredens and Goralewska–Lach, 1998; Foulkes and Barron, 2000
11. *Speaker identification by morphology and syntax*: Kredens and Goralewska-Lach, 1998

4.2.2   Acoustic Phonetics

Acoustic phonetics is the study of the physical characteristics of speech sounds as they leave their source (the speaker), move into the air, and gradually dissipate. The acoustic analysis of speech sounds requires laboratory observation with instruments and specialized (but readily available) computer hardware and software. A good overview of the acoustic approach to forensic examinations is found in French (1994:176).

Vowels and consonants are presented as waveforms having three features: *amplitude*, corresponding to loudness, *frequency* of complete repetitions, corresponding to high and low pitch, and *complexity*, corresponding to the periodic waves of a simple (pure) sound, or to a mixture of simple waves composing the sound.

When the vocal folds vibrate, they produce a complex periodic waveform made up of a fundamental and its harmonics. The fundamental is the frequency of vocal-fold vibration, so it is called the *fundamental frequency*. In addition to harmonics, there are areas in the frequency spectrum where energy is concentrated. These areas are called formant bands or *formants*, and they vary depending on the size and shape of the cavities of the vocal tract for the respective production of each different sound. For studies of vowels, positions and configurations of the first and second formants are often analyzed, but higher formants and formant trajectories are also used for specific purposes, such as voice identification. For studies of tone and intonation (pitch), the fundamental frequency is isolated and is especially useful in voice identification.

The waveforms are presented visually as a spectogram. On its horizontal, left-to-right plane, the spectogram indicates sound duration in milliseconds (ms). On its vertical (bottom-to-top) axis, the spectogram demonstrates various characteristics of speech sounds: the presence (markings) or absence (no markings) of sound, frequency position of sounds, i.e, waveform repetition in cycles per second (Herz), and formants and their positions. Figure 4.1 shows the waveform (top), intensity (middle), and fundamental frequency (bottom) for each of five isolated vowels recorded by an English-speaking American man: /i, e, a, o, u/, corresponding to the vowels in *beet, bait, pot, boat, boot*. Figure 4.2 is the spectogram of the same five vowels, showing the configurations and positions of formants 1 to 5, starting at the bottom with F1.

The primary area of acoustic analysis in forensic phonetics is speaker identification, but many studies have also been done to identify class characteristics of speakers, including physical height and weight, regional, social, or language group, voice and accent disguise, effect of intoxication on speech, and technical aspects of speech samples and recordings:

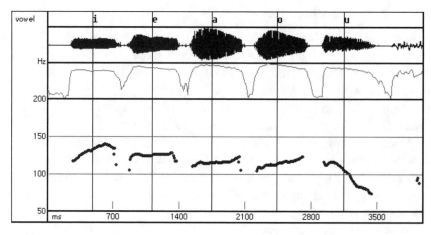

Notes:

1. Top: basic waveforms for /i e a o u/
2. Mid: intensity levels (loudness) for each vowel
3. Bottom: fundamental frequencies for each vowel
4. Vertical axis: frequency of sound in cycles per second (Hz)
5. Horizontal axis: time in milliseconds (ms)

Figure 4.1 Waveform, intensity contour, and fundamental for English vowels /i e a o u/.

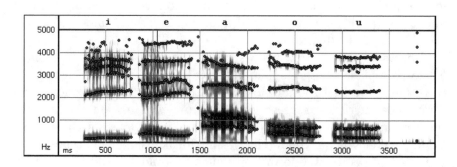

Notes:

1. Bottom-to-Top (c. 200 Hz to 4500 Hz): formants F1, F2, F3, F4, and F5 for /i e a o u/
2. Vertical axis: frequency of sound in cycles per second (Hz)
3. Horizontal axis: time in milliseconds (ms)

Figure 4.2 Spectogram for English vowels /i e a o u/.

1. *Speaker identification by phonetic analysis*: Tosi, 1979; Nolan, 1983; Baldwin and French, 1990; Hollien, 1990; Nolan, 1991; French, 1994; McClelland, 1994; Howard et al., 1995; Künzel, 1995; Boss, 1996;

Ingram et al., 1996; Jiang, 1996; Majewski and Basztura, 1996; Braun and Künzel, 1998; Kredens and Goralewska-Lach, 1998; Koolwaaij and Boves, 1999; Nolan, 1999; Foulkes and Barron, 2000, Hollien, 2001; Künzel, 2001

2. *Speaker identification by voice quality*, i.e., speaker-specific phonation type: Wagner, 1995; Michael Jessen, 1997; Moosmüller, 2001

3. *Speaker identification by phonological variation in diphthongs*: Moosmüller, 1997

4. *Speaker identification by speaking speed*: Künzel et al., 1994; Künzel, 1997

5. *Physical characteristics of speaker (height/weight) from format frequencies*: Greisbach, 1992.

6. *Speaker profiling related to regional and social group*: Labov, 1988; Moosmüller, 1997; Kredens and Goralewska-Lach, 1998

7. *Effects of intoxication on speech*: Hollien and Martin, 1996

8. *Phonetic manifestations of speaker's affective state, e.g., stress*: Hollien and de Jong, 1995; Klasmeyer and Sendlmeier, 1997; Jessen, 1997

9. *Foreign accent in voice discrimination*: Rogers, 1998

10. *Accent disguise or imitation*: Lindsey and Hirson, 1999; Markham, 1999

11. *Voice disguise*: Molina de Figueiredo and de Souza Britto, 1996; Künzel, 2000

12. *Voice characteristics of identical twins*: Nolan and Oh, 1996

13. *Comparability of speech samples*: Künzel, 1997

14. *Inference of voice loudness from measurement of pitch*: French, 1998

15. *Disambiguating speech from background sounds*: Hirson and Howard, 1994; Braun, 1994; Harrison, 2001

16. *Enhancement of audio records of disputed utterances*: Braun, 1994

4.2.3 Semantics: Interpretation of Expressed Meaning

Semantics is the study of meaning as expressed by words, phrases, sentences, or texts. The focus of semantic analysis in forensic contexts is on the comprehensibility and interpretation of language that is difficult to understand. Some studies combine the semantic and pragmatic approaches to meaning interpretation. Thorough introductions to this area are found in Solan (1998 and 1999); a recent example of the application of forensic semantics is the model used by Langford (2000) to interpret the meaning of expressions referring to crimes. The point of view that expert linguists do not play a role in helping judges interpret statutes is presented by Murphy (1998).

Primary areas of research in forensic semantics are the interpretation of words, phrases, sentences, and texts, ambiguity in texts and laws, and interpretation of meaning in spoken discourse, such as reading of rights and police warnings, police interviews, and jury instructions:

1. *Interpretation of words, phrases, and sentences*: Shuy, 1986; Cunningham, 1988; White, 1991; McMenamin, 1993; McMenamin and Lepken, 1993; Cunningham et al., 1994; Kaplan et al., 1995; Durant, 1996; Goddard, 1996; Green, 1996; McLeod, 1996; Langford, 2000

2. *Interpretation of texts (contracts, insurance policies, communications, restraining orders, statutes, contracts, legal texts)*: Labov and Harris, 1983; Labov, 1988; WULQ, 1995; Stratman and Dahl, 1996; Murphy, 1998; Solan, 1998

3. *Ambiguity in texts and laws*: Vishneski et al., 1991; Butters, 1993; Dumas and Short, 1998

4. *Interpretation of spoken discourse in reading of rights (Miranda warnings, police cautions) and in police interviews*: Gibbons, 1996; Shuy, 1997; Grisso, 1998; Cotterill, 2000; Russell, 2000, Shuy and Staton, 2000, Kurzon, 2000

5. *Interpretations of jury instructions*: Levi, 1993; Jackson, 1995; Tiersma, 1995

4.2.4 Discourse and Pragmatics: Interpretation of Inferred Meaning

Analysis of discourse is the study of units of language larger than the sentence, such as narratives and conversations. Discourse in spoken and written language can take many forms, especially in conversations tied to specific social contexts. The social context of discourse is determined by variable factors such as the speaker and hearer, their social roles, their personal or professional relationship, topic, purpose, time and place, etc.

Analysis of a speaker's intended meaning in actual language use is the study of pragmatics. Pragmatics is important for forensic purposes because speakers and writers do not always directly match their words with the meaning that they intend to convey. Since listeners and readers may also be unsuccessful in matching expression to intended meaning, the speaker's or writer's intended meaning is more open to interpretation by the listener or reader, sometimes resulting in mistaken understanding, miscommunication, and, eventually, conflict.

The linguist and practitioner (expert witness) who systematically developed forensic discourse analysis for a broad range of cases is Roger Shuy. These cases go back at least to the mid 1980s and are documented in his research, especially in *Language Crimes: the Use and Abuse of Language Evidence in the Courtroom* (Shuy, 1993), and in *The Language of Confessions, Interrogation and Deception* (Shuy, 1998). Other recent cases and surveys of forensic discourse analysis and pragmatics may be found in many of the works cited below.

Primary areas of discourse and pragmatics include analysis of spoken and written language, study of the discourse of specific contexts, such as dictation, conversations, hearings, etc., the language of the courtroom, i.e., of lawyers, clients, questioning, and jury instructions, and language of specific speech acts, such as threats, promises, warnings, etc.:

1. *Discourse and pragmatics*:
   Forensic discourse analysis: Coulthard, 1992
   Pragmatic analysis of linguistic and extralinguistic contexts of
      utterances: McLeod, 1996
   Pragmatic analysis of a will: Kaplan, 1998
   Perceived vs. intended meaning: McMenamin and Lepken, 1993
   Admissibility of expert evidence on discourse analysis: Wallace, 1986
2. *Discourse of specific contexts*:
   Analysis of dictation: Olsson, 1997
   Transcripts of recorded conversations: Solan, 1998; Gibbons, 2001
   Interviews of nonnative speakers of English: Hale, 1997
   Language of immigration hearings: Barsky, 1994
   Language of the defendants vis-à-vis that of the police transcribers:
      Gibbons, 1996; Rock, 2001
3. *Language of the courtroom*:
   Discourse of lawyers and clients: Maley et al., 1995; Hale, 1997
   Discourse of trial lawyers: Stygall, 1994
   Discourse of courtroom questions: Hale, 1999; Berk–Seligson, 1999;
      Rigney, 1999
   Language of jury instructions: Levi, 1993; Jackson, 1995; Tiersma,
      1995; Dumas, 2000
4. *Language of specific speech acts*:
   Threats: Storey, 1995; Fraser, 1998
   Promising: Fraser, 1998
   Warning: Fraser, 1998
   Offer and acceptance: Tiersma, 1986
   Defamation: Tiersma, 1987
   Denial: Brennan, 1994
   Perjury: Tiersma, 1990
   Sexual harassment: Ragan et al., 1996
   Sexual assault: Ehrlich, 2000; Trinch, 2000
   Car sales: Shuy, 1994

4.2.5 Stylistics and Questioned Authorship

The focus of forensic stylistics is author identification of questioned writings. Starting with mid-19th-century German scholars, methods for authorship identification were developed mainly for biblical and then literary purposes (see Chapter 5), such as determining the authorship of certain composite parts of the Old and New Testaments, or of questioned Shakespearean writings. Such applications of stylistic analysis to forensic authorship problems have now become common.

There are at least three types of questioned authorship problems. First, one may want to determine if one author wrote all the writings in a questioned set, i.e., if a particular writing, which may or may not be already accepted as part of a body (canon) of known writings, is consistent with the rest of the known writings. Second, one may be asked to compare a questioned writing with the writings of a large number of possible authors, if there are no obvious suspect authors. Third, the most common type of forensic problem is to assess the resemblance of a questioned writing to that of one author or a small number of candidate authors, if in fact possible suspect authors can be identified by external (nonlinguistic) means.

Linguistic stylistics uses two approaches to authorship identification: qualitative and quantitative. The work is qualitative when features of writing are identified and then described as being characteristic of an author. The work is quantitative when certain indicators are identified and then measured in some way, e.g., their relative frequency of occurrence in a given set of writings. Certain quantitative methods are referred to as stylometry. Qualitative and quantitative methods complement one another and are often used together to identify, describe, and measure the presence or absence of style-markers in questioned and known writings.

Figure 4.3 represents a qualitative description of a style feature, the spelling of the name *Maryanne* in the questioned and respective known writings of two suspect authors in a California questioned authorship case.

In contrast, Figure 4.4 contains an example of a quantitative description of two features in another California questioned-authorship case: abbreviation and spacing. The questioned and known writings in the case demonstrate a pattern of typewritten return addresses in which the state of California was abbreviated [**Ca.**], and the postal zip code was spaced two spaces after the state abbreviation, i.e., [**Ca. 91001**]. The preliminary description of this variable style of writing return addresses led the parties to question the significance (discriminating power) of such a combination marker, so a study of relative frequency of occurrence was done. Analysts assembled a corpus of 500 randomly selected California letter writers containing 686 return addresses on envelopes and letters. Observe in Figure 4.4 that 11% of the addresses contained the [**Ca.**] abbreviation, and 9% the two spaces between Ca. and the zip code: [**Ca. 91001**]. More importantly, only seven (1%) of the 686 addresses in the corpus demonstrated the simultaneous

QUESTIONED Letter	KNOWN Suspect Writer #1	KNOWN Suspect Writer #2
Mary Ann	Mary Ann	Maryanne
Mary Ann	Mary Ann	Maryanne
	Mary Ann	Maryanne
	Mary Ann	Maryanne
	Mary Ann	Maryann
		Maryann

Figure 4.3 Spelling of "Maryanne" in QUESTIONED and KNOWN writings.

Abbreviations for "California" (n = 686)								Spaces between State and Zip			
CA	CA.	Ca	Ca.	ca	ca.	Other	+	0 sp	1 sp	2 sp	no zip
514	39	31	76	1	1	24	6		558	60	62
75%	6%	5%	11%	0%	0%	3%	1%		81%	9%	9%

Notes:

1. "Other" = **Calif. / calif. / Cal. / Cal / cal**
2. The questioned and known writings consistently demonstrate the combination [**Ca. + 2 sp**]. The combination of the two variables occurs in seven (1%) of the 686 addresses from the corpus.

Figure 4.4 Quantitative description of corpus writings for state + zip code.

use of both characteristics. Variability results were similar for the same analysis done by writer instead of by address tokens.

References that follow are limited to recent forensic applications of stylistics. See McMenamin (1993) for earlier forensic and nonforensic references, and Chapter 5 for discussion of other recent studies.

1. *Descriptive methods of authorship identification*: McMenamin, 1993; Kniffka, 1996; Rudman, 1998 and 1999; Kniffka, 2000; McMenamin, 2001a

2. *Dialect evidenced in written language*: Lewis, 1994; McMenamin, 2001a
3. *Questioned time and occasion of writing*: Coulthard, 1997
4. *Stylometry and statistical methods in questioned authorship (forensic and literary)*: Finkelstein and Fairley, 1970 (Bayesian approach); Jackson, 1991 (function words); Burrows, 1992 (frequent and infrequent words); Dixon and Mannion, 1993 (various [22] variables); Greenwood, 1993 (common-word frequencies); Matthews and Merriam, 1993 (stylometry); McMenamin, 1993; Merriam, 1993; Schils and De Hann, 1993 (sentence length); Binongo, 1994 (high-frequency words); Holmes, 1994; Kjell, 1994 (letter-pair frequency); Louhivaara, 1994 (word order patterns); Merriam and Matthews, 1994 (stylometry); Rommel, 1994 (word cluster, conjunction and punctuation); Greenwood, 1995 (common-word frequencies); Holmes and Forsyth, 1995 (stylometry); Laan, 1995; Ledger, 1995 (orthographic variables); Mealand, 1995 (function words, letter variables, and parts of speech); Forsyth and Holmes, 1996 (textual feature finding); McKenna and Antonia, 1996 (most frequently occurring words); Merriam, 1996 (function words); Temple, 1996 (stylometry); Johnson, 1997; Coulthard, 1998; Gurney and Gurney, 1998a (stylometry); Gurney and Gurney, 1998b (word frequencies); Gurney and Gurney, 1998c (text subsets in stylometry); Holmes, 1998 (stylometry); Rudman, 1998 (stylistics); Tse et al., 1998 (function words); Tweedie et al., 1998 (frequently occurring words); Aoyama and Constable, 1999 (word length frequency); Binongo and Smith, 1999 (stylometry); Broeders, 1999 (probability scales); Champod and Evett, 2000 (probability scales); Craig, 1999 (common-word frequency); Forsyth, 1999 (stylometry); Forsyth et al., 1999 (stylometry); Hoorn et al., 1999 (letter sequences); Koolwaaij and Boves, 1999 (decision making); Mealand, 1999 (function word frequencies); Sjerps and Biesheuvel, 1999 (opinion scales); Taroni et al., 1999 (Bayesian approach); McKee et al., 2000 (vocabulary diversity); Merriam, 2000 (rare words and common function words); Waugh et al., 2000 (computational stylistics); Chask, 2001; Grant and Baker, 2001; McMenamin, 2001b; Elliott and Valenza 2001; Khmelev and Tweedy, 2001
5. *Corpus linguistics in forensic analysis*: Coulthard, 1994; Hänlein, 1999; Olsson, 2001
6. *Corpus linguistics*: An et al., 1995; Atkins et al., 1992; Fang and Nelson, 1994; Garside, 1993; Hunyadi, 1999; Kennedy, 1998; Kirk, 1994; Goutsos et al., 1994; Mair and Hundt, 2000; Meurman–Solin, 2001; Peranteau, 2000; Smith et al., 1998; Zampolli, 1994; Zampolli and Ostler, 1993

7. *Computer programs related to questioned authorship*: Johnson, 1997; Woolls and Coulthard, 1998; Barr, 2001
8. *Cumulative sum charts (CUSUM method) for authorship identification*: Canter, 1992; Hilton and Holmes, 1993; Sanford et al., 1994; Morton, 1995; Farringdon et al., 1996; Canter and Chester, 1997; de Haan, 1998; Smith, 1998

4.2.6 Language of the Law

Perhaps the most important development in the language of the law was begun by David Melinkoff in his 1963 book, *The Language of the Law*. Melinkoff pressed for clarity and brevity in the law, which extended to a later movement to simplify the language of laws, insurance policies, and consumer literature. He was very direct in his prescriptions for good writing, once saying that the most effective way of shortening law language is for judges and lawyers to stop writing.

Today, systematic analysis of legal language is represented by work such as that of Goodrich (1987), Conley and O'Barr (1998), and others; the plain language campaign has been taken up by Tiersma (1999), who has also expanded into other linguistically relevant aspects of legal language. Tiersma's website (see reference section) has internet links on plain legal language and language rights, and his attention to the pragmatics of courtroom language is cited elsewhere in this chapter.

4.2.7 Language of the Courtroom

The courtroom personae who speak are witnesses, lawyers, and judges. Research related especially to the discourse and pragmatic use of courtroom language has made this one area of forensic linguistics that holds considerable potential for affecting case outcomes. Studies of courtroom language are analyses of the language of all the players:

1. *Language of witnesses*:
   Witness examination: Conley et al., 1978; Cooke, 1996; Hale, 1999; Eades, 2000
   Sexual assault victims: Conley and O'Barr, 1998; Erlich, 2000; Trinch, 2000; Erlich, 2001
   Cross examination of child-victim witnesses: Brennan, 1994
   Disputes and mediation: Danet, 1980; Conley and O'Barr, 1998
   Language and gender in the courtroom: Conley and O'Barr, 1998
2. *Language of lawyers*:
   Lawyers and linguists: Kniffka, 1994
   Trial language: Stygall, 1994
   Language of lawyers: Tiersma, 1999; Tiersma, 2001

Legal-debate language: Penny et al., 1995
Language of closing arguments: Cotterill, 1998

3. *Language of judges:*
   Language of judges: Wetter, 1960; Solan, 1993a and 1993b; Phillips, 1998; Robershaw, 1998; Bernstein, 2001
   Language of jury instructions: Charrow and Charrow, 1979; Steele and Thornburg, 1988; Levi, 1993; Tiersma, 1993; Tiersma, 1999; Dumas, 2000

4.2.8   Interpretation and Translation

Interpreting is a complex skill under any circumstance, but it is especially difficult in forensic contexts. Interpretation studies such as those in Cooke et al. (1999) focus on interpretation tasks specific to questions and answers in testimony, the perceived role of the interpreter, interpreter education, the right to interpretation, etc.

Translating in the legal context requires much more than a literal, word-for-word match-up of two languages. Good translations are constrained by the intended meaning of the writer, the new text created by the translator, and the meaning given the translated text by the reader.

Forensic and academic scholars are giving more and more attention to the theory and practice of interpretation and translation, as evidenced by the following studies:

1. *Pre-trial interpreting* Hale, 1997; Berk–Seligson, 2000
2. *Courtroom interpretation*: Berk-Seligson, 1990; González et al., 1991; Laster and Taylor, 1994; Robinson, 1994; Carroll, 1995; Eades, 1995; Edwards, 1995; Morris, 1995; Palma, 1995; Colin and Morris, 1996; Gaiba, 1998; Lewis, 1998; Wadensjö, 1998; Cooke, Eades, and Hale, 1999; Lane et al., 1999; Moeketsi, 1999; Walsh, 1999; Russell, 2000
3. *Interpretation with cultural and dialect differences*: Hale, 1997; Mildren, 1999; Walsh, 1999
4. *Questioning in interpreted testimony*: Berk–Seligson, 1999; Hale, 1999; Rigney, 1999
5. *Absence of interpretation*: Gibbons, 1996; Lewis, 1998
6. *Courtroom role of the interpreter*: Morris, 1999
7. *Interpreter education*: Benmaman, 1999
8. *Translation*: Morris, 1995; Wu, 1995; Lane et al., 1999

4.3   Areas Directly Related to Forensic Linguistics

4.3.1   Document Examination

The examination of questioned documents relies on the scientific study of the physical evidence of a document. Physical traces that assist in the questioned document (QD) examination to uncover the history of a document are left in a number of ways: the writing instrument, i.e., pen and ink, pencil, typewriter, computer and printer, etc., the writing surface, such as paper, and information about the writer (or typist), such as physical position and physical, emotional, or mental state. For handwriting, the forensic document examiner observes various features: letter size, formation, and relative proportions, and letter slant, spacing, pressure, line quality, connecting strokes, etc. For typing, the document examiner observes characteristics of the typeface, font style, spacing between letters and lines, and association of a document with a particular machine or type of machine, i.e., typewriter, printer, or copier.

Previous QD studies indicate that the examination for authorship determination includes numerous characteristics of writing style, e.g., Conway (1959), Harrison (1958), Hilton (1982), and Osborn (1929), all reviewed in some detail in McMenamin (1993:113–120). Newer studies, however, are drawing a sharper line between QD and the elements of writing style that overlap into the field of linguistic stylistics. For example, Ellen (1997:23) recognizes that analysis of textual style may be of value and briefly describes the field of stylistic analysis of texts, noting that it is not usually considered part of document examination. He observes that typist identification may depend on characteristics such as line spacing, margin size, paragraph indenting, spaces after punctuation marks, capitalization, absence of mistakes, spelling mistakes, frequent use of certain words, and unconventional punctuation (Ellen, 1997:86). He adds, however, that the area of text analysis "is not normally considered as within the expertise of the forensic document examiner." Levinson (2001:41) takes much the same position about textual or syntax analysis and spelling errors, saying that "these approaches and their validity are outside the realm and training of the document examiner."

Huber and Headrick (1999:79) distinguish linguistics from QD examination as another kind of study having forensic application, but they emphasize the importance to QD analysis of abbreviations, diacritics, punctuation, and forms of dates (Huber and Headrick, 1999:110,114,167). On the other hand, the line between QD and stylistics is sometimes determined by the significant absence of a stated role for style characteristics within the QD examination. For example, Morris (2000:64) only makes passing reference to abbreviations and punctuation.

The overlap that exists between linguistics and document examination, minimal as it is, provides useful double coverage of stylistic markers in punctuation, spelling, abbreviations, forms of dates, etc. Many document examiners have the training and confidence to identify and use these features in their analyses. The opposite situation, however, is not common. Although there may be more, I know only one linguist who has the specialized training needed for document examination, over and above her graduate degree in linguistics. What this means is that the two fields and their practitioners are, for most part, in strict complementary distribution, i.e., the objects of analysis do not overlap.

In spite of this, some ambiguity is created in forensic linguistics by what appear to be efforts designed to increase communication between the fields of forensic document examination and forensic linguistics. For example, the journal *Forensic Linguistics* published two QD articles: one on ESDA analysis (Davis, 1994) and another on handwriting and signature comparisons (Found et al., 1994). Another example was a "specialist area" course in the U.K. on forensic handwriting analysis at a 2001 university summer school on forensic linguistics. The research and rigor that go into the development of a relatively new area in forensic science, like forensic linguistics, are sufficient to consume all resources and efforts. If crossover publications or activities are planned, one might clearly state the purpose to be communication between fields, thereby avoiding perceived ambiguity about the scope of the fields in the minds of attorneys, judges, juries, etc.

4.3.2   Software Forensics

Another interesting and recent development in forensic authorship identification is the application of stylistic analysis to computer programming. For example, two C++ code fragments written by two different programmers may well serve exactly the same function but demonstrate traceable differences in programmer coding style. Security analysts working on proprietary issues and virus sources have identified various metrics, i.e., style indicators, such as variable names, length of variable names, ratio of global to local variables, layout, upper- vs. lower-case letters, placement of comments, debugging symbols, mean line length, program statements per line, placement of syntactic structures, and ratio of white lines to code lines, etc. (Spafford and Weeber, 1992 and 1993; Krsul, 1994; Gray et al., 1997; Kilgour et al., 1997; Krsul and Spafford, 1996 and 1997).

Computer science professors suspicious of plagiarism are using software programs to identify suspiciously similar strings of code in programming assignments. The measure of software similarity (MOSS) program was widely applied after Alex Aiken at the University of California distributed it free to other professors in 1997.

4.3.3   Semiotics

Semiotics is the study of communication and language as systems of signs and symbols. Such systems are called codes and language is an example of a code with both verbal and nonverbal signs. The signs in the code have conventional meanings. Speakers and writers encode, and listeners and readers decode the system.

The International Journal for the Semiotics of Law applies forms of textual analysis to legal discourse, such as judicial argumentation (Adeodato, 1999), legal performatives (Cao, 1999), and judges' summations (Henning, 1999).

4.3.4 Plagiarism Detection

A computer program, designed by University of Virginia physics Professor Louis Bloomfield, searches for similar phrasing of six consecutive words or more in student papers. An internet service, *http://www.turnitin.com*, is said to take a so-called "digital fingerprint" of a student's paper, then searches the Internet and other databases for like language. Another site, *http://www.findsame.com*, scans the Internet for matching sentences or whole documents, instead of just single words.

4.4 Areas Inaptly Associated with Forensic Linguistics

4.4.1 "Psycholinguistics"

Psycholinguistics is a field that integrates the study of psychology, linguistics, and cognitive science. The comprehension and production of language is studied cognitively, neurologically, and conceptually. Typical courses for students of psycholinguistics include the study of general linguistics, first and second language acquisition, cognition, language and the brain, semantics, and pragmatics.

This characterization represents the actual academic discipline of psycholinguistics, but this is *not* what has been referred to as psycholinguistics within the forensic context. The late Murray S. Miron, a psychologist and consultant to the FBI and other government agencies for many years, developed the so-called "psycholinguistic approach." This approach examines written or spoken language for indications "as to the origins, background, and psychology of the originator" (Miron and Douglas, 1979:6), especially in contexts of threatening language.

A description and application of psycholinguistic analysis may be found in Miron (1990). This is a method of profiling a writer, but it is not really possible to predict its outcome or assess its reliability. First, it is difficult for a nonpsychologist (e.g., a judge or jury) to understand and evaluate the nexus made between a written-language threat and the diagnostic profile of the writer. Consider, for example, these statements from a case report which did not contain any supportive references to specific linguistic characteristics:

> The extortionist … exhibits many of the symptoms of bipolar manic psychosis. The language of both communications … is quite frenetic and manifests the exaggerated euphoria characteristic of manic psychosis. The

obvious dissimilarities, however, ... still suggest [the two letters] might be connected. It is not unusual to find the manic in and out of psychosis particularly if he is on a haphazardly kept regimen of medication (Miron, from author's files).

Second, the practice of psycholinguistics is risky when findings are dubious. In the 1993 Texas standoff at Waco, Miron is reported to have said that sect leader Koresh was not likely to respond to a tear gas attack by harming himself, but the compound burned, killing Mr. Koresh and 80 followers. Miron is quoted in *The New York Times* (Pace, July 18, 1995:A20) as saying, "We felt this was an individual who was extraordinarily vain and very fearful of physical injury." He was wrong.

One of the most recent and unusual applications of psycholinguistics was that of an American psychiatrist (Hodges, 2000) who analyzed the "thoughtprints" of the ransom note in the JonBenét Ramsey murder case. The linguistic characteristics of the ransom note (spelling, spacing, grammar) were said to be subconsciously coded by its writer to indicate that the killer was a woman and a cancer victim, she expected to be caught, her motive was anger and deep pain, the victim was dead before the note was written, etc. This kind of psycholinguistics is not forensic linguistics. Such things as subconsciously coded thoughtprints constitute some form of parapsychology, and threat-analysis profiling may fall somewhere within the field of psychology. Neither is best called "linguistics" or left to linguists for application or evaluation.

4.4.2 "Literary Forensics"

Literary forensics, also called "text analysis," is a recently created activity involving a kind of literary profiling similar to the psycholinguistic assessment of a writer's emotional or mental status. The approach is practiced by Donald Foster and described in the book, *Author Unknown: on the Trail of the Anonymous*, where the stated goal is to move "beyond the sphere of academics to criminal investigation and forensic linguistics" (Foster, 2000:17).

The contribution made by Foster is his emphasis on the need to search what he calls "text databases," but what are really large corpora of written language. His purposes for corpus searches are to identify class characteristics of writers (age, religion, education, etc.), to assess possible influences on writers who appropriate the language of what they read, and to determine how writers think: "The texts familiar to an unknown author are worth study, not only to locate borrowed phrasing and ideas but to develop an understanding of how the poet or felon *thinks*" (Foster, 2000:13).

Large corpora of spoken and written language are, in fact, used more and more in stylistics and authorship work for various purposes, one of which is to determine the relative frequency of variable style-markers. In addition to the focus on language corpora, Foster's broadest proposal for the "scientific analysis of text" for authorship identification is in the most general way based on strong theoretical ground: "It is the pattern of difference in each writer's use of language, and the repetition of distinguishing traits, that make it possible for a text analyst to discover the authorship of anonymous, pseudonymous, or forged documents" (Foster, 2000:5).

The "distinguishing traits" include formatting, punctuation, vocabulary, spelling, and grammar. If decisive authorship attribution is not possible in all cases, Foster is usually able to profile the writer ("narrow the field of suspects") by isolating the writer's motivation and ideology, and class features such as the author's age, religion, education, job, and the "geographic, ethnic, socioeconomic, corporate, or professional milieu to which the unknown writer belongs" (Foster, 2000:7).

Aside from its attention to the study of large corpora, text analysis defined this way has only the most tenuous of connections to linguistics or stylistics. It seems to be a hybrid form of what is generally known as text linguistics. At best, text analysis provides diversion for academic literati or, if cautiously used, may be a useful investigative tool; however, proposing text analysis as a reliable method of author identification is a paean to "a little bit of knowledge" and other dangerous things. The initially suggested "scientific analysis of text" remains a methodological secret throughout *Author Unknown* and is based on premises such as, "… how mind and hand conspire to commit acts of writing" (p. 4) and how "[h]uman beings … are prisoners of their own language" (p. 7).

A little bit of knowledge and other dangerous things: The "text analyst" will undoubtedly discover in a computer text search that the reference to "dangerous things" is influenced by my previous reading of Lakoff's (1987) *Women, Fire and Dangerous Things*, but indulge the impulse: women (however akin to fire and dangerous things) and fire do not come close to the dangers posed by a little bit of linguistic knowledge.

Dangers inherent in text analysis: One danger is to be wrong in linguistics. Although the text analyst appears to be identified as a linguist ("The linguist's first order of business …," [p. 209]), Foster's area of academic preparation is literature. Perhaps because of this, the approach to linguistics is impressionistic, with little pretense of science. As a result, mistakes appear in this work — some minor, others major, but all unexpected. Some examples: 1. the word *poeta* (p. 22) is from Sanskrit and Greek, not Latin, 2. the *that* in, "Monica's tendency to omit relative *that* in, 'I found out [that] she left…,' (p. 163) is not a relative *that* at all, and 3. "independent councel" (p. 187) is not spelled that way.

Author Unknown claims (p. 12) that "… the writer's syntax will usually remain fairly constant from one type of writing to another, whether it's a college essay, a letter to Mom, or a threat to kill the president." This is presented without empirical foundation. On the contrary, it is known that, while some aspects of syntax and language stay the same across domains, others (including syntax) change, sometimes very obviously, in different contexts of writing.

In another place (p. 11), *Author Unknown* notes that a suspect writer, "like the author of the anonymous letters, had chronic difficulty with the English present perfect (*he has gone*) and pluperfect (*he had gone*)." Foster surmises that the anonymous writer, like the suspect, must be a native speaker of Gujarati, reasoning that:

> In this Sanskrit-based tongue [Gujarati], the pastness of an action is indi-
> cated by the word placed at the end of a sentence, e.g., "[Dish broken] *tha*"
> (Gujarati syntax) for "the dish [has been, had been, was] broken" (English
> syntax), making it difficult for native speakers of Gujarati to master English
> tenses (Foster, 2000:11).

This was stated (p. 12) as one more reason to believe that the anonymous writer "was Indian-born and a speaker of Gujarati."

There are two problems underlying this analysis. First, the sentence-final example word *tha* is Hindi, not Gujarati. Second, there are millions of non-native English learners, speaking hundreds of languages other than Gujarati, who have trouble acquiring these English tenses. More specifically, assuming that the sentence-final tense marker in Hindi (or Gujarati) had something to do with the English tense problems of the anonymous writer, Gujarati is one of over 100 Indic languages that share this very same syntactic charac-teristic. So, if the writer were first to be somehow identified as a speaker of an Indic language, then he could be "narrowed down" to be one of about 512 million speakers.

Perhaps the most serious misstep a good scholar can take is to enter unknown territory (e.g., linguistics) as Columbus did in America, thinking that he is the first to arrive. Foster comments (emphasis added),

> I was now [1996] presented with a fresh challenge: *to develop a science of
> literary forensics*, to adapt for the courts and, later, for criminal investigations
> a methodology that was originally intended for the study of anonymous
> poems, plays, and novels (Foster, 2000:5).

Before 1996, hundreds of studies in the form of journal articles and books had been done on style, stylistics, and questioned authorship. German studies of Old Testament authorship date back at least to the middle of the 19th century. In addition, evidence has been presented in multiple court cases and numerous judicial opinions have been documented based on evidence of forensic stylistics. These cases date as far back as the 1728 *Trial of William Hales* in England and the 1846 *Pate v. People* case in the U.S. (McMenamin, 1993:110). Science progressively and slowly leads from ignorance to knowledge. The repetition of the cycle so constantly reminds most researchers of what is not yet known that the usual tendency is to understate one's role in the process, not the contrary.

Another danger is to be wrong in forensics. Text analysis seems to produce vague and ambiguous opinions that simply will not serve as a useful basis for expert testimony. For example, Foster makes various statements more consistent with literary criticism than linguistic science (italics inserted for emphasis):

> "... and this time [after a news report], *my confidence in Joe Klein's sole authorship* of the novel *was truly shaken*" (p. 76).
> "... *I don't know how to explain it*. All of the evidence points to Joe Klein" [quoting himself talking to a reporter] (p. 78).
> "I'm finishing the project [this book] on the fly, *just the way I've done everything else for the past four years* ..." (p. 277).

Most problematic is the vacillation resulting from opinions based on literary conjecture. For example, Foster's unsolicited involvement in the Jon-Benét Ramsey case is confusingly discussed in *Author Unknown* as the mistake of a novice expert witness (p. 16), but, the admission of the "beginner's mistake" is followed by "... I do stand by the statements that I have made for the record regarding the case ..." (p. 17). Foster's report to the Boulder police is reported to conlcude that Mrs. Ramsey had written the ransom note (Schiller, 1999). This is remarkable, given his mixed attempts to analyze the ransom note in the Ramsey case: 1. text analysis$_1$ was used to incorrectly identify an internet writer as the author, 2. then text analysis$_2$ was used to conclude in a letter to Mrs. Ramsey, "I know that you are innocent — know it, absolutely and unequivocally," then 3. text analysis$_3$ was apparently done for the Boulder police when, "I took the lesson to heart, started over, and did the best I could for justice and JonBenét." After all that, Foster apparently continues to maintain that "he was recruited for the JonBenét Ramsey murder investigation" (Roberts, 2001). Seesawing between protagonists may be fine for Shakespeare, but not for the witness in the courtroom.

Presenting no clear methodology for authorship identification is another danger. *Author Unknown* alludes to the work "of teasing out the identifiers that let us know with confidence that a found composition is ... a lost work of Shakespeare" (p. 1). There is mention of attention to linguistic characteristics at all levels of grammar, e.g., "flagging uncommon words" (p. 59), but no coherent system for finding and using identifiers is presented. In fact, sometimes the approach appears to be entirely subjective. For example, initial suspect writers for *Primary Colors* did not sound like the author because the writing was "too sincere," "too chaste," "too thoughtful," and "none seemed to share his fixation on race and aggressive women" (p. 64) or, "it does not take a Shakespearean scholar, or a computer, or a $40 million federal investigation, to see that 'points to make an affidavit' ... was written by somebody with legal training" (p. 167).

Moving back and forth between profiling and author identification is also a danger. *Author Unknown* is an amorphous melange of psycholinguistic profiling and hints for individual identification, e.g.,

> "I had a good fix on the text's orthography, diction, sentence construction, source material, political ideology, and points of anxiety; and I had inferred quite a bit about the author's psyche" (p. 60).
>
> "... I had found evidence of racial and sexual anxieties in [Joe Klein's] signed journalism and ... fiction" (p. 80).

Another danger is seduction of the expert by media attention. In a recent issue of *The Wine Spectator*, an I'm-not-a-wine-expert writer commented, "A little knowledge is not only dangerous — it's intoxicating." So are the media. Although the author of *Author Unknown* says that "the story I have to tell is least of all my own," the story is his. High profile cases are solicited, some analyzed by what would have been done had the assignment been given (not what was actually assigned and done), and all takes place within a narrative of personal vignettes, travel details, introspection, and calls from the media. Forensic science is seen as theater: "This [the Unabomber] was my first performance in the high-stakes game of criminal justice ..." (Foster, 2000:109).

Yet another danger is that text analysis will be used by law enforcement and attorneys. Most law enforcement professionals and attorneys will not be taken in by expert opinions that provide something of the aura but little of the substance of science. Many will successfully use text analysis for the investigative potential that it may have. However, if such a tool is used as evidence at trial, it should be with considerable caution. Its abuse by overzealous officers of the law or of the court, given the cloak of authority or respect their employing agency or position affords them, could mislead triers of fact.

A final and real danger of text analysis is to confuse it with stylistics. The judiciary has already confused the two in *U.S. v. Van Wyk*. In *Van Wyk* the FBI expert was reported to have conducted research on text analysis and to have worked on text analysis in a number of high-profile cases, including the Unabomber case. "Text analysis" and "forensic stylistics" are used interchangeably in the opinion, which examines, as the same thing, the reliability of "text analysis" on one line and "forensic stylistics" on the next. In this case, the Court admitted the expert's testimony of linguistic similarities and differences between questioned and known writings, but it barred conclusions regarding the identity of the author of the questioned writings (McMenamin, 2001).

In conclusion, everyone else would be well advised to come to the same point as has the author of *Author Unknown*: "I may give literary forensics a rest, at least for a while" (Foster, 2000:280).

References

Electronic Sources

American Association of Applied Linguistics
    http://www.aaal.org/

American National Corpus
    http://www.cs.vassar.edu/~ide/anc/

Center for Corpus Linguistics at the University of Birmingham:
    http://www.clg1.bham.ac.uk/index.html/

Corpus Linguistics (Michael Barlow):
    http://www.ruf.rice.edu/~barlow/corpus.html

Forensic Linguistics at the University of Birmingham:
    http://www.jiscmail.ac.uk/lists/forensic-linguistics.html

Forensic Linguistics: The International Journal of Speech, Language and the Law:
    http://www.bham.ac.uk/forensiclinguistics/

International Association of Applied Linguistics
    http://www.aila.ac/

International Association of Forensic Linguistics
    http://www.english.bham.ac.uk/forensic/IAFL/

International Association of Forensic Linguists: Bibliography
    http://www.iafl.org/

International Association for Forensic Phonetics
    http://www.iafp.net/

International Journal for the Semiotics of Law
    http://www.wkap.nl/journalhome/0952-8059/

Language in the Judicial Process, electronic newsletter of language and law
    http://www.outreach.utk.edu/ljp/

Linguist List Search Engine for Linguistics and Languages
    http://linguistlist.org/7tones.html/

Linguist List Archive of Lists on Linguistics and Languages
    http://linguistlist.org/multilist/searchall.html/

Plain Language — U.S.A.
http://www.plainlanguage.gov/
Plain Language — U.K.
http://www.plainenglish.co.uk/
P. M. Tiersma Website
http://www.tiersma.com/

Forensic Linguistics

Bryant, M., *English in the Law Courts: the Part that Articles, Prepositions and Conjunctions Play in Legal Decisions*, Frederick Ungar, New York, 1962.

Butters, R., *Forensic Linguistics*, Blackwell, London, 2001.

Conley, J. M. and O'Barr, W. M., *Just Words: Law, Language, and Power*, University of Chicago Press, Chicago, 1998.

Crystal, D., *The Cambridge Encyclopedia of the English Language*, Cambridge University Press, Cambridge, 1995.

Crystal, D., *The Cambridge Encyclopedia of Language*, Cambridge University Press, Cambridge, 1987.

Danet, B., Language in the legal process, *Law Soc. Rev.*, 14:3:445–564, 1980.

Eades, D., Forensic linguistics in Australia: an overview, *Foren. Linguis.*, 1:2:113–132, 1994.

Eades, D., *Language in Evidence: Issues Confronting Aboriginal and Multicultural Australia*, University of New South Wales Press, Sydney, 1995.

Gibbons, J., Ed., *Language and the Law*, Longman, New York, 1994.

Gibbons, J., Applied linguistics in court, *Appl. Linguis.*, 11:3:229–237, 1990.

Kniffka, H., *Texte zu Theorie und Praxis forensischer Linguistik*, Max Niemeyer Verlag, Tübingen, 1990.

Kniffka, H., Blackwell, S., and Coulthard, M., Eds., *Recent Developments in Forensic Linguistics*, Peter Lang, Frankfurt, 1996.

Lakoff, R. T., Talking Power: the Politics of Language in Our Lives, Basic Books, New York, 1990.

Levi, J. N., *Language and Law: a Bibliographic Guide to Social Science Research in the USA*, University of Chicago Press, Chicago, and American Bar Association, Washington, D.C., Teaching Resource Bulletin No. 4, 1994a.

Levi, J. N., Language as evidence: the linguist as expert witness in North American courts, *Foren. Linguis.*, 1:1:1–26, 1994b.

Levi, J. N. and Graffam Walker, A., Eds., *Language in the Judicial Process*, Plenum Press, New York, 1990.

Levi, J. N., *Linguistics, Language, and Law: a Topical Bibliography*, Indiana University Linguistics Club, Bloomington, 1982.

Melinkoff, D., *The Language of the Law*, Little, Brown, Boston, 1963.

Murphy, H. F., Linguistics and law: an overview of forensic linguistics, *J. Law, Intellectual Property Technol.*, 1:1–11, 1998.

O'Barr, W., *Linguistic Evidence, Language, Power and Strategy in the Courtroom,* Academic Press, New York, 1982.

Rieber, R. W. and Stewart, W. A., Eds., *The Language Scientist as Expert in the Legal Setting,* Annals of the New York Academy of Science, v. 606, New York, 1990.

Shuy, R. W., Language and the law, *Ann. Rev. Appl. Linguis.*, 7:50–63, 1986.

Shuy, R. W., *Language Crimes: the Use and Abuse of Language Evidence in the Courtroom,* Blackwell, Oxford, 1993.

Shuy, R. W., Linguistics in other professions, *Ann. Rev. Anthropol.*, 13:419–445, 1984.

Shuy, R. W., *The Language of Confessions, Interrogation and Deception,* Sage Publications, Los Angeles, 1998.

Tiersma, P. M., Linguistic issues in law, *Language,* 69:1:113–135, 1993.

Wetter, J. G., *The Styles of Appellate Judicial Opinions,* A. W. Sythoff, Leyden, 1960.

Auditory Phonetics

Bobda, A., Wolf, H., and Lothar, P., Identifying regional and national origin of English speaking Africans seeking asylum in Germany, *Foren. Linguis.*, 6:2:300–319, 1999.

Braun, A., Age estimation by different listener groups, *Foren. Linguis.*, 3:1:65–73, 1996.

Braun, A. and Köster, J. P., Eds., *Studies in Forensic Phonetics,* Wissenschaftlicher Verlag, Trier, 1995.

Broeders, A.P.A., Earwitness identification: common ground, disputed territory and uncharted areas, *Foren. Linguis.*, 3:1:3–13, 1996.

Clifford, B. R., Voice identification by human listeners: on earwitness reliability, *Law Human Behav.*, 4:373–394, 1980.

Deffenbacher, K. et al., Relevance of voice identification research criteria for evaluating reliability of an identification, *J. Psychol.*, 123:109–119, 1989.

Ellis, S., The Yorkshire Ripper enquiry: part I, *Foren. Linguis.*, 1:2:197–206, 1994.

Foulkes, P. and Barron, A., Telephone speaker recognition among members of a close social network, *Foren. Linguis.*, 7:2:180–198, 2000.

French, P., An overview of forensic phonetics with particular reference to speaker identification, *Foren. Linguis.*, 1:2:169–181, 1994.

Hecker, M. H. C., Speaker recognition: an interpretive survey of the literature, *Am. Speech-Language Hearing Assoc. Monogr.*, 16, 1971.

Hollien, H., Consideration of guidelines for earwitness lineups, *Foren. Linguis.*, 3:1:14–23, 1996.

Hollien, H. et al., Criteria for earwitness lineups, *Foren. Linguis.*, 2:2:143–153, 1995.

Hollien, H., Majewski, W., and Doherty, E. T., Perceptual identification of voices under normal, stress and disguise speaking conditions, *J. Phonet.*, 10:139–148, 1982

Hollien, H. and Schwartz, R., Aural-perceptual speaker identification: problems with non-contemporary samples, *Foren. Linguis.*, 7:2:199–211, 2000.

Huntley Bahr, R. and Pass, K. J., The influence of style-shifting on voice identification, *Foren. Linguis.*, 3:1:24–38, 1996.

Köster, O. et al., The correlation between auditory speech sensitivity and speaker recognition ability, *Foren. Linguis.*, 5:1:22–32, 1998.

Köster, O. and Schiller, N. O., Different influences of the native language of a listener on speaker recognition, *Foren. Linguis.*, 4:1:18–28, 1997.

Kredens, K. and Goralewska–Lach, G., Language as sole incriminating evidence: the Augustynek case, *Foren. Linguis.*, 5:2:193–202, 1998.

Künzel, H. J., Identifying Dr. Schneider's voice: an adventure in forensic speaker identification, *Foren. Linguis.*, 3:1:146–154, 1996.

Künzel, H., On the problem of speaker identification by victims and witnesses, *Foren. Linguis.*, 1:1:45–58, 1994.

Lloyd–Bostock, S. M. A. and Clifford, B. R., Eds., *Evaluating Witness Evidence: Recent Psychological Research and New Perspectives*, John Wiley & Sons, Chichester, 1983.

Masthoff, H., A report on a voice disguise experiment, *Foren. Linguis.*, 3:1:160–175, 1996.

McClelland, E., *Regina vs. Neil Scobie*, *Foren. Linguis.*, 1:2:223–228, 1994.

Newbrook, M. and Curtain, J. M., Oates' theory of reverse speech: a critical examination, *Foren. Linguis.*, 5:2:174–192, 1998.

Nolan, F., Forensic phonetics, *J. Linguis.*, 27:483–493, 1991.

Nolan, F. and Grabe, E., Preparing a voice lineup, *Foren. Linguis.*, 3:1:74–94, 1996.

Rose, P. and Duncan, S., Naive auditory identification and discrimination of similar voices by familiar listeners, *Foren. Linguis.*, 2:1:1–17, 1995.

Schiller, N. O. and Köster, O., The ability of expert witnesses to identify voices: a comparison between trained and untrained listeners, *Foren. Linguis.*, 5:1:1–9, 1998.

Schiller, N. O. and Köster, O., Evaluation of a foreign speaker in forensic phonetics: a report, *Foren. Linguis.*, 3:1:176–185, 1996.

Schiller, N. O., Köster, O., and Duckworth, M., The effect of removing information upon identifying speakers of a foreign language, *Foren. Linguis.*, 4:1:1–17, 1997.

Schlichting, F. and Sullivan, K. P. H., The imitated voice — a problem for voice line-ups? *Foren. Linguis.*, 4:1:148–165, 1997.

Stuart Laubstein, A., Problems of voice line-ups, *Foren. Linguis.*, 4:2:262–279, 1997.

Sullivan, K. P. H. and Kügler, F., Was the knowledge of the second language or the age difference the determining factor?, *Foren. Linguis.*, 8:2:1–8, 2001.

Sullivan, K. P. H. and Schlichting, F., Speaker discrimination in a foreign language: first language environment, second language learners, *Foren. Linguis.*, 7:1:95–111, 2000.

Yarmey, A. D., Earwitness descriptions and speaker identification, *Foren. Linguis.*, 8:1:113–122, 2001.

Acoustic Phonetics

Baldwin, J. and French, P., *Forensic Phonetics*, Pinter Press, London, 1990.

Boss, D., The problem of F0 and real-life speaker identification: a case study, *Foren. Linguis.*, 3:1:155–159, 1996.

Braun, A., The audio going with the video — some observations on the Rodney King case, *Foren. Linguis.*, 1:2:217–222, 1994.

Braun, A. and Künzel, H. J., Is forensic speaker identification unethical — or can it be ethical not to do it? *Foren. Linguis.*, 5:1:10–21, 1998.

Foulkes, P. and Barron, A., Telephone speaker recognition among members of a close social network, *Foren. Linguis.*, 7:2:180–198, 2000.

French, P., An overview of forensic phonetics with particular reference to speaker identification, *Foren. Linguis.*, 1:2:169–181, 1994.

French, P., Mr. Akbar's nearest ear vs. the Lombard reflex: a case study in forensic phonetics, *Foren. Linguis.*, 5:1:58–68, 1998.

Greisbach, R., Estimation of speaker height from formant frequencies, *Foren. Linguis.*, 6:2:263–277, 1999.

Harrison, P., GSM interference cancellation for forensic audio: a report on work in progress, *Foren. Linguis.*, 8:2:9-23, 2001.

Hirson, A. and Howard, D. M., Spectographic analysis of a cockpit voice recorder tape, *Foren. Linguis.*, 1:1:59–70, 1994.

Hollien, H., *The Acoustics of Crime: the New Science of Forensic Phonetics*, Plenum, New York, 1990.

Hollien, H., *Forensic Voice Identification*, Academic Press, New York, 2001.

Hollien, H. and de Jong, G., Psychological stress in voice: current references, *Foren. Linguis.*, 2:2:201–229, 1995.

Hollien, H. and Martin, C. A., Conducting research on the effects of intoxication on speech, *Foren. Linguis.*, 3:1:107–128, 1996.

Howard, D. M. et al., Spectography of disputed speech samples by peripheral human hearing modeling, *Foren. Linguis.*, 2:1:28–38, 1995.

Ingram, J.C.L., Prandolini, R., and Ong, S., Formant trajectories as indices of phonetic variation for speaker identification, *Foren. Linguis.*, 3:1:129–146, 1996.

Jessen, M., Phonetic manifestations of cognitive and physical stress in trained and untrained police officers, *Foren. Linguis.*, 4:1:125–147, 1997.

Jessen, M., Speaker-specific information in voice quality parameters, *Foren. Linguis.*, 4:1:84–103, 1997.

Jiang, M., Fundamental frequency vector for a speaker identification system, *Foren. Linguis.*, 3:1:95–106, 1996.

Klasmeyer, G. and Sendlmeier, W. F., The classification of different phonation types in emotional and neutral speech, *Foren. Linguis.*, 4:1:104–124, 1997.

Koolwaaij, J. and Boves, L., On decision making in forensic casework, *Foren. Linguis.*, 6:2:242–264, 1999.

Kredens, K. and Goralewska–Lach, G., Language as sole incriminating evidence: the Augustynek case, *Foren. Linguis.*, 5:2:193–202, 1998.

Künzel, H. J., Field procedures in forensic speaker recognition, in Lewis, J. W., Ed., *Studies in General and English Phonetics, Essays in Honour of J.D. O'Connor*, Routledge, London, 68–84, 1995.

Künzel, H. J., Some general phonetic and forensic aspects of speaking tempo, *Foren. Linguis.*, 4:1:48–83, 1997.

Künzel, H. J., Effects of voice disguise on speaking fundamental frequency, *Foren. Linguis.*, 7:2:149–179, 2000.

Künzel, H. J., Beware of the 'telephone effect': the influence of telephone transmissions on the measurement of formant frequencies, *Foren. Linguis.*, 8:1:80-99, 2001.

Künzel, H. J., Köster, J. P., and Masthoff, H. R., The relation between speech tempo, loudness, and fundamental frequency: an important issue in forensic speaker recognition, *Sci. Justice*, 35:291–295, 1994.

Labov, W., The judicial testing of linguistic theory, in Tannen, D., Ed., *Linguistics in Context: Connecting Observation and Understanding*, Ablex, Norwood, 159–182, 1988.

Lindsey, G. and Hirson, A., Variable robustness of nonstandard /r/ in English: evidence from accent disguise, *Foren. Linguis.*, 6:2:278–288, 1999.

Majewski, W. and Basztura, C., Integrated approach to speaker recognition in forensic applications, *Foren. Linguis.*, 3:1:50–64, 1996.

Markham, D., Listeners and disguised voices: the imitation and perception of dialectal accent, *Foren. Linguis.*, 6:2:289–299, 1999.

McClelland, E., Regina vs. Neil Scobie, *Foren. Linguis.*, 1:2:223–228, 1994.

Molina de Figueiredo, R. and de Souza Britto, H., A report on the acoustic effects of one type of disguise, *Foren. Linguis.*, 3:1:168–175, 1996.

Moosmüller, S., The influence of creaky voice on formant frequency changes, *Foren. Linguis.*, 8:1:100–112, 2001.

Moosmüller, S., Phonological variation in speaker identification, *Foren. Linguis.*, 4:1:29–47, 1997.

Nolan, F., Forensic phonetics, *J. Linguis.*, 27:483–493, 1991.

Nolan, F., *The Phonetic Bases of Speaker Recognition*, Cambridge University Press, Cambridge, 1983.

Nolan, F., Speaker identification and forensic phonetics, in Hardcastle, W. J. and Laver, J., Eds., *Handbook of Phonetic Sciences*, Blackwell, Oxford, 1999.

Nolan, F. and Oh, T., Identical twins, different voices, *Foren. Linguis.*, 3:1:39–49, 1996.

Rogers, H., Foreign accent in voice discrimination: a case study, *Foren. Linguis.*, 5:2:203–208, 1998.

Tosi, O. I., *Voice Identification: Theory and Legal Applications*, University Park Press, Baltimore, 1979.

Wagner, I., A new jitter-algorithm to quantify hoarseness: an exploratory study, *Foren. Linguis.*, 2:1:18–27, 1995.

Semantics

Butters, R. R., If the wages of sin are for death: the semantics/pragmatics of a statutory ambiguity, *Am. Speech*, 68:183–194, 1993.

Cotterill, J., Reading the rights: a cautionary tale of comprehension and comprehensibility, *Foren. Linguis.*, 7:1:4–25, 2000.

Cunningham, C. D., A linguistic analysis of the meanings of "search" in the Fourth Amendment: a search for common sense, *Iowa Law Rev.*, 73:3:541–609, 1988.

Cunningham, C. D. et al., Plain meaning and hard cases, *Yale Law J.*, 103:6:1561–1625, 1994.

Dumas, B. and Short, A. C., Linguistic ambiguity in non-statutory language: problems in "The Search Warrant in the Matter of 7505 Derris Drive," *Foren. Linguis.*, 5:2:127–140, 1998.

Durant, A., Allusions and other "innuendo meanings" in libel actions: the value of semantic and pragmatic evidence, *Foren. Linguis.*, 3:2:195–210, 1996.

Gibbons, J., Distortions of the police interview process revealed by video-tape, *Foren. Linguis.*, 3:2:289–298, 1996.

Goddard, C., Can linguists help judges know what they mean? Linguistic semantics in the courtroom, *Foren. Linguis.*, 3:2:250–272, 1996.

Green, D. W., Inferring health claims: a case study, *Foren. Linguis.*, 3:2:299–322, 1996.

Grisso, T., *Instruments for Assessing Understanding and Appreciation of Miranda Rights*, Professional Resource Press, Sarasota, FL, 1998.

Jackson, B. S., *Making Sense in Law*, Deborah Charles Publications, Liverpool, 1995.

Kaplan, J. et al., Bringing linguistics into judicial decision-making: semantic analysis submitted to the U.S. Supreme Court, *Foren. Linguis.*, 2:1:81–97, 1995.

Kurzon, D., The right to understand the right of silence: a few comments, *Foren. Linguis.*, 7:2:244–248, 2000.

Labov, W., The judicial testing of linguistic theory, in Tannen, D., Ed., *Linguistics in Context: Connecting Observation and Understanding*, Ablex, Norwood, 159–182, 1988.

Labov, W. and Harris, W., Linguistics evidence in the Thornfare case, cited in Labov, 1988, unpublished manuscript, 1983.

Langford, I., Forensic semantics: the meaning of *murder, manslaughter* and *homicide*, *Foren. Linguis.*, 7:1:72–94, 2000.

Levi, J. N., Evaluating jury comprehension of the Illinois capital sentencing instructions, *Am. Speech*, 68:20–49, 1993.

McLeod, N., Psycholinguistic analysis of tax judgments, *Foren. Linguis.*, 3:2:232–249, 1996.

McMenamin, G. R., *Forensic Stylistics*, Elsevier Science Publishers, Amsterdam, 1993.

McMenamin, G. and Lepken, L., Perceived vs. intended meaning in written language, in Nevis, J. A., McMenamin, G., and Thurgood, G., Eds., *Papers in Honor of Frederick H. Brengelman*, California State University Fresno, Fresno, 1993.

Murphy, H. F., Linguistics and law: an overview of forensic linguistics, *J. Law, Intellect. Property, Technol.*, 1:1–20, 1998.

Russell, S., "Let me put it simply …": the case for a standard translation of the police caution and its explanation, *Foren. Linguis.*, 7:1:26–48, 2000.

Shuy, R. W., Context as the highest standard of semantics: a lawsuit involving the meaning of "accuracy" in accounting, *J. Engl. Linguis.*, 19:2:295–303, 1986.

Shuy, R. W., Ten unanswered questions about Miranda, *Foren. Linguis.*, 4:2:175–196, 1997.

Shuy, R. W. and Staton, J. L., Review of *Grisso 1998*, *Foren. Linguis.*, 7:1:131–136, 2000.

Solan, L. M., Can the legal system use experts on meaning? *Tenn. Law Rev.*, 66:1167, Summer 1999.

Solan, L. M., Linguistic experts as semantic tour guides, *Foren. Linguis.*, 5:2:87–106, 1998.

Stratman, J. F. and Dahl, P., Readers' comprehension of temporary restraining orders in domestic violence cases: a missing link in abuse prevention, *Foren. Linguis.*, 3:2:211–231, 1996.

Tiersma, P. M., Dictionaries and death: do capital jurors understand mitigation? *Utah Law Review*, 1, 1995.

Vishneski, J.S. et al., The insurance industry's 1970 pollution exclusion: an exercise in ambiguity, *Loyola Univ. Chicago Law J.*, 23:1:67–101, 1991.

White, A. R., *Misleading Cases*, Clarendon Press, Oxford, 1991.

WULQ, *What Is Meaning in a Legal Text*, special issue of the *Wash. Univ. Law Q.*, 73:3, Hein & Co., Buffalo, 1995.

Discourse and Pragmatics

Barsky, R. F., *Constructing a Productive Other: Discourse Theory and the Convention Refugee Hearing*, John Benjamins, Amsterdam, 1994

Berk–Seligson, S., The impact of court interpreting on the coerciveness of leading questions, *Foren. Linguis.*, 6:1:30–56, 1999.

Brennan, M., The discourse of denial: cross-examining child victim witnesses, *J. Pragmatics*, 23:71–91, 1994.

Coulthard, M., Forensic discourse analysis, in Coulthard, M., Ed., *Advances in Spoken Discourse Analysis*, Routledge, London, 242–258, 1992.

Dumas, B. K., U.S. pattern jury instructions: problems and proposals, *Foren. Linguis.*, 7:1:49–71, 2000.

Ehrlich, S., The legitimization of pragmatic inappropriateness: language in sexual assault trials, paper presented at *Georgetown University Roundtable on Linguistics and the Professions,* Georgetown, May 2000.

Fraser, B., Threatening revisited, *Foren. Linguis.*, 5:2:159–173, 1998.

Gibbons, J., Distortions of the police interview process revealed by video-tape, *Foren. Linguis.*, 3:2:289–298, 1996.

Gibbons, J., Legal transformations in Spanish: an 'audiencia' in Chile, *Foren. Linguis.*, 8:2:24–43, 2001.

Hale, S., Clash of world perspectives: the discursive practices of the law, the witness and the interpreter, *Foren. Linguis.*, 4:2:197–209, 1997.

Hale, S., Interpreters' treatment of discourse markers in courtroom questions, *Foren. Linguis.*, 6:1:57–82, 1999.

Jackson, B. S., *Making Sense in Law,* Deborah Charles Publications, Liverpool, 1995.

Kaplan, J. P., Pragmatic contributions to the interpretation of a will, *Foren. Linguis.*, 5:2:107–126, 1998.

Levi, J. N., Evaluating jury comprehension of the Illinois capital sentencing instructions, *Am. Speech,* 68:20–49, 1993.

Maley, Y. et al., Orientations in lawyer–client interviews, *Foren. Linguis.*, 2:1:42–55, 1995.

McLeod, N., Psycholinguistic analysis of tax judgments, *Foren. Linguis.*, 3:2:232–249, 1996.

McMenamin, G. and Lepken, L., Perceived vs. intended meaning in written language, in Nevis, J. A., McMenamin, G., and Thurgood, G., Eds., *Papers in Honor of Frederick H. Brengelman,* California State University Fresno, Fresno, 1993.

Olsson, J., The dictation and alteration of text, *Foren. Linguis.*, 4:2:226–251, 1997.

Ragan, S. L. et al., *The Lynching of Language: Gender, Politics, and Power in the Hill–Thomas Hearings,* University of Illinois Press, Urbana, 1996.

Rigney, A. C., Questioning in interpreted testimony, *Foren. Linguis.*, 6:1:83–108, 1999.

Rock, F., The genesis of a witness statement, *Foren. Linguis.*, 8:2:44–72, 2001.

Shuy, R. W., Deceit, distress and false imprisonment: the anatomy of a car sales event, *Foren. Linguis.*, 1:2:133–150, 1994.

Shuy, R. W., *Language Crimes: the Use and Abuse of Language Evidence in the Courtroom,* Blackwell, Oxford, 1993.

Shuy, R. W., *The Language of Confessions, Interrogation and Deception,* Sage Publications, Los Angeles, 1998.

Solan, L. M., Linguistic experts as semantic tour guides, *Foren. Linguis.*, 5:2:87–106, 1998.

Storey, K., The language of threats, *Foren. Linguis.*, 2:1:74–80, 1995.

Stygall, G., *Trial Language: Differential Discourse Processing and Discursive Formation,* John Benjamins, Amsterdam, 1994.

Tiersma, P. M., Dictionaries and death: do capital jurors understand mitigation? *Utah Law Rev.,* 1, 1995.

Tiersma, P. M., The language of defamation, *Tex. Law Rev.,* 66:2:303–350, 1987.

Tiersma, P. M., The language of offer and acceptance: speech acts and the question of intent, *Calif. Law Rev.,* 74:1:189–232, 1986.

Tiersma, P. M., The language of perjury: "Literal truth," ambiguity, and the false statement requirement, *South. Calif. Law Rev.,* 63:2:373–431, 1990.

Trinch, S. L., Managing euphemism: transcending taboos and transforming Latinas' narratives of sexual violence in protective order interviews, paper presented at *Georgetown University Roundtable on Linguistics and the Professions,* Georgetown, May 2000.

Wallace, W. D., The admissibility of expert testimony on the discourse analysis of recorded conversation, *Univ. Fl. Law Rev.,* 38:69–115, 1986.

Stylistics, Questioned Authorship, and Corpus Linguistics

An, D. U., Kim, G. C., and Lee, J. H., Corpus-based modality generation for Korean predicates, *Lit. Linguis. Comput.,* 10:1:1–10, 1995.

Aoyama, H. and Constable, J., Word length frequency and distribution in English: part I. Prose, *Lit. Linguis. Comput.,* 14:3:339–358, 1999.

Atkins, S., Clear, J., and Ostler, N., Corpus design criteria, *Lit. Linguis. Comput.,* 7:1:1–16, 1992.

Barr, G. K., A computer model for the Pauline epistles, *Literary & Linguistic Computing,* 16:3:233–250, 2001.

Binongo, J. N. G., Joaquin's *Joaquinesquerie, Joaquinesquerie's* Joaquin: a statistical expression of a Filipino writer's style, Literary & Linguistic Computing, 9:4:267–280, 1994.

Binongo, J. N. G. and Smith, M. W. A., The application of principal component analysis to stylometry, *Lit. Linguis. Comput.,* 14:4:445–466, 1999.

Broeders, A. P. A., Some observations on the use of probability scales in forensic identification, *Foren. Linguis.,* 6:2:228–241, 1999.

Burrows, J. F., Computers and the study of literature, in C. S. Butler, Ed., *Computers and Written Texts,* Blackwell, Oxford, 167–204, 1992.

Canter, D., An evaluation of the "cusum" stylistic analysis of confessions, *Expert Evidence,* 1:2:93–99, 1992.

Canter, D. and Chester, J., Investigation in the claim of weighted cusum in authorship attribution studies, *Foren. Linguis.,* 4:2:252–261, 1997.

Champod, C. and Evett, I. W., Commentary on A.P.A. Broeders (1999) "Some observations on the use of probability scales in forensic identification," *Foren. Linguis.,* 6(2):228–241; *Foren. Linguis.,* 7:2:238–243, 2000.

Chaski, C. E., Empirical evaluations of language-based author identification techniques, *Foren. Linguis.*, 8:1:1–65, 2001.

Coulthard, M., A failed appeal, *Foren. Linguis.*, 4:2:287–302, 1997.

Coulthard, M., Making texts speak: the work of the forensic linguist, *Studia Anglica Posnaniensia*, 33:117–130, 1998.

Coulthard, M., On the use of corpus linguistics in the analysis of forensic texts, *Foren. Linguis.*, 1:1:27–44, 1994.

Craig, H., Authorial attribution and computational stylistics: if you can tell authors apart, have you learned anything about them? *Lit. Linguis. Comput.*, 14:1:103–114, 1992.

de Haan, P., Review [of Farringdon et al., 1996], *Foren. Linguis.*, 5:1:69–76, 1998.

Dixon, P. and Mannion, D., Goldsmith's periodical essays: a statistical analysis of eleven doubtful cases, *Lit. Linguis. Comput.*, 8:1:1–19, 1993.

Elliott, E. Y. and Valenza, R. J., Smoking guns and silver bullets: Could John Ford have written the Funeral Elegy? *Literary & Linguistic Computing*, 16:3:205–232, 2001.

Fang, A. C. and Nelson, G., Tagging the survey corpus: a LOB to ICE experiment using AUTASYS, *Lit. Linguis. Comput.*, 9:3:189–194, 1994.

Farringdon, J. M. et al., *Analysing for Authorship: a guide to the Cusum Technique*, University of Wales Press, Cardiff, 1996.

Finkelstein, M. O. and Fairley, W. B., A Bayesian approach to identification evidence, *Harv. Law Rev.*, 83:489, 1970.

Forsyth, R. S., Stylochronometry with substrings, or: a poet young and old, *Lit. Linguis. Comput.*, 14:4:467–478, 1999.

Forsyth, R. S. and Holmes, D. I., Feature-finding for text classification, *Lit. Linguis. Comput.*, 11:4:163–174, 1996.

Forsyth, R. S., Holmes, D. I., and Tse, E. K., Cicero, Sigonio, and Burrows: investigating the authenticity of the *Consolatio, Lit. Linguis. Comput.*, 14:3:375–400, 1999.

Garside, R., The large-scale production of syntactically analysed corpora, *Lit. Linguis. Comput.*, 8:1:39–46, 1993.

Goutsos, D., Hatzidaki, O., and King, P., Towards a corpus of spoken modern Greek, *Lit. Linguis. Comput.*, 9:3:215–224, 1994.

Grant, T. and Baker, K., Identifying reliable, valid markers of authorship: a response to Chaski, *Foren. Linguis.*, 8:1:66–79, 2001.

Greenwood, H. H., Common word frequencies and authorship in Luke's Gospel and Acts, *Lit. Linguis. Comput.*, 10:3:183–188, 1995.

Greenwood, H. H., St. Paul revisited — word clusters in multidimensional space, *Lit. Linguis. Comput.*, 8:4:211–219, 1993.

Gurney, L. W. and Gurney, P. J., The *Scriptores Historiae Augustae*: history and controversy, *Lit. Linguis. Comput.*, 13:3:105–110, 1998a.

Gurney, P. J. and Gurney, L. W., Authorship attribution of the *Scriptores Historiae Augustae*, *Lit. Linguis. Comput.*, 13:3:119–132, 1998b.

Gurney, P. J. and Gurney, L. W., Subsets and homogeneity: authorship attribution in the *Scriptores Historiae Augustae*, *Lit. Linguis. Comput.*, 13:3:133–140, 1998c.

Hänlein, H., *Studies in Authorship Recognition — a Corpus-Based Approach*, Peter Lang, Frankfurt, 1999.

Hilton, M. L. and Holmes, D. I., An assessment of cumulative sum charts for authorship attribution, *Lit. Linguis. Comput.*, 8:2:73–80, 1993.

Holmes, D. I., Authorship attribution, *Comput. Humanities*, 28:87–106, 1994.

Holmes, D. I., The evolution of stylometry in humanities scholarship, *Lit. Linguis. Comput.*, 13:3:111–118, 1998.

Holmes, D. I. and Forsyth, R. S., The *Federalist* revisited: new directions in authorship attribution, *Lit. Linguis. Comput.*, 10:2:111–127, 1995.

Hoorn, J. F. et al., Neural network identification of poets using letter sequences, *Lit. Linguis. Comput.*, 14:3:311–338, 1999.

Hunyadi, L., Linguistic analysis of large corpora: approaches to computational linguistics in Hungary, *Lit. Linguis. Comput.*, 14:1:77–88, 1999.

Jackson, M. P., George Wilkins and the first two acts of *Pericles*: new evidence from function words, *Lit. Linguis. Comput.*, 6:3:155–163, 1991.

Johnson, A., Textual kidnapping — a case of plagiarism among three student texts, *Foren. Linguis.*, 4:2:210–225, 1997.

Kennedy, G., *An Introduction to Corpus Linguistics*, Longman, London, 1998.

Khmelev, D. V. and Tweedie, F. J., Using Markov chains for identification of writers, *Literary & Linguistic Computing*, 16:3:299–308, 2001.

Kirk, J. M., Corpus — concordance — database — VARBRUL, *Lit. Linguis. Comput.*, 9:4:259–266, 1994.

Kjell, B., Authorship determination using letter pair frequency features with neural network classifiers, *Lit. Linguis. Comput.*, 9:2:119–124, 1994.

Kniffka, H., Forensische Linguistik: anonymous authorship analysis without comparison data? A case study with methodological implications, *Linguistische Berichte*, 182:179–198, 2000.

Kniffka, H., On forensic linguistic "differential diagnosis," in Kniffka, H., Blackwell, S., and Coulthard, M., Eds., *Recent Developments in Forensic Linguistics*, Peter Lang, Frankfurt, 1996.

Koolwaaij, J. and Boves, L., On decision making in forensic casework, *Foren. Linguis.*, 6:2:242–264, 1999.

Laan, N. M., Stylometry and method: the case of Euripides, *Lit. Linguis. Comput.*, 10:4:271–278, 1995.

Ledger, G., An exploration of differences in the Pauline epistles using multivariate statistical analysis, *Lit. Linguis. Comput.*, 10:2:85–98, 1995.

Lewis, J. W., The Yorkshire Ripper enquiry: part II, *Foren. Linguis.*, 1:2:207–217, 1994.

Louhivaara, S., Multiple authorship of the OE Orosius, in Fernandes, F., Fuster, M., and Calvo, J. J. Eds., *English Historical Linguistics, 1992: Papers from the 7th International Conference on English Historical Linguistics*, Amsterdam, John Benjamins, 343–352, 1994.

Mair, C. and Hundt, M., Eds., *Corpus Linguistics and Linguistic Theory*, Amsterdam, Rodopi, 2000.

Matthews, R. and Merriam, T., Neural computation in stylometry I: an application to the works of Shakespeare and Fletcher, *Lit. Linguis. Comput.*, 8:4:203–210, 1993.

McKee, G., Malvern, D., and Richards, B., Measuring vocabulary diversity using dedicated software, *Lit. Linguis. Comput.*, 15:3:323–338, 2000.

McKenna, W. and Antonia, A., "A few simple words" of interior monologue in Ulysses: Reconfiguring the evidence, *Lit. Linguis. Comput.*, 11:2:55–66, 1996.

McMenamin, G. R., *Forensic Stylistics*, Elsevier Science Publishers, Amsterdam, 1993.

McMenamin, G. R., A forensic analysis of writing style: an Indian English case, in Laury, R. et al., Eds., *Festschrift for P. J. Mistry*, New Delhi, Creative Books, 2001a.

McMenamin, G. R., Style markers in authorship studies, *Foren. Linguis.*, 8:2:93–97, 2001b.

Mealand, D. L., Correspondence analysis of Luke, *Lit. Linguis. Comput.*, 10:3:171–182, 1995.

Mealand, D. L., Style, genre, and authorship in Acts, the Septuagint, and Hellenistic historians, *Lit. Linguis. Comput.*, 14:4:479–506, 1999.

Merriam, T., *Edward III, Lit. Linguis. Comput.*, 15:2:157–186, 2000.

Merriam, T., Marlow's hand in *Edward III, Lit. Linguis. Comput.*, 8:2:59–72, 1993.

Merriam, T., Marlow's hand in *Edward III* revisited, *Lit. Linguis. Comput.*, 11:1:19–22, 1996.

Merriam, T. and Matthews, R., Neural computation in stylometry II: an application to the works of Shakespeare and Marlowe, *Lit. Linguis. Comput.*, 9:1:1–8, 1994.

Meurman-Solin, A., Structured text corpora in the study of language variation and change, *Lit. Linguis. Comput.*, 16:1:5–27, 2001.

Morton, A. Q., Response [to Sanford et al., 1994], *Foren. Linguis.*, 2:2:230–233, 1995.

Olsson, J., Review of H. Hänlein's *Studies in Authorship Attribution — a Corpus Based Approach, Foren. Linguis.*, 8:1:123–129, 2001.

Peranteau, P., *Corpus Linguistics: Lexical Grammar of English, Multimodal Dialogue*, John Benjamins, Amsterdam, 2000.

Rommel, T., "So soft, so sweet, so delicately clear." A computer-assisted analysis of accumulated words and phrases in Lord Byron's epic poem *Don Juan, Lit. Linguis. Comput.*, 9:1:7–12, 1994.

Rudman, J., The hypothetical and theoretical underpinnings of non-traditional authorship attribution studies: assumptions, presumptions, and verifiable constructs, paper presented at the conference of the *Association for Lit. Linguis. Comput.*, University of Virginia, Charlottesville, 1999.

Rudman, J., Non-traditional authorship attribution studies in the *Historia Augusta*: some caveats, *Lit. Linguis. Comput.*, 13:3:151–157, 1998.

Rudman, J., The state of authorship attribution studies: some problems and solutions, *Comput. Humanities*, 31:351–365, 1998.

Sanford, A. J. et al., A critical examination of assumptions underlying the cusum technique of forensic linguistics, *Foren. Linguis.*, 1:2:151–168, 1994.

Schils, E. and de Hann, P., Characteristics of sentence length in running text, *Lit. Linguis. Comput.*, 8:1:20–26, 1993.

Sjerps, M. and Biesheuvel, D. B., The interpretation of conventional and Bayesian verbal scales for expressing expert opinion: a small experiment among jurists, *Foren. Linguis.*, 6:2:214–227, 1999.

Smith, N., McEnery, T., and Ivanic, R., Issues in transcribing a corpus of children's handwritten projects, *Lit. Linguis. Comput.*, 13:4:217–226, 1998.

Smith, P., Review [Farringdon et al., 1996], *Foren. Linguis.*, 5:1:77–79, 1998.

Taroni, F., Champod, C., and Margot, P. A., Forerunners of Bayesianism in early forensic science, *Jurimetrics J.*, 38, 1998, and *J. Foren. Identif.*, 49:3:285–305, 1999.

Temple, J. T., A multivariate synthesis of published Platonic stylometric data, *Lit. Linguis. Comput.*, 11:2:67–76, 1996.

Tse, E. K., Tweedie, F. J., and Frischer, B. D., Unravelling the purple thread: function word variability and the *Scriptores Historiae Augustae*, *Lit. Linguis. Comput.*, 13:3:141–150, 1998.

Tweedie, F. J., Holmes, D. I., and Corns, T. N., The provenance of *De Doctrina Christiana*, attributed to John Milton: a statistical investigation, *Lit. Linguis. Comput.*, 13:2:77–88, 1998.

Waugh, S., Adams, A., Tweedie, F., Computational stylistics using artificial neural networks, *Lit. Linguis. Comput.*, 15:2:187–198, 2000.

Woolls, D. and Coulthard, M., Tools for the trade, *Foren. Linguis.*, 5:1:33–57, 1998.

Zampolli, A., Ed., Special section on corpora — part two, with seven separate articles, *Lit. Linguis. Comput.*, 9:1:21–86, 1994.

Zampolli, A. and Ostler, N., Eds., Special section on corpora, with ten separate articles, *Lit. Linguis. Comput.*, 8:4:212–292, 1993.

Language of the Law

Conley, J. M. and O'Barr, W. M., *Just Words: Law, Language, and Power*, University of Chicago Press, Chicago, 1998.

Goodrich, P., *Legal Discourse: Studies in Linguistics, Rhetoric and Legal Analysis*, St. Martin's Press, New York, 1987.

Melinkoff, D., *The Language of the Law*, Little, Brown, Boston, 1963.

Tiersma, P. M., *Legal Language*, University of Chicago Press, Chicago, 1999.

Language of the Courtroom

Brennan, M., The discourse of denial: cross-examining child victim witnesses, *J. Pragmatics*, 23:71–91, 1994.

Charrow, R. P. and Charrow, V. P., Making legal language understandable: a psycho-linguistic study of jury instructions, *Columbia Law Rev.*, 79:1306–1374, 1979.

Conley, J. M. and O'Barr, W. M., *Just Words: Law, Language, and Power*, University of Chicago Press, Chicago, 1998.

Conley, J. M, O'Barr, W. M., and Lind, E. A., The power of language: presentational style in the courtroom, *Duke Law J.*, 78:1375–1399, 1978.

Cooke, M., A different story: narrative vs. "question and answer" in semantics in the courtroom, *Foren. Linguis.*, 3:2:273–288, 1996.

Cotterill, J., "If it doesn't fit, you must acquit": metaphor and the O.J. Simpson criminal trial, *Foren. Linguis.*, 5:2:141–158, 1998.

Danet, B., Language in the legal process, *Law Soc. Rev.*, 14:3:445–564, 1980.

Dumas, B. K., U.S. pattern jury instructions: problems and proposals, *Foren. Linguis.*, 7:1:49–71, 2000.

Eades, D., *I don't think it's the answer to the question*: silencing Aboriginal witnesses in court, *Language Soc.*, 29:2:161–193, 2000.

Ehrlich, S., *Representing Rape: Language and Sexual Consent*, Routledge, London, 2001.

Ehrlich, S., The legitimization of pragmatic inappropriateness: language in sexual assault trials, paper presented at *Georgetown University Roundtable on Linguistics and the Professions*, Georgetown, May 2000.

Hale, S., Interpreters' treatment of discourse markers in courtroom questions, *Foren. Linguis.*, 6:1:57–82, 1999.

Kniffka, H., Understanding misunderstandings in court: La Serva Padrona phenomena and other miscommunications in forensic interaction, *Expert Evidence*, 2:4:164–175, 1994.

Levi, J., Evaluating jury comprehension of Illinois capital sentencing instructions, *Am. Speech*, 68:1:20–49, 1993.

Penny, L., Fitzhardinge, S., and Materne, H., The language of the suffrage debates in the South Australian parliament, 1885–94, *Foren. Linguis.*, 2:1:56–64, 1995.

Phillips, S. U., *Ideology in the Language of Judges: How Judges Practice Law, Politics, and Courtroom Control*, Oxford University Press, Oxford, 1998.

Solan, L. M., *The Language of Judges*, University of Chicago Press, Chicago, 1993a.

Solan, L. M., When judges use a dictionary, *Am. Speech*, 68:1:50–57, 1993b.

Steele, W. W. and Thornburg, E. G., Jury instructions: a persistent failure to communicate, *N.C. Law Rev.*, 67:77–119, 1988.

Stygall, G., *Trial Language: Differential Discourse Processing and Discursive Formation*, John Benjamins, Amsterdam, 1994.

Tiersma, P. M., Reforming the language of jury instructions, *Hofstra Law Review*, 22:37–78, 1993.

Tiersma, P. M., Jury instructions in the new millennium, *Court Review*, 36:2:28–36, 1999.

Tiersma, P. M., Textualizing the law, *Foren. Linguis.*, 8:2:73–92, 2001.

Trinch, S. L., Managing euphemism: transcending taboos and transforming Latinas' narratives of sexual violence in protective order interviews, paper presented at *Georgetown University Roundtable on Linguistics and the Professions*, Georgetown, May 2000.

Wetter, J. G., *The Styles of Appellate Judicial Opinions*, Sythoff, Leyden, 1960.

Interpretation and Translation

Benmaman, V., Bilingual legal interpreter education, *Foren. Linguis.*, 6:1:109–114, 1999.

Berk–Seligson, S., *The Bilingual Courtroom: Courtroom Interpreters in the Judicial Process*, University of Chicago Press, Chicago, 1990.

Berk–Seligson, S., The impact of court interpreting on the coerciveness of leading questions, *Foren. Linguis.*, 6:1:30–56, 1999.

Berk–Seligson, S., Interpreting for the police: issues in pretrial phases of the judicial process, *Foren. Linguis.*, 7:2:212–237, 2000.

Carroll, J., The use of interpreters in court, *Foren. Linguis.*, 2:1:65–73, 1995.

Colin, J. and Morris, R., *Interpreters and the Legal Process*, Waterside Press, Winchester, U.K., 1996.

Cooke, M., Eades, D., and Hale, S., Introduction to special issue on legal interpreting, with eight other articles, *Foren. Linguis.*, 6:1:1–5ff, 1999.

Eades, D., *Language in Evidence: Issues Confronting Aboriginal and Multicultural Australia*, University of New South Wales Press, Sydney, 1995.

Edwards, A. B., *The Practice of Court Interpreting*, John Benjamins, Amsterdam, 1995.

Gaiba, F., *The Origins of Simultaneous Interpretation: the Nuremberg Trial*, University of Ottawa Press, Ottawa, 1998.

Gibbons, J., Distortions of the police interview process revealed by video-tape, *Foren. Linguis.*, 3:2:289–298, 1996.

González, R. D., Vásquez, V., and Mikkelson, H., *Fundamentals of Court Interpretation*, Carolina Academic Press, Durham, NC, 1991.

Hale, S., Clash of world perspectives: the discursive practices of the law, the witness and the interpreter, *Foren. Linguis.*, 4:2:197–209, 1997.

Hale, S., Interpreters' treatment of discourse markers in courtroom questions, *Foren. Linguis.*, 6:1:57–82, 1999.

Lane, C., McKenzie–Bridle, K., and Curtis, L., The right to interpreting and translation services in New Zealand courts, *Foren. Linguis.*, 6:1:115–136, 1999.

Laster, K. and Taylor, V., *Interpreters and the Legal System*, Federation Press, Sydney, 1994.

Lewis, R., *Cyfiawnder Dwyieithog? Bilingual Justice*, Gomer, Llandysul, Wales, 1998.

Mildren, D., Redressing the imbalance: Aboriginal people in the criminal justice system, *Foren. Linguis.*, 6:1:137–160, 1999.

Moeketsi, R., *Discourse in a Multilingual and Multicultural Courtroom: a Court Interpreter's Guide*, J. L. van Schaik, Pretoria, 1999

Morris, M., Ed., *Translation and the Law*, American Translators Association Series, Vol. 8, John Benjamins, Amsterdam, 1995.

Morris, R., The gum syndrome: predicaments in court interpreting, *Foren. Linguis.*, 6:1:7–29, 1999.

Palma, J., Textual density and the judicial interpreter's performance, *Translation and the Law*, Scholarly Monograph Series VIII, American Translators Association, 219–231, 1995.

Rigney, A. C., Questioning in interpreted testimony, *Foren. Linguis.*, 6:1:83–108, 1999.

Robinson, L., *Handbook for Legal Interpreters*, The Law Book Company, Sydney, 1994.

Russell, S., "Let me put it simply …": The case for a standard translation of the police caution and its explanation, *Foren. Linguis.*, 7:1:26–48, 2000.

Wadensjö, C., *Interpreting as Interaction*, Addison Wesley Longman, Harlow, U.K., 1998.

Walsh, M., Interpreting for the transcript: problems in recording aboriginal land claim proceedings in northern Australia, *Foren. Linguis.*, 6:1:4–25, 1999.

Wu, W., Chinese evidence vs. the institutionalized power of English, *Foren. Linguis.*, 2:2:154–167, 1995.

Questioned-Document Examination

Conway, J. V. P., *Evidential Documents*, Charles C Thomas, Springfield, IL, 1959.

Davis, T., ESDA and the analysis of contested contemporaneous notes of public interviews, *Foren. Linguis.*, 1:1:71–90, 1994.

Ellen, D., *The Scientific Examination of Documents: Methods and Techniques*, 2nd Ed., Taylor & Francis, London, 1997.

Found, B., Dick, D., and Rogers, D., The structure of forensic handwriting and signature comparisons, *Foren. Linguis.*, 1:2:183–196, 1994.

Harrison, W. R., *Suspect Documents*, Sweet and Maxwell, London, 1958.

Hilton, O., *Scientific Examination of Questioned Documents*, Elsevier, New York, 1982.

Huber, R. A. and Headrick, A. M., *Handwriting Identification: Facts and Fundamentals*, CRC Press, Boca Raton, FL, 1999.

Levinson, J., *Questioned Documents: a Lawyer's Handbook*, Academic Press, San Diego, 2001.

McMenamin, G. R., *Forensic Stylistics*, Elsevier Science Publishers, Amsterdam, 1993.

Morris, R. N., *Forensic Handwriting Identification: Fundamental Concepts and Principles*, Academic Press, San Diego, 2000.

Osborn, A. S., *Questioned Documents*, 2nd Ed., Boyd Printing Company, Albany, NY, 1929.

Software Forensics

Gray, A., Sallis, P., and MacDonnell, S., Software forensics: extending authorship analysis techniques to computer programs, *Proceed. 3rd Ann. Conf. Int. Assoc. Foren. Linguists* (IAFL '97), Duke University, Durham, NC, 1–8, 1997.

Kilgour, R. I. et al., A fuzzy logic approach to computer software source code authorship analysis, paper presented at *The Fourth International Conference on Neural Information Processing, Annual Conference of the Asian Pacific Neural Network Assembly*, Dunedin, New Zealand, 1997.

Krsul, I., Authorship analysis: identifying the author of a program, *Technical Report CSD-TR-94-030*, Department of Computer Sciences, Purdue University, IN, 1994

Krsul, I. and Spafford, E. H., Authorship analysis: identifying the author of a program, *Technical Report CSD-TR-96-052*, Department of Computer Sciences, Purdue University, 1996.

Krsul, I., and Spafford, E. H., Authorship analysis: identifying the author of a program, *Comput. Security*, 16:3:233–257, 1997.

Spafford, E. H. and Weeber, S. A., Software forensics: can we track code to its authors? *Technical Report CSD-TR-92-010*, Department of Computer Sciences, Purdue University, 1992.

Spafford, E. H. and Weeber, S. A., Software forensics: can we track code to its authors? *Comput. Security*, 12:585–595, 1993.

Semiotics

Adeodato, J. M., The rhetorical syllogism (enthymeme) in judicial argumentation, *Int. J. Semiotics Law/Revue Internationale de Semiotique Juridique*, 12:2:133–150, 1999.

Cao, D., "Ought to" as a Chinese legal performative? *Int. J. Semiotics Law/Revue Internationale de Semiotique Juridique*, 12:2:151–167, 1999.

Henning, T., Judicial summation: The trial judge's version of the facts of the chimera of neutrality, *Int. J. Semiotics Law/Revue Internationale de Semiotique Juridique*, 12:2:169–210, 1999.

International Journal for the Semiotics of Law/Revue international de sémiotique juridique, vols. 1–13, 1988–2000: *http://www.wkap.nl/journalhome/0952-8059/*

Psycholinguistics

Hodges, A. G., *Who Will Speak for JonBenét?* Village House, New York, 2000.

Miron, M., Psycholinguistics in the courtroom, in Rieber, R. W. and Stewart, W. A., Eds., *The Language Scientist as Expert in the Legal Setting: Issues in Forensic Linguistics*, Annals of the New York Academy of Sciences, Vol. 606, New York, 1990, 55–64.

Miron, M. and Douglas, J. E., Threat analysis: The psycholinguistic approach, *FBI Law Enforcement Bull.*, September 1979, 5–9.

Pace, E., Murray Miron, 62, psychologist who aided F.B.I., *The New York Times*, July 28, 1995, A20.

Literary Forensics

Foster, D., *Author Unknown: on the Trail of the Anonymous*, Holt, New York, 2000.

Lakoff, G., *Women, Fire and Dangerous Things: What Categories Reveal about the Mind*, University of Chicago Press, Chicago, 1987.

McMenamin, G., *Forensic Stylistics*, Elsevier Science Publishers, Amsterdam, 1993.

Roberts, D., Don Foster has a way with words, *Smithsonian*, 100–111, September 2001.

Cases Cited

Pate v. People, 3 Gilman 644 (1846).

Trial of William Hales, 17 Howell State Trials 161 (1728).

United States v. Van Wyk, 83 F.Supp.2d 515 (D. New Jersey, 2000).

Style

GERALD R. McMENAMIN

5

5.1 The Concept of Style

Style is the variable element of human behavior. Common human actions such as getting dressed, eating, sweeping a room, saying hello and good-bye, driving, or playing the piano are behaviors that are largely invariant but also partly variable. The process and outcome of these actions are more or less the same for everyone, but *how* one moves through the process and arrives at the outcome will vary considerably from person to person.

There are various ways to understand this. If you attempt to teach a child to tie a shoe, or a teenager to drive a car, you must stop to think very explicitly about what to do with your fingers and the shoestring, or exactly how to coordinate clutch, gas, brake, shift, and steering, all the while coping with everyone's frayed nerves. Alternatively, think of the performance of a mime and why it is entertaining. The mime's skill lies in capturing the sequence and details of everyday human actions. People are so rarely able to observe themselves in such meticulous slow motion that a mime making them conscious of the mundane minutiae of their actions can be entertaining and, sometimes, even disturbing.

Style in behavior is acquired early by children. Style in music, theater, dance, etc. is acquired by performance artists as they develop their craft. Behavioral styles are seen as personal choices made on a continuum of consciousness; all become unconscious as they are constantly repeated and become more and more a part of the person.

Style, once developed, remains with one. Consider the paintings of the American artist, Willem de Kooning, who died in 1997 at the age of 92. A nascent artistic style from his Rotterdam teen years further developed, after moving to the U.S., during his 20s and 30s into "history's most eloquent brushstroke, which, thick or thin, communicates shape, line, substance, direction..." (Schjeldahl, 2001:98). Although he suffered from Alzheimer's and was unable even to sign his name after 1986, de Kooning's late body of work (over 340 canvases) demonstrates that "he didn't have to remember what he was about ... his art could more or less keep track of itself ... his hand never lost its cunning" (Schjeldahl, 2001:98). Oliver Sacks is cited by Schjeldahl as saying in a 1996 exhibition catalog that "'Style' neurologically is the deepest part of one's being, and may be preserved, almost to the last, in a dementia."

5.2   Style in Language

Style is not a uniform concept in language. Style in spoken language relates to linguistic variation resulting from the social context of conversation. The social context is defined by the topic and purpose of the interaction, as well as the social, cultural, and geographic characteristics of its speakers and listeners: their age, sex, race, ethnicity, education, income, occupation, links to social networks, group affiliations, places of residence, etc. Style in written language refers to the variable ways that language is used in certain genres, periods, situations, and individuals. While the link between writing style and situations shows that writing does share the spoken language connection to social context, written style is usually defined more narrowly for study and analysis, e.g., "[A] style is defined by the structural characteristics of texts" (Besnier, 1988:709).

Style in writing results from the recurrent choices that the writer makes. *Recurrent* reflects the writer's subconscious habits of regularly choosing one form over others to say the same thing. *Choices* are of two types: variation within a norm or deviation from a norm. Variation within a norm refers to choices among grammatical or acceptable ("correct") forms, e.g., *twenty-six/twenty six/26*. Deviation from a norm refers to choices that include ungrammatical or unacceptable ("incorrect") forms, e.g., *I might go./I could go./I might could go/I might could did go.* For someone from the west coast of the U.S., *I might could go* and *I might could did go* are mistakes, i.e., "deviant choices." But at least one of these, *I might could go,* is a correct form in the language of many English speakers and writers of the Gulf states of the American Southeast. As a result of such social and regional differences, the norm itself must be defined in order for it to be used as the standard for identifying variation within it or deviation from it.

A norm can be described in both linguistic and statistical terms. There are two kinds of linguistic norm: prescriptive and descriptive. A descriptive norm reflects speakers' and writers' knowledge of what is acceptable or grammatical in language form and function. A prescriptive norm is the social sense of what in language use is correct and appropriate. Linguistic norms are not static; they evolve over time in a social, cultural, and geographic community of speakers and writers. Linguistic norms are implicit in language use and in the perceptions of speakers and writers and are often explicitly described in dictionaries and grammars. A statistical norm is one that reflects a linguistic norm in the form of a certain frequency distribution for each of various linguistic forms in the population of speakers and writers of a speech community.

5.3 Evaluation vis-à-vis Description of Style

The purpose of evaluative stylistics is to identify the characteristics that make a piece of writing good or bad. This approach is prescriptive insofar as it specifies what is correct, good, and appropriate language. It is intuitive insofar as it focuses on a reader's subjective impressions of a writing. Prescriptive norms can be useful in authorship studies because they can be used to describe variation, but intuitive stylistics is best left to literary criticism.

The more objective study of descriptive stylistics reflects the analytical methods of linguistics and rejects casual observation of linguistic variation. This means that the structural and functional characteristics of writings are identified, catalogued, and analyzed for underlying regularities. In addition, the frequency of occurrence of linguistic features, which are qualitative, can often be quantified, providing a basis for statistical measurement of style.

5.4 Group vis-à-vis Individual Styles

Stylistic variation as a use of different variant forms to express a similar linguistic meaning is reflected in the distinct dialects of groups who speak the same language; it thus reflects the class characteristics of speaking and writing for the subgroup. For example, considerable research has been done on the form and function of women's language, and recent attention has also been focused on men's language (Johnson and Meinhof, 1997) – both socially defined groups. Geographically separate groups in English and many other languages have also been long studied. The little gray-black bug that curls up when touched is variably called *ball bug, doodle bug, pill bug, potato bug,* and *sow bug* throughout the U.S. An early index of geographically distinct lexical variants (Reed and DeCamp, 1951) includes over 1500 variant forms for approximately 500 variable words and expressions in American English.

Smaller groups within a community are often described and sometimes even defined by their register, jargon, or slang. A register is a socially constrained form of language often related to an occupational context, like the written language variables present in the structure and design of business letters (Mukomela, 1968). The jargon of medical residents is identified as "hospital lingo" in a recent *New York Times* article: *beans* = kidneys; *bed plug* = a patient in a bed that could be used for a more difficult case; *hit* = a new patient; *LOL* = little old lady, etc. (Khipple, 2001:7). The e-mail slang of teenagers is revealed in *The New Yorker*'s brief description of a questionable website. For example, a high school girl, reacting to the chagrin of her parents and teachers over the content of the website, is quoted as saying,

It's not that big a deal, the language. We call each other "ho's" all the time. It's nothing, but these girls on the list, the ones I heard about, really are ho's. I know someone who was on it. I talked to her, sort of. She seemed, like, happy to be, like, getting the attention, But, yeah, she was probably hurt, or whatever (Paumgarten, 2001:35).

Stylistic variation is also reflected in the idiolect of individuals who speak the same dialect and language, thus reflecting the individual characteristics of speakers and writers. The idiolect is "[t]he totality of the possible utterances of one speaker at one time in using a language to interact with one other speaker …" (Bloch, 1948:7). The range of linguistic variation in the writing style of a single person is identifiable as his or her idiolectal style, reflected as interwriter variation between that writer and other members of the same speech community, or as intrawriter variation occurring within that writer as a single member of the speech community. Interwriter variation is the basis for authorship identification and patterned intrawriter variation provides strongly identifying stylistic characteristics of a writer.

There is a qualitative relationship between individual and group variation. The idiolect of an individual speaker or writer demonstrates the same kind of variation as the dialect of a language. The difference lies in the quantity, with the range of variation less for the individual:

> … among communities there is … the Community of One. Every speaker has an *idiolect*, just as every collectivity of speakers has a *dialect*. We are most conscious of this in the pet words and expressions that individuals use. … Idiosyncrasies of speech can be used to caricature a person as effectively as the jut of a chin or the bulge of a nose. Idiolects differ from dialects just as dialects differ from languages: the range of variation in either case is narrower [by comparison to the larger group] (Bolinger and Sears, 1981:194).

References

Besnier, N., "The linguistic relationships of spoken and written Nukulaelae registers," *Language*, 64:4:707–736, 1988.

Bloch, B., A set of postulates for phonemic analysis, *Language*, 24:1:3–46, 1948.

Bolinger, D. and Sears, D. A., *Aspects of Language*, 3rd ed., Harcourt Brace, New York, 1981.

Johnson, S. and Meinhof, U. H., *Language and Masculinity*, Blackwell, Oxford, 1997.

Khipple, S., "Hospital lingo: what's a bed plug? An L.O.L. in N.A.D.," *The New York Times*, May 13, 2001, Sect. 4, p. 7.

Mukomela, K. D., The Structure and Design of Typewritten Business Letters: An Analysis of Selected Variables, University of North Dakota Ed.D. dissertation, 1968, University Microfilms, No. 69-8542, Ann Arbor, 1969.

Paumgarten, N., Kids today: the new bathroom wall, *The New Yorker*, 34–35, June 4, 2001.

Reed, D. W. and DeCamp, D., *A Collation of Check Lists Used in the Study of American Linguistic Geography*, University of California, Berkeley, 1951.

Schjeldahl, P., Ghosts: the dazzling mystery of de Kooning's last paintings, *The New Yorker*, 98–99, May 7, 2001.

Stylistics

6

GERALD R. McMENAMIN

6.1 Style in Language

Style in language has been studied on various levels. The focus of this book is linguistic stylistics, but it is important to understand nonlinguistic approaches in order to recognize how they differ from and have contributed to the study of linguistic stylistics.

The purpose of nonlinguistic stylistics is generally to evaluate either the esthetic quality or the prescriptive conformity of language used in speech or writing. Esthetic observations of style in written language reflect a reader's impression of excellence of expression. Prescriptive observations reflect how well the writer has followed stated rules of the language for correct writing and the social rules for good (appropriate) writing. Although the subjective nature of the intuitive evaluation of language precludes its use in linguistic methods of analysis, prescriptive norms for correct and good writing play a role in the objective analysis of style because writers can vary within or from that norm. See McMenamin (1993:162) for an extensive review of the aesthetic and prescriptive approaches to stylistics.

6.2 Linguistic Stylistics

Style is a reflection of group or individual variation in written language. Individual variation is a result of the writer's choices of one form out of the array of all available forms. Choices represent variations within a norm (different "correct" ways of saying the same thing), deviations from a norm (mistakes), and idiosyncrasies (author-specific forms). The style of a writer is demonstrated by his or her unique aggregate set of grammatical patterns, which is usually the result of the writer's recurrent (habitual) use of some or all of the forms in the set.

Linguistic stylistics is the scientific analysis of individual style-markers as observed and described in the idiolect of a single writer, as well as class style-markers as identified in the language or dialect of groups of writers.

Linguistic variation, whether variation within a norm or deviation away from a norm, presupposes the existence and identification of a norm. Although there are various theoretical issues related to defining linguistic norms (e.g., Lara, 1976), for all practical purposes, linguists formally identify linguistic norms, and speakers and writers of the language know and informally recognize them. The norm is made apparent in patterns of variation present in the language of the speech community: "The speech community is marked ... by participation in a set of shared norms; these norms may be observed in overt types of evaluative behavior, and in the uniformity of abstract patterns of variation..." (Labov, 1972:120).

Lara's definition of the norm complements Labov's insofar as it specifies the unlimited linguistic choices a speaker or writer has. The following is a free translation (not precisely quoted from the original Spanish) of Lara's definition of the norm:

> The *norm* is a model, a rule or a set of rules with a certain degree of obligatory application. The norm is imposed on the linguistic community by the speakers of the language, and it affects all manifestations of the linguistic *system*. The norm acts to dispose speakers and writers to select *acceptable* forms from among the unlimited variety of possible realizations in use (Lara, 1976:110).

Social or physical separation of groups will result in the formation of distinct communities and microcommunities. There are as many norms as there are groups and subgroups demonstrating some degree of relative isolation from one another.

Social norms relate to group acceptance of language forms and uses. Examples of norms for language behavior in communities or groups, as discussed by Eckert (1989:249), Grice (1975), Hudson (1980:116), Labov (1972:120), and Wolfram and Fasold (1974:17), include the following, which are neither exhaustive of the possibilities nor mutually exclusive:

1. Prestige norms (of acceptability by upper social classes)
2. Norms of social convention or necessity
3. Norms governing use of registers, varieties, and other languages
4. Class norms (of age, sex, ethnicity, race, socioeconomic status, etc.)
5. Regional norms (of geographic location)
6. Circumstantial norms (of situation: purpose, topic, reader, time, place, etc.)
7. Appropriate-language norms (of proper social behavior)
8. Correct-language norms (of correct linguistic behavior)

Language norms can be descriptive or prescriptive; they are revealed in the descriptive studies of linguists and sociolinguists, as well as in the prescriptive sets of rules codified by grammars of usage and dictionaries used in classrooms and workplaces. Language norms can also be defined in quantitative terms. Which forms speakers and writers of a community use can be counted vis-à-vis possible alternate forms, i.e., how often certain forms are

TYPE OF NORM	THE NORM	VARIATION WITHIN THE NORM	DEVIATION FROM THE NORM
PRESCRIPTIVE	*Examples*	*Examples*	*Examples*
Grammatically correct	I *am* going now.	I*'m* going now.	I *be* goin' now.
Socially appropriate	I'm afraid you're too late.	Sorry, the shop is closed.	Get the hell out of here!
DESCRIPTIVE			
Prestige: U.S. standard	We have enough money.	We*'ve got* enough money.	We *gots* enough money.
Choice of variety: teenage	*Hey, man!*	*Hey, dude!*	*Hello, sir.*
Class: age	That's a *cool* idea.	That's a *neat* idea.	That's a *swell* idea.
Regional: U.S. dialects	"a quarter *to* eleven"	is *before - / of - / till* - eleven	"eleven *less* fifteen"
Situational: at work	"Where's the *restroom?*"	"Where's the *bathroom?*"	"Where can I *take a leak?*"
QUANTITATIVE			
How often forms are used	*We are* here. (e.g., 10%)	*We're* here. (e.g., 80%)	*We* here. (e.g., 10%)
In a defined social context	It *is me. / It's me.* (85%)	It *is I.* (10%)	It *be me.* (5%)

Figure 6.1 Examples of linguistic norms.

used and in which specific linguistic and social circumstances. Figure 6.1 provides examples of linguistic norms.

6.3 Models of Analysis

All authorship cases analyzed in the present volume have been analyzed using one of Wachal's (1966:4) three models of authorship analysis: resemblance, consistency, and population. These are also outlined in McMenamin (1993:173).

The resemblance model is the most frequently used paradigm for authorship studies. When nonlinguistic evidence narrows the field of suspect authors to just one or a small number of writers, the authorship question is defined narrowly to exclude or identify just the one suspect writer. For example, a large U.S. telephone company received threatening letters containing information that only two people in the company had: the recipient and the suspected writer. For the analysis, both were considered possible authors. In another case, an attorney sought proof that his client was truthful in saying that he had not written (and posted) flyers defaming his soon-to-be ex-wife in the matter of their marriage dissolution. The requirements of the case itself dictated the use of the resemblance model.

The consistency model is used to determine whether two or more writings were written by the same author. This is a common task in forensic work. For example, numerous cases involve multiple questioned letters, all supposedly signed and written by different people. When all of those people deny writing the letters, the recipient wants to know if they were written by one or more than one person. Even when the letters purport to be from the same writer, the content or style of the writings sometimes suggest the possibility of multiple writers.

The population model is occasionally used in forensic contexts that do not provide external (nonlinguistic) evidence suggesting just one or two candidate writers. In one case, a high-level State of California official (and many other people) received a large set of writings exposing, in lurid detail, his personal relationships with office employees. The official knew from document examination evidence that the writer was likely to be one of 22 people who had access to a particular copy machine; thus, the population of possible writers was 22. In another case, an insurance company received potentially damaging letters about the manager of a large regional insurance office. Company security started their search for the writer by collecting writing samples of a population of 17 disgruntled employees and former employees.

Models of authorship analysis are often used in combination. For example, in the California case described above, the questioned writings were first analyzed for their internal consistency. When they were all found to share common stylistic characteristics, the known writings of the population of 22 possible writers were examined until all but three were excluded. Finally, the known writings of those three were analyzed for resemblance to the questioned writings, until two of the known writers were excluded and one identified.

The appropriate authorship model is frequently dictated by factors unknown to, or not under the control of, the linguist. For example, it is a good practice for the expert to maintain and demonstrate independence from the advocacy activity of a case by only getting enough information about the case to do the analytical work. The linguist may, and normally should not, be privy to nonlinguistic evidence that might support a particular authorship finding. Therefore, a client attorney may reasonably ask that the writings of a single suspect author be evaluated using a resemblance model because he or she is aware of external evidence that points to that person, thereby predefining the task and taking the decision as to authorship model out of the linguist's hands.

No matter what model is used to formulate the research questions in a case, the analytical tasks of observation, discovery, and comparison and contrast of style-markers in separate sets of questioned and known writings is the same.

6.4   Procedural Outline for Authorship Identification Studies

In the study of linguistic variation, there is a method for organizing observations that lends itself to the identification and separation of style-markers and to their subsequent systematic description and quantification. Similarities and differences in writing variation can be described and measured with some precision. The following is an adaptation to the forensic context of the general procedure for analyzing linguistic variation.

6.4.1   Organization of Case

Ask clients to submit writings with a letter containing four important parts: a request that you work on the case, a clear articulation of the authorship problem as they see it, a list of all accompanying documents, and an agreement as to conditions for expert-witness services.

Arrange documents into questioned writings and known exemplars, using logical bases such as chronological order, keyed in, typed, handwritten, or hand-printed, context of writing, i.e., personal letters, internal memos, business letters, diary entries, etc., and prepared by the author vs. by secretary. Photocopy all documents, preferably on nonwhite paper (e.g., light blue) to use as your working copies. Reserve copies received with the case to attach as exhibits with a final report. Retain all correspondence, courier and mailing receipts, notes of telephone conversations regarding the case, analytical notes, etc. Label successive pages of all documents in order, such as Questioned Q1, Q2, etc., and Known K1, K2, etc., and number lines on each page, counting by 1s, 5s, or 10s.

6.4.2   Problem

Articulate the authorship problem as you see it. Discuss this with the client, especially if it is different from the task as defined in the retention letter. Articulate the research questions for descriptive analysis. These will be stated again as the analysis proceeds and possibly reformulated (e.g., narrowed, broadened, or changed in other ways) based on findings as well as practical matters related to the availability of writings, etc.

Articulate the research questions for quantitative analysis. These will be stated again as the analysis proceeds, and possibly reformulated (e.g., narrowed, broadened, or changed) based on descriptive findings as well as practical matters related to the presence, absence, and frequency of occurrence of variables, etc. Select the appropriate authorship models: resemblance, population, or consistency (as outlined in Section 6.2).

6.4.3 Method

Before beginning any analysis, make every attempt to assemble all questioned materials and all available known materials whose context of writing is as close as possible to that of the questioned writings. The inclusion of writings after analysis begins, although sometimes inevitable, requires duplication of concordance and quantitative work, and is not cost effective.

Study the questioned writings and assess the range of stylistic variation, i.e., make lists of all variation, including variant as well as invariant forms of each variable. This allows identification of variation present in questioned writings that may or may not be present in the known. It also enables identification of variation in questioned writings that does not have the opportunity to occur in known (nonoccurring variables).

Study the known writings and assess the range of stylistic variation in the same way. This allows identification of variation present in known writings that may or may not be present in the questioned. It also enables identification of variation in known writings that does not have the opportunity to occur in questioned (nonoccurring variables).

Identify style-markers representing the range of variation by using the following two criteria: 1. deviations from any norm the writer may be influenced by, i.e., mistakes, and 2. variations within any norm of the writer, i.e., one or more variants of a form that may alternate within one speaker or among many speakers.

Note single occurrences of variation, as well as variations that occur more than once or represent recurring habits. If the samples of writing are large, OCR-scan or key all writings into a computer textfile and make a KWIC (key word in context) concordance of the entire text to help identify patterns and locate recurring variants. The concordance is a tool which will facilitate identification of many style-markers related to many levels of writing style. Review the concordance, item by item, on the computer for two reasons: a printed concordance can be hundreds of pages long, and one can cut and paste from the concordance window to a window containing the list of style-markers.

A KWIC concordance is useful for identifying words, phrases, and some syntactic patterns. Also, creating an ad hoc tagged corpus from the questioned and known writings will facilitate creation of a syntactic or pragmatic

Terms	Definitions
VARIATION	
Variable	A stylistic feature of the writing, also called *characteristic* or *style marker.*
Variation	The combination of all occurrences of the same variable found in a set of writings.
Similarity	A variable that is present in two sets of writings.
Dissimilarity	A variable that is present in one set of writings, but absent in another set.
Nonoccurring variable	A variable with no opportunity to occur in the language used in a set of writings.
INDIVIDUALIZATION	
Class characteristic	A variable that is found in the written dialect or language of a definable group.
Individualizing characteristic	A variable that is not a class characteristic, but not necessarily unique to the writer.
Idiosyncratic characteristic	A single variable that is unique to a given writer. This is infrequent in language.
Range of variation	The unique combination of all occurrences of all variables found in a set of writings.
WRITINGS	
Natural writing	Writing done in the context of its purpose, with little attention to the writing process.
Request writing	Writing done for the purpose of providing a writing sample, often via dictation.
Context of writing	Purpose, intended reader, topic, medium (paper), instrument (pen), time, place, etc.
Comparable writings	Two or more sets of writing that share the same or similar contexts of writing.
Quantity of writing	The amount of writing needed to assess the writer's range of variation.

Figure 6.2 Definitions related to variation, individualization, and writings.

concordance or database. A "KPIC" concordance containing just the punctuation present in the writings can be especially useful.

6.4.4   Findings

Definitions: The definitions provided in Figure 6.2 are directly related to the process of observing and describing stylistic variation, individualization, and the writings used for such analysis. They are adopted, or in some cases adapted, for language analysis from the Scientific Working Group for Forensic Document Examination's *Standard Guide for Handwriting* draft (SWGDOC, 2000), which is still subject to refinement and change in the SWGDOC process. However, they represent practical and theoretically sound starting points for handling linguistic variation in a forensic context:

Specify style-markers: Identify style-markers at all linguistic levels:

FORMAT or layout of the document itself (margins, spacing, etc.)
PUNCTUATION of all types
SPELLING (all the various kinds of patterned variants and mistakes)
WORD FORMATION (including inflectional variation)
SYNTAX (sentence structure, coordination, subordination, and punctuation)
LEXICAL VARIATION (choices of words and phrases)
SEMANTIC VARIATION (semantic features of words, phrases, and sentences)
FUNCTIONAL VARIATION of language use (match between structure and function)
INTERFERENCE features from other languages present in English writing

Descriptive analysis: Specify the range of variation by describing the aggregate set of all deviations and variations, at every linguistic level, for the questioned and known writings, based on the combination of markers identified from the reading analysis plus those from the concordance analysis.

Identify and separate as far as possible style-markers that are "class characteristics," i.e., dialect or language features of a definable group, e.g., social, regional, first language, age, etc. Then identify and separate style-markers that are "individual features," i.e., idiolectal (but not necessarily idiosyncratic) features of the writer. For example, the following examples represent repeated variation in one writer, and at least numbers 4, 5, and 10 are possible individual markers:

Punctuation: 1. I"LL (all contractions with quote marks for apostrophe)
Spelling: 2. PROBLY
     3. SECRATARY
     4. BEIGN (being)
     5. NNOT (not)
     6. THEN (than)
     7. THERE (their)
     8. PIST (pissed)

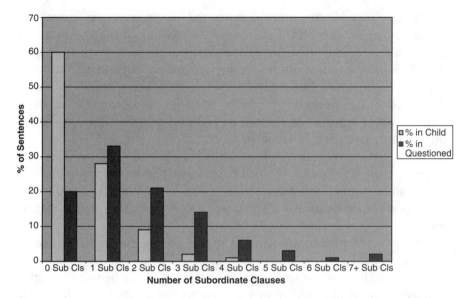

Figure 6.3 Sentences with subordinate clauses in known-child vs. questioned-letter.

Word Formation: 9. EVERYDAY (every day)
                    10. ALOT (a lot)
                    11. MKES (makes)

Quantitative analysis: Determine the need for quantitative analyses of selected style-markers. Analysis can start with descriptive statistics, such as the representation in Figure 6.3 of sentences with vs. sentences without subordinate clauses in a child custody case in which the mother was suspected of writing (by word processor) a letter from the child stating that he wanted to live with her instead of his father. The mother's writing included 243 sentences, the child's 376.

Appropriate statistical tests are used to evaluate the significance of such variables used to compare or contrast sets of writings. It is also possible to estimate the joint probability of occurrence of variables in compared writings by estimating the relative frequency of occurrence of each and all variables in a representative corpus of comparable writing (see Section 8.2).

In addition, there are numerous other quantitative approaches to the identification of style-markers used in authorship recognition and discrimination, e.g., orthographic (letter) variables and patterns, frequency distributions of low- and high-frequency words, function words, common words, and collocations of words, neural networks, and multivariate, principal component, cluster, correspondence, and discriminant analysis (see Section 8.3).

Results: Consider the hypothesis that the known candidate-writer is not the author of the questioned writings and determine if the known author can be excluded. Identify dissimilarities between the style-markers of questioned and known, then determine the significance of dissimilarities using appropriate linguistic and statistical criteria. If a known candidate-writer demonstrates significant differences vis-à-vis the questioned writing, determine to what degree he or she can be excluded as the writer, based on all other factors (see the next section).

A linguistically significant dissimilarity is a repeated individualizing characteristic present in one set of writings but absent in the other. A statistically significant dissimilarity is a characteristic present in questioned and known writings at respective relative frequencies of occurrence that *are* significantly different.

Next, consider the complementary hypothesis that the known candidate-writer is the author of the questioned material, and determine if the known candidate author can be identified. Identify similarities between the style-markers of questioned and known. Determine the significance of individual similarities using appropriate linguistic and statistical criteria. If the known candidate-writer demonstrates significant similarities vis-à-vis the questioned writing, determine to what degree he or she can be identified as the writer, based on all other factors (see the next section).

A linguistically significant similarity is a repeated individualizing characteristic shared by the respective sets of writings. A statistically significant similarity is a characteristic shared by the respective sets of writings that is repeated in the questioned and known writings at respective relative frequencies of occurrence that are not significantly different.

If possible, check linguistic and legal precedents to determine which of the style-markers used in the case have been used in other studies and cases of questioned authorship.

6.4.5 Conclusions

Conclusions regarding authorship are stated in terms of identification or exclusion on a five-, seven-, or nine-point continuum, such as the nine-point scale approved and used by the American Society for Testing and Materials (ASTM), or the similar scale presently under development by the Scientific Working Group for Forensic Document Examination (SWGDOC, 2000). Figures 6.4 and 6.5 represent a slight adaptation for language of a working SWGDOC proposal for handwriting conclusions. Figure 6.4 relates to conclusions concerning resemblance between questioned and known writings in population or resemblance studies (see Section 6.2). Figure 6.5 relates to conclusions concerning consistency among questioned writings. Figure 6.6 summarizes the criteria for determining levels of conclusion.

Did the suspect write it?	Scale	Conclusion
YES	9	Identification
	8	Highly probable - did write
	7	Probable — did write
	6	Indications — did write
INCONCLUSIVE	5	No conclusion
NO	4	Indications — did not write
	3	Probable — did not write
	2	Highly probable – did not write
	1	Elimination

Figure 6.4 Conclusions on resemblance between questioned and known writings.

Did one author write it?	Scale	Conclusion
YES	9	Definite — one writer
	8	Highly probable — one writer
	7	Probable — one writer
	6	Indications — one writer
INCONCLUSIVE	5	No conclusion
NO	4	Indications — more than one writer
	3	Probable — more than one writer
	2	Highly probable — more than one writer
	1	Definite — more than one writer

Figure 6.5 Conclusions on consistency within questioned writings.

6.4.6 Opinion

For every research question initially articulated, state your opinion for the Court: level of exclusion, level of identification, or inconclusive. An effective practice is to state your opinion up front, at the beginning of the report, then use the body of the report to support it.

6.4.7 Report

Write a report or a court declaration that follows the usual structure used in the sciences: problem, opinion, method, findings, discussion, conclusions, and appendices: 1. *curriculum vitae*, 2. copies of all documents used, 3. line numbered text file from concordance program, if one was used, and 4. list of all style-markers used for exclusion or identification, with all pertinent substantiating data.

RESEMBLANCE: Questioned vs. Known	CRITERIA	CONSISTENCY: Questioned vs. Questioned
9 **IDENTIFICATION** **(did write)**	1. Substantial significant similarities in the range of variation 2. No significant dissimilarities 3. No limitations present: nonoccurrence of variables, dissimilarities, quantity of writing	**9** **DEFINITE** **one writer**
8 **HIGHLY** **PROBABLE** **did write**	1. Substantial significant similarities in the range of variation 2. No significant dissimilarities 3. Limitations are present: nonoccurrence of variables, dissimilarities, quantity of writing	**8** **HIGHLY** **PROBABLE** **one writer**
7 **PROBABLE** **did write**	1. Some significant similarities in the range of variation 2. No significant dissimilarities 3. Limitations are present: nonoccurrence of variables, dissimilarities, individualizing characteristics, quantity of writing	**7** **PROBABLE** **one writer**
6 **INDICATIONS** **did write**	1. Few significant similarities in the range of variation 2. No significant dissimilarities 3. Limitations may be present: nonoccurrence of variables, dissimilarities, individualizing characteristics, quantity of writing	**6** **INDICATIONS** **one writer**
5 **NO** **CONCLUSION** **(Inconclusive)**	1. Insufficient significant similarities in the range of variation 2. Insufficient significant dissimilarities in range of variation 3. Limitations may be present: nonoccurrence of variables, individualizing characteristics, quantity of writing 4. There may be similarities and dissimilarities	**5** **NO** **CONCLUSION** **(Inconclusive)**
4 **INDICATIONS** **did not write**	1. Few significant dissimilarities in the range of variation 2. Limitations may be present: nonoccurrence of variables, individualizing characteristics, quantity of writing 3. There may be similarities.	**4** **INDICATIONS** **more than** **one writer**
3 **PROBABLE** **did not write**	1. Some significant dissimilarities in the range of variation 2. Limitations may be present, associated with: nonoccurrence of variables, individualizing characteristics, quantity of writing 3. There may be similarities	**3** **PROBABLE** **more than** **one writer**

Figure 6.6 Criteria for conclusions on authorship questions of resemblance or consistency.

RESEMBLANCE: Questioned vs. Known	CRITERIA	CONSISTENCY: Questioned vs. Questioned
2 **HIGHLY** **PROBABLE** **did not write**	1. Substantial significant dissimilarities in range of variation 2. Limitations are present: nonoccurrence of variables, individualizing characteristics, quantity of writing 3. There may be similarities	**2** **HIGHLY** **PROBABLE** **more than** **one writer**
1 **ELIMINATION** **(did not write)**	1. Substantial significant dissimilarities in range of variation 2. No limitations present: individualizing characteristics, quantity of writing 3. There may be nonoccurring variables 4. There may be similarities	**1** **DEFINITE** **more than** **one writer**

Figure 6.6 (Continued) Criteria for conclusions on authorship questions of resemblance or consistency.

References

Eckert, P., The whole woman: sex and gender differences in variation, *Language Variation and Change*, 1:3:245–267, 1989.

Grice, H. P., Logic and conversation, in Cole, P. and Morgan, J., Eds., *Syntax and Semantics 3: Speech Acts*, 41–58, Academic Press, London, 1975.

Hudson, R. A., *Sociolinguistics*, Cambridge University Press, Cambridge, 1980.

Labov, W., *Sociolinguistic Patterns*, University of Pennsylvania, Philadelphia, 1972.

Lara, L. F., *El Concepto de Norma en Lingüística*, El Colegio de México, México, D. F., 1976.

McMenamin, G. R., *Forensic Stylistics*, Elsevier Science Publishers, Amsterdam, 1993.

SWGDOC: Scientific Working Group for Forensic Document Examination, *Standard Guide for the Examination of Handwritten Items*, working version, Federal Bureau of Investigation, Laboratory Division, Washington, D.C., July 2000.

Wachal, R. S., Linguistic Evidence, Statistical Inference and Disputed Authorship, Ph.D. dissertation, University of Wisconsin, 1966.

Wolfram, W. and Fasold, R. W., *The Study of Social Dialects in American English*, Prentice Hall, Englewood Cliffs, N.J, 1974.

The Description of Style 7

GERALD R. McMENAMIN

7.1 The Qualitative Analysis of Style

The description of written language is the first means of discovering, analyzing, and interpreting style. While stylistic analyses are both qualitative and quantitative, the focus of the qualitative study of writing is on *what* forms are used by a writer, and *how* and *why* they are used (Johnstone, 2000:35).

Recent changes in the criteria for scientific evidence have emphasized the heuristic requirements of the scientific method traditionally used in the natural sciences. This is because, at worst, some proffered expert testimony did not have any scientific basis, and, at best, other methods of scientific inquiry were relative, i.e., more or less different from field to field and expert to expert. Although the methods of inquiry in the humanities and social sciences are of necessity more relative than those of the natural sciences, they nonetheless demonstrate sufficient rigor to produce objective observations of facts, reliable results, and valid conclusions.

Qualitative analysis will not result in absolute conclusions about any kind of indirect evidence, like sets of questioned and known writings. (For that matter, quantitative evidence will not either.) "But we can discover and say things that are plausible, relevant to practical problems, and important for our understanding of how language and society work" (Johnstone, 2000:60). There are at least three reasons for this:

1. Qualitative description is a first-order step; measurement depends on meaningful discovery, description, and categorization of linguistic elements.
2. In the courtroom, qualitative evidence is more demonstrable than quantitative evidence because it is the language data that are presented, in addition to their analysis, which may be one or two steps away from the data.
3. Qualitative results appeal to the nonmathematical but structured sense of probability held by judges and juries.

This third justification for use of qualitative analysis and court presentation of qualitative evidence is one of the most important. The nonmathematical but structured sense of probability is explained by Cohen (1977), who first considers the two usual ways to state probabilities: "an expert, exact, numerical way" for the natural and social sciences, and "a popular, loose, qualitative way" for everyday life. Both are assumed to be mathematical notions that differ only in precision and expertise:

> Both concepts of probability are assumed to conform in structure to the principles of the mathematical calculus of chance. It is just that in the one case, conformity is sharp, rigorous and computable, while in the other it is rough, indeterminate and a matter for judgment (Cohen, 1977:40).

However, Cohen proposes a third notion, that of "inductive probability," which "is not just a loose and popular form of mathematical probability," (Cohen 1977:40): "[Inductive probability] involves a comparative or ordinal gradation of probability rather than a quantitative or measurable one. So, it lends itself particularly well to use in areas of reasoning where it is not possible to count or measure the evidence" (Cohen, 1977:41).

Cohen argues that the obvious application of inductive probability is found in the nature of judicial proof in English, Australasian, and American courts, and "the probabilities with which certain conclusions are to be drawn from the evidence" (Cohen, 1977:44). He maintains that judges and juries are not using a mathematical concept of probability when circumstances concur and point to the same conclusion. In fact, he contends that "the notion of inductive probability exists alongside that of mathematical probability as a standing instrument of human reason" (Cohen, 1977:46), and the judicial concept for the high ("beyond reasonable doubt") level of probability so confidently used in criminal cases, as well as the lower ("preponderance of the evidence") level routinely used in civil cases, are both results of inductive probability. This view of probability is also articulated by others such as McAlexander et al. (1990) and Wolf (1928).

The method of qualitative inquiry is rigorously empirical insofar as it includes the elements for any such study: careful framing of questions or propositions to confirm or disconfirm, systematic observation, results that are the outcome of observation (data), reliable methods of description and analysis of data, including consideration of inadequate and disconfirming evidence, valid interpretation of results, including competing interpretations, and a statement of the basis for every conclusion.

For more detailed study and discussion of the elements of rigorous qualitative investigation, see Johnstone (2000) and Lofland and Lofland, (1995):

Observation (Johnstone, 2000:62–63)
Ways of framing answerable questions and forming propositions (Lofland and Lofland, 1995:123, 182)

Analytical methods (Johnstone, 2000:4; Lofland and Lofland, 1995:182)
Qualitative analysis as an emergent process (Lofland and Lofland, 1995:181–184)
Interpretation of data (Johnstone, 2000:36)
Validity and reliability in qualitative research (Johnstone, 2000:61–66).

7.2   An Example of Qualitative Analysis

Cohen (1977) mentions areas of reasoning where it is not possible to count or measure the evidence. While linguistic data frequently present countable variables, sometimes the linguistic significance of an identified variable is not captured by counting, or a variable is linguistically significant because it rarely occurs in the language, but it does not occur frequently enough in the data to be meaningfully counted. *The Estate of Violet Hussien* is a case related to linguistic disguise. It lends itself to demonstrating the importance of descriptive analysis and to the advisability of combining descriptive and quantitative analysis.

7.2.1   *In the Matter of the Estate of Violet Houssien*

This is the case of the contested will of a woman who was born in Japan, grew up in Hawaii, then later moved with her husband to Anchorage, Alaska. She was in frail health during the last years of her life and died in 1997 at the age of 85, leaving an estate of $1.6 million. Her will designated a neighbor couple as her heirs, but was contested by her sisters and brother. The will was a stationery-store will which was accompanied by photocopies of various letters indicating the decedent's desire to leave her large estate to them, not to her siblings.

The typed letters (Q1 to 5) were reportedly dictated by the decedent to a friend named Kim who acted as amanuensis. The neighbors presented the "Kim" letters as writings of the testator that represented her wishes. The decedent's sisters and brother, however, contended that the letters were not their sister's.

Nonlinguistic facts related to the five questioned "Kim" letters prompted questions about their origin, even apart from the parties' differing contentions. First, no one knew or could find Kim, the woman who reportedly acted as secretary. Second, the original letters were not to be found; the photocopies were reportedly found in the trunk of a car.

7.2.2   Linguistic Analysis

Linguistic facts related to the "Kim" letters also raise questions about their authorship. First, the decedent's known writings (and reportedly her spoken

	DELETION	PRESENT	ABSENT
		Examples from Q1–4	Examples from Q5
1	Article	... so I know you are **a** good man.	Know you good man and will do ....
2	Subject	**I** do not know what happened.	Do not know about him.
3	Object	Had her change **it** before	I get notarized.
4	Plural -s/-es	Only family know these **things**.	I tell you these thing so you know.
5	-t: *not* -> *no*	Make me think **not** want to leave	People say come to fix but no fix.
6	Auxiliary *do*	... but **do** not think he will take.	He say he not want my money.
7	Other Auxiliaries	I **was** losing hope then they come into	You tell me I taking to much ....
8	Tense Markers	The nurse **told** me that Ed asked the	Nurse tell me to put ....
9	Copula	I know you **are** a good man.	Know you good man and will do ...

Figure 7.1 Grammatical elements deleted in the questioned "Kim" writings.

English) evidenced some features of Hawaiian Creole English, but her writing was quite close to standard English. The "Kim" letters also demonstrated nine clearly observable features of Creole–English varieties spoken in Pacific area communities: article deletion, subject deletion, object deletion, plural -s/-*es* deletion, -*t* deletion in *no* for *not*, auxiliary "do" deletion, other auxiliary deletion, tense-marker deletion, and copula deletion. See Figure 7.1 for examples from the "Kim" letters.

Second, the "Kim" letters appeared to represent a creolized variety of English insofar as their nonstandard features were all simplifications of the system of standard English and were features found in English-based Creoles. However, the "Kim" letters had very high frequencies of Creole features, some of which were not evidenced in the known writings of the decedent.

Third and most importantly, all of the Creole characteristics in the "Kim" letters represented deletions of grammatical elements, as can be seen in Figure 7.1. There is no variety of English known to be defined by a single process of variation like deletion. In fact, the exclusive pattern of unexpectedly frequent deletions suggests that the letters were a poor imitation of a noncreole speaker's Creole stereotype.

Last, the one "Kim" letter that most overtly redirected the estate to the neighbors was Q5, seen in Figure 7.2. Not only did syntactic variation in Q5 consist of deletions of grammatical elements, but the relative frequencies of deleted forms were also much higher in Q5 than in the other "Kim" letters.

7.2.3   Linguistic Findings

Of most linguistic interest is the question related to whether a variety of English could ever be characterized by the single grammatical process of deletion. Although the linguist for the contestants of the will maintained that

ADDITION TO WILL

JANUARY 8, 1997

Need to do because mother and other come to me in dream.
I pay Ed $1000 for helping me. Think I should pay $2000 but do not think he will take.
So I write check for $1000. Elma and Ed come to house, he not take $1000. He say he not want any money but I say must pay. He say help because mother and father come to him in dream and ak him to help me. They tell him doctor going to kick me out of house if sewer not fix. He tell me other things they tell him that I only know but still do not believe. When I go to sleep they come to me. They say that Elma and Ed only ones that really help me when I really need. They talk to doctor when I very sick. Doctor not lie but leg get better fast after.
They tell me that I take to much dope. Not think straight. Stop taking and I feel much better.
They save me $20,000 on tax from bad accountant. I fire him later. Then I tell people that they do taxes bad. Bad thing for me to do. Do not know why I did. They come over late in night when man try to get into house. Danger. They scare man away. Ed come and fix roof when ceiling fall and almost kill me. Other people should have fixed during summer. Ed come over late at night when door can not close. Nurse tell me to put chair against door. No good. Call Ed and ne come right over. Sewer bad all summer nobody come to fix. People say come to fix but no fix. I pay bad people over $600C and they do nothing. Call Ed, know he fix. He fix. Man tell me going to cost $3500 for this and $4000 for other thing but only cost me $3700.
I think Ed pay $4000 but Elma say no. We talk and talk I want to pay him $1000. He keep saying that he not want anything. At end he take $500 but he say he not spend. Foolish if not spend I tell him. Will not spend. Good people. Last humans I know.
Mother and father tell me all this in dream. Say Elma and Ed only ones that protect me.
Say they went to sisters and brothers in dream but no help. Make me think not want to leave anything to them. But then think no still sisters and brother. So mother and father tell me to do this. If sisters and brother fight Elma and Ed over will they not get anything. And mother and father say they will be mad at them when they join them.
I want Elma and Ed to get all I own except what I say sisters and brother get. Know they will do good with that is why I keep everything together for them.
Please Elma and Ed make me happy and make mother and father happy. Please take what I give you in will.

I Violet M.B. Houssien being of sound mind and not crazy, will these things on January 8, 1997.

[signature]

Figure 7.2 'Kim' Letter Q5, "Addition to Will" directing estate to neighbors.

a Creole speaker like the decedent could demonstrate only deletions, he was not able to provide supporting evidence of such a claim in his deposition or later at trial. The pertinent part of the deposition transcript reads as follows:

Counsel:	Are you aware of any dialect of English that differs from standard English due solely to deletion of elements?
Linguist:	No, I don't believe there is any such variety, no.
Counsel:	How about English-based Creole, are you aware of any such Creoles that differ?
Linguist:	If we're talking about a Creole continuum and if we're talking about the registers of a Creole continuum that are closest to standard English, I would say that ... there would be not much else but deletion at that level. And I think that's the level that [the decedent] was at.
Counsel:	Can you refer me to any published sources identifying or discussing those issues?
Linguist:	Not offhand, no.

Additionally, the language and style of the questioned "Kim" and the known letters was markedly different. In her known writing, the decedent demonstrated Creole features other than deletions, e.g., absence of number concord between plural subjects and the verbs *have* and *be* ("All of them was tops."), mismatch between verb and complementizer ("no worth to catch only two"), mass nouns used as count noun ("our deepest appreciations"), etc. Judge Peter Michalski took note of such linguistic details, saying in his decision that "the language contained within the "Kim" letters generally lacks the use of articles and the proper use of the verb "to be." A reading of [the decedent's] correspondence ... makes it evident that she effectively used both."

The point of presenting this example in such detail is to demonstrate that linguistic facts can often be made apparent only by qualitative description. In considering all the "Kim" letters (Q1 to 5), four significant linguistic anomalies require qualitative description:

1. There is compelling qualitative evidence of disguise in the "Kim" letters, given the stylistic differences between one subset of the "Kim" letters (Q1 to 4) vis-à-vis another (Q5). These stylistic differences provide a basis for grouping the "Kim" letters into two subsets for analysis. Grouped in this fashion, the writings demonstrate that all nine dialect markers studied occur more frequently in Q5 than in all the other "Kim" letters.

2. All nine linguistic characteristics used to describe and define this variety of nonstandard English are of the same type: deletions. Nonstandard English is not simply standard English with many elements

deleted. Varieties of English contain various types of differences in addition to what can be explained as deletions. For example, although an auxiliary verb may be deleted ("I [*was*] taking too much dope") as it is in these data, one could also be added ("I might *could* take too much."), or be moved ("Wasn't nobody takin' too much.").

The extraordinary occurrence of various dialect markers that are only deletions may well be the result of a dialect imitator who stereotypically views Creole-English as just standard-English-with-things-missing. The imitator applies that understanding to a process of imitation by first writing something in standard English, then changing that writing to what he or she thinks is a nonstandard variety by going through it and simply removing elements.

3. The occurrence of the nine dialect features identified is asystematic throughout the "Kim" letters, i.e., their presence or absence is irregularly distributed throughout the writings. For example, the sequential occurrence of deletions is not evenly or randomly distributed in the texts but instead runs in contiguous sequences, especially in Q5.

4. Quite complex syntactic structures such as infinitives, gerunds, adjective clauses, sentence embeddings, and subjunctives occur without error in the "Kim" letters, side by side with the nine much less complex deletion markers of nonstandard English. In addition to these, there are various other indications of a standard-English writer in Q1 to 5: the articles that do occur all follow the rules of standard English, something that no individual that really had all the deletions in these letters could likely get correct; all adverbials are in the right places, something a speaker of nonstandard English or English language learner seldom gets right; and numerous correctly used idiomatic phrases throughout represent standard English as the first language of the writer.

All these characteristics of the "Kim" letters present the highly implausible prospect of a writer of English who uses a standard, syntactically complex, and very competent variety of English, but who simultaneously demonstrates the syntactic simplicity of a nonstandard variety in which many much less complex structures are missing.

7.2.4 Decision

Judge Michalski noted that "[t]he linguistic experts presented by the parties were helpful, … [but that] the linguists contradict each other and the court accepts as more convincing and believable the testimony of Professor McMenamin," and he found that "the evidence proves that the will and "Kim" papers were prepared by the [neighbors] or at their direction … [and that] the language usage ... of the supporting documents is concocted and a fraud." The final part of his decision reads: "The court finds that the will and the accompanying "Kim" letters are a fraudulent presentation to the court and, by these findings, the will of March 22, 1995, the accompanying writings and purported codicil are rejected as the Will of [the decedent]."

The decision of the State Superior Court was upheld in *Crittell v. Bingo* et al. by the Supreme Court of Alaska, whose decision reads in part: "Though denied by the [appellants], the evidence proves that the Will and "Kim" papers were prepared by the [appellants] or at their direction."

References

Cohen, L. J., *The Probable and the Provable*, Clarendon, Oxford, 1977.

Johnstone, B., *Qualitative Methods in Sociolinguistics*, Oxford University Press, New York, 2000.

Lofland, J. and Lofland, L. H., *Analyzing Social Settings: a Guide to Qualitative Observation and Analysis*, 3rd Ed., Wadsworth, Belmont, CA, 1995.

McAlexander, T. V., Beck, J., and Dick, R. M., Committee recommendations: the standardization of handwriting opinion terminology, paper presented at the 42nd annual meeting of the American Academy of Forensic Sciences, Cincinnati, OH, February 1990.

Wolf, A., *Essentials of Scientific Method*, 2nd Ed., George Allen & Unwin, London, 1928.

Case Cited

In the Matter of the Estate of Violet Houssien, Superior Court for the State of Alaska, Third Judicial District at Anchorage, Case No. 3AN-98-59 P/R, September 1999. Upheld in *Crittell v. Bingo* et al. by the Supreme Court of Alaska No. S-9468, November 9, 2001 Decision No. 5496.

The Measurement of Style

8

GERALD R. McMENAMIN

8.1 The Quantitative Analysis of Style

The measurement of variation in written language is a powerful complement to its description and is therefore important to the successful analysis and interpretation of style. While interpretations of stylistic data are both qualitative and quantitative, the focus of the quantitative study of writing is on how much and how often forms are used by a writer (Johnstone, 2000:35).

In the last chapter, for example, the seemingly simple but important observation was made that certain grammatical characteristics occurred more frequently in one set of documents than in another. Quantitative analysis of their respective frequencies would provide the analyst with the mathematical tools needed to test whether such differences are significant, i.e., have less than a 5% (or even 1%) chance of having occurred randomly.

Due to the multiple approaches toward graduate education in linguistics and differing training protocols in theoretical and empirical methodologies, some linguists simply do not understand variation. As a result, they have demonstrated at least two unsuccessful ways of handling it, as Anshen (1978:2–3) points out: they ignore it by not mentioning it or by calling it "free variation," or hope that they only find it in dialect groups and can say that it does not show up in the narrower context of individual language behavior (idiolects). Anshen's position is, of course, to recognize the fact that variation is there, in speech communities and in individuals, and to find ways to analyze it. This requires counting frequencies of assorted variants in various linguistic and social environments.

Early calls for critical attention to sampling methodology and careful quantitative analysis of linguistic variation were made by Reed (1949) and Pickford (1956), among others. These were largely ignored in the ensuing years of research emphasis on theory development, which put off the task of accounting for variation present in the language of real speakers by focusing only on the language of the "ideal speaker," who existed only as a mental construct outside the social and linguistic constraints of real-world communication. With the return of interest in language variation and change over the past 30 years, recent emphasis on quantitative methods for analysis of linguistic data is seen in work by Anshen (1978), Davis (1990), and Scholfield

(1995). As Anshen says, "With the advent of variation studies in linguistics … came the need for linguists to handle quantitative language data in a reasonably sophisticated way" (Anshen, 1978:ix).

Recent developments in the forensic sciences also suggest the need to develop methods to quantify the writing and language data of cases. Reactions in the forensic community to proposals for quantitative analysis range from cautious acceptance to rejection. On the one hand, such caution is well founded because of problems related to quantification. For example, as was seen in the last chapter, some language characteristics are very difficult to identify as discrete, countable units; sometimes, counting certain features makes little sense and does not seem to be related to their real identifying weight. Also, the absence of baseline data for comparison to particular case data is a limitation receiving current research attention. Other real obstacles may be less difficult to overcome, e.g., many forensic scientists need training in statistical analysis, counting is time consuming, labor intensive, and expensive, or a given case does not present sufficient data for valid quantification.

In spite of the obvious problems and limitations, present emphasis on quantification is important for two reasons: it will actually make decision-making related to hypothesis testing easier and more precise, and it meets internal (methodological) as well as external (judicial) requirements for scientific evidence. Such decisions should not be made totally on the weight of a statistical analysis because an opinion is based on the careful description and qualitative evaluation of all data. However, appropriate quantification is a valuable part of the presently used aggregate of tools (observation, description, and analysis) that form the basis for meaningful question formation, reliable procedures, objective findings, and valid conclusions — all of which lead to sound expert opinions.

In cases of disputed authorship, statistical tests lend themselves most to evaluating the significance of the relationship of variables across comparison writings. Various tests can be used in six general ways:

1. Frequency distributions: descriptions of the relative frequency of occurrence of variables needed to apply all tests
2. Evaluation of potential relationship among variables expressed as means in comparison writings: *standard error of difference* — s_D (Davis, 1990:26); *t-test* — t (Davis, 1990:30); *analysis of variance* — F (Davis, 1990:62)
3. Evaluation of potential relationship of variables expressed as percentages in comparison writings: *proportion test* — z (Davis, 1990:39)
4. Evaluation of potential relationship of variables expressed as frequencies in comparison writings: *chi square* — x^2 (Davis, 1990:42)
5. Evaluation of independence of variables in a corpus of writing: *coefficient of correlation* — r (Davis, 1990:54)

	Questioned		Known	
	n	p	n	p
can not	22	28.2%	37	27.6%
cannot	21	26.9%	41	30.6%
can't	35	44.9%	56	41.8%
TOTAL	78	100%	134	100%

Figure 8.1 Occurrence of written variants: *can not, cannot, can't.*

6. Estimate of the joint probability of occurrence of variables in questioned writings by estimating the same in a representative corpus of similar writing: frequency estimates — P, Olkin's likelihood ratio — lambda (Hilton, 1956; Wrenshall, 1956)

8.2 Statistical Tests for Significance of Variables

8.2.1 Frequency Distributions

Frequency distributions describe relative frequency of occurrence of variables. They are not tests. A frequency distribution describes the data, suggesting relationships or lack thereof. Consider in Figure 8.1 the similar frequency of occurrence of three variants of a CAN + NOT variable — *can not/cannot/can't* — in the questioned and known writings of a case.

In another case, an attorney brought an action against a judge, claiming that the judge wrote and mailed an anonymous and defamatory letter to several people, including a newspaper. Among the many stylistic characteristics of the questioned letter was the relative frequency of occurrence of the word *that* in a sentence like "he said *that* she left." The word *that* optionally precedes *she left* (the complement of the verb *said*), so it can be left out: "He said she left."

For the purpose of illustrating comparison of the descriptive data, the frequency table in Figure 8.2 demonstrates similarity in the respective relative frequencies of complementizer *that* as it occurs after verbs in the questioned and known writings.

In addition, *that* was interestingly used more after verbs of *saying* and less after verbs of *knowing*. Verbs like *say* included say [that], make it clear [that], advised me [that], confirmed [that], tell a good friend [that], held [that], agreed [that], stressed [that], indicate [that], and conclude [that]. Verbs like *know* included know [that], think [that], see [that], believed [that], and reason [that]. The similar and complementary frequencies of *that* in the

"He said *that* she left."	Questioned		Known	
"that"	n	p	n	p
Present	29	71%	52	68%
Absent	12	29%	24	32%
TOTAL	41	100%	76	100%

Figure 8.2 Frequency of complementizer *that* in questioned and known writings.

two respective contexts, *that* after *say*-verbs vs. *that* after *know*-verbs, is apparent in Figure 8.3.

8.2.2   Standard Error of Difference

The standard error of difference (s_D) compares two means in a large sample ($n < 30$). Here s_D is used to evaluate sameness or difference of a variable expressed in terms of mean averages in questioned and known writings.

In an acrimonious divorce case, a court-appointed psychiatrist received two anonymous letters describing the wife's unacceptable behavior toward her husband and children. The wife and her attorney thought the husband wrote the letters. She provided the questioned letters and three reference writings in the form of letters that her husband wrote to the same psychiatrist.

The questioned letters contained shorter sentences than the known letters, so sentence length was possibly a discriminating style-marker. Mean sentence length (by word) was 15.67 in the questioned letters and 17.80 in the known writings, raising the question of whether the difference between the two means was significant enough to use sentence length as a marker of style distinguishing the questioned and known writings. Corresponding to this question is the null hypothesis (H_0): there is no significant difference between sentence length in the respective questioned and known writings.

Here are data from the respective frequency distributions:

QUESTIONED LETTERS:
Number of sentences: $n_1 = 75$
Average number of words per sentence: $m_1 = 15.67$
Standard deviation from the mean: $s_1 = 8.24$

KNOWN LETTERS:
Number of sentences: $n_2 = 161$
Average number of words per sentence: $\mathbf{m_2 = 17.80}$
Standard deviation from the mean: $s_2 = 10.83$

"that"	QUESTIONED *that after* say-verbs:		KNOWN *that after* say-verbs		QUESTIONED *that after* know-verbs		KNOWN *that after* know-verbs	
	n_1	p_1	n_2	p_2	n_3	p_3	n_4	p_4
Present	17	81.0%	32	78.1%	12	60.0%	20	57.1%
Absent	4	19.1%	9	22.0%	8	40.0%	15	42.9%
TOTAL	21	100%	41	100%	20	100%	35	100%

Figure 8.3 Frequency of *that* after *say* and *know* verbs in questioned and known writings.

The standard error of difference is calculated:

$$s_D = \sqrt{\frac{s_1^2}{n_1} + \frac{s_2^2}{n_2}}$$

$$s_D = \sqrt{\frac{8.24^2}{75} + \frac{10.83^2}{161}}$$

$$s_D = 1.28$$

Next, the z score (the number of standard deviations on either side of the mean that include these results) is calculated by finding the differences between the means (m_1 and m_2), and dividing by the standard error s_D:

$$z = \frac{m_1^2 - m_2^2}{s_D}$$

$$z = \frac{15.67 - 17.80}{1.28}$$

$$z = -1.66$$

This resulting standard error of difference allows rejection of H_0, i.e., that sentence length in questioned and known writings is the same, only at a level of significance of $p < 0.10$, meaning that there is only a 10% probability that the differences are not significant. Since the $p < 0.10$ level is not generally considered enough to reject H_0, sentence length may *not* be a function of the samples from the different writers here and *cannot* be confidently used as a discriminator of the two sets of writings in this case.

	Q1		Q2		K1-2	
Subordinate Clauses	n_1	p_1	n_2	p_2	n_3	p_3
Ss with 0 sub clauses	9	39.1%	12	46.2%	0	0%
Ss with 1 sub clauses	9	39.1%	8	30.8%	7	20.0%
Ss with 2 sub clauses	2	8.7%	2	7.7%	2	5.7%
Ss with 3 sub clauses	2	8.7%	4	15.4%	6	17.1%
Ss with 4 sub clauses	1	4.3%	0	0%	8	22.9%
Ss with 5 sub clauses	0	0%	0	0%	12	34.3%
Total Sub clauses	23		24		121	
Total Sentences	23	100%	26	100%	35	100%
	m_1	s_1	m_2	s_2	m_3	s_3
	1.00	0.30	1.08	1.10	3.46	1.52

Figure 8.4 Number of subordinate clauses present in verb phrases of sentences. Note: $m_{1,2,3}$ = mean number of subordinate clauses per sentence; $s_{1,2,3}$ = standard deviation from the mean.

8.2.3 *t*-Test

The *t*-test (*t*) compares two means in a small sample. Here **t** is used to evaluate sameness or difference of a variable expressed in terms of mean averages in questioned and known writings.

In the case of a man accused of writing two anonymous and damaging letters about his former wife, two questions were posed. First, were the two anonymous letters written by the same person and, second, were they written by the former husband? One of the style characteristics in both sets of writings was the location of subordinate clauses in sentences.

A subordinate clause is a sentence that cannot stand apart from its matrix sentence. Subordination can occur before the subject noun phrase of a sentence ("*If you stay*, I'll cook dinner."), within the subject noun phrase ("The idea *that you might stay* makes cooking fun."), and in the verb phrase of a sentence ("I asked *if you could make a salad*.").

One characteristic difference in the writings was "left- and right-side" subordination in the questioned writing, i.e., subordinate clauses before and after the verb, and the presence of only right-sided verb phrase subordination in the known writing. Another difference was the frequent use of multiple subordinate clauses in the man's known writings (K1 to 2), which is one of the markers that helped clear him of the accusation. The similarities between Q1 and Q2 and the differences in Q1 and 2 vis-à-vis K1 and 2 in verb phrase subordination, described in Figure 8.4, may seem obvious, but the *t*-test can be used to confirm them.

First, the standard error of difference is calculated:

Q1 vis-à-vis Q2   **Q2 vis-à-vis K1–2**

$$s_D = \sqrt{\frac{(n1-1)s_1^2 + (n1-1)s_2^2}{n_1 + n_2 - 2}} \quad \sqrt{\frac{1}{n1} + \frac{1}{n2}} \qquad s_D = \sqrt{\frac{(n1-1)s_1^2 + (n1-1)s_2^2}{n_1 + n_2 - 2}} \quad \sqrt{\frac{1}{n1} + \frac{1}{n2}}$$

$$s_D = \sqrt{\frac{(22 \times .90) + (25 \times 1.21)}{48}} \quad \sqrt{\frac{1}{23} + \frac{1}{26}} \qquad s_D = \sqrt{\frac{(25 \times 1.21) + (25 \times 2.31)}{59}} \quad \sqrt{\frac{1}{26} + \frac{1}{35}}$$

$$s_D = 0.284 \qquad\qquad\qquad\qquad s_D = 0.316$$

Next, the *t* score is calculated by finding the differences between the means (m_1 and m_2), and dividing by the standard error s_D:

Q1 vis-à-vis Q2   **Q2 vis-à-vis K1–2**

$$t = \frac{m1 - m2}{s_D} \qquad\qquad t = \frac{m1 - m2}{s_D}$$

$$t = \frac{1.00 - 1.04}{0.284} \qquad\qquad t = \frac{1.04 - 3.48}{0.316}$$

$$t = -0.14 \qquad\qquad\qquad t = -7.72$$

For Q1 vis-à-vis Q2, the *t*-test demonstrates that H_0 (Q1 and Q2 are different) cannot be rejected at even the $p > 0.25$ level. For Q2 vis-à-vis K1 and 2, the *t*-test demonstrates that H_0 (Q2 and K1 and 2 are different) can be rejected at as much as the $p > 0.001$ level. In other words, with respect to subordination, there is significant similarity between Q1 and Q2, but significant difference between Q2 and K1 to 2.

8.2.4 Analysis of Variance

The analysis of variance (F) is used to compare more than two means. Here F is used to evaluate sameness or difference of a variable expressed in terms of mean averages in various questioned writings.

In an employment discrimination matter, a plaintiff found a set of four letters at his desk, each apparently written and signed by four other employees. Although the ultimate question of the employer was whether the plaintiff wrote the letters, the first task was to determine if the four letters demonstrated similar or different style characteristics.

Letters	0 Spaces	1 Space	2 Spaces
Q1	8%	56%	36%
Q2	10%	51%	39%
Q3	0%	48%	52%
Q4	7%	66%	27%
Mean	$m_1 = 6.25\%$	$m_2 = 55.25\%$	$m_3 = 38.5\%$
St. Dev.	$s_1 = 4.35$	$s_2 = 7.89$	$s_3 = 10.34$
St. Dev.^{2}	$s_1^2 = 18.92$	$s_2^2 = 62.25$	$s_3^2 = 106.92$

Figure 8.5 Spacing after sentence-final punctuation in four questioned letters.

Spacing after sentence-final punctuation varied from zero to two spaces in all four letters, prompting the need to know if the writings were related by this variable of their common variation in spacing after sentence-final punctuation. Specifically, if the four means were related, one would be able to reject H_0 that they are not related. Frequency data are presented in Figure 8.5, and the calculation of F follows:

Step 1: Calculate s^2

$$s^2 = \frac{18.92 + 62.25 + 106.92}{3}$$

$$s^2 = \mathbf{62.7}$$

Step 2: Calculate m

$$m = \frac{6.25 + 55.25 + 38.5}{3}$$

$$m = \mathbf{33.3}$$

Step 3: Calculate s_m^2

$$s_m^2 = \frac{4\left[(6.25 - 33.3)^2 + (55.25 - 33.3)^2 + (38.5 - 33.3)^2\right]}{2}$$

$$s_m^2 = \mathbf{2481.08}$$

	Questioned Writing		Suspect Writer 1		Suspect Writer 2		Suspect Writer 3	
Words	21,013		44,606		14,404		57,682	
	n_1	p_1	n_2	p_2	n_3	p_3	n_4	p_4
Periods	1650	51.7%	3408	52.2%	662	46.3%	2618	81.5%
Commas	1415	44.3%	3022	46.3%	716	50.0%	424	13.2%
Other Punct.	128	4.0%	103	1.6%	53	3.7%	169	5.3%
Total Punct.	3193	100%	6583	100%	1431	100%	3211	100%

Figure 8.6 Proportion of periods and commas to all punctuation in four sets of writing.

Step 4: Calculate F

$$F = \frac{2481.08}{62.7}$$

$$F = \mathbf{39.57}$$

Results: H_0 is that the differences between the four writers' mean use of 0, 1, or 2 spaces after sentence-final punctuation are not significant. F (df 2,9) requires a value higher than 4.26 to reject H_0 at $p<.05$ and higher than 8.02 to reject H0 at $p<.01$. Thus an F of 39.57 is significant at $p<.01$, allowing rejection of H0 at $p<.01$. The means are significantly different.

8.2.5   Proportion Test

The proportion test (z) is used to compare two percentages. Here **z** is used to evaluate sameness or difference of a variable expressed in terms of percentages in questioned and known writings.

A case example of a simple but significant punctuation feature is the presence of periods and commas in writing and their relative proportion one to the other. The data in Figure 8.6 represent the relative frequency of occurrence of commas and periods in four sets of writing: the questioned and known writings of a single case, and two sets of control data from other unrelated cases.

This frequency table is descriptive insofar as it enables the analyst to demonstrate easily two things to the trier of fact: first, the close similarity between questioned (Q) and suspect writer 1 (S1) and, second, their dissimilarity to suspect writers 2 (S2) and 3 (S3). But what if Q and S1 were not so close? How close must they be for the feature to constitute a similarity?

How far apart must they be for it to be a difference? For example, while S3 is very different from Q and S1, the proportions of periods and commas in S2 are closer to those in Q and S1. The descriptive table does not enable one to easily evaluate as significant or not their 51.7% vs. 46.3% difference in proportion of periods.

Such a problem calls for inferential analysis beyond the level of the frequency table description. The proportion test (Davis, 1990:39) can be used to determine whether there is no difference between each of the Q and S2 proportions, i.e., to test a hypothesis about whether the 5.4 point distance between the relative presence of periods to all punctuation in Q and S2 represents a difference between Q and S2.

The calculation of the proportion test for periods p_1 vs. p_2 and p_1 vs. p_3 follows:

Q's p_1 (51.7%) vis-à-vis S1's p_2 (52.2%)   Q's p_1 (51.7%) vis-à-vis S2's p_3 (46.3%)

$$\pi = \frac{v_1\pi_1 + v_2\pi_2}{v_1 + v_2}$$

$$\pi = \frac{n_1 p_1 + n_2 p_2}{n_1 + n_2}$$

$$\pi = \frac{(3193 \times .517) + (6583 \times .522)}{3193 + 6583}$$

$$\pi = \frac{(3193 \times .517) + (1431 \times .463)}{3193 + 1431}$$

$$\pi = .52$$

$$\pi = .50$$

$$z = \frac{\pi_1 - \pi_2}{\sqrt{\pi(1-\pi)\left(\dfrac{1}{v_1} + \dfrac{1}{v_2}\right)}}$$

$$z = \frac{p_1 - p_2}{\sqrt{\pi(1-\pi)\left(\dfrac{1}{n_1} + \dfrac{1}{n_2}\right)}}$$

$$z = \frac{.517 - .522}{\sqrt{.52(.48)(1/3193 + 1/6583)}}$$

$$z = \frac{.517 - .463}{\sqrt{.497(.503)(1/3193 + 1/1431)}}$$

$$z = \mathbf{0.47}$$

$$z = \mathbf{3.40}$$

Results: H_0 cannot be rejected at $p > .05$.

For Q vis-à-vis S2, the difference between the two proportions (0.517 vs. 0.463) was well within the acceptance range, allowing one to conclude what appears to be descriptively obvious, that their writers' respective uses of periods vs. commas were not significantly different. On the other hand, for K vis-à-vis control 1 and, more importantly, for K vis-à-vis control 2, the respective differences between their proportions (0.53 vs. 0.86, and 0.53 vs. 0.48) fell outside the acceptance range, thus allowing one to say that control 1, with a higher proportion of periods to commas than K, and control 2, with a lower such proportion than K, are significantly different in this respect than K.

The purpose of this discussion and example is to demonstrate that the increased precision sometimes offered by quantified data can help experts, attorneys, clients, juries, and judges to make more informed decisions. Even given the limitations of quantification in the analysis of writing and language, it is clear that some characteristics in certain cases may be appropriately analyzed in statistical fashion. If methods exist that will make testimony from linguistics clearer, more demonstrable, and thereby more convincing, one has the responsibility to learn and apply them.

8.2.6   Chi Square

Chi square (x^2) is used to analyze more than two percentages. Here x^2 is used to evaluate relative homogeneity of multiple variables expressed as actual frequencies in various questioned writings.

This is the case of the contested will (reviewed in Chapter 7) of the woman who was born in Japan, grew up in Hawaii, and then later moved with her husband to Anchorage, Alaska. Her will designated her siblings as her heirs, but it was contested by a neighbor couple who produced photocopies of a stationery store will and five letters indicating the decedent's desire to leave her large estate to the neighbors, not to her siblings. The typed letters included five (Q1 to 5) that were presented as known letters of the testator, reportedly dictated by her to a friend acting as a secretary. The neighbors claimed the letters were the decedent's and represented her wishes, but the woman's siblings contended that the letters were not their sister's.

Various characteristics of the five questioned letters prompted questions about their authorship, even apart from the parties' differing contentions. First, no one knew or could find the woman who reportedly acted as secretary. Second, while the decedent's known writings (and reportedly her spoken English) evidenced some features of Hawaiian Creole English, her writing was much closer to standard English. However, the questioned letters demonstrated very high frequencies of Creole features. Third, all of the Creole characteristics represented deletions of grammatical elements; however, no variety of English (or any other language, for that matter) is defined by a single process like deletion. In fact, the exclusive pattern of unexpectedly frequent deletions suggests that the letters were a poor imitation of someone's Creole stereotype. Fourth, the one letter (Q5) that most overtly redirected the estate to the neighbors contained only deletions in significantly higher proportions than the other four letters.

In Figure 8.7, deletion characteristics 1 to 8 (deletions) are presented in terms of how frequently the item is *present* in the writings. The case raises at least three important questions:

STYLE-MARKER	Q1–4			Q5		
	n Possible	n Present	% Present	n Possible	n Present	% Present
1. Article Deletion	54	19	35.1%	34	0	0%
2. Subject Deletion	244	221	90.6%	120	91	75.8%
3. Object Deletion	203	196	96.6%	81	68	84.0%
4. Plural -s Deletion	46	45	97.8%	12	11	91.7%
5. Auxiliary Deletion	63	56	88.9%	39	15	38.5%
6. -t Deletion: no for not	25	25	100%	17	15	88.2%
7. Tense Marker Deletion	199	181	91.0%	80	21	26.3%
8. Copula Deletion	68	53	77.9%	12	3	25.0%

Figure 8.7 Eight style-markers in a text disguised as Hawaiian Creole English (Q). Note: Deletion is described here in terms of variables present.

1. Do the known writings of the decedent match the questioned writings? Although Hawaiian Creole features occurred with a lesser frequency in the decedent's writing, the results of this comparison were given little evidentiary weight due to the difference in types of data: hand-written personal letters vs. typed, dictated letters.

2. Are the first four questioned writings (Q1 to 4) the product of one writer? It is necessary to establish Q1 to 4 as a set for subsequent contrast to Q5, given that the third question makes sense only if Q1 to 4 group together as the product of one writer. It is the internal relationship (consistency) of the first four letters that will presently serve to illustrate chi square. To determine if there is a relationship between the eight linguistic variables of deletion and the four questioned writings, it is necessary to ask if any one of the Q1 to 4 writings contains significantly fewer deletions than others. Chi square will be a means of testing H_0, that there is no relationship between the eight forms of deletion and the four questioned writings. Frequency data for each of the eight variables is presented in Figure 8.8, and the calculation of x^2 follows:

$$x^2 = \sum \frac{(\text{actual scores} - \text{expected scores})^2}{\text{expected scores}}$$

$$x^2 = 62.51$$

Results: The critical value must be at least 46.80 for X^2 to be significant at the p<.001 level (df = 21 with four rows and eight columns). Since X^2 at 62.51 is higher, H_0 is rejected at the highest level. Therefore, there is a strong relationship between the various forms of deletion in the four Questioned writings.

Variables	1	2	3	4	5	6	7	8	Total	%
Writings	tps/tkns	tps/tkns	tps/tkns	tps/tkns	tps/tkns	tps/tkns	tps/tkns	tps/tkns	tps/tkns	
Q1	3/14	49/48	55/59	13/13	13/16	8/8	31/41	8/16	180/225	19.07
Q2	6/20	58/69	54/56	4/5	13/15	4/4	52/56	13/18	204/243	21.61
Q3	9/14	80/81	56/56	16/16	13/15	7/7	68/71	22/22	271/280	28.71
Q4	1/6	34/36	31/32	12/12	17/19	6/6	30/31	10/12	141/154	14.94
Total	19/54	221/244	196/203	45/46	56/63	25/25	181/199	53/68		

Figure 8.8 Nondeleted forms for eight deletion variables. Note: tps/tkns = types/tokens = number of items present over number of items possible.

	n types	n tokens	p
Q1–4	106	902	11.75%
Q5	90	326	27.61%

Figure 8.9 Presence of standard forms in Q1 to 4 and Q5.

3. Is the fifth questioned writing (Q5) the product of a different writer? For the answer to this question, the proportion test for large samples (see the previous section) was used. Single variables that met the requirements for the proportion test demonstrate differences between Q1 to 4 and Q5. For example, for subject deletion, z = 3.95, allowing H_0, that subject deletion is not different between Q1 to 4 and Q5, to be rejected at the p > 0.001 level, and for object deletion, z = 3.75, allowing H_0, that object deletion is not different between Q1 to 4 and Q5, to be rejected at the p > 0.001 level.

Overall deletion of all variables in Q1 to 4 vis-à-vis Q5 is reflected in Figure 8.9. Application of the proportion test to the sum of all eight deletion variables yields z = –6.91, well beyond what is needed to reject H_0, i.e., to reject that there is not a difference between Q1 to 4 and Q5 for all deletion, at the p > 0.001 level.

8.2.7 Coefficient of Correlation

The Coefficient of Correlation (r) tests for relationship between two continuous variables. Here *r* is used to determine if two variables in a corpus of writing are independent.

If two variables are correlated in a corpus, their relationship may be one criterion for determining that they are class characteristics. On the other hand, if they are independent in the corpus, their combined appearance in a writing sample independent of the corpus may be a criterion for considering them to be, in combination, individual characteristics. A dialect of a language would represent the first case, wherein we would expect the linguistic variables that define the dialect to co-occur in a group-corpus from the speech community. Any other authorship case with unassociated markers occurring together in one author would be an example of the second, e.g., the JonBenét Ramsey ransom note vis-à-vis a representative corpus of writing (see Chapter 10).

For purposes of illustration, consider the following two style markers occurring in a small corpus of twelve men's writing. H_0 is that x and y are not correlated.

x = **Sentences containing one T-Unit** (vs. Sentences containing more than one T-Unit)

y = **Sentences starting with a function word: Article, Pronoun, Preposition, Conjunction** (vs. Sentences starting with a content word: Noun, Adjective, Verb, Adverb)

Note (from Section 1.3.5) that the terminable unit or *T-unit* is a measure of independent segments in discourse. Also note that examining the relationship between these two variables refers to their overall relative independence in the whole body of writing, not their co-occurrence in the same sentence. The data are found in Figure 8.10, and the calculation of r and t follow:

$$\Sigma x = 354.90 \qquad\qquad \Sigma y = 550.20$$

$$\Sigma x^2 = 17,764.93 \qquad\qquad \Sigma y^2 = 30,320.70$$

$$\Sigma xy = 16,155.44$$

$$(\Sigma x)^2 = 125,954.01 \qquad (\Sigma y)^2 = 302,720.04$$

$$r = \frac{n\Sigma xy - \left[(\Sigma x)(\Sigma y)\right]}{\sqrt{\left[n\Sigma x^2 - (\Sigma x)^2\right]\left[n\Sigma y^2 - (\Sigma y)^2\right]}}$$

$$= \frac{-1640.70}{73,020.31} = -0.0225$$

$$t = r\sqrt{\frac{n-2}{1-r^2}}$$

$$= 0.0225 \times \sqrt{\frac{10}{1-.0225^2}} = 0.071$$

Since t (df=10) is smaller than 1.372, H_0 cannot be rejected even at the p<.25 level, meaning that there is no relationship between x and y. Another way of saying this is that the two style-marker variables of sentence T-units and sentence-initial function words are independent in this corpus and could be confidently used in a calculation of the joint probability of occurrence of stylistic variables.

Writer	Sentences with 1 T-unit	Sentences with 2+ T-units	x % with 1 T-unit	Sentences starting with FW	Sentences starting with CW	y % Starting with FW
1	1	7	12.5	7	1	87.5
2	0	10	0	2	8	20
3	2	9	18.2	5	6	45.5
4	5	12	29.4	9	8	52.9
5	6	9	40	7	8	46.7
6	2	8	20	6	4	60
7	1	8	11.1	2	7	22.2
8	6	7	46.2	6	7	46.2
9	4	19	17.4	17	6	73.9
10	1	12	7.7	3	10	23.1
11	12	2	85.7	7	7	50
12	6	3	66.7	2	7	22.2
Totals			354.9			550.2

Figure 8.10 Sentences with one T-unit vis-a-vis sentences starting with a function word.

8.2.8 Frequency Estimates: *Regina v. Gurtler*

Frequency estimates are expressions of how many writers might possess the stylistic profile presented in the questioned writing, based on analysis of the joint probability of occurrence of a set of identification points, i.e., style-markers.

A Canadian woman was found dead of numerous stab wounds. Three apparent suicide notes were found at the scene, one on the computer screen and two others in computer files. The woman's husband was arrested for killing his wife, and the Crown prosecutor inquired as to the authorship of these notes. External circumstances indicated possible authors included only the husband and wife, so the specific questions of the prosecutor were:

1. Can the wife be eliminated or identified as the author of any or all of the notes? and
2. Can the husband be eliminated or identified as the author of any or all of the notes?

The Crown prosecutor subsequently mounted a circumstantial case against the husband, including testimony related to the language style of the suicide notes. The husband contended that his wife committed suicide, but

Stylistic Characteristics	QUEST Note 1	QUEST Note 2	QUEST Note 3	KNOWN Husband	KNOWN Wife
1. FORMAT: Closing: mid-page, CAPS, w/o end-comma	–	+	+	+	–
2. FORMAT: Salutation w/o end-comma or colon	+	+	+	+	–
3. SPELLING: *new* for *knew*	+		–	+	–
4. SPELLING: *to* for *too*	+	+	+	+	–
5. WORD FORM: *an* before word-initial consonant	–	+	+	+	–

Figure 8.11   Five style characteristics of questioned and known husband writings.

at trial he was convicted of murdering her. Part of the evidence against him were the suicide notes, which contained a set of style-markers that would serve both to exclude the wife and identify the husband as their author.

The questioned writings consisted of the three suicide notes. The known writings were eight separate computer-generated writings (450 lines of text) of the wife, and four computer-generated writings (350 lines of text) of the husband. Of the 15 style-markers used to describe the variation in the questioned and known writings, nine markers were isolated as most diagnostic, due to their relative rarity or their distance from possible conscious manipulation by the writer. Of these nine descriptive markers used for determining authorship of the suicide notes, five, presented in Figure 8.11, met the requirements for measurement of their individual and joint probabilities in a group of writers.

The letter-closings "LOVE LISA" found in two of the questioned notes, and "LOVE GARY" in the husband's known writing share many characteristics: same wording, centering (almost to the typed-space) at the bottom of these letters, written in all caps, and not followed by punctuation (a comma). The spelling of "new" for "knew" and the use of "an" for "a," common only to the questioned and the husband's known writings, are features not frequently found in writers such as these with some postsecondary education. The use of "to" for "too," also common only to the questioned notes and the husband's known writings, is more frequent but still significant for its presence in these writings.

The conditions applied for meaningful quantification were the following:

1. Instances of the variable ("variable events") must occur frequently enough to be meaningfully counted.
2. The variation in an event must be discretely discernible as present (occurrence) or absent (nonoccurrence).

3. Each one of possible variable occurrences must have an equal likelihood of occurring.
4. In determining the probability of several variable events occurring simultaneously (e.g., in the same writer), each variable must be independent of all others.

Language corpus: Two different corpora were used to establish a baseline relative frequency of occurrence for the four variables considered. For variables 1 and 2, a corpus of 742 letters was analyzed, and for variables 3 to 5, a corpus of 51,772 words from 154 letters, all from data gathered for the American Writing Project (see Section 8.4). The *new* for *knew* spelling was searched in the 51,772-word corpus, but the total possible occurrences of "knew" were unexpectedly only two, thus making their count impractical. Quantification of frequency estimates now turned on the four variables left.

Individual probability of occurrence calculations: The probability of occurrence was individually calculated for each of the four variables. Also, for later use, the probability of nonoccurrence was calculated for each one. Then, the joint probability of occurrence of the four individual probabilities was calculated.

Individual probabilities of occurrence in the corpus were based on the calculation:

$$p = \frac{occurrences}{occurrences + nonoccurrences}$$

Individual probabilities of nonoccurrence were based on this calculation in the corpus:

$$q = \frac{nonoccurrences}{occurrences + nonoccurrences}$$

Joint probabilities of occurrence calculation: The joint probability of all four individual variables occurring simultaneously (i.e., in the same writer) is the product of their individual probabilities:

$$P = p_1 \times p_2 \times p_3 \times p_4$$

Likelihood ratio statistic, "Olkin's *lambda*": The ratio of the probability of identity markers (occurrences) to the probability of nonidentity markers (nonoccurrences) is a measure of the probability of chance coincidence of factors (variables); it is a more conservative estimate than the calculation of joint probabilities of all factors.

The likelihood ratio (*lambda*) requires the calculation of nonoccurrence of each variable. Since the total of the probability ranges from 0 to 1, the probability of nonoccurrence is $1 - p$. For example, if the joint probability of occurrence (P) is 1/3, the joint probability of nonoccurrence is the 2/3, *lambda* = 0.5. The closer to 0, the less likely the joint probability of identity (occurrence) is due to chance.

$$lambda = \frac{\text{P of occurrence}}{\text{P of nonoccurrence}} = \frac{1/3}{2/3} = 0.5$$

Individual probabilities of occurrence and nonoccurrence:

	Occurrence		Nonoccurrence	
Marker 1	1/460	0.002	459/460	0.998
Marker 2	1/23	0.435	22/23	0.957
Marker 4	1/22	0.455	21/22	0.955
Marker 5	1/964	0.001	963/964	0.999

Marker 1: Letter-closing at mid-page, in CAPS, and without end-comma: **1/460**
   a. Of the 742 letters examined, those with the closing capitalized: 33/742 = 1/23
   b. Of the 742 letters examined, those without punctuation after close: 369/742 = 1/2
   c. Of the 742 letters examined, those appearing at center-page: 75/742 = 1/10
   d. The chance of a./b./c. occurring together is: $1/23 \times 1/2 \times 1/10 =$ **1/460**

Marker #2: Salutation without punctuation (end-comma or colon): **1/23**
   a. Of the 742 letters examined, no punctuation is present in: 33/742 = 1/23

Marker #4: Spelling of "too" as "to": **1/22**
   a. In the 51,772-word corpus, "too" is spelled "to": **1/22**

Marker #5: Use of article "an" for "a" before word-initial consonant: **1/964**
   a. In the 51,772-word corpus, "an" is used for "a": **0/964**

Joint probability of occurrence of markers 1, 2, 4, and 5:
   $1/460 \times 1/23 \times 1/22 \times 1/964 =$ **1/224,380,640**

Joint probability of nonoccurrence of markers 1, 2, 4, and 5:
   $439/440 \times 22/23 \times 21/22 \times 963/964 =$ **9/10**

The likelihood ratio of the joint probabilities of occurrence to nonoccurrence:

$$lambda = \frac{1/224,380,640}{9/10} = \frac{0.000000004}{0.9} = 0$$

The probability of all four variables occurring in one writer is one in 224.4 million. The likelihood of these four variables occurring together by chance is zero. The known writings of the husband, therefore, demonstrate a set of four style-markers *unique* to this writer. The fact that this set of characteristics is absent in the wife's known writings but present in the husband's known writings suggests two conclusions: that the wife be excluded as the writer of the questioned notes, and that the husband be identified as the writer of the questioned notes.

Note that the above analysis of data from *Regina v. Gurtler* can be considered a good example of how frequency estimates can be established based on reference to a corpus of writing. After extensive *voir dire* in this case, however, the Court excluded the foregoing quantitative analysis, admitting only the descriptive evidence of the linguist-witness. The defense successfully argued two limitations of the analysis, as stated by the linguist during direct and cross examination: the comparison of American writers from Canada to a reference corpus of American writing from the U.S., and the Crown's presentation of the expert to the Court as a linguist, not a statistician. Based on the evidence, which included the qualitative linguistic analysis, the jury convicted the defendant. This conviction, including challenges to the language evidence, has withstood all appeals to date.

8.3   Measures of Authorship Discrimination

Considerable research has been done on the identification and measurement of variables to serve as reliable markers for authorship discrimination recognition. Many of these are reviewed or cited in McMenamin (1993). Research in the past few years demonstrates some promising advances in this area. Examples of more recent work in this area are:

- Style-marker (variable) identification: Forsyth and Holmes, 1996; Forsyth, Holmes, and Tse, 1999; Chaski, 2001; Grant and Baker, 2001; McMenamin, 2001
- Intra-author vs. interauthor variation in stylometry: Laan, 1995
- Orthographic (letter) variables and patterns: Kjell, 1994; Ledger, 1995; Mealand, 1995; Hoorn et al., 1999
- Word clusters (collocations): Greenwood, 1993; Rommel, 1994
- Frequent and infrequent words: Burrows, 1992; Holmes and Forsyth, 1995

- Frequency distributions of function words: Merriam, 1993 and 1996; Mealand, 1995
- Frequencies of common words: Greenwood, 1995
- Neural networks: Kjell, 1994; Matthews and Merriam, 1993; Merriam and Matthews, 1994
- Principal component analysis: Dixon and Mannion, 1993; Greenwood, 1993; Baayen et al., 1996; Grant and Baker, 2001
- Cluster analysis: Dixon and Mannion, 1993; Greenwood, 1995
- Correspondence analysis: Dixon and Mannion, 1993; Mealand, 1995
- Discriminant analysis: Martindale and Tuffin, 1996
- Multivariate analysis: Ledger, 1995; Holmes and Forsyth, 1995; Mealand, 1995; Greenwood, 1995; Temple, 1996

8.4 Corpus Development of American English

While various English language corpora have been developed in the U.K. and in Commonwealth countries around the world such as Australia, the American National Corpus (ANC) project is just developing a corpus comparable to the British National Corpus. A committee of scholars and a consortium of publishers have combined their academic and financial resources to create a corpus of American English that is scheduled for release in late 2002 and will be managed by the University of Pennsylvania's Linguistic Data Consortium. The ANC website is *http://www.cs.vassar.edu/~ide/anc/*.

The American Writing Project (AWP) is a research initiative begun in 1998 with a goal to establish a large corpus and database of American writing from the U.S. and Canada as represented by letters to the editor from newspapers throughout the two countries. Other types of natural writing are also being collected for this corpus, such as fan letters to famous people and sports teams, as well as children's letters.

The AWP sample for the U.S. is now about one third completed. Participating newspapers represent proportionate populations in all census areas of the country, as summarized in Figure 8.12. The sample is designed to include unedited letters to the editor from 400 randomly selected newspapers, 100 from four urban-to-rural U.S. Census categories: 100 from metropolitan areas (250,000 population and up), 100 from urbanized areas (50,000 through 249,999 pop.), 100 from outside urbanized areas (2500 through 49,000 pop.), and 100 from rural areas (less than 1000 through 2499 pop.).

Although the goals and design of the AWP are linguistic (i.e., not forensic), the stylistic data present in the corpus are useful for establishing the relative frequency of occurrence of linguistic variables in this type of American writing, thereby facilitating the reliable and valid assessment of the importance of particular style-markers. Since the federal judiciary began to

AREA OF USA	% OF U.S. POPULATION	NO. OF PAPERS
NORTHEAST		
New England	5.3%	5
Middle Atlantic	15.1%	15
MIDWEST		
East North Central	16.8%	17
West North Central	7.1%	7
SOUTH		
South Atlantic	6.1%	6
East South Central	10.7%	11
West South Central	17.5%	18
WEST		
Mountain	5.4%	5
Pacific	15.7%	16
TOTALS	100%	100

Figure 8.12 AWP writing samples proportionate to population of U.S. Census areas.

apply the *Daubert* criteria for expert scientific testimony, the analytic basis for such linguistic testimony may include an estimation of the relative probability of occurrence of each maker in a large group of like-writers, as well as quantitative estimates of the joint probability of occurrence of multiple variables.

The AWP plain-text corpus of written language: A plain-text corpus of writing is a relatively unstructured compilation of digitized texts grouped into categories by variables that are external to language. The advantages of the AWP corpus are that it is large and contains randomly selected samples of nonrequest writing, and that subcorpora can be categorized by region, community size, typing or hand-printing or handwriting, and sex of writer. All writings in the AWP corpus are (slowly) being redacted to exclude writers' identifying information, then digitized as images and as text. The limitations of such a corpus are that, although letters to newspapers include a wide diversity of writers, the representativeness of the corpus is limited to those writers who would send a letter to the editor.

The AWP interpreted corpus of written language: An interpreted corpus of writing is a plain text corpus that has been "tagged" for selected linguistic and nonlinguistic variables, using an agreed upon format such as the SGML tagging system of the Text Encoding Initiative (TEI). Requirements of the AWP tagged corpus relate to the variables chosen for tagging. Although these choices are yet to be made, at least two criteria will apply: to include identification of variables at all linguistic levels, and to tag variables that appear frequently in writings studied. The advantage of an interpreted corpus is that it can be accessed as needed to create a database of selected style-markers, thus making it possible to efficiently analyze the frequency and type of markers, without the longer and slower search of the entire corpus required for markers not yet tagged or not included in this or any other database. The limitations of such a corpus are that tagging is labor intensive and slow, resulting in a tagging level that rarely meets the potential of the corpus.

The AWP linguistic database: A linguistic database is a digital repository of information structured according to categories of natural language and natural communicative interaction. The advantages of the AWP linguistic database relate to the accessibility of the corpora. A researcher can study a database already created, or create a new one from either or both source-corpora: all plain-text files can be searched or concorded, and all tagged files can be sorted by variable.

References

Anshen, F., *Statistics for Linguists*, Newbury House, Rowley, MA, 1978.

Burrows, J. F., Computers and the study of literature, in Butler, C. S., Ed., *Computers and Written Texts*, Blackwell, Oxford, 167–204, 1992.

Chaski, C. E., Empirical evaluations of language-based author identification techniques, *Foren. Linguis.*, 8:1:1–65, 2001.

Craig, H., Authorial attribution and computational stylistics: if you can tell authors apart, have you learned anything about them? *Lit. Linguis. Comput.*, 14:1:103–113, 1999.

Davis, L. M., *Statistics in Dialectology*, University of Alabama Press, Tuscaloosa, 1990.

Dixon, P. and Mannion, D., Goldsmith's periodical essays: a statistical analysis of eleven doubtful cases, *Lit. Linguis. Comput.*, 8:1:1–19, 1993.

Forsyth, R. S., and Holmes, D. I., Feature-finding for text classification, *Lit. Linguis. Comput.*, 11:4:163–174, 1996.

Forsyth, R. S., Holmes, D. I., and Tse, E. K., Cicero, Sigonio, and Burrows: investigating the authenticity of the *Consolatio, Lit. Linguis. Comput.*, 14:3:375–400, 1999.

Grant, T. and Baker, K., Identifying reliable, valid markers of authorship: a response to Chaski, *Foren. Linguis.*, 8:1:66–79, 2001.

Greenwood, H. H., Common word frequencies and authorship in Luke's Gospel and Acts, *Lit. Linguis. Comput.*, 10:3:183–188, 1995.

Greenwood, H. H., St Paul revisited — word clusters in multidimensional space, *Lit. Linguis. Comput.*, 8:4:211–220, 1993.

Grishman, R., *Computational Linguistics: an Introduction*, Cambridge University Press, Cambridge, 1986.

Hilton, O., The relationship of mathematical probability to the handwriting identification problem, *The Examination of Questioned Documents*, Seminar #4, RCMP Crime Detection Laboratories, Ottawa, May 10, 1956.

Holmes, D. I., Authorship attribution, *Comput. Humanities*, 28:87–106, 1994.

Holmes, D. I. and Forsyth, R. S., The Federalist revisited: new directions in authorship attribution, *Lit. Linguis. Comput.*, 10:2:111–127, 1995.

Hoorn, J. F. et al., Neural network identification of poets using letter sequences, *Lit. Linguis. Comput.*, 14:3:311–338, 1999.

Johnstone, B., *Qualitative Methods in Sociolinguistics*, New York, Oxford University Press, 2000.

Kjell, B., Authorship determination using letter pair frequency features with neural network classifiers, *Lit. Linguis. Comput.*, 9:2:119–124, 1994.

Laan, N. M., Stylometry and method: the case of Euripides, *Lit. Linguis. Comput.*, 10:4:271–278, 1995.

Ledger, G. "An exploration of differences in the Pauline epistles using multivariate statistical analysis, *Literary & Linguistic Computing*, 10:2:85–98, 1995.

Matthews, R. A. J. and Merriam, T. V. N., Neural computation in stylometry I: an application to the works of Shakespeare and Fletcher, *Lit. Linguis. Comput.*, 8:4:203–209, 1993.

McMenamin, G. R., *Forensic Stylistics*, Elsevier Science Publishers, Amsterdam, 1993.

McMenamin, G. R., Style markers in authorship studies, *Foren. Linguis.*, 8:2:93–97, 2001.

Mealand, D. L., Correspondence analysis of Luke, *Lit. Linguis. Comput.*, 10:3:171–182, 1995.

Merriam, T. V. N., Marlowe's hand in *Edward III*, *Lit. Linguis. Comput.*, 8:2:59–72, 1993.

Merriam, T. V. N., Marlowe's hand in *Edward III* revisited, *Lit. Linguis. Comput.*, 11:1:19–22, 1996.

Merriam, T. V. N. and Matthews, R. A. J., Neural computation in stylometry II: an application to the works of Shakespeare and Marlowe, *Lit. Linguis. Comput.*, 9:1:1–6, 1994.

Pickford, G. R., American linguistic geography: a sociological appraisal, *Word*, 12:2:211–233, 1956.

Reed, D. W., A statistical approach to quantitative linguistic analysis, *Word*, 5:3:235–247, 1949.

Rommel, T., 'So soft, so sweet, so delicately clear.' A computer-assisted analysis of accumulated words and phrases in Lord Byron's epic poem *Don Juan*, *Lit. Linguis. Comput.*, 9:1:7–12, 1994.

Scholfield, P., *Quantifying Language*, Multilingual Matters, Clevedon, 1995.

Temple, J. T., A multivariate synthesis of published Platonic stylometric data, *Lit. Linguis. Comput.*, 11:2:67–76, 1996.

Wrenshall, A. F. and Duke, D. M., Statistical methods and the examination of questioned documents, *The Examination of Questioned Documents*, Seminar #4, RCMP Fraudulent Cheque Section, Ottawa, May 10, 1956.

Cases Cited

In the Matter of the Estate of Violet Houssien, Superior Court for the State of Alaska, Third Judicial District at Anchorage, Case No. 3AN-98-59 P/R, September 1999. Upheld in *Crittell v. Bingo* et al. by the Supreme Court of Alaska No. S-9468, November 9, 2001 Decision No. 5496.

Regina v. Gurtler, Court of Queens Bench, Saskatoon, Saskatchewan, 1996; 7134, Sask. C.A., Sask. D. Crim. 260; 10.35.00-08, 1998.

Forensic Stylistics 9

GERALD R. McMENAMIN

9.1 Forensic Applications of Linguistic Stylistics

Forensic stylistics is the application of the science of linguistic stylistics to forensic contexts. The focus of forensic stylistics is written language and, sometimes, spoken language represented in writing, e.g., transcripts of tape recorded conversations, depositions, interviews, etc. The primary application of forensic stylistics is in the area of questioned authorship. Other frequent applications relate to the analysis of meaning in documents such as wills, insurance policies, contracts, agreements, laws, and the analysis of meaning in spoken discourse.

9.1.1 Questioned Authorship

Forensic authorship identification is accomplished through the analysis of style in written language, i.e., linguistic stylistics. Stylistics exploits the two principles of inherent variability in language (see Chapter 3): no two writers of a language write in exactly the same way, and no individual writer writes the same way all the time.

Forensic stylistic analysis makes use of stylistic analysis (stylistics) to reach a conclusion and opinion related to the authorship of a questioned writing within the context of litigation. Stylistics is the scientific study of patterns of variation in written language. The object of study is the language of a single individual (idiolect), resulting in a description of his or her identifying linguistic characteristics.

Typical cases of questioned authorship present a questioned writing to be compared or contrasted to the known reference writings of one or more candidate authors. Such an analysis is accomplished by examining the writing style of all available questioned and known writings. The writing style is exhibited in underlying linguistic patterns internal to the habitual language used by the author. Results of this analysis may be 1) determination of resemblance of questioned writings to a common cannon of known writings, 2) elimination or identification of one or more suspect authors, or 3) inconclusive with respect to data that support neither elimination nor identification. Models for the study of questioned authorship are presented in Chapter 6. Various types of authorship cases are summarized in Chapter 11, and examples of style-markers from various authorship cases are provided there also.

This approach to author identification is based on two well-documented facts: author-specific linguistic patterns are present in unique combination in the style of every writer, and these underlying patterns are usually established enough to be empirically described and measured by careful linguistic observation and analysis, making author identification possible.

A language is at one and the same time *owned* by its whole group of speakers and uniquely *used* by individuals from that group. Why one writer chooses one linguistic form over another is the result of differences in what each individually knows of the language, as well as differences in how each one uses the core linguistic knowledge shared by speakers and writers of English.

Individual differences in writing style are, therefore, due to the writer's choice of available alternatives within a large, shared common stock of linguistic forms. At any given moment, a writer picks those elements of language that will best communicate what he or she wants to say. The writer's "choice" of available alternate forms is often determined by external conditions and then becomes the conscious, semiconscious, subconscious, or (usually) unconscious result of habitually using one form instead of another.

Individuality in writing style results from a given writer's own unique set of habitual linguistic choices. Identification and analysis of a writer's choices, i.e., of his or her style-markers, constitute stylistic analysis, which is well established as a method of author identification in literary and forensic contexts.

9.1.2   Semantic and Pragmatic Interpretation of Meaning

The analysis of semantic meaning in words relates to the sense of a word vis-à-vis other words in the language, or to a word's reference to things, actions, and situations in the world. The analysis of pragmatic meaning in words and sentences is the study of intended meaning, which is distinct from semantic meaning in that a given utterance is interpreted based on the intention of the speaker or writer.

Disputes about the meanings of words and phrases arise when different readers of the same document do not agree as to one or more of the following:

1.   The relationship between a word and its defined sense
2.   The relationship between a word and its referent
3.   The meaning of a word in the context of the phrase, clause, or sentence
4.   The meaning of words and phrases in language units beyond the sentence
5.   The intended meaning of a word or phrase as different from its linguistic meaning

9.2   Legal Definitions of Stylistics

Definitions of forensic stylistics are found in Chapter 4 of McMenamin (1993), which cites two principal sources: Black et al. (1990) and Moenssens et al. (1986:579), both of which are based on the linguistic principle stated by Moenssens et al. that, "… while … a common language is very much rule-governed, there are a great number of underlying parts of the use of language that are characterized by idiosyncratic and individualistic factors and habits" (1986). (Note that the naming confusion between the overarching field of forensic linguistics and one of its subareas, forensic stylistics, is unfortunately reflected in these sources.)

Black et al. define *comparative stylistics*, and *forensic linguistics*:

Comparative stylistics. An evidential technique focusing on nonidentity of typist of questioned writings. Matter-of-fact solutions are premised on comparisons of the numerous stylistic alternatives in grammar and format, and the individualized habits and routine practices inherent in the repetitive reduction of like writings to paper, with emphasis on typewritings. (Black et al., 1990:282)

Forensic linguistics. A technique concerned with in-depth evaluation of linguistic characteristics of text, including grammar, syntax, spelling, vocabulary and phraseology, which is accomplished through a comparison of textual material of known and unknown authorship, in an attempt to disclose idiosyncrasies peculiar to authorship to determine whether the authors could be identical. (Black et al., 1990:648)

Moenssens et al. define forensic linguistic analysis based on *United States v. Clifford* (1983):

The discipline consists of an evaluation of linguistic characteristics of communications — either written text or the spoken word, including the grammar, syntax, spelling, vocabulary, and phraseology. The evaluation involves a comparison of one or more texts, or one or more samples of speech, that are of known origin for the purpose of disclosing idiosyncrasies peculiar to individuals in order to determine whether the authors or speakers could be identical. (Moenssens et al., 1986:578)

Legal precedents related to authorship identification and stylistic analysis may be found in McMenamin (1993, Chapter 5) and at *36 ALR4th 598* (1985).

9.3   Linguistic Stylistics as Evidence

To determine whether a theory or technique is scientific knowledge that will assist the trier of fact so as to be the basis of admissible evidence under Rule

702 of the Federal Rules of Evidence, *Daubert v. Merrell Dow Pharmaceuticals* (1993) proposes key questions to be answered, but "the inquiry is a flexible one, and the focus must be solely on principles and methodology ...." The questions are:

1. Can the theory or technique be tested?
2. Has it been tested?
3. Has the theory or technique been subjected to peer review and publication?
4. Is the known or potential rate of error of the particular scientific technique known?
5. Can a relevant scientific community be identified?
6. Is there an expressed degree of acceptance of the theory or technique within that community?

The answer to these questions as they relate to linguistic stylistics is yes, with some qualification: the process of testing the theory and practice of authorship identification is continuous (e.g., Brengelman and McMenamin, 2000), and the study of error rates is just beginning, with the first serious attempt in a forensic context to be Chaski (2001).

Since the appearance of *Daubert*, there have been many interpretations of exactly how to apply it to particular sciences and cases. One example is Risinger and Saks' (1996:31) specification of questions for the field of forensic document examination. What follows is an adaptation of this list of questions to language and linguistic stylistics, most of which have been discussed in other parts of this book:

1. What characteristics of the language are relevant to specific identification (individuation)?
2. Which of these characteristics can be separated one from another?
3. Is it possible to assess interdependence among characteristics that are not separable?
4. Is it possible to assess interdependence among those that are separable?
5. Have base-rate incidences been established for each of those characteristics in the population of candidates for the source of the writing?
6. Is it possible to distinguish intra- from intersource variation, given: source variation, i.e., that writings from the same source may differ each time, and intercandidate similarity, i.e., different sources may be capable of producing a writing indistinguishable from the writing in question?
7. Can the linguist separate important from unimportant characteristics? How is this done?

8. Is there a means for gathering and publishing observations?
9. Is there an established taxonomy for organizing observations that lends itself to their systematic description and quantification?
10. Is there a process for generating new hypotheses (to answer the above questions) consistent with all known observations, and potentially able to be falsified through empirical observation?
11. Is there an established protocol for attempting to empirically falsify new hypotheses?
12. Do the linguists who perceive similarities and differences in writings use standardized measurements of some precision?
13. Is the database of examples that defines which characteristics are common and which are unusual open for inspection and evaluation by other linguists or by any interested person?
14. How do linguists explain their findings? (The authors note that describing similarities and differences, asserting that they are common or uncommon, and assigning some to interwriter difference and others to intrawriter variation do not suffice as a scientific explanation of these same phenomena.)

There are three possible reactions to *Daubert*; the last of these is the most responsible and constructive direction to follow at present:

1. Settle for the status of linguistic stylistics in federal court to simply be "expert nonscientific testimony" and continue professional and research activities as currently practiced.
2. Resist the suggestions that accompany *Daubert's* very narrow definition of science, then attempt to change (broaden) the federal court's notion of science to include as sufficiently scientific the traditional activities of observation, identification, classification, description, and demonstration, in addition to experimental investigation and theoretical explanation.
3. Take the position that this is a call to action for forensic linguists, which would mean examining closely the *Daubert* test with questions like those posed by Risinger and Saks (1996), and setting about doing the research necessary to completely meet the test.

It is also important to take advantage of every possible case that would serve to demonstrate the increasing scientific reliability and validity of linguistic stylistics. At present, *U.S. v. Van Wyk* has been cited as a case demonstrating the weakness of forensic stylistics, so it bears examination.

In Van Wyk, it is clear that the principal focus of the Court's objections to forensic stylistics was on the witness, an FBI agent who: 1. was not a linguist, 2. had no undergraduate or graduate degree in anything related to language, 3. had no training in linguistic stylistics, 4. had experience only in Foster's (2000) text analysis, rejected as nonscientific by linguists, 5. was pointedly proffered as an expert in text analysis, not forensic stylistics, 6. had "attended threat assessment, psychotherapy assessment, and risk assessment seminars that have involved matters related to the assessment of text, taught and conducted research in text analysis, analyzed text …" i.e., all unrelated to stylistics, 7. and in the judge's words, "relie[d] on 'external' and background information, the sum of which is to cast Defendant as a 'terrorizer' of women, or as a 'very bad' person. [The agent] in effect states that Van Wyk is the author because he is the aggressor, whereas the issue is whether he is the aggressor because he is the author. … [his] testimony regarding these external or extratextual factors is barred."

It is also important to note that, while the witness was not permitted to testify to his conclusion as to the identity of the author of the unknown writings in *U.S. v. Van Wyk*, the Court did in fact admit his testimony regarding "the comparison of characteristics or 'markers' between writings known to have been authored by Defendant and the writings in which authorship is 'questioned' or unknown."

Allowing such testimony has been repeated in at least one other recent case, *U.S. v. Spring* (2001), wherein the Court's response to a request for a *Daubert* hearing was as follows:

> The distinctiveness of any individual, whether it's a term of expression, tone of voice, accent, vehicles of expression, peculiar words, words attributable to his or her profession or peculiar expertise, all of those … are things that can be considered by a jury in determining the identity of a person … I think it's absolutely legitimate, and that's what I'm going to rule.

There will be more opportunities to present the scientific strength of linguistic stylistics, but it must be done by experienced linguists who have a strong background in the analysis of linguistic variation and in the requirements (discussed here) for scientific evidence (McMenamin, 2001b).

9.4   Issues in Forensic Stylistic Analysis

Various issues have been raised regarding linguistic approaches to questioned authorship cases, both in documented research and criticism, as well as in the direct- and cross-examination testimony of various expert witnesses (linguists and nonlinguists). The principal focus of concern is the methodology used to exclude or identify potential writers as authors.

A critical focus on method is helpful because it forwards the process of testing and improving the theory and of unifying applications of it. To be ignored, of course, are isolated instances where some investigators take themselves far too seriously on their detour as critics. For example, upon seeing how his own research is used to support nearly all other studies of individuality in writing, Crystal (1995:382) laments for himself and a coauthor, "If we were dead, we would turn in our graves." Alas, poor Yorick! And, after inaccurately representing that American questioned document examiners claim a zero error rate, Chaski (2001:11) bravely tumbles her straw man with the comment that "such claims should make any scientist shudder in disbelief."

The most constructive critical commentaries related to recent developments in questioned authorship studies are those of Finnegan (1990), Crystal (1995), Goutsos (1995), and Grant and Baker (2001). Many of the issues that they raise have been consolidated in the questions and responses that follow.

9.4.1 Stylistics

Is stylistics an established field? Stylistics is a well established field in literary and linguistic studies. Its history of study is broad based and long, spanning many countries and nearly two centuries, and its documented bibliography contains hundreds of works in and on various languages. However, older techniques for establishing authorship are continually under the test of scientific scrutiny, and new methods are being progressively proposed and tested.

9.4.2 Variation

What is the norm and how can it be established? Since variation presupposes a norm, it is necessary to establish the norm to describe variation within or from it. The analyst must be able to establish the norms of language behavior associated with writings studied (see Section 5.2). Although norms may be difficult to identify in precise terms, speakers and writers do not find it difficult to identify variation, which means that they have at least an unconscious knowledge of the norms governing their language use. Any social, geographic, or situational norm can be used as the basis for describing variation in writing.

What is conscious and what is unconscious in composition? Related questions concern the possibility of forgery or disguised writing. Not enough is known about composition to establish precisely what in writing is conscious or unconscious. The reasons for this are the difficulties associated with such studies, i.e., that every writer's level of conscious choice of forms in writing is different, and that writers demonstrate varying levels of consciousness in language production, e.g., unconscious, subconscious, semiconscious, and conscious.

A reasonable assumption is that there are linguistic levels more distant from the conscious choice of a writer. For example, words and phrases are viewed as more consciously chosen than syntactic structures. Chaski (2001:8) says, "... syntactic processing is automatized, unconscious behavior and therefore is difficult either to disguise or imitate ...," but she refers to this as a "fundamental idea about language individuality," i.e., still an assumption.

A solution to this problem is to exploit the relationship known to exist between natural language and patterned variation. *Natural language*: what can be applied of Labov's (1966:100) definition of casual speech to written language is that natural language in writing is everyday writing used in informal situations, where little or no attention is directed to the writing process. *Patterned variation*: countless studies demonstrate linguistic variation to be structured, meaning that the pattern of linguistic and nonlinguistic constraints on the presence and probability of occurrence of each variable can be specified.

The less attention paid to language production, the more regularly structured (real) the variation will be. On the other hand, if considerable attention is given to the writing process, especially in the contexts of imitation or disguise, variation will be unstructured, unpredictable, and different from that present in like writings of the same author. (See Sections 5.2 and 8.2.6 for examples.)

As a practical matter, then, the analyst can do at least two things to take full advantage of a writer's entire range of variation (important in authorship cases), while mitigating the possibility of imitation or disguise. First, every effort should be made to obtain comparison writings of similar context and purpose. Second, if possible disguise is an issue, the analyst can include all variation as part of a given writer's range of variation, then determine the validity of every variable based on its internal structure.

With respect to attempts to replicate another writer's style, it has already been demonstrated earlier (*Oregon v. Crescenzi* in Chapter 3, and *Estate of Violet Houssien* in Chapters 7 and 8) that it is not always so difficult to identify attempted disguise in written language. Imitators cannot recognize the type or frequency of the variables in another writer's range of variation. It is well known, for example, that the American radio comedians of decades past, Amos 'n' Andy, were two white men imitating African-American English. Although they both had considerable lifetime contact with speakers of African American English, they really only succeeded in using a few stereotypical dialect features, and even those were not used at frequencies matching those of the speech community (Snyder, 1989).

What is a sufficient sample size? There are very many stylistic studies demonstrating various sample sizes (see McMenamin, 1993), yet an absolute low-end sample size has not been successfully determined as adequate for authorship studies. The reason for this lies in the diversity of language itself. The sample of language is adequate when stylistic variables occur with sufficient frequency to establish patterns of variation. Although the test for what constitutes a pattern may be qualitative or quantitative, one of the long established requirements for a good linguistic variable is frequency of occurrence. Of course, on the high end, the larger the sample, the more chance that linguistic patterns will demonstrate their structure.

9.4.3   Method of Data Analysis

How do different models of stylistic analysis relate to practical cases? The consistency model (as reviewed in Chapter 6) is used in many cases wherein the single or multiple authorship of various writings is in question. For example, an insurance company wanted to know if ten different witness statements were actually written by the people who signed them, or if they were all authored by the claimant and then presented for signature to the ten different writers. Sometimes the consistency of a set of writings is questioned in anticipation of using them as a single-author set of questioned writings to compare to those of a known suspect writer.

The resemblance model is the one most frequently applied. When content or external circumstances permit identification of just one suspect writer, the authorship question is limited to the resemblance between the questioned writings and known writings of that candidate.

The population model is an extension of the resemblance task. When content or external circumstances permit identification of a limited population of writers, the authorship question is narrowed to the resemblance between the questioned writings and known writings of a limited number (closed-set) of writers.

What is the method of analysis?

1. *Get organized:* arrange and organize questioned and known writings into manageable sets.
2. *State the problem:* articulate the authorship problem as you see it. Articulate the research questions for descriptive analysis and quantitative analysis. Select the appropriate authorship models.
3. *Procedural steps:* assemble all questioned and known writings with the same or similar context of writing. Assess the range of stylistic variation in each set. Identify style-markers: deviations from or variations within any appropriate norm. Note single occurrences of variation as well as habitual variation. If the writings are extensive, make a KWIC concordance to help identify variables. If variation so indicates, make a KPIC concordance of the punctuation in the writings.

4. *Specify descriptive results:* specify individual style-markers at all linguistic levels. Specify the range of variation: the aggregate set of all deviations and variations. Identify and separate style-markers that are class and individual characteristics.

5. *Specify quantitative results:* give results of statistical tests used to evaluate the significance of variables. Estimate the joint probability of occurrence of variables in compared writings. Apply other appropriate quantitative approaches to style marker identification.

6. *Specify exclusion conclusion:* identify dissimilarities between the style-markers of questioned and known writings. Determine linguistic or statistical significance of dissimilarities. Determine to what degree the candidate writer can be excluded.

7. *Specify identification conclusion:* identify similarities between the style-markers of questioned and known writings. Determine linguistic or statistical significance of similarities. Determine to what degree the candidate writer can be identified.

8. *Precedent cases:* check linguistic and legal precedents related to style-markers used.

9. *State an opinion:* state an opinion for the court: exclusion level, identification level, or inconclusive.

10. *Write a report if so requested:* write a report or declaration that follows the structure used in the sciences.

How are style-markers identified? This question is the single most important issue raised in current research on questioned authorship and is posed in various other ways, e.g.,: how are criteria for identification motivated? and how are stylistic variables selected and justified?

The single most important starting point for selecting style-markers is to work within a theoretical model of linguistics that views stylistic variation as inherent to the system of language itself, i.e., not a characteristic of language performance. This will assure the discovery of the patterned variation needed for authorship identification, as opposed to the accidental and less than systematic characteristics of performance.

The second analytical requirement is to recognize that unique markers are extremely rare, so authorship identification requires the identification of an aggregate of markers, each of which may be found in other writers, but all of which would unlikely be present together in any other writer. This means that it is highly unlikely that any single marker of writing style could be used to identify all writers of a language or dialect, or even one writer's idiolect.

Therefore, the approach is to identify the whole range of variation in a given set of writings, and analyze it in any acceptable descriptive or quantitative way. The theoretical limitation to this, of course, is the recognition and definition of the norm within or from which the language varies. This, however, does not present significant practical obstacles, except for an analyst who does not know the governing norms or who cannot identify the variation.

One recent attempt to tackle the issue of style marker identification (Chaski, 2001) is only marginally successful because it assumes that style-markers are like the same relatively small set of chromosomes used for DNA analysis, thereby ignoring the whole range of linguistic variation presented in writing (McMenamin, 2001). However, Grant and Baker (2001:76) and others have proposed a very promising approach to style marker identification, and it is consistent with the (above-mentioned) principles of stylistic variation: principal component analysis. This approach makes eminent sense. First, it recognizes that authorship identification is achieved through an array of markers: "Components would consist of those markers which collectively account for the most variance in the texts" (Grant and Baker, 2001). Second, it recognizes the near impossibility of identifying style-markers that are generally valid and reliable for all writers (Grant and Baker, 2001). This indicates that they understand the inherent variability of language, i.e., that stylistic variation, whether dialectal or idiolectal, must be analyzed as part of the underlying competence of speakers and writers, not as a never-to-be-found universal of linguistic performance.

9.4.4 Qualitative Analysis

What is the role of the analyst's intuition? Intuition is the analyst's use of his or her own judgment to discover linguistic variation and suggest initial hypotheses to investigate. As a speaker or writer of the language and as a linguist, the analyst uses introspection to start the process of analysis. Lakoff comments on the use of introspection and informal observation that, "... any procedure is at some point introspective ..." (Lakoff, 1975:5). A good discussion of the methodological role of intuition in linguistic research can be found in Johnstone (2000).

Are qualitative statements impressionistic? This is also asked in other ways: Is not qualitative analysis subjective and quantitative analysis objective? Is this description without analysis? While this question is elaborated on in Chapter 7, it bears repeating that stylistic analyses are both qualitative and quantitative, but the description of written language is the first and most important means for discovering style variation. The focus of the qualitative study of writing is a systematic linguistic description of what forms are used by a writer, and how and why they may be used.

What is the process of argumentation? The scientific basis of the argument is that of any empirical study: observation, description, measurement, and conclusion. In the specific case of authorship studies, the argument is as follows:

Notice these style-markers in the corpus of writing.

The array of patterned markers is described as *a, b, c, ...*

Each of these markers has *x* probability of occurring in the writing of the speech community.

Taken as an aggregate set, they have *y* probability of occurring together in one writer.

The author-specific markers and their joint probability of occurrence are either the same as or different from those of a comparison corpus of writing.

9.4.5   Quantitative Methods of Data Analysis

Is statistical analysis necessary? As stated in Chapter 8, the measurement of variation in written language complements its description and is therefore important to the successful analysis and interpretation of style. The focus is on how much and how often forms are used by a writer, which is necessary to satisfy current requirements for the study of linguistic variation, as well as to satisfy external requirements for expert evidence as imposed by the judiciary.

Are there baseline norms for frequency statements? Baseline norms can be established on a case-by-case basis. Written language corpora are becoming more available, although it may not always be possible to match exactly the context of writing presented by documents in a particular case. Often, civil and criminal clients can produce an appropriate corpus from their own workplace or other writings produced in a context similar to those being analyzed. Specialized corpora developed by specialists in other fields can sometimes be found e.g., a corpus of suicide notes collected by a coroner.

How is frequency defined and what is its significance? In descriptive studies, one instance of a style variant does not constitute a pattern, unless it can be demonstrated to be unique through frequency estimates based on large corpora. However, a pattern (whose relative strength increases with frequency of occurrence) can be established with two or more instances. For example, the appearance of "confidentuality" in a questioned document and its double repetition in known writings is a definite pattern of variation. In quantitative studies, the determination of frequency is somewhat easier insofar as statistical tests specify minimum numbers of instances necessary for their reliable use.

9.4.6   Other Questions

Does not the use of a suspect writer's own name suggest that he is not the writer? No, it is well known in the field of questioned document examination that anonymous writers often use their own names to encourage investigators to see them as victims rather than possible perpetrators.

Does the analyst fail to look at other possible writers? The specific task determines the model of analysis to be used. If the population model is appropriate to the problem, then other possible writers are studied. If external information dictates the use of the resemblance model, then only one writer is considered. In those cases for which clients cannot articulate the problem and clearly indicate the task, this must be done with the linguist's help before analysis is started.

Does the analyst look for exculpatory characteristics? Whether certain evidence is incriminating or exculpatory is the concern of the client and the trier of fact, not the expert witness. The linguist analyzes the writings presented for both similarities and differences vis-à-vis comparison writings, then states his or her findings, conclusions, and opinions. The linguist's participation usually stops there if the evidence is not consistent with the expectations of the client. The linguist may testify at deposition or in court if it is the case that his or her evidence supports the client's position.

9.5 The Linguist as Expert Witness

9.5.1 Qualifications

There are two ways to talk about a linguist's qualifications: what level of professional preparation in linguistics and forensic science the individual should have, and what the Court determines is necessary to qualify the linguist as an expert. Although most forensic linguists who now testify in court have a doctorate, a lesser degree, graduate or undergraduate, would suffice when combined with sufficient case experience in analysis and in court. The Court will usually qualify the linguist as an expert in the field if the combination of education and experience demonstrates that the linguist can, in fact, provide evidence that will help a jury make an enlightened decision.

The Federal Rules of Evidence (FRE 702) state three requirements for an expert witness:

1. The witness must qualify as an expert by knowledge, skill, experience, training, or education greater than the average layperson in the area of his or her testimony. Since the expert is there to help the jury resolve a relevant issue, his or her relative level of expertise may affect the weight the judge or jury gives the opinion, but not its admissibility.
2. The expert must testify to scientific, technical, or other specialized knowledge. The reliability of the testimony is based on valid reasoning and a reliable methodology, as opposed to subjective observations or speculative conclusions.

3. The expert's testimony must assist the trier of fact, i.e., be relevant to the task of the judge or the jury to understand the evidence or determine disputed facts.

To be avoided is the imposition of artificial requirements that have nothing to do with the linguist's ability or FRE 702. In one case, an opposing linguist implied that his opinion should carry more weight, noting that, while the other linguist was a professor at a state university, he taught at a well known private university elsewhere in California. In another case, a linguist proposed the narrow requirement that a good expert linguist be a graduate of one of a select few East Coast universities in the U.S. There are, in fact, excellent linguistics programs throughout the U.S. and the world, and thousands of good linguists (now more than 14,000 on *The Linguist List*), many capably handling cases in forensic linguistics.

9.5.2 Reports

The structure of the linguist's statement will follow the report style of the empirical sciences, something along these lines:

1. Summary (equivalent to the abstract of an academic paper)
2. Articulation of problem (research problem and statement of hypotheses)
3. Upfront statement of opinion (usually at the end of an academic paper)
4. Previous work
   Linguistic studies related to identified variables
   Legal precedents related to problem or variation (often best handled by attorney)
5. Method
   Outline of research tasks that match the specified problem
   Data collection and organization
   Data analysis
6. Findings
7. Discussion
8. Conclusion
   (9.) Identification
   (8.) Highly probably did write
   (7.) Probably did write
   (6.) Indications did write
   (5.) Inconclusive
   (4.) Indications did not write
   (3.) Probably did not write
   (2.) Highly probably did not write
   (1.) Elimination

In studying various reports and testimony of opposing linguists a number of observations can be made. First, forensic linguists must learn to function in the oftentimes aggressive context of litigation without getting angry, defensive, petulant, or aggressive — behaviors learned anywhere, but not infrequently reinforced in academia.

Second, linguists should be reserved about the outcomes of cases, even if their testimony was important to the Court's decision. The contrary communicates lack of scientific detachment, even possible advocacy, and, puffery on a website or overstating the importance of testimony in an academic article is unseemly. Also, linguistics testimony is rarely the only evidence. The linguist may not (and should not) know what other external (nonlanguage) evidence is used to support his or her client's case, all of which can have a significant bearing on the outcome of the case. In addition, differences of professional opinion and trial outcomes may also result from linguists on opposing sides having different data to work with, or having the occasional client who cares more about his or her advocacy role than the truth. There is also the danger, as once happened, that a linguist rushes into print with "the truth," only to discover that the other side won a $6 million judgment against his client.

Some linguists are actually quite careful about this. In one case, reviewed by Kaplan (1998), significant differences in linguistic analyses and testimony existed. Kaplan's presentation of the evidence clearly documents his analysis (with some reference to the differences), states the positive outcome for his client, and in no way exaggerates the issues.

Third, some linguists do not conduct their own analysis, but simply evaluate the analysis of an opposing linguist. As a trial consultant, the client may certainly limit the role of the linguist to the evaluation of the other side's position. However, if the linguist will be a witness and present testimony at trial, such an approach will not work. It is important that he or she study the issue and take a position, as well as evaluate the opposition's work.

Fourth, linguists must learn how to reflect the rigor of their analysis in their reports. If they cannot do this, the analysis is weak and should not be reported on or testified to. The following are a few examples of unexpected statements from the reports of linguistics witnesses in authorship cases:

"I have also subjected the document to analysis through a Grammatik 5 computer program, which compares the document in question against other writing styles ..."
"I reached the conclusion that the document is the work of an experienced writer who has a vivid imagination."
"We need to rely on all evidence, linguistic as well as nonlinguistic, that may be useful in identifying an author."
"There is no significant link in the ideas expressed in the writings."

"These comments indicate a person whose anxiety ... is so intense that ..."
"The quality of the language submitted ... is polished and free of serious
    grammatical problems."
"Their level of English is similar."
"The writer is a fairly fluent English speaker."
"Due to the press of time, I took a cursory look at the writing."

9.5.3 Testimony

Roger Shuy (emeritus, Georgetown University) is frequently heard to say that
a forensic linguist is really just a good linguist who happens to be applying
what he or she does to a forensic purpose. This means that the forensic
linguist must first be a linguist, but also that he or she must still learn the
principles and practices of forensic science, such as how to prepare for testimony and present evidence in court. Any linguist who faces the prospect
of court testimony would do well to consult Shuy (2000), who clearly reviews
the mandates and constraints of trial preparation and testimony.

The goal of the expert witness is to communicate to the judge and jury.
The single most important way to do this is to use plain language, thereby
avoiding what appears to be the hypertechnical language of linguistics. This
may be a more challenging tasks for the witness than the analysis itself. For
example, a previous chapter referred to the "explicit knowledge of and experience with language," which could have more easily been called *paralinguistic
awareness*. However, use of the longer, more roundabout, and less technical
phrase (technically called *periphrasis*) usually contributes to more comprehensible and efficient witness responses.

One of the best ways to assure success in presenting testimony is to
prepare questions for direct examination. The client can then take the linguist
through the questions in what he or she believes to be the most appropriate
manner for the Court, e.g., question and answer or narrative format. An
example of direct examination recently prepared for a prosecutor presenting
evidence to a Grand Jury may be seen in Appendix 1.

There are many books and treatises available on deposition and court
testimony, e.g., Storey–White (1997). One of the best is the San Francisco
Police Department's in-office guide for criminalistics trainees, prepared by
Susan Morton of the SFPD's crime lab. Morton's *Expert Testimony* is reproduced in Appendix 2.

References

Black, H. C., Nolan, J. R., and Nolan–Haley, J. M., *Black's Law Dictionary*, 6th ed.,
    West Publishing, St. Paul, 1990.

Brengelman, F. and McMenamin, G., Two independent studies of the same ques-
    tioned-authorship case, paper presented at Georgetown University Round
    Table in Linguistics (GURT): Languages of the Professions, May 6, 2000.

Chaski, C. E., Empirical evaluations of language-based author identification techniques, *Foren. Linguis.*, 8:1:1–65, 2001.

Crystal, D., Review of *Forensic Stylistics, Language*, 71:381–384, 1995.

Finnegan, E., Variation in linguists' analyses of author identification, *Am. Speech*, 65:4:334–340, 1990.

Foster, D., *Author Unknown: on the Trail of the Anonymous*, Holt, New York, 2000.

Goutsos, D., Review article: *Forensic Stylistics, Foren. Linguis.*, 2:1:99–113, 1995.

Grant, T. and Baker, K., Identifying reliable, valid markers of authorship: a response to Chaski, *Foren. Linguis.*, 66–79, 2001.

Johnstone, B., *Qualitative Methods in Sociolinguistics*, Oxford University Press, New York, 2000.

Kaplan, J. P., Pragmatic contributions to the interpretation of a will, *Foren. Linguis.*, 5:2:107–126, 1998.

Labov, W., *The Social Stratification of English in New York City*, Center for Applied Linguistics, Washington, D.C., 1966.

Lakoff, R., *Language and Woman's Place*, Harper & Row, New York, 1975.

McMenamin, G., *Forensic Stylistics*, Elsevier Science Publishers, Amsterdam, 1993.

McMenamin, G., Style markers in authorship studies, *Forensic Linguistics*, 8:2:93–97, 2001b.

Moenssens, A. A., Inbau, F. E., and Starrs, J. E., *Scientific Evidence in Criminal Cases*, 3rd Ed., Foundation Press, Mineola, NY, 1986.

Risinger, D. M. and Saks, M. J., Science and non-science in the courts: *Daubert* meets handwriting identification expertise, *Iowa Law Review*, 82:21, 1996.

Snyder, C. A., A closer look at Amos 'n' Andy, unpublished paper prepared for Linguistics 148, California State University, Fresno, 1989.

Shuy, R., Breaking into language and law: the trials of the insider-linguist, paper presented at Georgetown University Round Table in Linguistics (GURT): Languages of the Professions, May 4, 2000.

Storey–White, K., KISSing the jury: advantages and limitations of the "Keep it Simple" principle in the presentation of expert evidence to courts and juries, *Foren. Linguis.*, 4:2:280–286, 1997.

Cases Cited

36 *ALR4th* 598, 1985.

Daubert et ux. et al. *v. Merrell Dow Pharmaceuticals, Inc.*, 509 U.S. 579, 1993.

U.S. v. Spring, No. 5:00-CR-168-1F3, U.S. Dist. Court, Eastern District of NC, 2001.

U.S. v. Van Wyk, 83 F. Supp. 2d 515; D. N.J., 2000.

U.S. v. Clifford, 704 F.2d 86, 1983.

Case Study: JonBenét Ramsey

10

GERALD R. McMENAMIN

10.1 Introduction

Six-year-old JonBenét Ramsey was found dead in her home on December 26, 1996. Before she was found, a three-page ransom letter (Figure 10.1) was discovered in the Ramsey home, precipitating the search for the missing child. In early January, 1997, attorneys for John and Patricia Ramsey anticipated the need to determine if each parent could be excluded as the writer of the ransom letter. Therefore, they sought assistance on the Ramsey matter, requesting a forensic stylistic analysis of the questioned ransom note vis-à-vis the known reference writings of each parent.

The district attorney, for reasons seemingly related to other available evidence, focused less on John Ramsey and more on Patricia Ramsey as the potential writer of the ransom letter. Linguistic findings regarding both the ransom letter and the known Ramsey writings were first reported to their attorneys in January 1997. This chapter reports elements of the linguistic analysis principally related to Patricia Ramsey.

10.2 Method

Four tasks were undertaken in order to accomplish this assignment. First, I established the range of variation present in the questioned ransom letter. I then did the same for the known reference writings of John and Patricia Ramsey, which consisted of three types of hand-printed texts for each of them: 1. one requested writing in the form of a hand-printed repetition of the ransom letter, produced as a result of dictation of the letter to each person on separate occasions, 2. two requested writings in the form of hand-printed repetitions of the ransom letter, produced as a result of each person copying their first dictated letter on separate occasions, and 3. a limited sample of nonrequest "natural" writings, produced before December 26, 1996, in the form of personal notes, calendar entries, and letters. Also, since Patricia Ramsey remained a suspect-writer after initial investigative efforts, she later produced from dictation another two hand-printed versions of the ransom note.

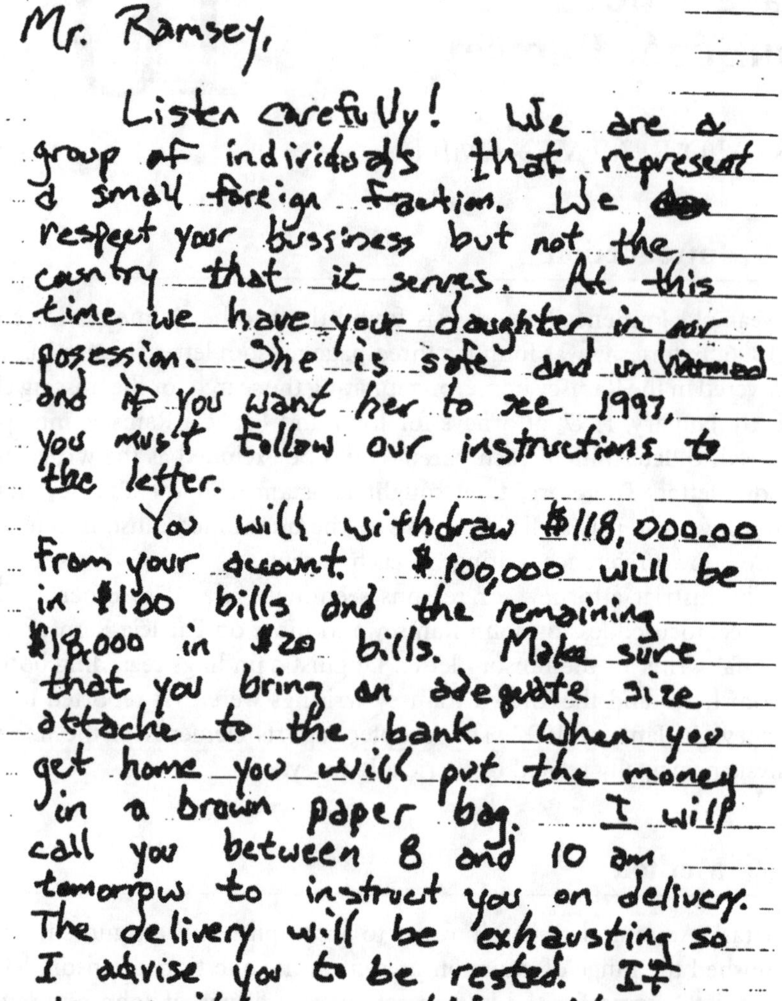

Mr. Ramsey,

   Listen carefully! We are a group of individuals that represent a small foreign faction. We do respect your bussiness but not the country that it serves. At this time we have your daughter in our posession. She is safe and unharmed and if you want her to see 1997, you must follow our instructions to the letter.

   You will withdraw $118,000.00 from your account. $100,000 will be in $100 bills and the remaining $18,000 in $20 bills. Make sure that you bring an adequate size attache to the bank. When you get home you will put the money in a brown paper bag. I will call you between 8 and 10 am tomorrow to instruct you on delivery. The delivery will be exhausting so I advise you to be rested. If we monitor you getting the money eatly, we might call you early to arrange an earlier delivery of the

Figure 10.1 Ramsey ransom note of 12/26/96.

Second, I entered all requested writings into a computer textfile and set up questioned and known writings on successive pages in a vertical score format (analogous to the musical score of a conductor), facilitating easy reference to variable markers of style across all writings. All style-markers are identified in the score text by means of a half-tone overlay on each variant. This was done for Mr. and Mrs. Ramsey; Mrs. Ramsey's can be examined in Figure 10.2.

money and hence d earlier
delivery pick-up of your daughter.
Any deviation of my instructions
will result in the immediate
execution of your daughter. You
will also be denied her remains
for proper burial. The two
gentlemen watching over your daughter
do particularly like you so I
advise you not to provoke them.
Speaking to anyone about your
situation, such as Police, F.B.I., etc.,
will result in your daughter being
beheaded. If we catch you talking
to a stray dog, she dies. If you
alert bank authorities, she dies.
If the money is in any way
marked or tampered with, she
dies. You will be scanned for
electronic devices and if any are
found, she dies. You can try to
deceive us but be warned that
we are familiar with Law enforcement
countermeasures and tactics. You
stand a 99% chance of killing
your daughter if you try to out
smart us. Follow our instructions

Figure 10.1 (Continued) Ramsey ransom note of 12/26/96.

Third, style-markers in the respective known request writings of Mr. and Mrs. Ramsey were found to contrast with those found in the questioned ransom note. And, last, I examined the available sample of John and Patricia Ramsey's pre-December 1996 natural writings (all cursive handwritings) to discern the presence or absence of the Ramsey's respective style-markers in before-the-fact, nonrequest writing.

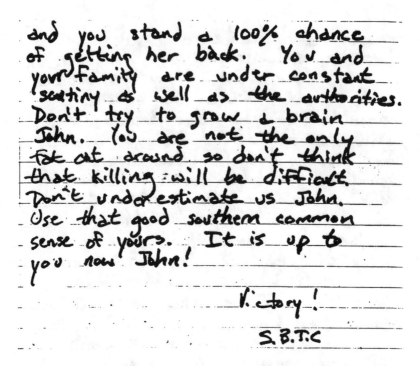

and you stand a 100% chance
of getting her back. You and
your family are under constant
scutiny as well as the authorities.
Don't try to grow a brain
John. You are not the only
fat cat around so don't think
that killing will be difficut.
Don't underestimate us John.
Use that good southern common
sense of yours. It is up to
you now John!

Victory!

S.B.T.C

Figure 10.1 (Continued) Ramsey ransom note of 12/26/96.

10.3   Findings: Qualitative

The questioned ransom letter contains many markers of style that contrast with the known writings of John and Patricia Ramsey. A contrast of the ransom note vis-à-vis John Ramsey's known request writings demonstrates 15 stylistic differences, as outlined in Figure 10.3. The contrast of the ransom note to Patricia Ramsey's known request writings shows 18 stylistic differences, as seen in Figure 10.4. It is also clear that John and Patricia Ramsey's respective known request writings are very different from one another, thereby necessitating separate contrasts to the questioned letter.

There are five style-markers that the Ramseys share and which also contrast to the questioned letter. The respective summary lists of the style-markers appearing in Figures 10.3 and 10.4 demonstrate forms in the known request writings altogether different from those that appear in the questioned ransom letter. Specific variables with their contrasting variants in the questioned letter and Mrs. Ramsey's known request writings may be seen in Figures 10.5 (spelling), 10.6 (capitalization and punctuation), 10.7 (word formation), and 10.8 (money amounts).

Letter	Qp:line =	**Questioned Ransom Letter**
Patricia KP1	=	**1ˢᵗ KNOWN writing, dictated to Patricia Ramsey, 1/4/97**
KP2	=	2ⁿᵈ KNOWN writing, copied from KP1 by Patricia Ramsey, 1/4/97
KP3	=	3ʳᵈ KNOWN writing, copied from KP1 or 2 by Patricia Ramsey, 1/4/97
KP4	=	4ᵗʰ KNOWN writing, dictated to Patricia Ramsey, 2/28/97, thin-tip pen
KP5	=	5ᵗʰ KNOWN writing, dictated, of Patricia Ramsey, 2/28/97, thick-tip pen

RANSOM LETTER (Q) AND FIVE COMPARISON WRITINGS (KP)

Letter Q1:1	**Mr.**	**Ramsey,**			
Patricia KP1	**Mr.**	**Ramsey,**			
KP2	Mr.	Ramsey,			
KP3	Mr.	Ramsey,			
KP4	Mr.	Ramsey,			
KP5	Mr.	Ramsey,			

Letter Q1:2	**Listen**	**carefully!**	**We**	**are**	**a**
Patricia KP1	**Listen**	**carefully!**	**We**	**are**	**a**
KP2	Listen	carefully!	We	are	a
KP3	Listen	carefully!	We	are	a
KP4	Listen	carefully.	We	are	a
KP5	Listen	carefully.	We	are	a

Letter Q1:3	**group**	**of**	**individuals**	**that**	**represent**
Patricia KP1	**group**	**of**	**individuals**	**that**	**represent**
KP2	group	of	individuals	that	represent
KP3	group	of	individuals	that	represent
KP4	group	of	individuals	that	represent
KP5	group	of	individuals	that	represent

Letter Q1:4	**a**	**small**	**foreign faction.**	**We**	
Patricia KP1	**a**	**small**	**foreign faction.**	**We**	
KP2	a	small	foreign faction.	We	
KP3	a	small	foreign faction.	We	
KP4	a	small	foreign faction.	We	
KP5	a	small	foreign faction.	We	

Letter Q1:5	**respect**	**your**	**bussiness**	**but**	**not**	**the**
Patricia KP1	**respect**	**your**	**business**	**but**	**not**	**the**
KP2	respect	your	business	but	not	the
KP3	respect	your	business	but	not	the
KP4	respect	your	business	but	not	the
KP5	respect	your	business	but	not	the

Letter Q1:6	**country**	**that**	**it**	**serves.**	**At**	**this**
Patricia KP1	**country**	**that**	**it**	**serves.**	**At**	**this**
KP2	country	that	it	serves.	At	this
KP3	country	that	it	serves.	At	this
KP4	country	that	it	serves.	At	this
KP5	country	that	it	serves.	At	this

Figure 10.2 Comparison of known Patricia Ramsey writings to ransom letter.

The stylistic variables identified in Mr. and Mrs. Ramsey's pre-December 1996 nonrequest writings were found, with one exception, to be consistent between request and nonrequest writings. In John Ramsey's nonrequest writing, markers J1, J2, J5, J7, J10, and J15 occurred, and all occurred in the same words or in the same fashion as in his request writing. In Patricia Ramsey's natural writing, markers P9, P11, P14, and P18 occurred, and the last three

Letter Q1:7	time	we	have	your	daughter	in	our
Patricia KP1	time	we	have	your	daughter	in	our
KP2	time	we	have	your	daughter	in	our
KP3	time	we	have	your	daughter	in	our
KP4	time	we	have	your	daughter	in	our
KP5	time	we	have	your	daughter	in	our

Letter Q1:8	possession.		She	is	safe	and	un harmed
Patricia KP1	possession.		She	is	safe	and	unharmed
KP2	possession.		She	is	safe	and	unharmed
KP3	possession.		She	is	safe	and	unharmed
KP4	possession.		She	is	safe	and	unharmed
KP5	possession.		She	is	safe	and	unharmed

Letter Q1:9	and	if	you	want	her	to	see	1997,
Patricia KP1	and	if	you	want	her	to	see	1997,
KP2	and	if	you	want	her	to	see	1997,
KP3	and	if	you	want	her	to	see	1997,
KP4	and	if	you	want	her	to	see	1997,
KP5	and	if	you	want	her	to	see	1997

Letter Q1:10	you	must	Follow	our	instructions	to
Patricia KP1	you	must	follow	our	instructions	to
KP2	you	must	follow	our	instructions	to
KP3	you	must	follow	our	instructions	to
KP4	you	must	follow	our	instructions	to
KP5	you	must	follow	our	instructions	to

Letter Q1:11	the	letter.
Patricia KP1	the	Letter.
KP2	the	Letter.
KP3	the	letter.
KP4	the	letter.
KP5	the	letter.

Letter Q1:12	You	will	withdraw	SII 118,000.00
Patricia KP1	You	will	withdraw	one hundred eighteen thousand dollars
KP2	You	will	withdraw	SII 118,000.
KP3	You	will	withdraw	SII 118,000.
KP4	You	will	withdraw	SII 118,000.
KP5	You	will	withdraw	SII 118,000

Letter Q1:13	From	your	account.	SII 100,000	will	be
Patricia KP1	from	your	account.	One hundred thousand dollars	will	be
KP2	from	your	account.	SII 100,000.	will	be
KP3	from	your	account.	SII 100,000.	will	be
KP4	from	your	account,	SII 100,000 dollars	will	be
KP5	from	your	account	SII 100,000	will	be

Letter Q1:14	in	SII 100	bills	and	the	remaining
Patricia KP1	in	100 dollar	bills	and	the	remaining
KP2	in	100 dollar	bills	and	the	remaining
KP3	in	SII 100 dollar	bills	and	the	remaining
KP4	in	100 dollar	bills	and	the	remaining
KP5	in	one hundred dollar	bills	and	the	remaining

Figure 10.2 (Continued) Comparison of known Patricia Ramsey writings to ransom letter.

Letter Q1:15	SII 18,000		in	SII 20	bills.	Make	sure
Patricia KP1	eighteen thousand dollars		in	20 dollar	bills.	Make	sure
KP2	SII 18,000		in	20 dollar	bills.	Make	sure
KP3	SII 18,000.		in	SII 20 dollar	bills.	Make	sure
KP4	SII 18,000 dollars	will be	in	20 dollar	bills.	Make	
sure							
KP5	eighteen thousand		in	twenty dollar	bills.	Make	sure

Letter Q1:16	that	you	bring	an	adequate	size
Patricia KP1	that	you	bring	an	adequate	size
KP2	that	you	bring	an	adequate	size
KP3	that	you	bring	an	adequate	size
KP4	that	you	bring	an	adequate	size
KP5	that	you	bring	an	adequate	size

Letter Q1:17	attache	to	the	bank.	When	you
Patricia KP1	attache	to	the	bank.	When	you
KP2	attache	to	the	bank.	When	you
KP3	attache	to	the	bank.	When	you
KP4	attache	to	the	bank.	When	you
KP5	attache	to	the	bank.	When	you

Letter Q1:18	get	home	you	will	put	the	money
Patricia KP1	get	home	you	will	put	the	money
KP2	get	home	you	will	put	the	money
KP3	get	home	you	will	put	the	money
KP4	get	home	you	will	put	he	money
KP5	get	home	you	will	put	the	money

Letter Q1:19	in	a	brown	paper	bag.	I	will
Patricia KP1	in	a	brown	paper	BAG.	I	will
KP2	in	a	brown	paper	bag.	I	will
KP3	in	a	brown	paper	bag.	I	will
KP4	in	a	brown	paper	bag.	I	will
KP5	in	a	brown	paper	bag.	I	will

Letter Q1:20	call	you	between	8	and	10	am
Patricia KP1	call	you	between	8	and	10	a.m.
KP2	call	you	between	8	and	10	a.m.
KP3	call	you	between	8	and	10	a.m.
KP4	call		between	8	and	10	a.m.
KP5	call		between	8	and	10	A.M.

Letter Q1:21	tomorrow	to	instruct	you	on	delivery.
Patricia KP1	tomorrow	to	instruct	you	on	delivery.
KP2	tomorrow	to	instruct	you	on	delivery.
KP3	tomorrow	to	instruct	you	on	delivery.
KP4	tomorrow	to	instruct	you	on	delivery.
KP5	tomorrow	to	instruct	you	on	delivery.

Letter Q1:22	The	delivery	will	be	exhausting	so
Patricia KP1	The	delivery	will	be	exhausting	so
KP2	The	delivery	will	be	exhausting	so
KP3	The	delivery	will	be	exhausting	so
KP4	The	delivery	will	be	exhausting	so

Figure 10.2 (Continued) Comparison of known Patricia Ramsey writings to ransom letter.

KP5	The	delivery	will	be	exhausting	so

Letter Q1:23	I	advise you	to	be	rested. IF	
Patricia KP1	I	advise you	to	be	rested. If	
KP2	I	advize you	to	be	rested. If	
KP3	I	advize you	to	be	rested. If	
KP4	I	advize you	to	be	rested. If	
KP5	I	advize you	to	be	rested. If	

Letter Q1:24	we	monitor	you	getting the	money
Patricia KP1	we	monitor	you	getting the	money
KP2	we	monitor	you	getting the	money
KP3	we	monitor	you	getting the	money
KP4	we	monitor	you	getting the	money
KP5	we	monitor	you	getting the	money

Letter Q1:25	early,	we	might call	you	early	to
Patricia KP1	early,	we	might call	you	early	to
KP2	early,	we	might call	you	early	to
KP3	early,	we	might call	you	early	to
KP4	early,	we	might call	you	early	to
KP5	early	we	might call	you	early	to

Letter Q1:26	arrange	an	earlier delivery	of	the	
Patricia KP1	arrange	an	earlier Delivery	of	the	
KP2	arrange	an	earlier Delivery	of	the	
KP3	arrange	an	earlier Delivery	of	the	
KP4	arrange	an	earlier delivery	of	the	
KP5	arrange	an	earlier delivery	of	the	

Letter Q2:1	money and	hence a	earlier	
Patricia KP1	money and	hence a	earlier ~~delivery~~	
KP2	money and	hence an	earlier ~~delivery~~	
KP3	money and	hence an	earlier ~~delivery~~	
KP4	money and	hence an	earlier	
KP5	money and	hence an	earlier	

Letter Q2:2	pick-up	of	your	daughter.
Patricia KP1	pick up	of	your	daughter.
KP2	pick up	of	your	daughter.
KP3	pick up	of	your	daughter.
KP4	pick up	of	your	daughter.
KP5	pick up	of	your	daughter.

Letter Q2:3	Any	deviation	of	my	instructions
Patricia KP1	Any	deviation	of	my	instructions
KP2	Any	deviation	of	my	instructions
KP3	Any	deviation	of	my	instructions
KP4	Any	deviation	of	my	instructions
KP5	Any	deviation	of	my	instructions

Letter Q2:4	will	result in	the	immediate
Patricia KP1	will	result in	the	immediate
KP2	will	result in	the	immediate
KP3	will	result in	the	immediate
KP4	will	result in	the	immediate
KP5	will	result in	the	immediate

Figure 10.2 (Continued) Comparison of known Patricia Ramsey writings to ransom letter.

Letter	Q2:5	execution	of	your	daughter.	You	
Patricia	KP1	**execution**	**of**	**your**	**daughter.**	**You**	
	KP2	execution	of	your	daughter.	You	
	KP3	execution	of	your	daughter.	You	
	KP4	execution	of	your	daughter.	You	
	KP5	execution	of	your	daughter.	You	

Letter	Q2:6	will	also	be	de/inied	her	remains
Patricia	KP1	**will**	**also**	**be**	**denied**	**Her**	**remains**
	KP2	will	also	be	denied	her	remains
	KP3	will	also	be	denied	her	remains
	KP4	will	also	be	denied	her	remains
	KP5	will	also	be	denied	her	remains

Letter	Q2:7	for	proper	burial.	The	two	
Patricia	KP1	**for**	**proper**	**buriel.**	**The**	**two**	
	KP2	for	proper	buriel.	The	two	
	KP3	for	proper	buriel.	The	two	
	KP4	for	proper	buriel.	The	two	
	KP5	for	proper	buriel.	The	two	

Letter	Q2:8	gentlemen	watching	over	your	daughter	
Patricia	KP1	**gentlemen**	**watching**	**over**	**your**	**daughter**	
	KP2	gentlemen	watching	over	your	daughter	
	KP3	gentlemen	watching	over	your	daughter	
	KP4	gentlemen	watching	over	your	daughter	
	KP5	gentlemen	watching	over	your	daughter	

Letter	Q2:9	do	not	particularly	like	you	so	I
Patricia	KP1	**do**	**not**	**particularly**	**like**	**you**	**so**	**I**
	KP2	do	not	particularly	like	you	so	I
	KP3	do	not	particularly	like	you	so	I
	KP4	do	not	particularly	like	you.	So	I
	KP5	do	not	particularly	like	you	so	I

Letter	Q2:10	advise	you	not	to	provoke	them.	
Patricia	KP1	**advis/ze**	**you**	**not**	**to**	**provoke**	**them**	
	KP2	advis/ze	you	not	to	provoke	them	
	KP3	advis/ze	you	not	to	provoke	them	
	KP4	advize	you	not	to	provoke	them.	
	KP5	advize	you	not	to	provoke	them.	

Letter	Q2:11	Speaking	to	anyone	about	your	
Patricia	KP1	**speaking**	**to**	**anyone**	**about**	**your**	
	KP2	speaking	to	anyone	about	your	
	KP3	speaking	to	anyone	about	your	
	KP4	Speaking	to	anyone	about	your	
	KP5	Speaking	to	anyone	about	your	

Letter	Q2:12	situation,	such	as	Police, F.B.I.,	etc.,	
Patricia	KP1	**situation,**	**such**	**as**	**police, F.B.I.,**	**etc.,**	
	KP2	situation,	such	as	police, F.B.I.,	etc.,	
	KP3	situation,	such	as	Police, FBI,	etc.,	
	KP4	situation	such	as	police, FBI,	etcetera	
	KP5	situation	such	as	police, FBI	etcetera,	

Figure 10.2 (Continued) Comparison of known Patricia Ramsey writings to ransom letter.

Letter Q2:13	will	result	in	your	daughter	being	
Patricia KP1	will	result	in	your	daughter	Being	
KP2	will	result	in	your	daughter	being	
KP3	will	result	in	your	daughter	being	
KP4	will	result	in	your	daughter	being	
KP5	will	result	in	your	daughter	being	

Letter Q2:14	beheaded.	If	we	catch	you	talking	
Patricia KP1	beheaded.	If	we	catch	you	talking	
KP2	beheaded.	If	we	catch	you	talking	
KP3	beheaded.	If	we	catch	you	talking	
KP4	beheaded.	If	we	catch	you	talking	
KP5	beheaded.	If	we	catch	you	talking	

Letter Q2:15	to	a	stray	dog,	she	dies.	If	you
Patricia KP1	to	a	stray	dog,	she	dies.	If	you
KP2	to	a	stray	dog,	she	dies.	If	you
KP3	to	a	stray	dog,	she	dies.	If	you
KP4	to	a	stray	dog	she	dies.	If	you
KP5	to	a	stray	dog	she	dies.	If	you

Letter Q2:16	alert	bank	authorities,	she	dies.	
Patricia KP1	alert	bank	authorities,	she	dies.	
KP2	alert	Bank	authorities,	she	dies.	
KP3	alert	bank	authorities,	she	dies.	
KP4	alert	bank	authorities,	she	dies.	
KP5	alert	bank	authorities,	she	dies.	

Letter Q2:17	If	the	money	is	in	any	way
Patricia KP1	If	the	money	is	in	any	way
KP2	If	the	money	is	in	any	way
KP3	If	the	money	is	in	any	way
KP4	If	the	money	is	in	any	way
KP5	If	the	money	is	in	any	way

Letter Q2:18	marked	or	tampered	with,	she	
Patricia KP1	marked	or	tampered	with,	she	
KP2	marked	or	tampered	with,	she	
KP3	marked	or	tampered	with,	she	
KP4	marked	or	tampered	with,	she	
KP5	marked	or	tampered	with	she	

Letter Q2:19	dies.	You	will	be	scanned	for	
Patricia KP1	dies.	You	will	be	scanned	for	
KP2	dies.	You	will	be	scanned	for	
KP3	dies.	You	will	be	scanned	for	
KP4	dies.	You	will	be	scanned	for	
KP5	dies.	You	will	be	scanned	for	

Letter Q2:20	electronic	devices	and	iF	any	are
Patricia KP1	electronic	devices	and	if	any	are
KP2	electronic	devices	and	if	any	are
KP3	electronic	devices	and	if	any	are
KP4	electronic	devices	and	if	any	are
KP5	electronic	devices	and	if	any	are

Figure 10.2 (Continued) Comparison of known Patricia Ramsey writings to ransom letter.

Letter Q2:21	**found, she**	**dies.**	**You**	**can**	**try**	**to**	
Patricia KP1	**found, she**	**dies.**	**You**	**can**	**try**	**to**	
KP2	found, she	dies.	You	can	try	to	
KP3	found, she	dies.	You	can	try	to	
KP4	found, she	dies.	You	can	try	to	
KP5	found she	dies.	You	can	try	to	

Letter Q2:22	**deceive**	**us**	**but**	**be**	**warned**	**that**
Patricia KP1	**deceive**	**us**	**but**	**Be**	**warned**	**that**
KP2	deceive	us	but	be	warned	that
KP3	deceive	us	but	be	warned	that
KP4	deceive	us	but	be	warned	that
KP5	deceive	us	but	be	warned	that

Letter Q2:23	**we**	**are**	**familiar**	**with**	**Law**	**enforcement**
Patricia KP1	**we**	**are**	**familiar**	**with**	**law**	**enforcement**
KP2	we	are	familiar	with	law	enforcement
KP3	we	are	familiar	with	Law	enforcement
KP4	we	are	familiar	with	law	enforcement
KP5	we	are	familiar	with	law	enforcement

Letter Q2:24	**countermeasures**	**and**	**tactics. You**
Patricia KP1	**counter measures**	**and**	**tactics. You**
KP2	counter measures	and	tactics. You
KP3	counter measures	and	tactics. You
KP4	counter measures	and	tactics. You
KP5	counter measures	and	tactics. You

Letter Q2:25	**stand**	**a**	**99%**	**chance**	**oF**	**killing**
Patricia KP1	**stand**	**a**	**99%**	**chance**	**of**	**killing**
KP2	stand	a	99%	chance	of	killing
KP3	stand	a	99%	chance	of	killing
KP4	stand	a	99%	chance	of	killing
KP5	stand	a	99%	chance	of	killing

Letter Q2:26	**your**	**daughter**	**iF**	**you**	**try**	**to**	**out**
Patricia KP1	**your**	**daughter**	**if**	**you**	**try**	**to**	**outsmart**
KP2	your	daughter	if	you	try	to	outsmart
KP3	your	daughter	if	you	try	to	outsmart
KP4	your	daughter	if	you	try	to	outsmart
KP5	your	daughter	if	you	try	to	outsmart

Letter Q2:27	**smart**	**us.**	**Follow our**	**instructions**
Patricia KP1		**us.**	**Follow our**	**instructions**
KP2		us.	Follow our	instructions
KP3		us.	Follow our	instructions
KP4		us.	Follow our	instructions
KP5		us.	Follow our	instructions

Letter Q3:1	**and**	**you**	**stand**	**a**	**100%**	**chance**
Patricia KP1	**and**	**you**	**stand**	**a**	**100%**	**chance**
KP2	and	you	stand	a	100%	chance
KP3	and	you	stand	a	100%	chance
KP4	and	you	stand	a	100%	chance
KP5	and	you	stand	a	100%	chance

Figure 10.2 (Continued) Comparison of known Patricia Ramsey writings to ransom letter.

Letter	Q3:2	**oF**	**getting her**	**back.**	**You**	**and**	
Patricia	KP1	**of**	**getting her**	**back.**	**You**	**and**	
	KP2	of	getting her	back.	You	and	
	KP3	of	getting her	back.	You	and	
	KP4	of	getting her	back.	You	and	
	KP5	of	getting her	back.	You	and	

Letter	Q3:3	**your**	**family are**	**under**	**constant**	
Patricia	KP1	**your**	**family are**	**under**	**constant**	
	KP2	your	family are	under	constant	
	KP3	your	family are	under	constant	
	KP4	your	family are	under	constant	
	KP5	your	family are	under	constant	

Letter	Q3:4	**scruitiny**	**as**	**well**	**as**	**the**	**authorities.**
Patricia	KP1	**scruitiny**	**as**	**well**	**as**	**the**	**authorities**
	KP2	scruitiny	as	well	as	the	authorities.
	KP3	scrutiny	as	well	as	the	authorities.
	KP4	scrutiny	as	well	as	the	authorities.
	KP5	scrutiny	as	well	as	the	authorities.

Letter	Q3:5	**Don't**	**try**	**to**	**grow**	**a**	**brain**
Patricia	KP1	**Don't**	**try**	**to**	**grow**	**a**	**brain**
	KP2	Don't	try	to	grow	a	brain,
	KP3	Don't	try	to	grow	a	brain
	KP4	Don't	try	to	grow	a	brain,
	KP5	Don't	try	to	grow	a	brain

Letter	Q3:6	**John.**	**You**	**are**	**not**	**the**	**only**
Patricia	KP1	**John.**	**You**	**are**	**not**	**the**	**only**
	KP2	John.	You	are	not	the	only
	KP3	John.	You	are	not	the	only
	KP4	John.	You	are	not	the	only
	KP5	John.	You	are	not	the	only

Letter	Q3:7	**fat**	**cat**	**around**	**so**	**don't**	**think**
Patricia	KP1	**fat**	**cat**	**around**	**so**	**don't**	**think**
	KP2	fat	cat	around	so	don't	think
	KP3	fat	cat	around	so	don't	think
	KP4	fat	cat	around	so	don't	think
	KP5	fat	cat	around	so	don't	think

Letter	Q3:8	**that**	**killing**	**will**	**be**	**difficult.**
Patricia	KP1	**that**	**killing**	**will**	**be**	**difficult.**
	KP2	that	killing	will	be	difficult.
	KP3	that	killing	will	be	difficult.
	KP4	that	killing	will	be	difficult.
	KP5	that	killing	will	be	difficult.

Letter	Q3:9	**Don't**	**under estimate**	**us**	**John.**
Patricia	KP1	**Don't**	**underestimate**	**us**	**John.**
	KP2	Don't	underestimate	us	John.
	KP3	Don't	underestimate	us	John.
	KP4	Don't	underestimate	us	John.
	KP5	Don't	underestimate	us	John.

Figure 10.2 (Continued) Comparison of known Patricia Ramsey writings to ransom letter.

Letter Q3:10	Use	that	good	southern	common	
Patricia KP1	**Use**	**that**	**good**	Southern	**common**	
KP2	Use	that	good	Southern	common	
KP3	Use	that	good	Southern	common	
KP4	Use	that	good	Southern	common	
KP5	Use	that	good	Southern	common	

Letter Q3:11	sense	of	yours.	It	is	up	to
Patricia KP1	**sense**	**of**	**yours.**	**It**	**is**	**up**	**to**
KP2	sense	of	yours.	It	is	up	to
KP3	sense	of	yours.	It	is	up	to
KP4	sense	of	yours.	It	is	up	to
KP5	sense	of	yours.	It	is	up	to

Letter Q3:12	you	now	John!	
Patricia KP1	**you**	**now**	**John!**	
KP2	yo	now	John!	
KP3	you	now	John.	
KP4	you	now	John.	
KP5	you	now	John.	

Letter Q3:13	Victory!
Patricia KP1	**Victory!**
KP2	Victory,
KP3	Victory,
KP4	Victory.
KP5	Victory.

Letter Q3:14	S.B.T.C
Patricia KP1	**SBTC**
KP2	SBTC
KP3	SBTC
KP4	SBTC
KP5	SBTC

Figure 10.2 (Continued) Comparison of known Patricia Ramsey writings to ransom letter.

occurred as they do in her request writing. Mrs. Ramsey's marker P9, the abbreviation of *a.m.* with periods present, is the single contrast to the *am/pm* abbreviations without periods found in her nonrequest writing.

In addition to the style-markers noted, the paragraph formats of all three sets of writings are in contrast. John Ramsey indents less than the questioned writer, and Patricia Ramsey blocks and skips a line between paragraphs.

10.4   Findings: Quantitative

The relative diagnostic power of style-markers depends on their substance and strength. Substance relates to the type and amount of variation, and strength to the significance (relative importance) of the variation. Considering the range of variation presented by Mrs. Ramsey's writing only, the presence of substantial dissimilarities in her stylistic profile vis-à-vis that of

Number	Location	Style-Marker in John Ramsey's Writing
John Ramsey	Ransom Note	
		SPELLING
JR1	Q1:4	Misspelling of *foreign* as **foriegn**
JR2	Q1:5	Correct spelling of **business**
JR3	Q1:6	Correct spelling of **possession**
JR4	Q2:6	Absence of correction in writing the word **denied**
		PUNCTUATION
JR5	Q1:1	Absence of period after **Mr** in KJ1 & KJ2
JR6	Q1:18	Presence of comma after **When you get home,** clause
JR7	Q2:12	Absence of periods after initials in **FBI**
JR8	Q3:14	Presence of period after last letter **C.** in KJ1 & KJ2
		WORD FORMATION
JR9	Q1:17	Use of longer form, **attache**, in KJ2
JR10	Q1:20	Use of a plus-like **&** sign instead of the word *and*
JR11	Q2:2	Use of single word for **pickup**
JR12	Q2:26	Use of single word for **outsmart**
JR13	Q3:9	Use of single word for **underestimate**
		SYNTAX
JR14	Q1:6	Absence of relative pronoun **that** in KJ2 & KJ3
		MONEY AMOUNTS
JR15a	Q1:12	Use of only one vertical stroke in **dollar sign**
JR15b	Q1:13	Use of only one vertical stroke in **dollar sign**
JR15c	Q1:14	Use of only one vertical stroke in **dollar sign**
JR15d	Q1:15	Use of only one vertical stroke in **dollar sign**
JR15e	Q1:15	Use of only one vertical stroke in **dollar sign**

Figure 10.3 Style-markers of John Ramsey that contrast to questioned ransom note. Note: Style-markers JR1, JR2, JR5, JR7, JR10, and JR15 were found in John Ramsey's pre-12/26/96 natural writing, and they appear just as they do in the samples of his post-12/26/96 requested writing.

the evidence sample is readily established by the qualitative description of all variables in Section 10.3.

However, limitations of the data (see Section 10.6) suggest that measurement of the strength of single style-markers and of the aggregate profile of all markers within the questioned letter itself would more objectively establish the uniqueness of the stylistic profile demonstrated by the ransom letter.

Number	Location	Style-Marker in Patricia Ramsey's Writing
Patricia Ramsey	Ransom Note	
		SPELLING
PR1	Q1:5	Correct spelling of **business**
PR2	Q1:8	Correct spelling of **possession**
PR3	Q1:23	Misspelling of *advise* as **advize**
PR4	Q2:6	Absence of correction in writing the word **denied**
PR5	Q2:7	Misspelling of *burial* as **buriel**
PR6	Q2:10	Misspelling (and correction) of *advise* as **advize**
PR7	Q3:4	Misspelling of *scrutiny* as **scruitiny** in KP1 & KP2
PR8	Q3:10	Use of capital *S* on the word **Southern**
		PUNCTUATION
PR9	Q1:20	Presence of periods in **a.m.** abbreviation
PR10	Q3:13	Use of **periods** (instead of !) in KP2 & KP3
PR11	Q3:14	Absence of periods after capitalized initials **SBTC**
		WORD FORMATION
PR12	Q1:8	Use of single word for **unharmed**
PR13	Q2:1	Addition of correct form of article **an** in KP2 & KP3
PR14	Q2:2	Use of two words without hyphen for **pick up**
PR15	Q2:24	Use of two words for **counter measures**
PR16	Q2:26	Use of single word for **outsmart**
PR17	Q3:9	Use of single word for **underestimate**
		MONEY AMOUNTS
PR18a	Q1:12	Use of **decimal point** without cents marker
PR18b	Q1:13	Use of **decimal point** without cents marker
PR18c	Q1:14	Use of word **dollar** without dollar sign: $
PR18d	Q1:15	Use of **decimal point** without cents marker in KP3
PR18e	Q1:15	Use of word **dollar** without dollar sign: $

Figure 10.4 Style-markers of Patricia Ramsey that contrast to questioned ransom note. Note: Style-markers PR11, PR14, and PR18 were found in Patricia Ramsey's pre-12/26/96 (i.e., precrime) natural writing, and they appear just as they do in the samples of her post-12/26/96 requested writing.

The significance of selected variables in the questioned letter can be established using base rates of individual occurrence of each variable and of estimated frequency of joint occurrence of all variables. In other words, how many writers in a representative population have the profile of joint occurrence of all style variables identified in the questioned letter?

Questioned RANSOM NOTE	Q1:5 "bussiness"	Q1:8 "posession"	Q1:23 "advise"	Q2:10 "advise"	Q2:6 "di/enied"	Q2:7 "burial"	Q3:4 "scrutiny"
12/26/96	bussiness	posession	advize	advise	denied	burial	scrutiny
Known P. RAMSEY WRITINGS	K "business"	K "possession"	K "advize"	K "advis/ze"	K "denied"	K "buriel"	K "scruitiny"
1/4/97-1	business	possession	advize	advise	denied	buriel	scruitiny
1/4/97-2	business	possession	advize	advise	denied	buriel	scrutiny
1/4/97-3	business	possession	advize	advise	denied	burie)	Scrutiny
2/28/97-1	business	possession	advize	Advize	denied	buriel	scrutiny
2/28/97-2	business	possession	advize	advize	denied	buriel	scrutiny

Figure 10.5 Ransom note vis-à-vis Patricia Ramsey writings: spelling.

Questioned RANSOM NOTE	Q3:10 southern	Q1:20 10 am	Q3:14 S.B.T.C
12/26/96	*southern*	10 am	S.B.T.C
Known P. RAMSEY WRITINGS	K Southern	K 10 a.m.	K SBTC
1/4/97-1	Southern	10 a.m.	SBTC
1/4/97-2	Southern	10 a.m.	SBTC
1/4/97-3	Southern	10 a.m.	SBTC
2/28/97-1	Southern	10 A.m.	SBTC
2/28/97-2	Southern	10 A.M.	SBTC

Figure 10.6 Ransom note vis-à-vis Patricia Ramsey writings: capital S and punctuation.

In cases involving the matching of profiles of stylistic variables, the question is: what is the probability that someone other than the known writer could have authored the questioned material? In a case with no apparent association between reference and evidence writings, it makes little sense to continue to contrast Mrs. Ramsey's stylistic characteristics to that of the questioned letter. However, one question that can be asked is: does the questioned writing contain enough variation to estimate the probability that anyone other than its author could match the stylistic profile of the questioned letter?

Since observation of the differences between the questioned letter in evidence and Mrs. Ramsey's known writings indicates that an association does not exist between them, the reference writings of Mrs. Ramsey are used at this point only to provide alternate variants (variant number 2 in following figures) for stylistic variables found in the ransom letter. What is measured is the significance of a potential association between the stylistic profile of the questioned letter and the writing of any other writer, Mrs. Ramsey included.

For purposes of this analysis, the American Writing Project (see Chapter 9) made available a subcorpus of writings from Colorado. The subcorpus contains 338 pieces of writing, each representing a separate writer. Subsets of typed writings (197) and hand-writings (141) were identified, but these were combined for the analysis of most stylistic variables. The purpose of studying a set of Colorado writings was to determine how often a matching profile could be expected to occur in a population of Colorado writers, i.e., in a corpus of writing most likely reflecting the speech community of the author of the ransom note. This requires that three things be determined: the relative frequency of occurrence of each style marker, the degree of independence of each style variable, and an estimate of their joint probability of occurrence.

Questioned RANSOM NOTE	Q2:1 a earlier	Q1:8 un harmed	Q3:9 under estimate	Q2:2 pick-up	Q2:24 countermeasures
12/26/96	d earlier	un harmed	under estimate	pick-up	countermeasures
Known P RAMSEY WRITINGS	K an earlier	K unharmed	K underestimate	K pick up	K counter measures
1/4/97-1	a earlier	unharmed	underestimate	pickup	counter measures
1/4/97-2	an earlier	unharmed	underestimate	pick up	Counter measures
1/4/97-3	an earlier	unharmed	underestimate	Pick up	Counter measures
2/28/97-1	an earlier	unharmed	underestimate	pick up	counter measures
2/28/97-2	an earlier	unharmed	underestimate	pick up	counter measures

Figure 10.7 Ransom note vis-à-vis Patricia Ramsey writings: word formation.

QUESTIONED RANSOM NOTE 12/26/96	Q1:12 $118,000.00	Q1:13 $100,000	Q1:14 $100 [bills]	Q1:15 $18,000	Q1:15 $20 [bills]
	$118,000.00	$100,000	$100	$18,000	$20
KNOWN P. RAMSEY WRITINGS	K	K	K	K	K
1/4/97-1	one hundred eighteen thousand dollars	One hundred thousand dollars	100 dollar	eighteen Thousand dollars	20 dollar
1/4/97-2	$118,000.	$100,000	100 dollar	$18,000	20 dollar
1/4/97-3	$118,000	$100000	$100 dollar	$18,000	$20 dollar
2/28/97-1	$118,000.	$100,000 dollars	100 dollar	$18,000 dollars	20 dollar
2/28/97-2	$118,000	$100,000	one hundred dollar	eighteen thousand	twenty dollar

Figure 10.8 Ransom note vis-à-vis Patricia Ramsey writings: money amounts.

A set of 13 variables was used to establish the stylistic profile of the questioned writing; see Figure 10.9. Nine of the variables (PR 1, 2, 3, 4, 9, 11, 12, 13, and 14) were identified in the independent analysis of the questioned letter. Four of the variables (PR 5, 6, 18a, and 18c) were identified based on the independent analysis of Mrs. Ramsey's known writings. Six stylistic variables from the questioned letter were selected for quantitative analysis, based on their frequent occurrence in the randomly selected handwritten and typed texts of the subcorpus of 338 Colorado writers. The variables studied appear in Figure 10.10, along with their variants: variant 1 from the questioned letter and variant 2 from Mrs. Ramsey's request and nonrequest writings.

10.4.1 Joint Probability of One Writer Using All Variables

Individual probability of writer-use of each variable: Frequency of occurrence may be related to number of occurrences of a given variable in the overall corpus or to the number of writers in the corpus who use a particular variant. This is an analysis of the number of writers in which each variable occurred one or more times. The probability *p* of use by a writer was individually calculated for each of six variables in the 338 writers of the corpus. Individual probabilities of writers using variant number 1 of each variable in the corpus are presented in Figure 10.11. (There are various ways to count variables and calculate individual and joint probabilities. The statistical bases for these calculations are presented in Chapter 6.).

Independence of variables: The multiplication rule for independent events is used below to determine the probability of the joint occurrence of two or more style variables in one writer. This means that the calculation of joint probabilities is based on the assumption that all variables used are independent, i.e., that the occurrence of one will not affect the probability of occurrence of another.

As a matter of fact, of the six categorical variables used, very few of the marked variants (variant number 1) co-occur in the same writer, but there is no linguistic reason why they should. Consider all six variables. The most suspicious pair is that of detached *un-* and *under-*. One might assume that spacing the prefix *un-* away from its following root might co-occur with spacing *under-* away from the second part of a compound word. These are both morphological phenomena, but *un-* is a derivational prefix and *under-* is a free root compounded to another root. There is no evidence of their association in these data or elsewhere to indicate that a writer who separates a prefix will also separate joined compounds. Also, given enough occurrences in a reference corpus of writing, the independence of linguistic variables to be used can be statistically evaluated by a measure such as the coefficient of correlation (see Section 8.2.7).

Variables	Ransom Note	Patricia Ramsey	Writers Total n	Writers Total %	Variant 1 in Corpus	Writers n	Writers %	Variant 2 in Corpus	Writers n	Writers %
SPELLING										
PR1 business[2]	bussiness	business	15	4.4%	bussiness	2	13%	business	13	87%
PR2 possession	posession	possession	0	0%	possession	0	0%	possession	0	0%
PR3 advise	advise	advize	0	0%	advize	0	0%	advise	0	0%
PR4 denied	dinied	denied	11	3.3%	dinied	0	0%	denied	11	100%
PR5 burial	burial	buriel	0	0%	buriel	0	0%	burial	0	0%
PR6 scrutiny	scrutiny	scruitiny	0	0%	scruitiny	0	0%	scrutiny	0	0%
PUNCTUATION										
PR9 a.m./p.m.	am	a.m.	5	1.5%	a.m.	3	60%	am	2	40%
PR11 initials	S.B.T.C	SBTC	146	43.2%	S.B.T.C.	58	40%	SBTC[4]	88	60%
WORD FORMATION										
PR12 prefix un-[3]	un harmed	unharmed	108	32.%	un harmed	6	6%	unharmed	102	94%
PR13 an + noun	a earlier	an earlier	100	29.6%	a earlier	0	0%	an earlier	100	100%
PR17 under-	under estimate	underestimate	26	8%	under estimate	0	0%	underestimate	26	100%
MONEY AMOUNTS										
PR18a cents	$118,000.00	$118,000.	28	8.3%	$118,000.	19	73%	$118,000.00	9	27%
PR18c no. words	$100	100 dollar	59	17.5%	100 dollar	31	53%	$100	28	47%

Notes:

[1] Of the 338 writers, 197 letters were typewritten and 141 handwritten.

[2] Bolded variables 11 to 18c are those that occurred frequently enough for measurement.

[3] When a writer mixed both variants, the writer was not counted for this analysis.

[4] Two capitalized initials (G.I.S and R.R) occurred with the last period missing, as in "S.B.T.C"

Figure 10.9 Relative frequency of selected variables in a corpus of 300 Colorado writers.[1]

VARIABLE TYPE	Style Marker Variable	Variant 1 Ransom Letter	Variant 2 Patricia Ramsey
1. PUNCTUATION	PR11 initials w/ periods	S.B.T.C	SBTC
2. WORD FORMATION	PR12 prefix *un-* spaced	un harmed	unharmed
3. WORD FORMATION	PR13 *a* + V-initial noun	a earlier	an earlier
4. WORD FORMATION	PR17 *under-* spaced	under estimate	underestimate
5. MONEY AMOUNTS	PR18a decimal w/ cents	$118,000.00	$118,000.
6. MONEY AMOUNTS	PR18c numbers or words	$100 bill	$100 dollar bill

Figure 10.10 Six variables selected for quantitative analysis.

Writers Using Each Variable	Variable 1	Variable 2	Variable 3	Variable 4	Variable 5	Variable 6
p = Individual Probabilities of Writer Use	58/146 pl = .397	6/108 p2 = .056	5/100 p3 = .050	5/26 p4 = .192	19/28 p5 = .679	31/59 p6 = .525

Figure 10.11 Individual probabilities of writer use of variables 1 to 6.

Joint probabilities of occurrence: The joint probability P of all six individual variables occurring simultaneously in one writer was calculated for the corpus. The joint probability of the simultaneous occurrence of two or more variables is the product of the separate probabilities of all individual variables:

$$P = .397 \times .056 \times .050 \times .192 \times .679 \times .525 = 0.000076$$

Joint probabilities of nonoccurrence: The joint probability of all six individual variables not occurring simultaneously in one writer is $1 - P$:

$$Q = 1 - 0.000076 = 0.999924$$

10.4.2   A More Conservative Analysis of Joint Probability

Likelihood ratio statistic, Olkin's *lambda*: The ratio of the probability of identity markers (occurrence of variables in a writer) to the probability of nonidentity markers (nonoccurrence of variables in a writer) is a measure of the probability of chance coincidence of factors (variables) and is a more conservative estimate of chance coincidence than the calculation of joint probabilities of all factors.

It is the likelihood ratio (*lambda*) that requires the calculation of nonoccurrence of each variable. Since the total of the probability ranges from 0

	Variable 1	Variable 5	Variable 6
Individual Probabilities of Occurrence: p	58/146	19/28	31/59
	40%	68%	53%

Figure 10.12 Individual probabilities of writer use of variables 1, 5, and 6.

to 1, the probability of nonoccurrence is 1 – P. In this case, the joint probability of occurrence in a writer P is 0.000076, and the joint probability of nonoccurrence in a writer is 0.999924, so *lambda* = 0.000076. The closer to 0, the less likely the joint probability of identity (occurrence in a writer) is due to chance.

$$lambda = \frac{\text{P of occurrence}}{\text{P of nonoccurrence}} = \frac{0.000076}{0.999924} = 0.000076$$

The probability of all six variables occurring in one writer is 0%, or just over one in 13,000. The likelihood of these six variables occurring together by chance is also zero.

10.4.3   The Most Conservative Analysis of Joint Probability

Individual probability of occurrence calculations: The most conservative analysis of joint probability would be to contrast the variants of just the three variables of the questioned letter that also occur in Mrs. Ramsey's before-the-fact, nonrequest writings: variables 1, 5, and 6, from Figure 10.10. Individual probabilities of occurrence of corpus writers using variant number 1 of variables 1, 5, and 6 may be found in Figure 10.12.

Joint probabilities of occurrence calculation: The joint probability of just these three individual variables occurring simultaneously in the same writer is the product of their individual probabilities:

$$P = .397 \times .679 \times .525 = 0.1415$$

Joint probabilities of nonoccurrence calculation: The joint probability of all six individual variables not occurring simultaneously in the same writer is 1 – P:

$$Q = 1 - .1415 = 0.8585$$

Likelihood ratio statistic, Olkin's *lambda*: In the case of these three variables, the joint probability of occurrence P is 0.1415, and the joint probability of nonoccurrence is 0.8585, so *lambda* = 0.1648. The closer to 0, the less likely that the joint probability of identity (occurrence in a writer) is due to chance.

$$lambda = \frac{.1415}{.8585} = 0.1648$$

The probability of these three variables occurring in one writer is 14%, or one in seven. The likelihood of these three variables occurring together by chance is 17%.

10.5　Discussion

Exclusion of Mrs. Ramsey as the author of the questioned letter is indicated because the stylistic profiles of her reference writings and the evidence writing are different. There are 18 to 20 variables (depending on how they are counted) with contrasting variants in the two sets of writings. Further, the questioned letter contains sufficient variability to estimate the probability at zero that its stylistic profile could be randomly matched. In the most conservative of analyses, in examining just the three variables that occur in and also differ from Mrs. Ramsey's precrime, nonrequest writing, the probability of these three variables randomly occurring in any one writer is estimated at 14 to 17%.

10.5.1　Strength of Findings

Authorship exclusion requires presence of significant differences; identification requires absence of significant differences as well as presence of significant similarities between questioned and known writings. In this case, the substance and strength of differences between the questioned ransom letter and the known Ramsey writings are sufficient to exclude Mrs. Ramsey as the writer of the ransom letter. The differences are substantial and strong insofar as they show the broad range of individual difference in the language system of each writer.

For example, note that the questioned writer's hyphenation of the compound word "pick-up," contrasts with the Ramseys' probably unconscious habits of writing it as one word (John's *pickup*), or as two words without hyphen (Patricia's *pick up*). The remaining respective habits of style used by John and Patricia Ramsey all show, in varying degrees, underlying language systems very different from each other, as well as from the writer of the questioned letter.

10.5.2   Limitations of Findings

There are two known limitations of the data: the request writings produced just after the first one are not from dictation, making conscious manipulation of the reference samples possible, and not all variables occur in Mrs. Ramsey's nonrequest writings. Two additional limitations relate to the frequency estimates of the patterned stylistic profile of the questioned letter: one is that the qualitative analysis does not take into account the possibility of attempted disguise; another is that the corpus of baseline writing used is from Colorado writers, and the questioned writer may not be from Colorado (e.g., the Ramseys).

With respect to the possibility of attempted disguise, manipulation of the nonrequest, precrime samples in the known Ramsey reference writings was not possible. Additionally, most variables identified in the Ramseys' request writings, in writings used here to exclude the Ramseys as writers of the ransom letter and in those not used (e.g., dictated word lists), contain such a patterned level of consistency that the conscious manipulation of even the most carefully executed request writings is highly improbable, given the circumstances of their production.

10.6   Conclusion

Patricia Ramsey is excluded as the writer of the questioned ransom letter. This conclusion is based on three facts:

1. There are substantial and significant dissimilarities between her range of variation and that of the ransom letter.
2. Limitations present in the available data (i.e., lack of more than one contemporaneous, dictated request sample, nonoccurrence of some variables in the nonrequest samples, and chance of disguise in evidence or reference writings) do not diminish the significance of reliable available data or indicate language disguise.
3. The range of variation measured in the questioned letter constitutes sufficient basis for comparison to any suspect writer, given that the probability of replicating it by chance in other than its own writer is near zero.

Stylistic Variation in Authorship Cases

11

GERALD R. McMENAMIN

11.1 Cases in Forensic Linguistics

The purpose of this chapter is to provide citations of adjudicated cases in which forensic stylistics testimony was given, as well as examples of unadjudicated cases wherein forensic stylistics evidence was prepared and may have played some role in case settlement. In addition, style-markers from 80 cases of questioned authorship are summarized in Section 11.3. Although such a summary does not provide the aggregate stylistic profile of writings pertinent to each case, it does allow study of actual style-markers as well as their occurrence by case.

Linguists have testified in many cases on various language-related issues. Although a comprehensive list of case citations for the U.S. and other countries has yet to be compiled, this author can characterize and cite his cases. Linguistic analysis during the period from 1982 to 2001 was done for 240 cases, 201 (88%) civil and 30 (12%) criminal, as summarized in Figure 11.1.

Three types of cases are presented: questioned authorship, questioned meaning, and discourse analysis. Of these, questioned authorship cases represent most (93%) of the work of forensic stylistics. Discourse analysis is an area of specialization in linguistics distinct from stylistics. The author's involvement in matters related to discourse analysis is mostly associated with Spanish language cases.

Of all 240 cases, 24 (10%) were adjudicated at trial. It is evident, therefore, that most cases are settled out of court for one reason or another, usually after evidence is presented in report form or at deposition. The adjudicated cases of this writer (except for three presented in confidential venues) are cited in the next section.

11.2 Adjudicated Cases

Appellate Decisions:

- *In the Matter of the Estate of Violet Houssien, 3AN-98-59 P/R, Superior Court for the State of Alaska, Anchorage, 1999.* A will and supporting letters (typed by an unknown person, "Kim") were purported to have been authored by the decedent and were presented by her former

CASES 1982–2001	CIVIL		CRIMINAL		TOTAL	
Case Type	n	%	n	%	n	%
Questioned Authorship	201	96%	23	76%	224	93%
Questioned Meaning	9	4%	2	7%	11	5%
Analysis of Discourse	0	0%	5	17%	5	2%
TOTAL	210	100%	30	100%	240	100%

Figure 11.1 Civil and criminal cases by case type. Note: 240 total cases: 88% civil, 12% criminal.

neighbors, but their authorship was disputed by contestants. The Court decided in favor of the decedent's siblings, rejecting the will. From the Sept. 23, 1999 Decision. The decision was upheld in *Crittell v. Bingo* et al. by the Supreme Court of Alaska No. S-9468. From the Nov. 9, 2001 Decision No. 5496: "Though denied by the [appellants], the evidence proves that the Will and "Kim" papers were prepared by the [appellants] or at their direction." This decision is discussed in Chapter 7, and can be accessed at *http://www.touchngo.com/sp/html/sp-5496.htm*.

- *In the Matter of the Appeal by Amarjit (Jack) Saluja, 30082 and 94-16, 1994, California State Personnel Board, 1994.* This case is found at *www.spb.ca.gov/spblaw/pdsindx.htm*. In this state employment dismissal case, the employee denied writing letters harmful to other employees. The court found that he did write them.
- *Oregon v. Crescenzi, CA A90559, Court of Appeals of Oregon, 152 Ore. App. 567; 953 P.2d 433; 1998 Ore. App., 1998, Deschutes County Circuit Court. No. 94-CR-0258-ST, affirmed without opinion.* The defendant denied writing a letter sent to the Bend Police Department with details of his wife's death. The case is reported in *The Bend Bulletin*, June 8 and 11, 1995.
- *Regina v. Gurtler, 7134, Sask. C.A., Sask. D. Crim. 260; 10.35.00-08, 1998.* The accused was convicted of the second degree murder of his wife. At trial, the accused's position was that his wife committed suicide, leaving suicide notes on her computer; however, the Crown adduced direct and circumstantial evidence to link the accused with the homicide, including linguistic evidence that the accused wrote the wife's purported suicide notes. The Court dismissed an appeal against conviction on the ground that the verdict was unreasonable and not supported by the evidence saying, "In this case, there was cogent evidence for the jury to weigh and consider. On the evidence, the jury was satisfied beyond a reasonable doubt that the accused killed his wife. The evidence was reasonably capable of supporting the jury's conclusion."

U.S. Federal Cases:

- *Dewey v. Western Minerals and Wytana, CV 86-97-BLG-JFB, U.S. District Court, District of Montana, 1990.* The plaintiff was determined to have manufactured and mailed letters in an attempt to fabricate evidence in support of a previously unsuccessful claim of blacklisting by his employer. From the Decision of February 20, 1990:

  > Plaintiff had access to the legitimate letters of reference written by Decker employees ... Comparison of the linguistic characteristics of the two paste-up letters with those of various other documents known to have been written by the persons in question led one of defendants' experts to the conclusion that both letters were written by one person, or two persons working in collusion. ... The expert also found that the letters exhibited linguistic patterns and traits markedly different from those of documents known to have been authored by the purported signatories.

- *Ilic v. Liquid Air, 92-199-CIV-ORL-22, U.S. District Court, Middle District of Florida, 1993.* The plaintiff claimed that memos affecting his employment were written by a supervisor, who denied writing them.
- *CIGNA v. Polaris, 1997.* The defendant made a large insurance claim for a yacht that sank. The plaintiff investigated the claim because the defendant had three previous yachts that sank. The authorship issue related to the value of the yacht, which progressively increased as it was bought and sold by three apparently different companies. However, the letters and written documentation of all the "different" companies appeared to have one author, the defendant. The case was reported in the *Los Angeles Daily Journal*, 110:138:1, July 18, 1987.

Superior Court Civil Cases:

- *Beard v. Wittern, V-014504-4, Superior Court of Alameda County, California, 1999.* This case was indirectly related to another matter in which many anonymous letters were received by a company that wanted to know if all were authored by the same person and if one candidate writer was the author.
- *Boyar v. Boyar, Superior Court of Los Angeles County, California, 1986.* In a marriage dissolution matter, the husband denied writing a letter regarding settlement of community property. The issue was whether either the husband or wife could be excluded or identified as its author.
- *Brisco v. VFE Corp, and Related Cross-Action, 272028-2, Superior Court of Fresno County, California, 1984.* The defendant suffered losses as

result of an anonymous letter that accused the defendant of engaging in criminal business practices to secure business. The Court found that the plaintiff wrote the anonymous letter. From the July 9, 1984 decision: "12. On or about May of 1982, [Plaintiff] authored an anonymous letter.... 14. Authorship of this anonymous letter was determined by expert linguistic testimony." Aspects of this case are documented in Finnegan (1990); the case is also reported in *The Fresno Bee*, July 12, 1984.

- *Butte College v. CSEA Member, California Office of Administrative Hearings, Sacramento, California,* 1994. The respondent in this case tape recorded and transcribed conversations in an employment matter; the question related to whether the transcription actually represented spoken language or not.
- *Estate of Merrill Miller v. Gunderson, Superior Court of Orange County, California,* 1994. The issue here was which of two attorneys drafted the will of the decedent.
- *Goeddel v. Rawlins, 657688, Superior Court of San Diego County, California,* 1993. This was a case of alleged unfair competition between ex-spouses; one received interest in their communal business at the dissolution of their marriage and the other started a competing business after the dissolution. In question was the linguistic similarity of written educational materials used by both businesses.
- *In Re Estate of Sam Zakessian, 39269, Superior Court of Marin County,* 1997. At issue was the meaning of the language in a brief holographic will. Aspects of this case are documented in Kaplan (1998).
- *In Re The Marriage of Kepic and O'Bara, RFL 35956, Superior Court of San Bernardino County, California,* 1999. At a child custody hearing, petitioner Kepic maintained that the child's letter requesting to live with respondent O'Bara was not written by the child.
- *State Farm v. Toabe, Superior Court of Fresno County, October 15, 1986.* The question in this case related to the meaning of the phrase "bodily injury" as it was used in the State Farm auto insurance policy.
- *Villafranca v. Soukup, CV 751860, Superior Court of Santa Clara County, California,* 1998. The defendant was accused of writing a widely distributed note, the content of which was harmful to the plaintiff.

Superior Court Criminal Cases:

- *Arizona v. Calo, CR 89-02973, Superior Court of Maricopa County, Arizona,* 1991. The defendant's wife maintained a typewritten diary documenting activities of her husband and an accomplice. The diary could be used as evidence against the accomplice, but the woman denied writing it.

- *Arizona v. Muzakkir and Rasul, CR-29681 and CR-29722, Superior Court of Pima County,* 1990. The name of a third party was signed on anonymous letters related to this criminal matter, making her appear to be their author.
- *California v. Armas, NA 023430, Superior Court of Los Angeles County, California,* 1996. The defendant maintained that he did not author or write a confession allegedly signed by him. This case is documented in Chapter 12.
- *California v. Whitham, C 10514, Superior Court of Kings County, California,* 1993. The defendant was convicted of murdering her 11-year old foster daughter by feeding her pudding laced with toxic amounts of drugs, because of fear the girl had told others of being sexually abused. The defendant denied dictating the suicide note written by the girl. The case was reported in *The Fresno Bee*, July 28, October 15 and 19, 1993.
- *Colorado v. Johnson, Superior Court of El Paso County, Colorado,* 1989. The defendant was appealing his conviction for arson when three anonymous letters confessing to the arson were sent to his attorney. The letters contained many features of the English spoken by many African Americans in the U.S., but defendant is white. The case was reported in *The Colorado Springs Gazette Telegraph*, February 7, 8, and 21, 1989.

11.3   Examples of Unadjudicated Cases

11.3.1   Civil Cases

Employment:

- An employee who received an anonymous letter regarding her performance believed her boss to be the author.
- An employee was severely burned in a restaurant accident and an engineering firm was asked to assess the equipment failure that caused the injury. A long, very negative evaluation appeared on the engineering firm's letterhead, but the firm denied preparing such a letter. The restaurant's insurance company wanted to know if the injured employee had written the letter.
- A supervisor denied writing certain memoranda about a former employee. The writings had the supervisor's name on them and the employee wanted to know if it could be demonstrated that the supervisor had actually written them.
- An equipment manufacturer wanted to know if certain anonymous letters to employees were coming from one suspect employee.

- A hospital employee received a lengthy disciplinary letter from a medical supervisor who denied writing the letter. The hospital wanted to know if the employee or the supervisor had written the letter.

Business:

- A bank customer was the subject of a letter to the editor of a large newspaper, the apparent writer of which was a bank employee who denied authorship.
- A small business received four anonymous and harassing letters. They wanted to know if they were all written by the same person and if that person was the former spouse of the owner.
- A propane gas explosion killed a homeowner whose survivors wanted to determine the technical skills and training of the delivery driver. The issue related to whether the narrative answers written on the state competency tests of various drivers were their individual answers or were copied from a single sample test with answers already completed.
- A bank received various anonymous letters advising against financing a large business project. The company provided a list of likely suspect writers.
- A large hospital received a number of anonymous letters threatening an administrator. The hospital identified a number of present and former employees as possible writers.
- A large company began receiving letters threatening and degrading a woman employee. The company suspected the author to be another employee with whom she had had a previous personal relationship.
- A company received a series of anonymous letters and wanted to know if they were written by an employee of a competing company.
- A series of anonymous flyers was distributed around a large baking company, alleging racial discrimination and harassment by management. The company presented known writings of various employees whom they considered possible writers.
- A frequent flyer alleged that an employee of a large airline was sending him offensive and anonymous letters. The airline wanted to know if the customer had actually sent the letters as part of a continuing campaign of complaints against the company.
- A deceased entertainer was the purported writer of an agreement to give a percentage of his earnings to an agent. The agent claimed a part of the estate, representatives of which wanted to know if the entertainer had actually authored and prepared the letter.
- A man was filmed on a security camera faxing an offensive anonymous letter to his employer; however, he said that he did not write the letter, but that someone else had written it and asked him to fax it. The

company wanted to know if he or the other employee could be excluded or identified as author.

- An Australian contractor was interested in discovering the author of various anonymous letters that revealed proprietary information to other companies bidding on the same projects. The content of the letters was so specific that the author was indicated as one of a small number of employees who had that information.
- A damaging letter arrived at a hospital on the letterhead of an equipment distributing company. The company stood to lose the hospital's business as a result and denied writing it. The business provided writing samples of every person in the company for the purpose of excluding all possible internal writers.
- The board of directors of a large transport company received anonymous letters regarding the sexual exploits of male employees with one administrative secretary. The board had no suspects, but eventually provided comparison writings of some possible writers.
- A letter of agreement related to a real estate transaction was thought to contain an added paragraph which was not part of the original document when it was signed. The issue was whether the questioned paragraph matched the language of the rest of the letter.
- Various letters of agreement and contracts were prepared and signed, all relating to the same business transaction and containing similar language. One, however, was alleged to have been fabricated in a hotel room in Italy. The issue was whether or not all but one of the agreements demonstrated similar characteristics.

Public Policy:

- An activist from an environmentalist group received a threatening letter, which was matter for great concern because a member of the group had already suffered physical violence. The group presented sample writings from various possible suspect writers.
- A nonprofit organization received anonymous letters about the drug habits of one of its employees. The issue was to exclude or identify as their author the client who denied writing the letters but whose signature appeared on them.

Law:

- Two documents, an "opening brief" and a "motion to compel," were the subject of a dispute among attorneys, each of whom claimed to have written one. Their paralegal, however, asserted that he wrote and typed all of one and parts of the other document.

- A Belgian judge ordered the examination of two English-language agreements for the purpose of determining if they shared a single author.
- A judge was accused of writing offensive letters under the name of an attorney and another judge. The question was whether the judge could be excluded as the author of the letters.
- A judge in the Philippines was accused of having an interested party to a case draft his judgment in the case. One of the litigants in the case wanted to know if the judgment was consistent with past written decisions of the same judge.

Education:

- Damaging anonymous letters were being written to a high school faculty; based on content and a typewriter identification, the administration suspected one employee of writing them.
- A college student was accused of an honor code violation, i.e., turning in a term paper written by someone other than the student. The student wanted an evaluation of the professor's reasons for reporting this as plagiarism and also a demonstration based on attested writings that the paper was his own work.

Medicine:

- A physician's cases were scrutinized by six reviewers; he wanted to know if the six resulting reviews were written by six different authors or just one.
- In a medical malpractice case, a doctor denied making an entry on a chart. The handwriting analysis was inconclusive, so the doctor's insurance company wanted to know if the entry was consistent or not with other entries known to have been made by the same physician.

Wills and Estates:

- A large promissory note appeared in the settlement proceedings of an estate wherein the executors were feuding among themselves. The issue was whether the note was prepared by the decedent or by its intended beneficiary, one of the executors.
- A holographic will was written by a woman with a diagnosed multiple personality disorder. The issue was to determine if her known diary-type writings could be differentiated by respective personalities, then if the written language of any one or all of the personalities could be associated with the language of the will.

Family:

- A woman received a letter purportedly from her husband confessing indiscretions and his contracting a serious sexually transmitted disease. The husband denied writing the letter.
- A series of underground newsletters that defamed members of a well-known family were circulated for a time in a community. The family suspected one person to be the author of at least one of the newsletters.
- Immediately after the dissolution of his marriage, a man was fired from his position as CEO of a company whose board of directors had received a letter from an anonymous shareholder who exposed unusual personal activities of the man. The man wanted to know if his former wife was the "shareholder" who had written the letter.

Religion:

- An anonymous letter was distributed reporting that a very high-level cleric was engaged in pedophilia. Church officials wanted to know if one of a few suspect writers could be identified as the author of the letter.

Media:

- A TV news program asked for an evaluation of the report of a self-proclaimed linguistics expert profiling the writer of a letter about a juror in the O.J. Simpson trial.
- An investigative reporter for a newspaper submitted a letter with comparison writings of the alleged writer, wanting to know if there was evidence to exclude or identify him.
- A Los Angeles newspaper was interested in knowing what the stylistic characteristics were in the Unabomber manifesto.

Meaning:

- Litigants disagreed over the meaning of language in their written agreement regarding the planting of trees on agricultural land. The issue related to determining whether the language of the agreement could be unambiguously interpreted.

11.3.2 Criminal Cases

- A confession was in the defendant's handwriting, but he testified at trial that it had actually been written by another suspect and simply copied by the defendant.

- U.K. solicitors handling a murder appeal for defendants asked for an evaluation of previously used evidence and for a new analysis of the evidence. The issue was that one defendant insisted that the words in his confession statement, dictated to and written down by police, were not his.
- A defendant was accused of murder and made various statements to police and others, who in turn repeated and transcribed the unrecorded statements. The defense questioned the veracity of the transcription of one incriminating statement. Transcriptions of recorded statements attested to be the defendant's were available for comparison.
- An African-American man asked an undercover police officer, "What's chillin'?" He was promptly arrested for soliciting drugs or a drug deal. The issue was whether or not, "What's chillin'" was such a request in the contemporary slang of African American youth.

11.4   Style-Markers Found in 80 Authorship Cases

Numbers after specific variables indicate the number of cases (out of 80) in which this variable played a role.

11.4.1   Text Format

Variation in Format	Examples
Variation in memo format: 3	date, to, from, subject, etc.
General layout/format: 4	postscript, page layout
Text division: 8	titles, centering, subsections, columns, etc.
Distinctive spacing in address and letter: 1	spacing of address, salutation, and body of letter
Position of page numbers at top: 6	circled numbers at top center; -2- top center; *Page 2* at top left; *3)* at top left; *Page −2* at top left; *2.* top right
Running-head on pages: 1	
Form of date: 15	*'94; 7/25/95; 29 June 1996; September 14, 1988* vs. *15 September 1988*; dates within Text: Month and Year with/without Specific Day; no date; vertical position of date; horizontal position: left (4), middle (2), right (3), bottom center (1); ordinal numbers in date
Date followed by period: 1	*January 24, 1997.*
Absence of title for addressee: 2	*James Hargrove* w/o *Mr.* or *III*, no *Mr.* or *Justice*

Presence of title for addressee: 1	title *Regent* with first and last name
Full forms in address used instead of abbreviations: 7	*Street, Boulevard, Avenue, East, West*
Absent punctuation in address: 2	
Position of address: 2	arrangement of date, address, return address
Zip codes: 4	nine-digit zip code; position and spacing of zip code
Salutation followed by colon or comma: 10	*Gentlemen:* or *Dear Sir,*
No punctuation after salutation: 7	*Dear Marie*
Spacing of salutation above body of letter: 6	2 spaces; 3–5 spaces
Blocked vs. indented salutations: 1	
First name as salutation: 2	*Charlotte,*
Variable spacing between address and salutation: 2	
Letter opening: 1	*I am writing …*
Distinctive spacing: 24	word, line, paragraph
Spacing between word and punctuation: 16	0–3 spaces before and after word or quote marks
Spacing between period and following word: 14	0–3 spaces
Comma spacing: 2	no space after; one space on either side
Spacing of parentheses: 4	one space after left parenthesis only; left and right parenthesis one space away from word inside; more than one space away from words outside
No space between initial and name:	*Peter W.McAuliff*
Narrow right margin: 2	
Right margin narrows from top to bottom: 2	
Right margins not justified: 10	
Right margins justified: 1	
Left margins uneven: 2	
Left and right margins combined features:	
Text lines — variations: 4	text extends across page; typed-text continues on following line with room left on previous line; relative variance of line-endings at the right margin
Paragraphs indented 1–13 spaces: 10	

Paragraphs blocked: 13	
Paragraph spacing 1–3 spaces: 8	
Paragraph spacing 4 or more spaces: 1	alternating spacing; only first paragraph indented
No paragraph divisions: 1	
Font size for emphasis: 1	
Underlining for emphasis: 14	
Bolding for emphasis: 2	
Bold + italic for emphasis: 1	
Bold + underline for emphasis: 1	
Bold + underline + italic for emphasis: 3	
Capital letters for word emphasis: 11	
Capitals for phrase emphasis: 3	
Capitals for whole sentences for emphasis: 1	
Capitals + underlining for emphasis: 3	
Combination of capitals, bold, underline for emphasis: 1	
Specific font sizes and types: 3	mixture of size and type: 12 and 14
Asterisks: 2	footnotes * ** ***; double asterisk for later insertion
Subparagraphs ordered by numbers: 3	number starting at left margin; number +), e.g.,: 2); sub-sections occurring outside running text
Line-end word division: 4	*com- mitments, condi- tioned, facili- ties syna- gogue, construc- tion, arrange- ments, des- cribed, etc.*
Specific ending-sentence of a letter: 4	*Thank you for …; thanks in advance …*
Specific letter closing: 8	*night night; Yours truly, Yours very truly, Very truly yours; Thank you. (3); Regards; no capital letters in closing*
No punctuation after closing: 3	*Sincerely*
Position of closing: 8	left; centered
Closing space from text: 10	1–5 spaces from text
Letter signed with no caps: 2	*a friend*
Signed name under typed name in close: 2	

11.4.2 Numbers and Symbols

Variation in Numbers and Symbols	Examples
Characteristic usage of number-words: 2	twenty-second street (use of words, no caps); distribution of number-words (vs. numerals)
Number-word followed by numerals in parenthesis: 1	twenty-seven (27)
Numerals 1–10 instead of number-words: 5	*There are 6 students.*
Variation in parentheses, dashes, and periods in telephone number: 2	*559.787.9653; 800-555-1212; (800) 555-1212*
Written structure of money amounts: 3	*$500,0000.00; (Three thousand and five hundred dollars and 00/100)*
Absence of place in thousands marker in money amounts: 1	absence of one place in "000" thousands marker in money amounts: *$30,00.00*
Cents-places + decimal or cents marking: 3	large money amounts with cents places marked
Number or cents-places typed with small zero: 2	*1oo (100); $500.oo*
Dollar sign: 6	one vertical stroke in dollar sign; $ for word "money"; word "dollars" for $
Numbers in ( ) followed by number words: 1	($500) five hundred dollars
Numerals in parenthesis with no accompanying words: 1	*($70,000)*
Technical convention for writing proportions: 1	*70:30 mixture*
Written structure of time of day: 3	AM/PM; numbers followed by small pm with no space of periods
Bullets: 9	written as *o* at left margin, then text indented 5 spaces; no bullets; lettered lists of the form a., b., etc.; numbered lists of the form 1., 2., etc.
Equal sign: 1	equal sign = without spacing on either side
Written *plus,* not + sign: 1	plus (+)

11.4.3 Abbreviations

Variation in Abbreviations	Examples
Abbreviated/unabbreviated state: 3	*Ca* (small a, no period), *CALIFORNIA* within text

Varying abbreviations of state: 2	Variable abbrev. California in addresses: *CA, Calif.*
Title abbreviation: Ms.: 1	*Ms.* vs. *Mrs.* or *Miss*
Middle initial in name: 1	Full name + middle initial + last name
General use of abbreviations: 5	*wks, apprx. #*, phone numbers, *corp/corpor.*
All capital letter abbreviation: 3	*OK* (*okay* or *ok*), Postscript *PS:*, *ASAP*
Full forms vs. abbreviations: 6	*Eastern Telecommunications Philippines, Inc.*, vs. *Eastern* vs. *ETPI*; Full forms: *Street, Avenue, Boulevard, West + street*, and *East + street*
Abbreviation marked with or without apostrophe: 1	*FBI's* vs. *FBIs*
Abbreviation with or without periods: 3	*a.m., Attn*
Abbreviations + periods and spacing: 3	U S WEST: no periods and space between U S
Abbreviations in all lower case lettering: 1	*st., ln., ave.*
Nonstandard abbreviations: 4	*para* (paragraph), *SSAN* (SSN), *ibs* (*lbs*), *No./N./North*

11.4.4   Punctuation

Variation in Punctuation	Examples
COMMA	
Comma for apostrophe: 1	*John,s*
Comma +/- before final word in a series: 1	…cars, trucks and rv's.
Commas for periods in run-on sentences: 5	They were leaving, I was arriving.
Comma present/absent in date: 4	January 22 1999
Intrusive commas: 18	*I hope, that you are able to go.*
No comma following S-initial adverbial: 9	*After seeing that I was …*
No comma after S-initial adverb: 6	*Well let's …, Simply one of the …*
No comma after S-initial subordinate clause: 7	*When you get home don't forget …*
No comma before S-final phrases and clauses: 6	*She forgot it since nobody reminded her.*
No comma before a tag question: 1	She was there wasn't she?
No comma before Ss conjoined by *and, but, or*: 14	[Often a specific comma distribution with conjunctions]
No commas around parenthetical phrases/clauses: 5	The office since it was open became a target.

No commas around unrestricted relative clauses: 8	She admitted it which means she's the one.
No comma around name of person, company, title: 1	We asked you Ray to call right away.
No comma after name or title: 8	Allen you messed up!
No comma before/after abbreviation: 2	No comma before etc., or after Ltd.
No comma before "too": 3	We bought tickets too.
No comma before quotes: 6	The witness said "I was walking …
Comma one space after preceding word: 3	They took it, and I never saw it again.
Double spacing after a comma: 1	The bus was late, but we never lost …
PERIOD	
Period present/absent with initials: 4	*S.B.T.C, FBI*
Period in the place of a comma: 1	*After they arrived. we thought we would …*
Double period with S ending in abbreviation: 1	*… all of it, etc..*
Period for exclamation: 1	*What a drag.*
Period for interrogative: 2	*Were you listening.*
Period after specific line of format: 6	*topic line, list items, address lines, signature, cc line*
Spacing around periods and S-final punctuation: 11	*They left on time .*
Period inside/outside at end of quote: 3	*… all of that." … at the time."*
Absence of period: 8	*Mr McMahon*
Total or partial absence S-final punctuation: 11	*The others were here*
Total absence of all punctuation: 1	*[Throughout the writing]*
Double or triple S-final punctuation: 3	*… new guys.!*
SEMICOLON	
Frequent use of semi-colon: 2	*Every day is better; we are making it.*
Semi-colon for full stop: 1	*Every day is better; We are making it.*
Semi-colon for comma: 4	*Every day is better; and we are making it.*
Semi-colon for colon: 4	*These are the rules; first, …*
COLON	
Variable use of colon: 6	*[for period, comma, semicolon]*
Absence of colon: 1	*try the following first start …*
Presence of colon with dash: 1	*:-, -:,: -, -:*
Colon present/absent with *SUB:*, *RE:*, and *CC*: 2	*Subj:, SUB*

Colon spaced away from preceding word: 2	*Title:*
EXCLAMATION	
Multiple exclamation marks: 12	*!!! !!!! !!!!!*
Exclamation marks spaced apart: 1	*! ! ! ! !*
Spacing between S-final word and exclamation: 2	*everyone !*
QUESTION	
Double question marks: 3	*When??*
Multiple question marks (3 or more): 3	*When????*
Question mark after declarative sentence: 2	*We were watching?*
Question mark after indirect question: 2	*I asked what they were doing?*
Question mark inside/outside quote marks: 1	*… there?" …there"?*
Absent S-final question mark: 1	*When did they see him.*
Question marks spaced apart: 2	*? ? ? ? ? ?*
DASH (HYPHEN)	
Dash to separate clauses or embedded Ss: 3	*The books arrived — and all the materials were late.*
Dash to separate joined compound words:	*full-time, old-time*
Dash as separator of made-up compounds: 2	*a just-to-be-talking-about-it comment*
Dash for comma: 7	*…working,-then she will …*
Dash for period: 3	*Everyone saw it — I saw it, too.*
Double and triple dashes: 6	*… all at once — — everything happened.*
Long dashes (4–61 dashes): 2	*— — — — — — -*
Dash after number of heading: 1	*1-, 2-, etc.*
Dash(s) with no spacing between words: 2	*… arrived on time-that is, at 8pm*
SUSPENSION POINTS	
Suspension points after S-initial clauses: 1	*After we got there … we met the Smiths.*
Suspension points conjoining sentences: 1	*We were having dinner … They saw us in the window.*
Suspension points before tag construction: 7	*He did it anyway…right or wrong!*
S-final suspension points for suspense: 1	*And, that was saying a lot … You know what he said?*
Suspension points after S-initial exclamation/topic: 1	*Ah…. a million here, a million there. Carl.*
Suspension points after topic statement: 1	*"100% service.it failed*

Suspension points to replace missing material: 1	*The ... company will not do it.*
Suspension points to pause in discourse: 5	*Well ..., who knows?*
S-final suspension points, trailing off...: 1	*You asked for it ...*
Double suspension points: 3	*The fact is ... he doesn't know.*
Triple suspension points + variable spacing: 4	*Whenever I go ...he goes, too.*
Multiple suspension points (4 or more): 3	*What are you going to do ...... stop?*
No space between words and suspension points: 3	*School is getting better...now that I have a job.*
SLASH	
Slash to separate words: 8	*and/or, he/she, month/year numbers*
Slash in the place of a period: 1	*They left/We're still here/*
Single space after slash, no space before: 1	*either/or*
QUOTES	
Quote marks on top of punctuation: 2	[handwritten or typed on a typewriter]
Variation in quotes within quotes: 2	*He said, "We don't "do" that anymore."*
Quotes around single words: 6	*The "happy" ones are gone.*
Quotes around phrases: 7	*The "first to go" have already left.*
Quotes for emphasis: 3	*I don't want "any" of it.*
Spacing around periods and open/close quotes: 3	*She said, " Why not? "*
APOSTROPHE	
Intrusive apostrophe: 4	*it's (its),*
Absence of apostrophe: 14	*its (it's)*
Possessive apostrophe for plural	*book's (books)*
PARENTHESIS	
Parentheses only around examples or notes: 2	*(e.g., and (Note:*
Parentheses to enclose phrase or sentence: 3	*The worst (very worst) part is over.*
Parentheses to enclose single word: 2	*I thought he (they) might be here.*
Parentheses in the place of commas: 1	*The last ones (John and Tom) closed up the place.*
Double parentheses: 1	*((He's here to stay.))*
Square brackets for references: 1	*She quoted the dictionary [Websters].*
ITALICS	
Absence of underlining or italics: 2	*The* Los Angeles Times *carried the ...*

11.4.5   Capitalization

Variation in Capitalization	Examples
Superfluous capitals: 13	*And* in "Saint John's Hospital And Health Center"; *At* and *Of* in names and titles; *River* in joined compound "SunRiver"; first and second letter of word, *Beverly HIlls, YOur committee;* last word in a sentence, They are *THROUGH*; in content words: The *Airport*" is five minutes away.
Absence of capitals: 9	*State Employees credit union*
All capitals applied to a word or document: 8	*DATED, NOT, YES*
Small letters vs. capital letters in one writer: 11	*sixth floor/Sixth Floor, Minutes/minutes of the Congregational Meeting, Joint Venture/joint venture, AM/a.m.*
Absent capitalization in names or titles: 3	*mr. and mrs. Floyd*
Use of capital letters in distinguishing manner: 2	*Southern charm*
Use of small letters in distinguishing manner: 1	*los angeles, california*

11.4.6   Spelling

Variation in Spelling	Examples
Separated compounds: 1	a while, when ever
Unseparated compounds: 2	donot, upto
Homonyms or close-homonyms: 18	*fair* (fare), *new* (knew), *soul* (sole), *their* (there) (2), *their* (they're), *there* for their (3), *they're* (their), *then* (than) (3), *to* (too) (4), *were* (where), *you* (you're) (2), *your* (you're)
Alternate spelling choice: 10	*nite, theatre, thru, till* (to mean as long as, not until), *mine* (my), *while*
The *short e* sound: 1	*streached* (stretched)
Reduced vowel sound: 5	*confidentuality, buriel* (burial), *summery, travling*
Words with -ei- and -ie-: 2	foreign, retrived
Non-doubling of consonants: 6	backstaber, folowing, inocent, literaly, occurrences, posession
Doubling of consonants: 15	ammaized, bussiness, fullfill, loose (lose) (2), occassions, opperations, oppinion, peoplle, powerfull, slid of (off), ussual

Regional variants: 5	colour, learnt, while
Variation in spelling proper names: 11	*Ann* (Anne), *Terrance* (Terrence), *Bobbie* (Bobbi), *Garry* (Gary), *Barbato* (Barbado), *Shimomeguro* (Shimomeguru), *Wood* (Woodd), *Allan* (Allen), *Rosenblaum* (Rosenblum), *Kattenkamp* (Katenkamp), *Sanjay* (Sanjaya)
Final *silent e* absent before suffix: 5	*unfortunatly, involvment, sombodys, cloths* (clothes)
Deletion of final *e*: 3	*th* (the), *Sincerly* (2)
Consonant cluster reduction: 2	unterained (untrained), Appox. (Approx.)
Consonsant cluster creation: 3	intresting, surpreme, order (odor)
Phonetic or near-phonetic spellings: 12	*cheep, dispise, envolved, equiptment, fucken, govenor, our* (or), *peer ticks* (protects), *prejudice* (prejudiced), *spacius, strives* (strides), *thay* (they), *they* (there), *this* (these), *tradgedy, want* (what), *wheater* (weather)
Phonetic spelling of auxiliary verbs: 3	*half to* (have to), *use to* (used to)
Alternation of c/s/z: 12	presious, *advize*
Homorganic consonant loss or change: 1	*exemt* (exempt), *discusting* (disgusting)
Patterned or random typographical errors: 9	*form* (from), *I* (It), *if* (is), *inquires* (inquiries), *jor* (job), *sypervisors* (supervisor's), *uou* (you), *we* (were), *subtergufe* (subterfuge)
Plural of words ending in -*eys* or -*ies*: 1	moneys/monies, attonerys/attornies
Silent *e* retained with addition of suffix: 5	disableing, enableing, handeling, hopeing, inquirey, judgment, noisey, storey, Truely
Ill-formed contraction in both spelling and punctuation: 3	*doenn't, doesn,t, does'nt* (doesn't)
Miscellaneous spellings:	ect., *scruitiny* (scrutiny), *lense* for lens

11.4.7 Word Formation

Variation in Word Formation	Examples
Article *an* for *a*: 2	an pillow
Plural for singular form: 1	women [woman]
Absent inflections (other than -*ed*): 3	he was walk, ten book
Absent inflection -*ed*: 4	render[ed], ask[ed]
Intrusive inflection -*ed*: 1	caughted
Perfect form for simple past: 3	it sunk, he seen it
Present form for simple past: 1	yesterday he goes to school
Single verbs for two-part verbs: 1	lookat me

Singular for plural verbs: 2	they asks
Ampersand in place of *and*: 10	bread & butter
Absence of apostrophe in possessive: 2	sombodys
Absence of apostrophe in contraction: 9	its [it's], whats, lets, wont, dont
Possessive apostrophe for plural: 5	the season's of the year, van's are expensive
Two-way confusion of it's and its: 2	its here, it's tail
Patterned presence of certain contractions: 13	how're vs. how is, he'd vs. I would
Misplaced apostrophe in contraction: 1	didnt', cant', its' mine
Separation of joined compound words: 23	can not, lady friend, any way, grave yard, with out
Fusion of separate words into a joined compound: 9	todate, alot, cleanoff
Intrawriter variation in writing compounds: 2	cannot + can not
Creation of new compounds with hyphen: 1	the get-there-on-time type
Separation of prefixes with intrusive hyphen: 2	pre-dict, un-favorable, de-duct
Unsystematic word division at line-ends: 1	inv- olved, sec-ured, vi- sually
Clipping a proper name: 1	*shayn* for *shayna*

11.4.8   Syntax

Variation in Syntax	Examples
Sentence structure: 8	long, short, linear complexity, embedding complexity, unpunctuated sentences, adverb position, auxiliary position
Commands: 2	*Ask..., You will ... and You won't ...*
Questions: 6	Rhetorical, direct, how-questions, lists of questions, series of quasi-rhetorical questions after a statement; mixing real with rhetorical
Subject-verb agreement (concord): 9	*Why isn't there more supervisors? What does a girl usually wears? My supervisor keep me ... Quality employees comes from ... Decisions that helps ...*
Sentence fragments: 8	*Just when he got up.*
Run-ons with/without punctuation: 13	*You wouldn't know it he's blind without glasses.*

Words in a series, e.g., triplets: 4	*Well well well …, … you were vindictive, vengeful hateful.*
Nonstandard constructions: 3	nonstandard phrase/clause/sentence formations, nonstandard sequence of tenses
Direct discourse for indirect: 2	*He asked me will you go.*
Passive voice: 1	*The building was painted by all the volunteers.*
Periodic sentences: 2	unit between the sentence and paragraph
S-initial modifiers: 24	*Again (5), Also (5), Always, Anyway, Consequently, Finally, Furthermore, Hopefully, However, (3), Indeed, Meanwhile, No, Now, Therefore, (2), Today, Unfortunately, Well, Yes (2), As stated, In addition, In fact, In reality,*
S-initial conjunctions: 4	*And, But, Or,*
Other Sentence openers: 6	*I … (2), Never …, Not …, You …, Please …, [vocative],*
S-initial subordinate clause: 7	*Because …, If …, You are right …,*
Topic-comment: 3	Short, declarative topic sentences; S-initial topic with S-final question; S-initial topic with S-final comment
Subjectless sentences: 2	*Sorry about the accident. Don't know when I'll see you.*
S-internal subordination: 2	*after …, before …*
Phrase insertion marked with commas: 2	*…, and ultimately, and …, say,*
Absolute constructions: 1	*You, by the grace of God, will not follow the same path.*
Phrase insertion marked with parentheses: 1	*The rest of us (God willing) will be here with you.*
S-final subordination: 3	*…, which. …, if elected. …, because .*
S-final phrases: 3	*…, within one year. …, in the treasury of the congregation*
Subordinate clauses: 4	nonstandard subordination; left- or right-heavy subordination; internal clause set off by commas
Subordinate clauses beginning with as: 4	*as* meaning *since*
Intrusive article: 3	*The happiness is very important.*
Absence of article: 6	*… only in United States. You were sent by Turkish.*
Count/Non-count nouns: 2	non-count for count nouns: *What interests does it pay?*

Pronouns: 10	first and third person alternation, personal and possessives, relatives, demonstratives, case variation after preposition, restrictive *that* for *who*, *mine* for *my*, royal *we*.
Prepositions: 3	... in revenge of what you did. ... your influence *in* me was high. ... in return *with* sexual favors. ... receive recognition *from* doing.
Verbs: 5	forms unmarked by all verb inflections; transitive with no object; past-perfect for simple past
Absent Verb Particles: 1	*We looked the word in the dictionary.*
Auxiliary verbs: 4	combinations *would + have* and *could + have*; emphatic *do* and *did*; *didn't* for *haven't + verb*
Complementizers: 5	Structure, frequency, and function of complementizer *that*; incorrect complementizer
Modifiers: 9	nouns with multiple modifiers; adjective with adverb modifiers, e.g., qualitative adv + adj; *approximately* with all numbers; adverb + verb order
Conjunctions other than and, but, or: 3	*however, nor, yet*
Double marking comparative adverb: 1	*more clearer*

11.4.9   Discourse

Variation in Discourse	Examples
Concluding forms in letters: 2	*Thank you for VERB +ing; In conclusion, ...*
Distinctive text openings: 2	*On or about the time of 7:00 to 7:30 AM...; I am pleased to ...*
Topic/purpose stated overtly at outset: 2	Sets up a topic to comment on; purpose of writing stated at outset
Frequent verb changes: 1	change of verb tense between present and past
Sequence of tenses: 1	*I hoped that you will be there.*
Ordering of ideas with first,...second,...third: 1	Writer lists order of points, *first...*, *second...*, *third...*,
Indirect/direct speech: 4	indirect discourse; quoted direct speech
Commands: 1	*Wise up! Think about it — -*
Questions in discourse: 3	direct questions; questions with insulting intent; rhetorical questions

Common themes: 3	repeated themes: *I'm sorry, I love you, I can change; protect my kids, a little girl*
Near identical wording in questioned and known: 1	
Short paragraphs: 3	Short paragraphs functioning like sentences
Calling addressee by first name: 1	vocative: calling addressee by first name
Reference to time and place: 2	exact dates and time references; exact addresses and place references

11.4.10   Errors and Corrections

Similar corrections in questioned and known: 2	shared corrections in spelling
Additions made later to text: 6	-ing on verb *include* added later
Strikeovers: 6	strikeover indicating first spelling like other variable spelling
Cross-outs: 4	used as evidence of composition, not copying; words crossed-out with combination of [/] and [x]
Word run-ons: 5	no space between words: *Iam*
Typing anomalies: 6	*April* as *Aoruk* in questioned and known; line 46 begins with #@; repeated words: *Jane Jane, will will, and and*
Discarded pages: 1	discarded draft pages compared to actual letter
Error/correction symbol: 1	*sic* interspersed in writing

11.4.11   High-Frequency Words and Phrases

Variation in Words and Phrases	Examples
Frequent words: 34	*advise* (advice); *backoff* [one-word verb]; *boy!*; concerns; destroy; destructive; disrupt; executed; experiences; expertise; eyes; felt; footstool; foreigner; further; God!; heretofore; immediate; mates; Mediterranea; mench; mendacity; Naples vs. Napoli; note; numerous; OK [in caps]; persona; productivity; proforma (written as one word); rating; serious; set forth; silliness; spick; staff; subbies; subordinates; such; then; various; via; words related to cleanliness; words related to clothes; words related to holidays; words related to jewelry; words related to negative emotions

Frequent phrases: 78	*(here) at the Airport; [am/are] a big boy; [have/has] always done the best [she can/I could]; agreed to proceed with; Airport structure; along with; also mentioned that; and also; as a result of; as defined in the above mentioned letter; as for …; as well (as); as you already know; As you know; at best/worst; at this point; based upon vs. based on; Best wishes; between the parties concerned; bible quotes; By the time [that] you read this …; career pathing; City staff, employees, crew, staff; coaches and sponsors; consists of; easier to; even if; Expression of not wanting a funeral + just .; following or the following; forms of dates; funding possibilities; getting worse; had made a miracle; have heard; house and rooms of the house; I am acknowledging the information; I believe (that); I believe …; I feel …; I had wanted that she should be cut down; I happen to know; I have always; I still love you …; I urge you to …; I would like to go on record as saying…; in behalf; in order to used exclusively in place of to; In other words; in regards to (vs. in/with regard to, regarding, etc.); In/on one occasion; interest rates; investment portfolio; It appears …; it appears that; It is difficult; It is interesting to note that …;It is not fair …; it is time to …; it was agreed that; Latin phrases; lose weight; measures of time; my job title is surplus; My name … and My name is …; neither … nor expressed as neither … or; once in awhile; one more thing; or so … appearing after an expression of quantity or time; our jobs; pay upstream …; Personal and Confidential; personally and professionally; Please be advised that; properly functioning; quality of information systems; recorded in/on the books; rendering asunder; scatology; she is a mega brain of knowledge; Sheriff's Personnel; so as to; someone else; such as a noun; Thank you and best wishes; that I can get; the driver behind; the fact that; the following; the public; the straight scoop; this company; this letter … and writing you this letter …; those that vs. those who; time phrases; time-telling; to go ahead and; to make witness; two/both parties concerned; with regards to; work hard; would be wise; You will retain…*
Frequent word in different forms (parts of speech): 1	*ironic, ironically, irony*
Frequent word with specific meaning attached: 5	*means* in expressions like *securement means, address* meaning consider, *Joint Venture* used in nonlegal way, *faithful* to designate alignment with insurance company, *said* as in *said machine*
Frequent use of close-meaning words in couplets: 2	*customs and practices*

Frequent phrase types: 10	ADJ + *type* + NOUN (as opposed to ADJ type of NOUN); *all* + MODIFIER + NOUN (vs. *all* + of + MOD + NOUN); amounts (not numbers) used with count nouns; VERB + *that*; NOUN + *that*; ADJ + *that*; Please consider … + numbered list; *I sincerely* + VERB; *the next few* + a time period; *the above* + NOUN; *Please* + Command; *attempt to* + VERB
Words specific to a particular discipline or occupation: 3	psychological vocabulary; technical ecclesiastical language; sports terms

References

Finnegan, E., Variation in linguists' analyses of author identification, *Am. Speech*, 65:4:334–340, 1990.

Kaplan, J. P., Pragmatic contributions to the interpretation of a will, *Foren. Linguis.*, 5:2:107–126, 1998.

Style and Stylistics in Spanish Writing

12

GERALD R. McMENAMIN

Abstract

El propósito de este capítulo es enfocar la investigación actual sobre tres áreas relacionadas: el estilo, la estilística, y la estilística forense. Hay una muy larga tradición de estudios sobre el estilo y la estilística de la lengua española. Éstos se ubican dentro de varios marcos teóricos, tanto literarios como lingüísticos, casi todos elaborados durante el siglo pasado.

Se trata ahora de tomar estos avances teóricos ya hechos y de abarcar sobre un campo nuevo y estrecho dentro de la estilística aplicada: la *estilística forense*. En mayor parte, la estilística forense incluye dos tipos de estudios: la identificación de autores desconocidos, por estudiar el lenguaje de escritos conocidos frente a los escritos anónimos; y la interpretación semántica del lenguaje de documentos como contratos, testamentos, acuerdos, etc. Además, el campo general de la *lingüística forense* incluye el análisis del discurso de entrevistas policiacas, lo cual es muy importante en lugares bilingües como el suroeste de los Estados Unidos.

Se da primero un breve bosquejo de la investigación sobre el estilo y la estilística en español, incluyendo los siguientes tópicos: el estilo, la estilística tradicional, la estilística lingüística, el grupo frente al individuo, la variación estilística, y una incipiente bibliografía sobre estos temas. Entonces, se consideran los rasgos estilísticos que se observan en las redacciones de alumnos universitarios, inmigrantes de primera hasta tercera generación e hispanohablantes, pero sólo medio literatos en la lengua. Finalmente, se presentan cinco casos forenses, dos del análisis de discurso de entrevistas policiacas, una del análisis del discurso de la conversación grabada, y dos de escritos desconocidos: una confesión sí firmada por el acusado pero, según él, no escrito por él; y unas cartas anónimas escritas por un bilingüe español-inglés.

12.1 Spanish-Language Style and Stylistics

12.2.1 Style

The definitions of style in Spanish revolve around two concepts: choice and aggregate of features. The writer's choice to say the same thing in different ways is the fundamental essence of style, each choice becoming a marker of style. Every writer must make choices:

> *En el estilo se elige. … Es más, definimos el estilo por la obligación de elegir.*
> *… el hablante tiene que escoger entre las opciones: no puede evitar hacerlo.*
> *Este rasgo diferencia aún más al estilo de los otros fenómenos de variación*
> (Garrido Medina, 1997:124)

The aggregate of choices represents the writer's range of stylistic variation:

> *"… [Amado Alonso] caracteriza el estilo como la totalidad de los medios de expresión artística de un autor…."* (Robb, 1965)
> *"… los estilos son opciones que, en bloque, distinguen un autor, un grupo social, etc."* (Garrido Medina, 1997).
> *"Cada opción es una marca de estilo … y un estilo consiste en un conjunto integrado de marcas"* (Garrido Medina, 1997).
> *"… verdadero estilo, como conjunto de opciones de espresión"* (Hagège, 1996, 240).

Style is also seen as dependent on the social context of the writing, i.e., its purpose, intended reader, topic, medium, etc. Styles correspond to text types, e.g., general writing, business letters, memoranda, reports, technical writing, documentation, proposals, newspaper and magazine writing, publicity, fiction, etc.

12.1.2   Traditional Stylistics

There are many ways to analyze style, thus causing the definition of stylistics to depend on the purpose of the analysis. As Gariano (1968:14) observes, *"Qué es la estilística no es cosa fácil de definir."*

Traditionally, Spanish stylistics draws from the French tradition of clarity of expression and author's choice of forms. Translation studies have also focused on stylistic characteristics. In addition, the more subjective currents of literary criticism are present in traditional Spanish stylistics, viewing style types as humble or subtle, medium or moderated, and serious or sublime. There are also numerous prescriptive studies that focus on correct and appropriate language, e.g., good vocabulary, well-constructed sentences, etc.

12.1.3   Linguistic Stylistics

The linguistic analysis of style is descriptive or quantitative. The focus of descriptive stylistics is on the linguistic characteristics of the writing:

> *El estilo se intenta definir mediante propiedades lingüísticas* (Garrido Medina, 1997:32)
> *… la descripción del estilo indivdual del autor mediante métodos lingüísticos* (Garrido Medina, 1997:28)

... la estílistica ... estudio de los medios de espresión disponibles a una lengua (Yllera, 1974:14)

Quantitative approaches to studying Spanish language stylistic variation are developed in the same way that they are for other languages. Some Spanish language style researchers (*estilólogos*) have expressed more or less reasonable caution, e.g., "*De otro lado, dejemos a los cándidos obreros de la técnica del cuentahilos su inocente manía*" (Alonso, 1981:12).

On the other hand, with easier access to computers and keener understanding of the relationship between the study of linguistic variation vis-à-vis frequency of occurrence of variables, serious quantitative and digital analysis is being done on Spanish language and style, e.g.,: Lara et al., 1979; de Kock et al., 1983; Ballester et al., 1993; Valderrábanos et al., 1994; and Bia and Pedreño, 2001.

12.1.4   The Group and Individual

There is a clear recognition and distinction of group vs. individual styles in Spanish language stylistic analysis. Style refers to the language of a single author or to that of a group of writers identified by time, place, or cultural and social factors. Consider the observation of Menéndez Pidal almost a half century ago: "*El arte colectivo del estilo tradicional es 'una armoniosa cooperación de creaciones individuales.' El estilo individual es la 'suma de fuerzas colectivas inconscientes' ... en su autor comienza y en su autor acaba*" (Menéndez Pidal, 1957:384).

The Spanish language *estilólogos* view style as necessarily individual, as do their French counterparts, e.g., "*El estilo se concibe como trabajo individual de estructuración*" (Garrido Medina's translation of Granger, 1968). However, they are less apt to oppose individual to group styles than to consider the two as complementary but necessary ingredients of a single definition of style:

> *... el estilo se da en cualquier hablante, en todos y en cada uno de los miembros de un mismo grupo ...* (Garrido Medina, 1997:101)

> *... se ha considerado el estilo como resultado de la raza, o de la nación o de la comunidad a la cual pertenece el artista; o también como efecto de la cultura o del espíritu de los tiempos en que se forma; o como compuesto de agentes psícicos, históricos y hasta geográficos. En fin, se ha vuelto otra vez a lo individual, ...*" (Gariano, 1968:14)

12.1.5   Variation: Markers of Style

Style is a result of variation marked by the diversity of choices made by writers:

Y esta situación [que se da dentro de cada variedad, de cada lengua] es la de diversidad interna: la existencia de opciones léxicas, de pronunciación o de construcción, que están disponibles para cualquier hablante. Aquí no hay variedades ya hechas, sino casos de variación, de diversidad dentro de una misma variedad. Este es el terreno del estilo: las opciones internas a una variedad (Garrido Medina, 1997:103).

Stylistic variation is marked in any variable element of the language: "... *la mera agrupación de palabras, o por la peculiares selecciones gramaticales, sintácticas o aparentemente causales de vocabulario, etc. ... o hasta un mero detalle de puntuación ... como 'un guión"* (Robb, 1965:17).

Examples of stylistic variation are provided in just about every study. The following short but representative list of style-markers can be found in Alcalá Arévalo (1991:202):

Recursos gráficos
  los entrecommillados
  cambio de tipografía
  signos de puntuación
    puntos suspensivos
    utilización doble o triple de signos de puntuación
    fragmentación entre palabras
    cambio de los signos diacritícos por palabras
    paréntesis
    ausencia de signos de puntuación
las mayúsculas
utilización de signos no codificados (nuevos)
unión de palabras diferentes en una sola
empleo de grafías para caracterizar el habla
unión no normativa de las sílabas
introducción de otros elementos gráficos
las canciones

12.1.6   The Study of Spanish Style and Stylistics

The scope of this book does not allow significant review or even an annotated bibliography of Spanish language work on style and stylistics. However, it is possible to provide a resource bibliography (see end of chapter) to facilitate further study. Works are categorized in the following five areas, but the categorization is of necessity a loose one, given the great amount of overlap in most of the research.

1. Theory of style: Báez San José, 1971; Marichal, 1957; Marichal, 1984; Montes, 1975; Spitzer, 1980; Ullman, 1968; Verdín Díaz, 1970; Vossler, Spitzer, and Hatzfield, 1942

2. Prescriptive Stylistics: Allés and Abad, 1971; Clarín, 1997; Diario Perfil, 1998; Lagmanovich, 1997; Martín Vivaldi, 1972; *La Voz de Galicia*, 1992
3. Literary stylistics: Alazraki, 1974; Alcalá Arévalo, 1991; D. Alonso, 1981; S. Alonso, 1981; Baroja, 1983; Bello Vazquez, 1988; Ciplijaus-kaite, 1972; Criado de Val, 1953; Galmés de Fuentes, 1981; Gonzalez Maldonado, 1968; Herrero Mayor, 1972; Lapesa, 1988; Lorenzo–Riv-ero, 1977; Martín, 1974; Menéndez Pidal, 1957, 1958; Menéndez Pidal, 1957; Robb, 1965; Román, 1993; Yllera, 1974; Young, 1978
4. Linguistic stylistics: M. Alonso Pedraz, 1975; deKock, Geens et al., 1983; Haverkate and Dehennin, 1994; Hengeveld, 1994; Galmés de Fuentes, 1996; Gariano, 1968; Garrido Medina, 1997; Gutiérrez Mar-rone, 1978; Heger, 1982; Martín, 1973; Sebeok, 1974; Spillner, 1979
5. Stylistic analysis: Beltrán, 1990; Castagnino, 1974; Escartin Gual and Martinez Celdran, 1983; Fernandez, 1972; Guiraud, 1967; Hatzfeld, 1975; Lopez-Casanova and Alonso n/d; Paz Gago, 1993

12.2 Style Markers: A Small Corpus of Mexican-American Writing

A study was done of the spontaneous writing in Spanish of 22 college students whose first language was Spanish, and who were enrolled in an upper division writing class in the U.S. (Herrera, 2000). The corpus consists of 306 short essays e-mailed to the professor for review and correction. Corrected essays, rewritten before or during class, are not in corpus.

Even though these writers were Spanish speakers, they had little or no Spanish language schooling. Due to their developing literacy skills, therefore, most of the obvious style-markers were deviations from the Mexican–Spanish norm, i.e., mistakes. Examples of representative style-markers are provided in Figure 12.1. Some represent problems that any Spanish learner would have, e.g., spelling sound-alike letters and homonyms. Others are indicative of interference from English, e.g., double-letter spellings and the absence of subjunctive verb forms. The most frequently occurring characteristic related to orthographic accents, their omission in words like *asi, crimenes, creia, alli, aprendi, ¿como?, accion*, etc., as well as their superfluous or misplaced presence in words like the following:

ó, sí, él, está, hacía, éste, qué, cómo, marcó, mí
vivír, escribír, págar
competencía, preparatoría, ordinaría, diarías, materia, estudíantes
novío, limpío, obvío
generaciónes, correcciónes, millónes

VARIATION	STANDARD FORM
Spelling: Sound-Alike Letters	
meresen	merecen
enserrados	encerrados
comienso	comienzo
relasiona	relaciona
ase nueve años	hace
hiso/hico daño	hizo
la misma ves	vez
come sacate	zacate
estubiera	estuviera
ayudava	ayudaba
hambiente	ambiente
aberme permitido	haberme
armonía	harmonía
Spelling: Double Letters	
addicción	adicción
appropiada	apropiada
contradición	contradicción
carera	carrera
Spelling: Homonyms	
y **ser** ejercicio	hacer
para **hacer** ingeniero	ser
voy **hacer** maestra	a ser
debe de **ver** penas	haber
a **ha** tener	a
no me **a** parado	ha
ahí ciertos requisitos	hay
asta la noche	hasta
Spelling: Like Pronunciation	
siguido	seguido
desiara	deseara
ojiar revistas	ojear
Written Accent: Absent	
para mi	mí
ayer me aconsejo	aconsejó
algun día	algún
aqui	aquí
asi	así
creia	creía
mama	mamá
musica	música
periodico	periódico

Figure 12.1 Variation in the Spanish writing of Mexican–American college students.

VARIATION	STANDARD FORM
Written Accent: Intrusive	
él único	el
unicó	único
mí libro	mi
ésta elección	esta
Capitalization	
Mayo	mayo
lengua Española	española
Martes	martes
Word Formation: Separation	
A si	Así
sí no que	sino
a un más	aun
de el criminal	del
amedia noche	a medianoche
me gustó **por que** ...	porque
Word Formation: Joining	
ala misma vez	a la
voy **adar** mi opinión	a dar
amí se me hace ...	a mí
apesar de que	a pesar
haveces	a veces
compiter **haber** cuál ...	a ver
enveces	en veces
nomas	no más
patras	para atrás
porfavor	por favor
¿**Porque** está ...?	¿Por qué?
al fin de **alcabo**	al fin y a cabo
nostan	nos están
Word Formation: Verbs	
ju**e**gaba	jugaba
v**e**niendo de México	viniendo
toy estudiando	estoy
lleg**e**	llegué
mirába**nos**, estába**nos**, llevába**nos**	mirábamos
	estábamos
	llevábamos

Figure 12.1 (Continued) Variation in the Spanish writing of Mexican– American college students.

VARIATION	STANDARD FORM
Agreement	
una carrera buen**o**	buen**a**
mi propi**o** clase	propi**a**
la escuela secundari**o**	secundari**a**
vari**os** veces	vari**as**
Articles	
la área	el
el intención de ir	la
los clases	las
Absence of Subjunctive Verb Forms	
hasta que no la **termino** ...	termine
como si nada **pasó** ...	pasara
imagina si **fue** víctima ...	fuera
antes que se **baja** el sol ...	bajara
Code Switching	
No es muy **safe** cargar mucho dinero. Estoy en mi **senior year.** Nostan enseñando hacer fuertes **and to** **believe in ourselves.** Nostoros podemos hacer **anything we put** **our minds to**, y que nadien ...	
False Cognates	
atendiendo la escuela	asistiendo a
realizar que	darse cuenta de
Example of Habitual Phrasing (1 writer)	
... matemáticas **y todo.** ... que seguía **y todo.** ... platicaba bien **y todo.** ... él venía a visitarme **y todo.**	

Figure 12.1 (Continued) Variation in the Spanish writing of Mexican– American college students.

creciendo, mintiendo
túve, tuvé, dierón
rápidez, mártes, escogído, jóvencitas, jovén, déporte, tiempó

While this corpus is small and only narrowly representative of the Spanish language spoken throughout the world, the writing of this particular community of speaker-writers serves well to provide one example of Spanish-language stylistic variation.

12.3   Spanish-Language Cases: Linguistics and Stylistics

12.3.1   Analysis of Interpreted or Translated Discourse

12.3.1.1   Case 1: California v. Defendant (1996)

A monolingual Spanish-speaking farmworker was arrested for the murder of a fellow worker. The man's defense attorney requested a linguistic analysis of his initial postarrest police interview in 1995, which contained a confession. The primary purpose of the analysis was to analyze the language of the interview and confession to determine if the defendant's "Miranda rights" were explained and understood.

This police interview, as well as case 3 below, were really interrogations which demonstrate almost all the pitfalls discussed in previous work on such Miranda warnings and police cautions. Paraphrasing (Cotterill, 2000) is a problem here, as well as coerciveness of questions, questionable volition, comprehension, agreement, etc. (Shuy, 1997).

The English-language transcript of the defendant's taped interview and confession was studied and the Spanish-language tape of the same was analyzed. Pertinent segments in Spanish were then translated to English; see Figures 12.2 to 12.7. The Spanish-language transcript facilitated comparison of the detective's reading of the defendant's rights to the "Miranda card" he used to read them from. It also made it possible to identify and isolate five sections of the taped interview related to the issue of the defendant's rights:

Section 1. Officer's reading of Miranda rights: The detective's fluency in Spanish, as observed throughout the tape, is quite good. However, certain word endings, verb forms, and more complex syntactic structures absent in his use of the language make his speech at times ungrammatical and unintelligible. See Figure 12.2.

In contrast, the Miranda rights, as translated to Spanish on the card, contain a complex array of linguistic forms. This difference between the detective's linguistic competence in Spanish and the language complexity of the card, lead him to compensate in two ways. First, he made some changes, possibly to simplify the language for the listener. Second, he began to mumble and became incomprehensible at certain brief points in the reading. (The card itself does not help the reader, in that it does not have important accents on words, which might change their meaning if not pronounced as intended.) See Figure 12.3.

The results of this are twofold. First, certain mistakes in Spanish can change meanings and will affect comprehension by the listener (defendant), as in these examples:

1. Is:"*… puedes usar …*"
1. Should be:"*… se puede usar/puede usarse …*"

SPANISH: From Tape	ENGLISH: Translation
Detective: "Ese, vamos a hablar de ..., de este caso."	Well, we are going to talk about ..., about this case.
Defendant: Umm.	*Umm.*
Detective: La ley dice que puede escuchar sus derechos que usted tiene, [UI + ¿Ok?]	The law says that you can hear your rights that you have, [unintelligible + Ok?]
Defendant: OK.	OK.
Detective: OK, bien, primero, usted tiene el derecho de quedarse callado.	OK, well, first, you have the right to remain silent.
Defendant: OK.	OK.
Detective: Cualquier cosa que usted diga, puedes usar [UI] y sí usa contra de usted en una corte de leyes.	Anything that you say, you can use [UI] and yes [UI] use against you in a court of law.
Usted tiene derecho de hablar con un abogado, y de tenerlo presente antes y durante los preguntes.	You have the right to speak with an attorney, and to have him present before and during the questions.
Si usted no tiene dinero para contratar un abogado, se le nombrará uno gratis [UI] antes y durante los preguntes.	If you do not have money to hire an attorney, one will be named free [UI] before and during the questions.
¿Entiende usted cada de los derechos que expliqué ahorita?	Do you understand each of the rights that I explained just now?
Defendant: Umm.	Umm.
Detective: ¿Sí o no?	Yes or no?
Defendant: Sí, ¿pero por qué me detienes a mí?	Yes, but why are you holding me?

Figure 12.2 Officer's reading of Miranda rights.

2. Is: "... *y si usa contra* ..."
2. Should be: "... *y se use contra* ..."

3. Is: "... *los preguntes* ..."
3. Should be: "... *las preguntas* ..."

Second, certain points of unintelligible speech will also affect comprehension by the listener (defendant). In Figures 12.2 to 12.7, such unintelligible segments are marked by a bracketed [UI] (unintelligible) in the transcription.

Differences in the "Miranda card" vs. the detective's reading of the card consisted mainly of certain simplifications to the language of the card, but

"Miranda Card" [sic]	What Detective Said in Spanish	Translation of Detective's Words
ADVERTENCIA DE SUS DERECHOS LEGALES	"La ley dice que puede escuchar sus derechos que usted tiene, ..."	"The law says that you can hear your rights that you have, ..."
1. Usted tiene el derecho de no decir nada.	"... primero, usted tiene el derecho de quedarse callado."	"... first, you have the right to remain silent."
2. Cualquier cosa que usted diga puede usarse contra usted y se usara contra usted en una corte de leyes.	"Cualquier cosa que usted diga, puedes usar [UI] y sí usa contra de usted en una corte de leyes."	"Whatever you say, you can use [unintelligible] and yes use against you in a court of law."
3. Usted tiene el derecho de hablar con un abogado, y de tener un abogado presente antes y durante cualquier interrogacion.	"Usted tiene derecho de hablar con un abogado, y de tenerlo presente antes y durante los preguntes."	"You have the right to speak with an attorney, and to have him present before and after the questions."
4. Si usted no puede pagarle a un abogado, uno le sera nombrado gratis para que le represente a usted antes y durante la interrogacion.	"Si usted no tiene dinero para contratar un abogado, se le nombrará uno gratis [UI] antes y durante los preguntes."	"If you do not have money to hire an attorney, one will be named free [UI] before and during the questions."
RENUNCIA	**WAIVER** [Not referred to.]	**WAIVER** [Not referred to.]
1. ¿Entiende usted cada uno de los derechos que acabo de explicarle a usted? ¿Sí o no?	"Entiende usted cada de los derechos que expliqué ahorita?	"Do you understand each of the rights that I explained just now?"
2. ¿Teniendo en cuenta estos derechos suyos, desea usted hablar con nosotros ahora? ¿Sí o no?	[Not asked.]	[Not asked.]

Figure 12.3 The "Miranda card" vis-à-vis what the detective said.

the principal difference between what the defendant was told and what is on the "Miranda card" was that he was not asked the last question: "*¿Teniendo en cuenta estos derechos suyos, desea usted hablar con nosotros ahora? ¿Sí o no?*" ("Taking into account these right of yours, do you wish to speak with us now? Yes or no?")

In addition, the detective's interview style of language during his questioning of the defendant was very different from his style of language when reading the defendant's rights to him. During questioning, the detective varied his speed, often speaking slowly, repeating questions, pausing, and speaking loudly and clearly in many instances. During the rights-reading,

SPANISH: From Tape	ENGLISH: Translation
Detective: "Antes cuando hablemos, eh, expliqué sus derechos, eh, ¿éste es verdad?"	"Before when we spoke, eh, I explained your rights, eh, is this true?"
Defendant: "Uh, uh."	"Uh, uh."
Detective: "Y, ... también, sabe que esos derechos está en efectivo por [UI] ¿Ok?"	"And, ... also, you know those rights are in cash [effect] for [UI] Ok?"
Defendant: [inaudible response]	[inaudible response]

Figure 12.4 Officer's first request for confirmation of rights-understanding.

SPANISH: From Tape	ENGLISH: Translation
Detective: "[Apellido], este, ¿podemos seguir hablando? ¿No problema?"	"[Surname], ah, can we keep on talking? No problem?"
Defendant: "No problema."	"No problem."

Figure 12.5 Officer's second request for confirmation of rights-understanding.

SPANISH: From Tape	ENGLISH: Translation
Detective: "Bueno, ya lo pensaste, [UI]"	Well, you thought about it. [unintelligible]
Defendant: [Pause, UI]	[Pause, UI]
Detective: "OK, ¿Qué fue los que pasó?"	OK, what was it that happened?
Defendant: "¿Sí puedo agarrar un abogado yo, no?"	Yes, I can get a lawyer, can't I?
Detective: "Sí, la corte, cuando llegas a corte, la corte no te va a dejar sin abogado, que no tiene dinero.	Yes, the court, when you get to court, the court is not going to leave you without a lawyer, one that does not have money.
Defendant: [25 second pause, then ...] OK.	Defendant: [25 second pause, then ...] OK.

Figure 12.6 Defendant's first request for representation.

SPANISH: From Tape	ENGLISH: Translation
Detective: "OK, ¿hay alguna otra cosa que nos quieres decir acerca de [UI]?"	OK, is there anything else that you want to tell us about the [unintelligible]?
Defendant: "No, pues, ya no más, pues como fue por defensa propia, no más quiero un abogado."	No, well, no more now, well since it was in self defense, I just want a lawyer.
Detective: "[UI] OK."	[UI] OK.

Figure 12.7 Defendant's second request for representation.

the detective spoke fast, in a softer and lower voice, using unclear and unintelligible language in at least three instances.

Section 2. Officer's first request for confirmation of rights understanding: After a break in the interview, a second detective confirmed with the defendant that he had been explained his rights. His second question to the defendant contained the Spanish words "in cash" as opposed to "in effect," and ended unintelligibly. See Figure 12.4.

Section 3. Officer's second request for confirmation of rights understanding: Upon return to questioning from a break, the interviewing officer asked the defendant, "… can we keep on talking? No problem?" The defendant replied, "No problem." See Figure 12.5.

Section 4. Defendant's first request for representation: Immediately following the police confirmation, the defendant made his first request for an attorney and was told he could have one when he got to court. When the officer answered "yes" to the defendant's request, it was with rising intonation, indicating question or surprise. When the defendant finally and quietly said what sounds like "OK," it was after a long 25-second pause, indicating possible lack of understanding or agreement. See Figure 12.6.

Section 5. Defendant's second request for representation: Near the very end of the interview, the defendant again asked for a lawyer, saying, "… well, since it was in self-defense, I just want a lawyer." See Figure 12.7.

There are six factors present in the circumstances of the defendant's interview and confession that could negatively affect his ability to understand his rights:

1. The detective's mistakes in spoken Spanish and his momentary lapses into unintelligible speech during the Miranda reading could have significantly inhibited comprehension.
2. The detective's distinctly rapid, low-pitched, unpaused reading style of the Miranda rights was much less intelligible than his normal speaking and questioning style on the rest of the tape.
3. The last direct Miranda question — the one related specifically to defendant's waiver of his rights, "Do you wish to speak with us now?" — was not asked.
4. The officer's first request for comprehension of rights from the defendant contained mistakes in Spanish, as well as mumbled speech, affecting comprehension.
5. It is likely that, after a rest break, the questioning officer's purpose in asking the defendant, "Can we keep on talking? No problem?" was to renew what had previously been taken as his agreement to waive his rights and agree to talk. However, due to the defendant's probable lack of initial understanding and to this absence of specific reference to the

initial rights-reading, no indication is in the conversation that the officer's probable intent constituted a mutual understanding between him and the defendant. The defendant's response, "No problem," was very likely his verbal indicator of readiness to continue the process, reflecting an understanding only of the conversational imperative of the moment. The defendant's lack of understanding of the question is confirmed by his subsequent long pause after another question from the interviewing officer, then his first request for an attorney.

6. The defendant tested his own understanding of his rights on the two occasions during the interview, when he asked for legal representation but did not receive it. His first request for an attorney was met with a "yes" response, with high and rising intonation, which indicates surprise or questioning, not affirmation. Then, the actual response to the question was, "… when you get to court…," implying that he was not entitled to one at that moment, even though the detective had previously told him, "*Usted tiene derecho de hablar con un abogado, y de tenerlo presente antes y durante los preguntes* [sic]," i.e., "You have the right to speak with an attorney and to have him present before and during the questions." Then, after this response from the officer, the defendant paused a full 25 seconds before mumbling, "OK," indicating probable incomprehension of his rights to an attorney, at least during the process of arrest and questioning. The defendant's second request for an attorney did not prompt a response from the officer. The result of these failed attempts to obtain an attorney may have indicated to him (on the first request), and then confirmed for him (on the second request), that his understanding of his rights was mistaken, when in actual fact it was correct, i.e., that he could have an attorney at that time of the questioning.

There are also at least four important indicators that the defendant did not, in fact, understand his rights or what the interviewers were really saying when he was read his rights:

1. After his rights were read, the defendant had to be prompted twice to say, "Yes," then he moved immediately to his own different agenda and question, "Yes, but why are you holding me?" In other conversational contexts, "Yes, but …," can be taken as an indication that the speaker was not listening to or objects to what the previous speaker was saying. In this case, there is no discourse indicator (i.e., response) in the conversation to indicate that he was focused on what was being said. His focus was on his arrest.

2. In the officer's first request for rights-comprehension, there is no audible response from the defendant to the officer's second question about rights still being in effect.
3. The defendant's first request for legal representation came moments after an interviewing officer's request for confirmation that it was OK to continue, indicating that the defendant might have begun to understand his right to representation. However, when he was put off by the officer ("Yes ... when you get to court"), the defendant did not insist; instead, he paused for a very long time.
4. The defendant connected his last request for a lawyer to a claim of self-defense. This indicates that he may have then understood his right to legal representation to be associated only with a position of self-defense: "... well, since it was self-defense, I just want a lawyer."

Conclusions: The circumstances of the police interview of the defendant are sufficient to lead to three conclusions: first, it is highly probable that the "Miranda rights" as read were not comprehensible to the defendant; second, the factors that negatively affected the defendant's comprehension are objectively demonstrable; third, the defendant demonstrated his probable lack of comprehension in significant and multiple ways.

Opinion: The defendant did not understand his Miranda rights or the circumstances surrounding references to his rights during his 1995 interview and confession.

12.3.1.2 *Case 2: U.S. v. Defendant (2000)*

An FBI wire tap produced multiple recordings of the Spanish-language telephone conversations of a man suspected of participating in a large-scale drug making operation in California. The government maintained that its transcript of the English interpretation of the conversations demonstrated the speaker's significant involvement in the operation.

Two independent translators listened simultaneously to nine of the recorded conversations considered to be the most incriminating. Their evaluation of the respective translations from the Spanish tape to the English transcript revealed many errors in the government's English interpretations of the conversations. The conversation sample was large enough, and the errors found were varied enough in type and frequent enough in occurrence, for the defendant's defense counsel to question seriously the reliability of the interpretation of the entire corpus of telephone conversations.

Upon completion of the assessment of the conversations, interpretation or translation errors were grouped into various types, examples of which are presented in Figure 12.8. Error-types are as follows:

SPANISH: Tape Recording	ENGLISH: Government Transcript	ENGLISH: Two-Person Translation
	Mistranslation: **positive → negative**	
Válgame	Damn!	Gosh! [expression of surprise or disgust]
	Mistranslation: **positive → vulgar**	
A que a toda madre que me habla	What a fucking surprise that you call me.	How great that you call me.
	Mistranslation: **neutral → vulgar**	
tiene los *diches* puestos allí	he's got the fuckers posted there	he has the ditches set up there.
para tumbar el *diche*	to know the fucking ...	to break down the ditch
	Mistranslation: **neutral → vulgar**	
Andamos en chinga.	Here we are, fucking.	Here we are working hard.
Ando en chinga.	I'm really fucking.	I'm really working hard.
un puto	a faggot	a "dummy"
el puto	the faggot	the "dummy"
un cabrón trabajador	a bastard worker	a "dumb ass" worker
	Mistranslation: **small → large scale**	
cinco fransquillos	five baskets sacks [sic]	five small jars
cuadrillo	the land	small plot of land
Para eso de las semillas	This business of the seeds	That thing of the seeds
	Word Addition	
los tractores	the fucking tractors	the tractors
usted se la lleva tranquilo allí en la troca	you are all cool and calm in the truck	you're there all calm in the truck
Digo, no, no le preguntó a don ... ?	I saying, you did not find Mr. Roberto?	I'm saying, you did not ask Mr. ... ?

Figure 12.8 Comparison of two English translations from Spanish wire-tap recording.

1. *Mistranslation: making the English more negative or vulgar than the Spanish is.* These errors are potentially very serious because they go beyond linguistic differences, demonstrating a possible prosecutorial

agenda, conscious or unconscious, on the part of the translator. The role of the translator should be to provide a neutral bridge between the two languages, not to enhance the meaning in any way during the translation process. Such translations make the speaker appear (e.g., to the trier of fact) to use more negative and vulgar language than he really does.

2. *Mistranslation: using English that exaggerates what was actually said in Spanish.* These errors also reflect a potential translator's agenda because such magnification of reality in the English translations might make activities discussed in the telephone conversations appear more compatible with a large-scale drug operation than the actual conversation indicates.

3. *Mistranslation: addition of material in English.* Additions are potentially serious because adding a word like "fucking" to a phrase that does not contain it reflects negatively on the speaker (defendant). Also, adding the name "Roberto," which was reportedly related to a "respected" player known to be long-active in local drug activity, goes beyond interpreting something *that was actually said* as drug-related; it is effectively inserting drug-related language where there was none in the conversation. Such interpretative enhancement might possibly be the role of others involved in such a case, but it is definitely not the role of the translator.

4. *Mistranslation: translating unintelligible material.* At various points in the recorded conversations, the two independent translators listened to the recording various times and with different tape recorders but were not able to ascertain what was said in Spanish. Yet, unambiguous translations for some of these sections were reflected in the transcripts without the usual UI (unintelligible) notation.

5. *Interpreted translation: translator extending meaning beyond what is said in Spanish.* This is another case of the translator consciously or unconsciously demonstrating something more than a linguistic agenda in the translation process.

The translator demonstrated in various ways that he was not altogether familiar with colloquial Spanish. On the one hand, he mistranslated *todo el pedo* as "the whole fart" (which is meaningless in English) instead of something more like the colloquial English, "all that shit," and he did not know that the commonly used *raite* is a word borrowed from English meaning "ride." On the other hand, he readily interpretted *milpas* and *muebles* as possibly drug-related words, as indicated by the quote marks put around both words in the translation ("milpas" and "furniture") and by the suggestion of "[thousand dollars?]" in brackets for *milpas*.

SPANISH: From Tape	ENGLISH: Translation
Detective: "Tiene derecho de *permanecerse* callado, ¿entiendes?"	**Detective:** You have the right to remain quiet, do you understand?
Defendant: "No sé mucho de eso. Yo nunca estaba así, en estas cosas."	**Defendant:** I don't know much about that. I was never, like this, in these things.

Figure 12.9 Dialog relating to, "Did he understand his rights?"

The translator's role does not include extending the meaning of translated words to include anything more than what is said. In this case, however, the translator has given considerable evidence that he has provided a less than linguistically objective interpretation of what was said in the taped conversations.

Findings: There are two serious problems with the English translations of these tape-recorded Spanish conversations. First, the translation process and the relative competence of the translator in both languages can be questioned due to irregularities such as the following: the translation contains phrases that have no meaning in English, some material present in Spanish is omitted in English, words unintelligible or absent in Spanish are unambiguously translated to English without a "UI" designation, and familiarity with colloquial Spanish is demonstrated to be inconsistent.

Second, the misplaced prosecutorial bias of the government's translator is evident in translations that 1) demonstrate English words and phrases more negative or vulgar than their Spanish sources, 2) are amplified in the English toward meanings more consistent with the drug-making charges, or 3) are added to the English seemingly for the same purpose.

12.3.1.3 Case 3: California v. Defendant (2001)

This is a case of a monolingual Mexican national who was facing charges related to the sexual abuse of a minor. The detective in the case prepared a "synopsis" of the interview, wherein he made two claims important to the case: 1) "The following is a synopsis of the taped interview, conducted in Spanish" and 2) "I advised [defendant] of his Miranda rights in Spanish." Defense counsel wanted to know if these statements were consistent with what was said in the police interview, articulating her specific request in questions A, B, and C below:

A. *Did he understand his rights?* The defendant indicated that he did not understand his rights. When directly asked the first time (see Figure 12.9), he said no. Nothing was done at that point to stop the conversation or otherwise mitigate his lack of understanding. In fact, the detective reported, "He stated he understood each of his rights."

B. *Did he give a knowing and intelligent waiver of his rights?* The subsequent discourse between detective and defendant indicates that the defendant did not waive his rights. This conversation, represented in Figure 12.10, demonstrates this in various ways:

1. He gave three minimal responses (*uh, uh* or *um, hum*), which do not necessarily indicate understanding.
2. As a result, the defendant had to be prompted three times to answer *yes* or *no*.
3. In one instance, after prompting ("Yes?"), he did not give an audible answer.
4. When he did answer *yes* (three times), it is not clear what the *yes* was a response to — the question or the prompting to say *yes* or *no*.
5. Grammatical mistakes in the detective's Spanish make it hard to follow: switching between *tú* and *usted* forms; *a quedarse silencio*; *mientras que hagaren*; *se le daré*; *antes que hague*.
6. When asked directly if he wanted to speak about why he was arrested, the defendant said he wanted to know why.

The function of the detective's question, "... and do you want to speak with us about why you were arrested?" seems to be one of requesting the defendant to waive his right not to speak. However, the defendant's response ("I would like to know why I was arrested.") indicates that he saw the question as the detective's offer to explain why they arrested him. Such a response is not a waiver of his right to remain silent. Nevertheless, the detective's report says, "He ... agreed to speak to me about this case and why he was arrested."

C. *Did the defendant understand the nature of the questions he was responding to when describing what he did?* The detective did not speak Spanish well enough to successfully conduct such an interview. He made repeated lexical and grammatical errors in Spanish, many of them making the meaning of what he was saying impossible to interpret. He sometimes used English when he did not know a term or phrase in Spanish; however, the defendant did not speak English. At other times the detective mumbled unintelligibly when he did not know a term or phrase in Spanish. He also asked the defendant questions about how to say certain things in Spanish, especially terms relating to body parts and intercourse.

The most obvious of the many examples of the detective's problems with the Spanish language was the multiple use of the well-known false cognate, *molestar*, which means *to bother* in Spanish but looks like the English word *molest*. He told the defendant that the alleged victim of abuse indicated that "*él la estuvo* **molestando**," and the defendant quizzically responded, "*¿ ... que*

SPANISH: From Tape	ENGLISH: Translation
Detective: "Bueno, sí, tiene derecho de quedarse callado o no decir nada. Ah, tiene derecho a quedarse *silencio* silencioso ... UI. ¿Entiende eso?"	**Detective:** Ok, you do have the right to remain quiet or not say anything. Ah, you have the right to remain silence silent ... UI. Do you understand that?
Defendant: Uh, uh.	**Defendant:** Uh, uh.
Detective: ¿Sí?	**Detective:** Yes?
Defendant: ---	**Defendant:** [No audible answer.]
Detective: "Cualquiera cosa que diga se puede usarse en su contra en una corte, ¿entiendes?"	**Detective:** Anything you say can be used against you in court. Do you understand?
Defendant: "Um, hum."	**Defendant:** Um, hum.
Detective: "Díme sí o no, por favor."	**Detective:** Tell me yes or no.
Defendant: "Sí."	**Defendant:** Yes.
Detective: "Tiene el derecho de tener un abogado antes que y mientras que hagaren cualquier preguntas, ¿entiendes?"	**Detective:** You have the right to have an attorney before and while they ask any questions, do you understand?
Defendant: "Sí."	**Defendant:** Yes.
Detective: "Si no tiene con que pagarle a un abogado se le daré uno sin costo antes que hague cualquier preguntas, ¿entiendes?"	**Detective:** If you do not have money to pay the lawyer, one will be I will give you one without cost before ask any questions. Do you understand?
Defendant: "Um hum."	**Detective:** Um, hum.
Detective: "¿Entiendes?"	**Detective:** Do you understand?
Defendant: "Sí."	**Defendant:** Yes.
Detective: "Ok, ¿y sí gusta hablar con nosotros de por qué estuvo arrestado?	**Detective:** Ok, and you do want to speak with us about why you were arrested?
Defendant: "Pues, sí me gustaría saber por qué. Yo no sé por qué, me cae de sorpresa, verdad.	**Defendant:** Well, I *would* like to know why. I do not know why, it comes as a surprise to me, truly.

Figure 12.10 Dialog relating to, "Did he give an intelligent waiver of his rights?"

la estuve molestando hace una semana … ?" — as if to ask why he would be arrested for bothering her.

Conclusion: The "synopsis" of the police interview provided in the detective's report is at best inaccurate due to his lack of Spanish language proficiency. At worst, it is simply untruthful. Whatever the cause of such miscommunication, its consequences are serious.

This type of situation could be readily avoided by creating a Spanish-language transcript of the police interview before an English-language translation or summary is made. For example, in addition to the discourse-related problems described above, the defendant in this case repeatedly denied penetrating the victim, which is not reflected in the police summary. A carefully prepared transcript of the police interview in the language used during the interview would protect victim and accused alike. If the accuracy of such a record were stipulated to by all parties, all other translations, "synopses," and the like could emanate from and be checked against that source document.

12.3.2 Questioned Authorship

12.3.2.1 Case 4: California v. Armas (1997)

A child died as the result of injuries related to either physical abuse or an accident, i.e., falling down a flight of stairs. The prosecutor's position was that the death was not an accident. The defendant was being tried on murder charges, and his attorney requested an analysis of a 1995 confession allegedly written by the defendant. The defendant agreed that the signature was his, but that the confession itself was not.

As occasionally happens, a linguistic analysis was sought as the result of differences in the opinions of the forensic document examiners. The prosecutor's document examiner maintained that, "Exemplar writer [defendant] wrote the signature found on the document in question. Also, there is strong evidence that the same writer wrote the handprinting on the face of the document …" However, the defense's document examiner concluded that, "The … evidence indicates that there are some differences which indicate the possibility that the questioned writing was prepared by another writer."

The linguistic analysis: The Spanish language confession that the defendant was alleged to have written is reproduced below (Figure 12.11). The defendants's known writings were also examined. These consisted of two types of texts: three "requested" writings in the form of handwritten repetitions of the confession elicited from dictation, and two multipage "natural" writings in the form of personal letters to relatives. The principal court exhibit was a line-by-line (score-format) comparison of the confession to the three dictated confessions (Figure 12.12).

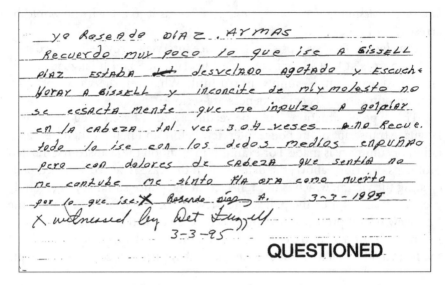

Figure 12.11 Questioned confession.

This analysis facilitated identification and isolation of 24 style-markers as diagnostic of authorship in the comparison and contrast of the questioned confession vis-à-vis all the known writings analyzed in this case. Five of these were markers of similarity and 19 were markers of difference between the questioned confession and known writings.

Results of this analysis are summarized in Figure 12.13. While this shows some similarities, it demonstrates numerous differences between the questioned confession and the known request writings. With respect to the similarities between the questioned confession and the defendant's known writings, these are style-markers of a frequency and type that mark the writing of very many undereducated writers of Spanish in Mexico. Writing without punctuation and accents is common, and the frequent pronunciation and spelling of *siento* as *sinto* (and like-words containing this and similar diphthongs) is well documented in research on the process of monophthongization in Mexican–Spanish dialects.

The -cs- *ecsactamente* spelling of *exactamente* is a conservative form of -*x*- documented since at least the 15th century (Patón, 1965), which still turns up in the writing of undereducated Mexican writers (in linguistically conservative areas) because of their documented frequent use of older linguistic forms and because of the close connection of -*cs*- to the actual sound produced by the -*x*- in words such as *exactamente*.

With respect to the differences between the questioned confession and the defendant's known writings, these are also style-markers of a frequency and type that mark the writing of very many undereducated writers of Spanish

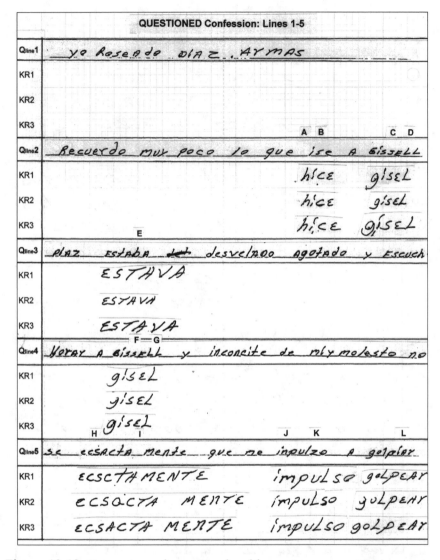

Figure 12.12 Comparison of questioned and known request writings, page 1.

in Mexico. However, these marked differences are much more significant than the similarities (discussed above) for a number of important reasons. First, they are greater in number, with only 20% of the markers being similarities but 80% differences. Second, chance similarities between two different writers are much more possible than chance differences in a single writer. It is possible that these five similarities co-occur in questioned and known by chance, but nearly impossible that the other 19 markers contrast (differ) in the writings of one and the same author, no matter how common each style marker may be in written Spanish.

QUESTIONED Confession: Lines 6-10			
	M	N O	P
Qline6	en la cabeza tal ves 3 o 4 veses a.no Recue.		
KR1	CAVEZA VEZ 34 VEZES		
KR2	CA.VEZA VEZ 34 VEZES		
KR3	CAVEZA VEZ 34 VEZES		S
	Q - R		
Qline7	tode lo ise con los dedos medios enpuñao		
KR1	hice		EMPUÑADOS
KR2	hice		empuÑados.
KR3	hice	T	EMPUÑAdos
Qline8	pere con dolores de cabeza que sentia na		
KR1	CAVEZA		
KR2	CAVEZA		
KR3	U V W CAVEZA.	X	Y
Qline9	ne contube me sinto Ha ora como muerta		
KR1	conTUVE Mi sinto Ahora MUERTA		
KR2	conTUVE Mi sinto Ahora MUEYTA		
KR3	Z1- Z2 contuve mi sinto Ahora muerta		
Qline10	per lo que see X Resardo Diap A. 3-3-1995		
KR1	hice		
KR2	hice		
KR3	hice		
Qline11	X witnessed by Det Duggell 3-3-95		

Figure 12.12 Comparison of questioned and known request writings, page 2.

Third, *Gisel* is written with double -*ss*- and double -*ll* in the questioned confession, a form closer to an English or French spelling. The defendant repeatedly writes it in the Spanish form, *Gisel* with one -*s*- and one -*l*. The double-letters spelling would be unusual for a speaker or writer of Spanish as a first language, and any such spelling difference in a known proper name would be unexpected in any single writer.

Last, *todo lo que hice* ("all that I did") is realized in the question confession without the required relative *que* ("that"): *todo lo ise*. Although the *que* is also absent in the dictated known request writings, it is present in all cases in the defendant's self-produced known letter writing. It is significant that the English equivalent of *que* ("that") is optional in the corresponding English construction. The defendant is a completely monolingual Spanish speaker; if he were the writer of the questioned confession, where would the absence of *que*, a likely case of interference from English, and for that matter the non-Spanish spelling of *Gisel*, come from? Both variations are possible signs of a writer whose first language is not Spanish.

Conclusions: These findings provide observable and demonstrative bases for three conclusions: first, the similarities shared by the questioned confession and the known writings are very likely due to chance coincidence, given their small number (relative to differences) and their frequent presence as class features in the writing of undereducated writers of Mexican–Spanish. Second, the differences between the questioned and known writings cannot be accounted for by chance, due to their large number (20) and quality. Third, the number and quality of differences between the questioned and known writings are sufficient to exclude the defendant, at more than reasonable-doubt level, as the author of the questioned confession.

12.3.2.2   Case 5: Corporation v. Defendant (1997)

A bilingual woman was allegedly harassed at work by her foreman. A strategy she used to combat the harassment was to send anonymous letters to her foreman and his wife. Letters appeared in Spanish, in English, and in both languages mixed together. As a part of the resolution to the case, the company wanted to know if, indeed, the letters were written and sent by the complainant.

A large number of style-markers (40) resulted from the analysis of variation in both languages, and in the questioned letters and known reference writings of the woman. Figure 12.14 contains a summary list of variation present in both languages; limited examples from five of these style-markers (number 17, 19, 27, 35, and 36) appear in Figure 12.15.

STYLE MARKER	CONTEXT	VARIATION	IN QUESTIONED WRITING? Yes-No/ # of Tokens	IN KNOWN REQUEST WRITING? Yes-No/ # of Tokens	IN KNOWN NATURAL WRITING? Yes-No/ # of Tokens
MARKERS OF SIMILARITY					
1 Punctuation			No	No	No
2 Accent Marks			No	No	No
3 x -> cs	EXACTAMENTE	ECSACTA MENTE	Yes/1	Yes/3	-
4 Space before suffix	EXACTAMENTE	ECSACTA_MENTE	Yes/1	Yes/2	-
5 ie -> i	SIENTO	SINTO	Yes/1	Yes/4	Yes/1
MARKERS OF DIFFERENCE					
1 Format of date	3-3-95	3-3-1995	Yes/1	No/2	-
2 Movement of h	AHORA	HA ORA	Yes/1	No/3	No/1
3 Ahora -> 2 words	AHORA	HA_ORA	Yes/1	No/3	No/3
4 Loss of h	HICE	ISE	Yes/3	No/9	-
5 c -> s	HICE	ISE	Yes/3	No/9	-
6 c -> s	VECES	VESES	Yes/1	No/3	-
7 c -> z	VECES	VEZES	No/1	Yes/3	-

	TAL VEZ	TAL VES			
8 z -> s	TAL VEZ	TAL VES	Yes/1	No/3	-
9 s -> ss	GISEL	GISSELL	Yes/2	No/6	-
10 l -> ll	GISEL	GISSELL	Yes/2	No/6	-
11 s -> z	IMPULSÓ	INPULZO	Yes/1	No/3	-
12 m -> n	IMPULSÓ	INPULZO	Yes/1	No/3	-
13 b -> v	CABEZA	CAVEZA	No/2	Yes/6	-
14 b -> v	ESTABA	ESTAVA	No/1	Yes/3	Yes/2
15 v -> b	CONTUVE	CONTUBE	Yes/1	No/3	-
16 ea -> ia	GOLPEAR	GOLPIAR	Yes/1	No/3	-
17 -o -> -a	MUERTO	MUERTA	No/1	Yes/3	-
18 me -> mi	ME SIENTO	MI SINTO	No/1	Yes/3	-
19 o -> -	3 O 4 VECES	3-4 VESES	No/1	Yes/3	-
20 Absence of que	TODO LO QUE ISE	TODO LO ISE	Yes/1	Yes/3	No/5

Figure 12.13 Summary of style-markers in questioned and known writings.

STYLE MARKERS	QUEST. ENGLISH	QUEST. SPANISH	KNOWN ENGLISH	KNOWN SPANISH
FORMAT				
1 Numbered street names without ordinal marker: 34 STREET	+	+	+	+
2 Numbered street names with incorrect ordinal marker: 42nd vs. 42st STREET	+	+	+	+
3 No space between "30AVE"	+		+	
4 Placement of period after zip code	+	+	+	
5 Placement of zip code on a separate line	+		+	
6 Hours/minutes in time-of-day divided with period and colon: 1.15 and 1:15	+	+	+	+
7 Form of date: "FRIDAY 18"	+			+
PUNCTUATION				
8 Abbreviated titles without period: MR / MRS / MS	+	+	+	+
9 Period absent after "AVE," "ST", and "BLVD"	+	+	+	+
10 Spacing between text and following punctuation	+	+	+	+
11 Colon for period or comma	+	+	+	+
12 Semicolon for comma	+		+	
13 Multiple sentence-final punctuation marks: comma + period	+	+	+	+
14 Multiple sentence-final punctuation marks: period + period	+	+		+
15 Word division at line-end using the underscore as a hyphen	+		+	+
16 Apostrophe absent in contractions	+		+	
SPELLING				
17 Metathesis of "-HT" to "-TH" in "-GHT" words	+		+	
18 "TH" for "THE"	+		+	
19 "WIT" for "WITH"	+		+	+
20 "LOOSE" for "LOSE"	+		+	
21 "HARRASMENT" for "HARASSMENT"	+		+	
22 "RESPET" for "RESPECT"	+		+	
23 "THRU" for "THROUGH"	+		+	
24 "TO" for "TOO"	+		+	
25 Other misspellings: "FRUSTRADED" and "MEKE"		+	+	
26 Spanish /s/ sound: RESE/REZE for RECE, COMIENZE for COMIENCE				+

	Questioned English	Known English	Questioned Spanish	Known Spanish
WORD FORMATION				
27 Substitution of "A" for "I'LL"	+	+	+	+
28 Two words run together as one	+	+	+	+
29 One word separated into parts	+	+	+	+
30 Writing "LaSalle" as two words: "LA SALLE"	+	+		+
31 Substitution of "IS" for "IF"	+	+		
32 Substitution of regularized past-tense form "LOSTED" for "LOST"	+	+		
33 Substitution of "THAT" for "THAN"	+	+		
34 Substitution of plural "WOMEN" for singular "WOMAN"	+	+		
35 Substitution of subject pronoun for possessive: e.g., "HE" for "HIS"	+	+		
36 Substitution of "NO" for "NOT"	+	+		+
37 Substitution of "HE" for "SHE"	+	+		+
38 Absence of "-s" inflections	+	+		
39 Absence of "-ed" inflection	+	+		
SENTENCE SYNTAX				
40 Spanish–English code switching or language mixing	+	+	+	+

Data Sources

QUESTIONED ENGLISH: Letters and envelopes (24 pp)
KNOWN ENGLISH: Letters and envelopes of bilingual writer (322 pp)
QUESTIONED SPANISH: Letters and envelopes (13 pages)
KNOWN SPANISH: Letters and envelopes of bilingual writer (35 pp)

Figure 12.14 Summary of 40 style-markers in bilingual (Spanish and English) writings.

QUESTIONED - English	KNOWN - English and Spanish
#17. *-GTH for -GHT in words ending in -GHT*	
FIGTHING	*nigth*
NIGTH	*nigth*
FIGTH	*Rigths*
#19. *WIT for WITH*	
WIT ALL	*wit on em*
	wit MiKe
#27. *A for I'LL*	
A SEEYOU	*a See you*
A SEE YOU	
#35. *Subject pronoun for possessive: HE for HIS*	
YOU NICE ASS	*Hey lawyer*
he day time	*he feet*
YOU REPUT	
#36. *NO for NOT*	
NO SUPOSE	*no supose*
NO A PORTER	*no showing*

Figure 12.15 Selected examples of style-markers in bilingual (Spanish and English) writings.

References

Alcalá Arévalo, P., *Sobre recursos estilísticos en la narrativa de Miguel Delibes*, Universidad de Extremadura, Cáceres, 1991.

Alonso, D., *Poesía española: Ensayo de métodos y límites estilísticos*, 5a ed., 3a reimp., Gredos, Madrid, 1981.

Ballester, A., Santamaría, C., and Marcos-Marín, F., Transcription conventions used for the corpus of spoken contemporary Spanish, *Lit. Linguis. Comput.*, 8:4:283–292, 1993.

Bia, A. and Pedreño, A., The Miguel de Cervantes digital library: the Hispanic voice on the web, *Lit. Linguis. Comput.*, 16:1:161–177, 2001.

Cotterill, J., Reading the rights: a cautionary tale of comprehension and comprehensibility, *Foren. Linguis.*, 7:1:4–25, 2000.

de Kock, J. et al., *Elementos para una estilística computacional*, Tomos I y II, Coloquio, Madrid, 1983.

Gariano, C., *El enfoque estilístico y estructural de las obras medievales*, Alcalá, Madrid, 1968.

Garrido Medina, J., *Estilo y texto en la lengua*, Gredos, Madrid, 1997.

Granger, G-G., *Essai d'une philosophie du style*, Armand Colin, Paris, 1968.

Hagège, C., *L'enfant aux deux langues*, Jacob, Paris, 1996.

Herrera, A., Análisis estilístico de un cuerpo lingüístico de 30 escritores mexicoamericanos, unpublished paper, California State University, Fresno, December 2000.

Lara, L. F., Ham Chande, R., and García Hidalgo, M. I., *Investigaciones Lingüísticas en Lexicografía*, CELL, Jornadas 89, El Colegio de México, México, D. F., 1979.

Menéndez Pidal, R., *Poesía juglaresca, y orígenes de las literaturas románicas*, Instituto de Estidios Políticos, Madrid, 1957.

Patón, B. J., *Epítome de la ortografía latina y castellana, Instituciones de la gramática española*, Eds., Quilis, A. and Rozas, J. M., Consejo Superior de Investigaciones Científicas, Madrid, 1965.

Robb, J. W., *El estilo de Alfonso Reyes*, 2a ed., Fondo de Cultura Económica, México, 1978.

Shuy, R., Ten unanswered language questions about Miranda, *Foren. Linguis.*, 4:2:175–196, 1997.

Valderrábanos, A. S., Díaz, E. T., and de Pineda Pérez, M. A., An automatic information extraction system for the *Diccionario Ideológico de la Lengua Española* by Julio Casares, *Lit. Linguis. Comput.*, 9:3:203–214, 1994.

Yllera, A., *Estilística, poética y semiótica literaria*, Alianza, Madrid, 1974.

Adjudicated Cases Cited

California v. Armas, Los Angeles County Superior Court (Long Beach), Case No. NA 023430, 1996.

Bibliography: Spanish Style and Stylistics

Alazraki, J., *La prosa narrativa de Jorge Luis Borges: temas, estilo*, 2da ed. aumentada, Biblioteca Románica Hispánica, Gredos, Madrid, 1974.

Alcalá Arévalo, P., *Sobre recursos estilísticos en la narrativa de Miguel Delibes*, Universidad de Extremadura, Cáceres, 1991.

Allés, F. and Abad, P., *Cómo dar más estilo a vuestro español*, De Vecchi, Barcelona, 1971.

Alonso, D., *Poesía española: Ensayo de métodos y límites estilísticos*, 5a ed., 3a reimp., Gredos, Madrid, 1981.

Alonso Pedraz, M., *Ciencia del lenguaje arte del estilo*, 12a ed., Aguilar, Madrid, 1975.

Alonso, S., *Tensión semántica (lenguaje y estilo) de Gracián*, Institución Fernando el Católico, Zaragoza, 1981.

Báez San José, V., *La estilística de Dámaso Alonso*, 2a ed. corregida, Universidad de Sevilla, Sevilla, 1971.

Baroja, P., *La intuición y el estilo*, ed. conmemorativa del centenario del nacimiento de Pío Baroja, Caro Raggio, Madrid, 1983.

Bello Vazquez, F., *Lenguaje y estilo en la obra de Pío Baroja*, Universidad de Salamanca, Salamanca, 1988.

Beltrán, V., *El estilo de la lírica cortés: para una metodología del análisis literario*, Promociones y Publicaciones Universitarias, Barcelona, 1990.

Castagnino, R. H., *El análisis literario: Introducción metodológica a una estilística integral*, 9a ed., Nova, Buenos Aires, 1974.

Clarín. Manual de estilo, Clarín/Aguilar, Buenos Aires, 1997.

Ciplijauskaite, B., *Baroja, un estilo*, Insula, Madrid, 1972.

Criado de Val, M., *Análisis verbal del estilo: índices verbales de Cervantes, de Avellaneda y del autor de "La Tía Fingida,"* RFE, Madrid, 1953.

de Kock, J. et al., *Elementos para una estilística computacional,* Tomos I y II, Coloquio, Madrid, 1983.

Diario Perfil. Cómo leer el diario: gramática y estilo, documentación enciclopédica actualizada, contexto social, jurídico y económico, Perfil, Buenos Aires, 1998

Escartin Gual, M. and Martinez Celdran, E., *Comentario estilístico y estructural de textos literarios,* Vol. 1 teoría y comentarios, PPU, Barcelona, 1983.

Fernandez, P. H., *Estilística: Estilo, figuras estilísticas, tropos,* José Porrúa Turanzas, Madrid, 1972.

Galmés de Fuentes, Á., *Influencias sintácticas y estilísticas del árabe en la prosa medieval castellana,* 2a ed., Gredos, Madrid, 1996.

Galmés de Fuentes, Á., Lengua y estilo en la literatura aljamiado-morisca, *Nueva Revista de Filología Hispánica,* 30:2, 420–440, 1981.

Gariano, C., *El enfoque estilístico y estructural de las obras medievales,* Alcalá, Madrid, 1968.

Garrido Medina, J., *Estilo y texto en la lengua,* Gredos, Madrid, 1997.

Gonzalez Maldonado, E., *El arte del estilo en José Enrique Rodó: Análisis de El Camino de Paros,* Edil, San Juan, Puerto Rico, 1968.

Guiraud, P., La estilística, trad. esp. de *La stylistique* (Presses Universitaires de France, Paris, 1961), Nova, Buenos Aires, 1967.

Gutiérrez Marrone, N., *El estilo de Juan Rulfo: estudio lingüístico,* Bilingual Press/Editorial Bilingüe, New York, 1978.

Hatzfeld, H., *Estudios de estilística,* Planeta, Barcelona, 1975.

Haverkate, H. and Dehennin, E., Presentación, Lingüística y estilística de textos, en *Foro Hispánico: Revista Hispánica de los Países Bajos,* Rodopi, Amsterdam, 8:7–29, 1994.

Heger, K., *Báltasar Gracián, estilo lingüístico y doctrina de valores: estudio sobre la actitud literaria del conceptismo,* Institución "Fernando el Católico," Zaragoza, 1982.

Hengeveld, K., El discurso reproducido: análisis lingüístico, en *Foro Hispánico: Revista Hispánica de los Países Bajos,* Rodopi, Amsterdam, 8:31–39, 1994.

Herrero Mayor, A., *El castellano de Rubén Darío: Idioma y estilo,* Ministerio de Cultura y Educación, Buenos Aires, 1972.

Lagmanovich, D., *Libro de estilo para universitarios,* Universidad Nacional de Tucumán, 1997.

Lapesa, R., *De Ayala a Ayala: estudios literarios y estilísticos*, Bella Bellatrix, ISTMO, 1988.

Lopez-Casanova, A. and Alonso, E., *El análisis estilístico: (poesía/novela)*, Bello, Valencia, undated.

Lorenzo-Rivero, L., *Larra: Lengua y estilo, Colleción Nova Scholar*, Playor, Madrid, 1977.

Marichal, J., *La voluntad de estilo: teoría e historia del ensayismo hispánico*, Seix Barral, Barcelona, 1957.

Marichal, J., *Teoría e historia del ensayismo hispánico*, Alianza, Madrid, 1984.

Martín, J. L., *Crítica estilística*, Gredos, Madrid, 1973.

Martín, J. L., *La narrativa de Vargas Llosa: acercamiento estilístico*, Gredos, Madrid, 1974.

Martín Vivaldi, G., *Curso de redacción: teoría y práctica de la composición y del estilo*, Paraninfo, Madrid, 1972.

Menéndez Pidal, R., *La lengua de Cristóbal Colón: el estilo de Santa Teresa y otros estudios sobre el siglo XVI*, 4a ed., Espasa–Calpe, Madrid, 1958.

Menéndez Pidal, R., *Poesía juglaresca, y orígenes de las literaturas románicas*, Instituto de Estudios Políticos, Madrid, 1957.

Montes, H., *Ensayos estilísticos*, Gredos, Madrid, 1975.

Paz Gago, J. M., *La estilística*, Síntesis, Madrid, 1993.

Robb, J. W., *El estilo de Alfonso Reyes*, 2a ed., Fondo de Cultura Económica, México, 1965.

Román, I., *La creatividad en el estilo de Galdós*, Cabildo Insular de Gran Canaria, Las Palmas de Gran Canaria, 1993.

Sebeok, T. A., *Estilo del lenguaje*, Cátedra, Madrid, 1974.

Spillner, B., *Lingüística y literatura: investigación del estilo, retórica, lingüística del texto*, versión española de Elena Bombín de *Linguistik und Literaturwissenschaft, Stilforschung, Rhetorik, Textlinguistik* (1974), Gredos, Madrid, 1979.

Spitzer, L., *Estilo y estructura en la literatura española*, Crítica, Barcelona, 1980.

Ullman, S., *Lenguaje y estilo*, traducción del inglés por Juan Martín Ruiz-Werner de *Language and Style* (1964), Aguilar, Madrid, 1968.

Verdín Díaz, G., *Introducción al estilo indirecto libre en español*, RFE, Madrid, 1970.

Vossler, K., Spitzer, L., and Hatzfield, H., *Introducción a la estilística romance*, traducción y notas de Amado Alonso y Raimundo Lida, 2a ed., Instituto de Filología, Universidad de Buenos Aires, Buenos Aires, 1942.

La Voz de Galicia. Manual de estilo, Galicia, La Coruña, 1992.

Yllera, A., *Estilística, poética y semiótica literaria*, Alianza, Madrid, 1974.

Young, R. J., *Introducción al arte y estilo literario*, UNAM, México, 1978.

Stylistic Features of Gujarati Letter Writing: A Note

13

P. J. MISTRY

Abstract

આ "કરણ ગુજરાતીમાં લખાયેલા કાગળો પરત્વે છે. એમાં એક વ્યક્તિએ લખેલા છ કૌટુંબિક કાગળોમાં જોવા મળતાં લક્ષણો ચર્ચ્યાં છે. અક્ષરોના વળાંકો, શબ્દો-શબ્દો અને વાક્યો-વાક્યો વચ્ચેનું અંતર જેવી તરત નજરે ચઢતી સામ્યતા ઉપરાંત વિભાગો, વિરામચિહ્નો, જોડણી જેવી દસ આંતરિક બાબતોનું સામ્ય એમાં બતાવ્યું છે. આ સમાન લક્ષણો તેર વર્ષના ગાળા દરમ્યાન લખાયેલા છએ છ કાગળોમાં છે અને લખનારની જ વિશિષ્ટતાઓના ધોતક છે. આમ અવાજની માફક લખાણમાં પણ વ્યક્તિની ઓળખની ચાવી મળે છે.

13.1 Introduction

This chapter presents some orthographic and linguistic features found in personal letters written in Gujarati that help to single out the writer. Formal letters are quite rigid in following conventions and prescriptive standards with respect to general format, fixed expressions, and salutations. Personal correspondence, however, is less observant of such regulations in other aspects of phrasing and even in the act of writing. More often than not these are speedy and spontaneous compositions which are revealing sources for distinguishing stylistic attributes of the author. Unlike typed or printed documents, handwritten materials additionally embody orthographic peculiarities of their writers. The data have been chosen for these reasons. Also provided is information about differentiating traits from a language typologically different from English and with a nonalphabetic writing system; it also delves into the type of literacy among a majority that is notably different in level and restricted in function.

13.2 Language

Gujarati is a descendant of Sanskrit and a sister language of Bengali, Hindi, Sinhalese, and other Indo–Aryan languages. The official language of the state of Gujarat located on the western coast of India, it has more than 42 million speakers with a 62% literacy rate. Sizable numbers of Gujarati speakers are settled in Africa, Great Britain, and North America, as well as in other states of India. For a brief account of the language see Mistry (2001).

Written documents are of interest for the encoded message accessible to those who know the writing system and the represented language. The knowledge entails erudition of a specific script and how it is applied to an individual language and used by individual members.

13.3 Writing System

Gujarati uses a modified version of the Devanagari script used in writing Sanskrit and such modern languages as Hindi, Marathi, and Nepali. It consists of 45 notations, presented mostly in their native order in Figure 13.1.

For other consonant clusters, the consonant symbol other than the last one loses the space or the vertical stroke located to its right, e.g., જ્ય /jy/, and સ્ય /sy/. In addition to the notations for consonants and vowels, there is a diacritic for nasalization, a dot above the *akṣara*, e.g., માં /mã/.

The system used in representing Gujarati is the same across languages with Devanagari or Devanagari-based script. It has the *akṣara*, which is a vowel or a sequence of a consonant and a vowel as a unit. Symbols for consonants are all *akṣara* since they have the vowel *a* inherently. The symbol મ represents /ma/. Other vowels are represented by specific diacritics attached to the consonants, e.g., મા /maa/, મુ /mu/ and મે /me/. For more details, see Lambert (1953), Cardona (1965), and Mistry (1996).

The writing system thus does not fit in the traditional division of alphabetic and syllabic. It has been called "alphasyllabary" (Bright, 1996) to refer to the dual types of features associated with it. In this diacritic-based syllabic system, graphic similarities match with phonemic similarities.

13.4 Literacy

The 62% literacy rate among the speakers of Gujarati is comparatively high for the region; however, the range varies noticeably from the minimum to the ideal. In the idealized variety, the standard-setting status of Sanskrit prevails in the selection and in the spelling of words. Opting for Sanskrit loans — many with clusters — and retaining in writing the distinction of short:long for high vowels, three-way distinctions among sibilants (š, ṣ, s), the vocalic ṛ, etc., no longer present in the phonemic system of the language are the hallmarks of this level of literacy. The fluency in this variety exists among a small group who are exposed extensively to compositions containing

GUJARATI CHARACTERS With Transliteration					
Nine Vowels	અ	આ	ઈ	ઈ	
	/a/	/aa/	/i/	/ii/	
	ઉ	ઊ	એ	ઓ	ઋ
	/u/	/uu/	/e/	/o/	/r̥/
Two Diphthongs	ઐ	ઔ			
	/ai/	/au/			
Thirty-Two Consonants	ક	ખ	ગ	ઘ	
	/k/	/kʰ/	/g/	/gʰ/	
	ચ	છ	જ	ઝ	
	/c/	/cʰ/	/j/	/jʰ/	
	ટ	ઠ	ડ	ઢ	ણ
	/ṭ/	/ṭʰ/	/ḍ/	/ḍʰ/	/ṇ/
	ત	થ	દ	ધ	ન
	/t/	/tʰ/	/d/	/dʰ/	/n/
	પ	ફ	બ	ભ	મ
	/p/	/pʰ/	/b/	/bʰ/	/m/
	ય	ર	લ	વ	
	/y/	/r/	/l/	/v/	
	શ	ષ	સ		
	/š/	/ṣ/	/s/		
	હ	ળ			
	/h/	/ḷ/			
Two Conjuncts	ક્ષ	જ્ઞ			
	/kṣ/	/gn/			

Figure 13.1 Gujarati characters.

these characters and for whom reading and writing is central to their life and profession. They write in different genres, often produce carefully crafted compositions after several different drafts, and exhibit an elated degree of diglossia. This high-status literacy (HSL) is considered the norm and is used in education, literature, and printed documents.

What is referred to as HSL is in a somewhat fluid state. Even among the small minority commanding HSL, there are three groups. One adheres to the prescribed conventions, a second adopts an extra overdifferentiation with two more notations in the script, and the third has mainly discarded the long:short distinction of high vowels. A majority of publications follows the prescribed conventions of the first group.

The vast majority of writers, however, are not particular about the prescriptive standards; for them literacy is restricted to a narrow range of functions: they comprehend written materials that they occasionally come across in their day-to-day activities and write simple messages in much the way that they speak. Their writings are primarily personal letters written in a customary layout and marked with deviations from conventional spellings and with regional and individual features.

13.5 The Letters

The six letters examined here were written by an elderly relative of the author, who grew up in a village and had a seventh-grade education. These are all the letters that could be found, i.e., they are not selected by any other criterion. The letters span a period of 13 years from October 1987 to October 2000. Figure 13.2 contains the number assigned to each letter and the date of its writing, as well as an extracted segment.

13.6 Ten Characteristics Common to All Letters

In addition to the graphic similarities among the six letters, i.e., size and shape of characters, spacing between words and lines, and general layout, several other characteristics are common across this time span and exhibited in all the letters. Ten of these will be discussed in the following sections.

13.6.1 Format

All of the letters have six components:

1. Name of the village and the date at the top on the right; letters written by others have either place or date, the complete address with or without the date, or nothing.
2. The salutation addressing all members of the family; other letter writers may address only one family member.
3. The sender's name with blessings; other writers may mention other family members as well.
4. The customary opening, "we are fine, hope you are fine." Not all writers have this expression or component in their letters.
5. Main body of the letter
6. The same closing salutation; other writers may use other available expressions.

Letter Number	Date	Sample Segment
1	October 5 1987	
2	August 14 1989	
3	May 17 1994	
4	June 12 1999	
5	August 31 2000	
6	October 4, 2000	

Figure 13.2 Six Gujarati letters with the same component from each letter.

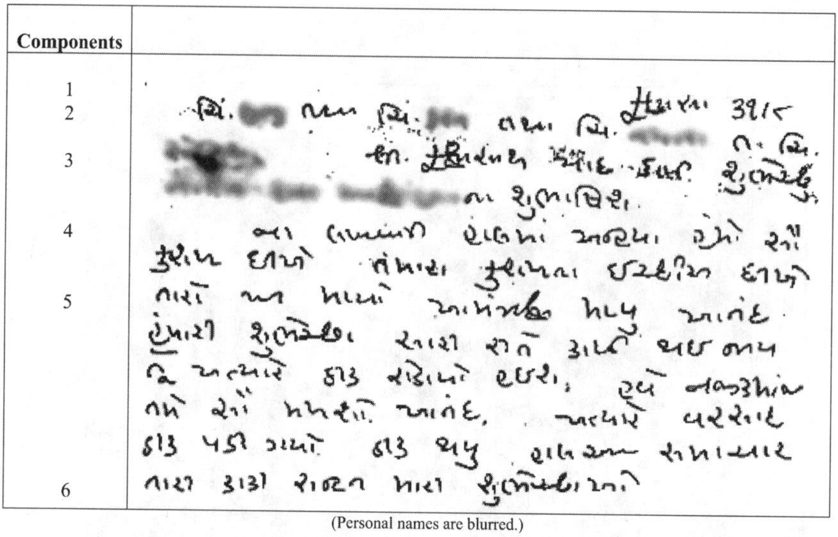

(Personal names are blurred.)

Figure 13.3 Letter 5 with six components identified.

Except for the main body of the letter, the other components are almost identical in these letters. Figure 13.3 is a short letter with these six components identified.

13.6.2 Punctuation

Letters vary with respect to punctuation marks, from completely absent to all adequately present, thus revealing the individual writer's preference. These letters show no consistent punctuation markings. Out of the 16 possible sites for punctuation marks in letter 6, the question mark is appropriately present at three places. The period, on the other hand, is present at four places and absent at nine. Another notable feature of the letter is a slightly longer space between sentences than between words.

13.6.3 English Loans

Words from English have penetrated all regional and social groups of Gujarat and, in some instances, have replaced native words. These letters contain both the day-to-day words (*minita* "minute," *phona* "phone," *ṭaaima* "time") and the learned words (*cekapa* "check up," *ṭrita menṭa* "treatment"). While many prefer to write learned words in the Roman alphabet, the author of these letters writes everything in the native orthography only. Note the use of the notation for the long *i* for "minute" and "treatment."

In writing English loans, there is a lack of uniformity, especially with respect to the long:short notations for high vowels, even in HSL. Thus, the Gujarati weekly, *Gujarat Times*, has the word *matrimonial* occurring twice

Example	Letters	HSL
(a)	sacavaaya jaaya	sacavaai jaaya
(b)	thaya gayaa	thai gayaa
(c)	thaya hati	thai hati
(d)	gai haše	gai haše
(e)	thaya gai che	thai gai che
(f)	thai gai haše	thai gai haše

Figure 13.4 Examples of *ya* for *i*.

on page 3 of its September 21, 2001, issue. The second syllable is printed with long *i* in the first occurrence and short *i* in its second occurrence.

13.6.4 *Ya* or *i* for Postvocalic Final *i*

What is represented by the notation for *i* in the postvocalic position in HSL is spelled *ya* by a large segment of Gujarati speakers. In the letters examined, there is fluctuation between these two ways of representation. Figure 13.4 contains some examples from the letters, along with their counterparts in HSL. Examples (a), (b), and (c) show the *ya:i* correspondence between the writer and HSL, whereas in (d) the same *i:i* is found. The phrase in (e) has two items, the first with *ya:i* correspondence and the second with *i:i*. The phrase in (f) also has two items, both written with *i:i* correspondence. Note that the transliterated *i* in such instances is random since the Gujarati notations for long *i* ૐ and short *i* ૐ are exceedingly similar in shape, and, consequently, the one targeted by a writer remains unclear.

13.6.5 Regional Vowel Nasalization

These letters come from Southern Gujarat, a region noted for minimum nasalization of word-final vowels (Mistry, 1997). This regional feature prevails in these letters, as shown in Figure 13.5.

13.6.6 Murmur

Another regional feature that marks these letters is the form of the first person exclusive plural pronoun. What is written *ame* (nominative) and *amaarii* (genitive) in HSL consistently appear as *hame* and *hamaarii* in these letters. Additionally interesting is the consistent appearance of a graphic notation for nasalization on the first syllable of this pronoun (see Figure 13.2). The presence of initial *h* is attributable to the "murmured" *a* as the first segment of this pronoun. It is this murmuring that is quite prominent in Southern Gujarat, and that surfaces as *h* in the writer's spelling of the pronoun.

Example	Letters	HSL
(a)	caalu	caalũ
(b)	ahi	ahĩ
(c)	tyaanaa	tyããna
(d)	saaru	saarũ
(e)	ochu	ochũ
(f)	thayu	thayũ

Figure 13.5 Nasalization of vowels in Southern Gujarat.

13.6.7 Sibilants

Gujarati orthography overdifferentiates by having three notations for sibilants: શ for /š/, ષ for /ṣ/ and સ for /s/. The conventions for writing them do not match the facts of pronunciation, causing confusion for representing a two-way phonemic distinction. Thus, each letter contains the unusually spelled word *šubhaaṣiša* (*šubhaasĩṣa* in HSL). Similarly, letter 2 of August 14, 1989 has *kamanašiiba* (*kamanahiba* in HSL). The name "Sonia" also appears with initial notation varying between *sa* and *ša*, even in the same letter.

13.6.8 Long-Short *i*

Another writing convention at odds with pronunciation relates to high vowels with the long:short distinction in notation. After several years of schooling, the large majority remains uncertain about how to split a single unit of sound into two distinct notations. Writers face no difficulties in their written communication by using either notation. The writer of these letters uses the notation for short *i* for personal names and for some learned Sanskrit words. However, English words are written with the notation for the long *i* (see the words for "minute" and "treatment" discussed in 13.7.3), and the same notation prevails in writing many other words, e.g., *tabiiyata* (*tabiyata* in HSL), *mããgaliika* (*mããgalika* in HSL).

13.6.9 Hypercorrection

One feature singularly and consistently present in these letters is the use of the notation for the short *i* in a specific construction. In a verbal complex, the first verb that should end with a notation for a long *i* always has a short *i* in these letters, as may be seen in the examples in Figure 13.6. Like other features, this individual feature is present from the first letter (October 5, 1987) through the last one (October 4, 2000).

Example	Letters	HSL
(a)	aawi gayaa	aawii gayaa
(b)	laawi hati	laawii hati
(c)	ajamaawi jou	ajamaawii jou
(d)	aawi gai	aawii gai

Figure 13.6 Hypercorrection of long *i* to short *i*.

Sentence	Gujarati Transliteration	English Translation
1	taaro patra maḷyo your letter received	Received your letter.
2	aamãtraṇa maḷyu invitation received	Received the invitation.
3	aanãda glad	Very happy.
4	hamaarii šubhecchaao our best wishes	(We send) our best wishes.
5	saarii riite kaama thai jaaya good manner-in work happen go	Hope the event takes place successfully.
6	tu atyaare ṭhiika rokaayo haiša you at present much occupied will be	You must be very busy at present.
7	have najiihamãã ja tame sau malšo now near in [emph] you all will meet	All of you will get together in the near future.
8	aanãda glad	Very happy.
9	atyaare varasaada ṭhiika pai gayo at present rain much fell went	It rained well.
10	ṭhiika thayu good happened	That was good.

Figure 13.7 Transliteration of letter 5 (August 31, 2000).

13.6.10 Telegraphic Language

Another noticeable characteristic of these letters is the occurrence of a high proportion of truncated expressions as exemplified in the transliterated version of the main body of letter 5 (August 31, 2000) presented in Figure 13.7. Sentence numbers are inserted at the left to indicate that the 31 words in lines 6 to 10 of the letter divide into ten (fragmentary) sentences. These letters are written on aerograms that also contain letters from other members of the family. A simple comparison of letters from different family members shows that this specific truncated style is not associated with letter writing but with the writer.

13.7 Concluding Remarks

The uniformity in the shape of the alphabetic characters that one finds in print is not present in handwritten materials. Not only are there differences due to different individuals, but handwriting styles of the same individual may also reflect shaping the same character differently, due to factors such as the haste with which it is written or how it connects with the neighboring characters. Further scrutiny brings forth a host of other stylistic features, many of them exclusive to the writer. The scanning of these six letters has shown a repository of such features. Though these features are shown to be present from 1987 to 2000, one can justifiably assume their presence earlier and predict their continued presence throughout the writer's lifetime.

As there are markers of individual uniqueness in speech, similar characteristics exist in writing as well. One's ears can identify a specific individual out of a familiar group by his or her voice quality, with voice prints displaying physical features exclusive to that individual. In much the same fashion, one's eyes can detect the writer of a document. The type of analysis presented here pinpoints distinguishing graphic and stylistic clues for such detection.

References

Bright, W., The Devanagari script, in Daniels, P. and Bright, W., Eds., *The World's Writing Systems*, Oxford University Press, 384–390, Oxford, 1996.

Cardona, G., *A Gujarati Reference Grammar*, University of Pennsylvania Press, Philadelphia, 1965.

Lambert, H. M., *Introduction to the Devanagari Script*, Oxford University Press, Oxford, 1953.

Mistry, P. J., Gujarati, in Garry, J. and Rubino, C., Eds., *Facts about the World's Languages: an Encyclopedia of the World's Major Languages, Past and Present*, H. W. Wilson Co., 274–277, New York, 2001.

Mistry, P. J., Gujarati phonology, in Kaye, A. S., Ed., *Phonologies of Asia and Africa*, Eisenbraun, Winona Lake, 653–673, 1997.

Mistry, P. J., Gujarati writing, in Daniels, P. and Bright, W., Eds., *The World's Writing Systems*, Oxford University Press, 391–394, Oxford, 1996.

The Stylistic Analysis of Korean Writing

14

DONGDOO CHOI

Abstract

문체론 (Stylistics) 은 응용언어학의 한 분야인 법언어학 (Forensic Linguistics) 에서 사용되는 방법론으로서 글쓰기에 나타나는 문체적 특징들을 추적하여, 그 저자를 식별하는데 도움을 준다. 문체론에 관한 연구는 영어와 유럽언어들을 중심으로 발전되어 왔기에, 아시아 언어들, 특히 한국어에 관한 문체론 연구는 찾아 보기 힘들다. 따라서 본 연구의 목적은 한국어의 글쓰기에서 나타나는 일련의 특징들을 제시, 분석함으로써, 한국어 문체론 연구를 한 단계 발전시키고자 하는 데 있다.

이러한 연구 목적을 위해서, 총 서른 한 명의 한국인이 쓴 오십한편의 글쓰기 표본을 수집하였다. 이 언어 자료들은 스물 여섯명이 쓴 마흔 여섯 통의 편지와 다섯 명의 초등학교 삼 학년 학생들의 글쓰기 과제물로 구성되어있다. 서른 한명의 글쓴이들은 연령 면에서 보면 아홉 살에서 예순 네 살에 이르는 넓은 분포도를 그리며, 성별로는 여성이 열 일곱, 남성이 열 네 명이다. 이들이 아흔 두 장에 쓴 약 만 여 개의 단어들로 구성된 언어자료에 근거한 본 연구는 한국어에 나타나는 신뢰도있는 문체변인들을 제공한다.

연구 자료에서 발견된 구체적인 문체적 특징들로는 한자의 사용, 알파벳의 사용, 아라비아 숫자의 사용, 발음나는 대로 쓴 철자법, 구두점, 다양한 띄어쓰기의 용례 등을 들 수 있다. 각각의 특징들에 대한 묘사와 설명 그리고 그 특징들이 함축하고 있는 문체 표시자로서의 중요성에 대한 논의가 연구 자료에서 선택된 보기들과 함께 제시된다. 본 연구는 특히 띄어쓰기와 관련하여 나타나는 다양한 문체적 특성들의 문체 표시자 (Style Marker) 로서의 풍부한 잠재성에 주목하고, 띄어쓰기의 개별적, 집단적 용례에 보다 심도있는 언어학적 분석을 시도하였다.

14.1   Introduction

14.1.1   Korean Writing Style

Style reflects variation within a single writer and among various writers. Writers are constantly selecting among various forms: "In the process of expressing meaning and purpose, every writer selects some linguistic structures at the resultant expense of rejecting many other possible forms" (McMenamin, 1993). The selected linguistic features present style-markers that help determine the authorship of written documents to which the linguistic features belong.

Although considerable research has been done on the Korean language, previous studies provide little insight into the style and stylistics of Korean writing. The goal of the present paper is to describe selected variables of writing style in Korean, with the specific objective of providing a preliminary list of style-markers for further study in Korean stylistics.

The elements of this chapter are ordered as follows: a brief description of the Korean writing system, how the data used in this study were collected and analyzed, examples and discussion of style characteristics found in the corpus of writing, and a focus on aspects of Korean word spacing as a potentially strong characteristic of writing style.

14.1.2   The Writing System of Korean

The Korean alphabetic system, called Hangul, was developed in the 15th century by King Sejong and a group of scholars. While the original Korean alphabet had 28 letters, four of them are now obsolete, leaving 14 consonants and 10 vowels in the current system (Sampson, 1985; Hannas, 1997; Taylor and Taylor, 1995). The Korean alphabet is phonetic; in other words, one can articulate the sounds in words with a high degree of accuracy by following the representation of each Korean letter.

In written Korean, a word is formed by assembling a vowel and a consonant or two. Each written word forms a syllable block representing one of two possible combinations of consonants (C) and vowels (V): CV or CVC. For example, a common family name, 박 /pak/ is a bundled combination of a consonant ㅂ /p/, a vowel ㅏ /a/, and a consonant ㄱ /k/. By contrast, a word in English contains a linear sequence of letters.

Syntactically, Korean is a subject–object–verb (SOV) language, i.e., the verb comes at the end of sentence. In both spoken and written Korean, the subject is a loose element which is usually left out when that to which the subject refers can be identified from the context.

In the Korean lexicon, words borrowed from Chinese account for about half of the Korean vocabulary (Choo and O'Grady, 1996). These are referred to as Sino–Korean words. They are pronounced in the Korean way but can be written in Chinese characters or in Hangul.

In contrast to English, the Korean writing system is prescriptively governed by officially established rules. This chapter follows the *Revised Korean Spelling System* and *Korean Standard Language* announced in 1988 and currently in effect (Lee, 1988). For more on the Korean writing system, see Hannas (1997), Kim–Renaud (1997), Martin (1992), Sampson (1985), Sohn (1999), and Taylor and Taylor (1995).

14.2 Method

14.2.1 Data Collection

For this study, 51 writing samples were collected, which consist of 92 pages, containing about 10,000 word segmentations: among 51 samples, 46 personal letters were written by 26 different writers, and five single samples of writing assignments were authored by five third-grade Korean elementary school students. The student samples were made available by the author's sister, who is an elementary school teacher in Changwon, a city in southeastern Korea; they include the grades that teachers gave to each assignment.

Among the 31 writers, 17 are female, and 14 are male. The range of age of the writers is from 9 to 64. Except for the elementary school students, most of the writers are college-educated or college students: 23 are college students or college-educated, one is a high school graduate, and two are high school students. The letters are mostly between friends; some are love letters. There are letters between a father and son, and between a sister and a younger brother. See Figure 14.1 for actual writing from the corpus.

With respect to the methods used for writing, 10 letters are typed and the rest are hand-written. Noticeably, one adult writer and the five children use what Koreans call 'manuscript sheets' that have 200 small sequential quadrangles. Each quadrangle contains a written syllable, and word segmentations are divided by leaving one intervening quadrangle blank. Elementary school students are required to use the manuscript sheets for writing assignments in order to learn word spacing in Korean, which is why the five students in this study used this type of paper. The receiver of the adult letter written on manuscript sheets said that it was the first time she had received such a letter from the writer. The writer might have had only the manuscript sheets available when she wrote the letter. Before the 1990s, when personal computers were not widely available, writing on manuscript sheets was a requirement for college assignments. See Figure 14.2 for actual manuscript-sheet writing from the corpus.

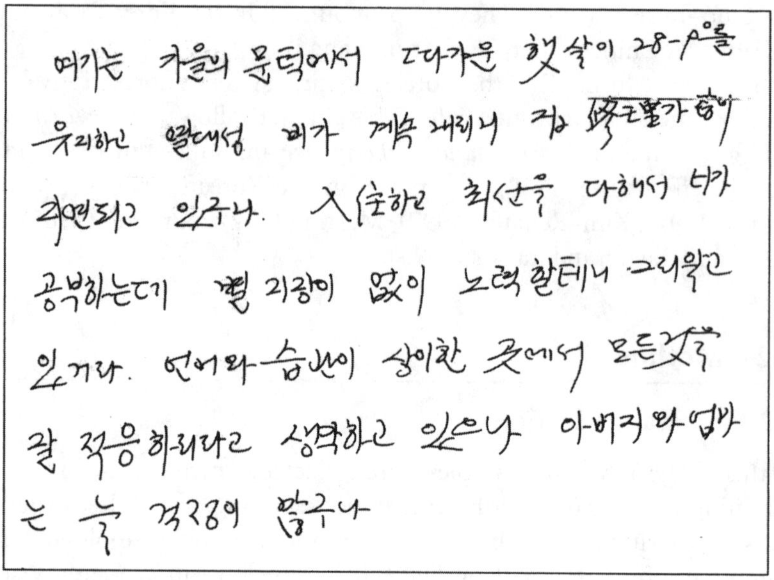

Figure 14.1 Example of Korean writing from corpus.

Figure 14.2 Example of Korean handwriting on manuscript sheet.

14.2.2 Data Analysis

As a preliminary step for the data analysis, observed stylistic variations (style characteristics) were isolated, counted, and compared with the frequency of appearance of the same characteristics in letters of the other writers. This process made it possible to identify a list of surface style characteristics used by some writers but not by others.

The word spacing analysis in particular required several steps. First, more than 500 examples were highlighted as nonstandard variants, following the criteria of the 1988 *Korean Orthographic Rules* (KOR). This step required morphological and syntactic decisions, given that the KOR specifies spacing only with respect to morpheme types. Then, the selected examples were broadly divided into two categories: incorrectly not-spaced and incorrectly spaced. Next, confirmation of the spacing criteria was sought in two computer word processing programs, *Hangul Word Processor 97* (HWP) and the Korean version of *Microsoft Word Processor 97* (MWP), both of which help identify incorrect spellings and forms, including spacing errors.

Instances of word spacing were identified as "problematic" if differences between the author's assessment and that of either word processor indicated uncertainty in determining their correctness; these examples were excluded from the data of this study. In the process of identifying clear instances of spaced and nonspaced words, an interesting third group of words was found: ambiguous spacing in handwritten letters not on manuscript sheets. Some writers put a shorter distance between words than they usually do, thereby causing the reader difficulty in determining whether the words were spaced or not, and possibly reflecting the writers' uncertainty. All possible ambiguous spacing examples were isolated, then each was determined to be ambiguous or not by agreement between two native speakers of Korean. Instances for which the two observers could not agree were excluded from the data set. See examples of spacing in Figure 14.4, and the spacing rule and its exceptions in Section 14.4.2.

14.3 Findings and Discussion

14.3.1 Chinese Characters for Sino–Korean Words: *Hanja*

As mentioned earlier, there are a number of Sino–Korean words in the Korean lexicon which can be written in Chinese characters. In fact, it is not unusual to see simple Chinese characters such as 月 or 日 in Koreans' writing. In fact, of the total 34 occurrences of Chinese characters in the corpus, 15 are of just these two characters. The other 18 Sino–Korean words reflect use of Chinese characters that are more complex, for example:

긍정적으로 思考하고 現實에 적응하기 바란다.
kungjungjokuro sagohago hyunsil-e jokunghaki paranta.
positively thinking reality-to accustomed hope
'I hope that you would be thinking positively and accustomed to reality.'

The Chinese characters used above can be expressed by Korean letters as 사고 for 思考 and 현실 for 現實. This example is from a hand-written letter by a 64-year-old man. Although the data do not include letters of any other older writers, use of Chinese characters is a writing characteristic of older and educated people. The writer of the example above has a high school education, which is a relatively high level of education for his age. In the years when he received official education and had an active social life, Chinese characters were highly valued in school and in social life.

Although the Korean alphabet was invented more than five and a half centuries ago, only around the turn of the last century did Koreans begin widely using it. By law, Chinese characters began to lose their place in the Korean writing system in 1945 (Hannas 1995). For instance, some 30 years ago, elementary school students were taught 400 Chinese characters, but not now. Currently, middle- and high school students are taught Chinese characters in a separate course called *hanmun* 'Chinese word', from the course of National Language, a symbolic sign that Chinese characters are no longer part of Korean. As this development of educational policy for Chinese characters indicates, when the oldest writer in the present corpus was educated over 40 years ago, much more importance was given to knowledge of Chinese characters. At that time, lack of such knowledge meant near social illiteracy. For example, reading newspapers just 15 or 20 years ago required recognition of many Chinese characters expressing lexical words.

Since most Sino–Korean words are lexical nouns, as Kim–Renaud (1997) states regarding the reasons for use of Chinese characters, official documents and law are written with Chinese characters and Hangul to disambiguate intended meanings. Additionally, using Chinese characters not only helps avoid ambiguity but also has a way of making the writer appear educated or knowledgeable. This might explain the use of Chinese characters by the other two writers in the present corpus, i.e., both are law students for whom knowing Chinese characters is integral to success in their studies and bar examination. Chinese characters in writing, therefore, represent "class characteristics" of older and/or educated people, thus indicating something of the social background of writers.

14.3.2   Roman Alphabetic Letters from English

As with the case of Chinese characters, Korean writers sometimes use simple English words in their writing. The writings of 22 of the 31 letter writers exhibit Roman letters, English words, and some English sentences. Such writings share the feature that the foreign alphabetic letters are used to articulate proper names, such as MBC (the name of a company), or unit words such as kg (kilogram), and to express short English expressions or simple words such as *good bye, from, to, pen,* etc. Even two elementary students used English words such as IQ and CD.

Of the total 125 occurrences of English used by the 22 writers, 47 examples are used as loan words or simple English words. Four writers show a strong tendency (71 of the 125 occurrences) to use English letters, words, and sentences. Two of these came with their parents to the U.S. when they were 12 and 10, a third is an international student at an American university, and the fourth is an English major in a Korean university. Their use of English words seems to be associated with mutual understanding of English, i.e., their and the receiver's knowledge of English. The remaining seven examples of English letters in the writings are used to articulate the sound of laughter: *haha* (3 occurrences in a female writer and one in a male writer), and the pronunciations of some Korean words such as *oppa* 'older brother called by sisters or younger females' (three occurrences in the same female writer).

14.3.3   Arabic Numbers for Korean Number Words

As in English, the numeric concepts in Korean can be cardinal or ordinal. Ordinal numeric concepts are used to show an order and cardinal numbers are used for the other cases of expressions of numeric concepts. In the latter case, depending on the concepts that the numbers are needed to express, whether to use Arabic numbers or corresponding Korean words is generally determined by custom.

In order to see the cases where Koreans tend to use Korean or Arabic numbers, I with another Korean native speaker made a list of possible cases of number use and five different Korean native speakers were asked whether they would use Korean words or Arabic numbers to express the listed cases. The results of this survey reveal significant divisions among the cases. They unanimously said that ordinal numbers should be used in Korean in expressing duration and passage of time, the number of times, items, and in counting the number of kinds. In contrast, those questioned showed a tendency to use Arabic numbers for cases such as telephone numbers, time, grades, dates, weight, year, etc.

The data demonstrate that the three divisions showed in Figure 14.3 are true to a degree. Of all the 193 number-related expressions, only seven of them are ordinal, with 47 phrases corresponding to the second category; the remaining 139 fall under the third category. Among seven ordinal numeric phrases, six are written in Korean and one in Arabic, as shown in Figure 14.3. Of the 47 phrases of the second category, 14 are written in Arabic numbers

	First Category (Should be Korean)	Second Category (Usually Korean)	Third Category (Usually Arabic numbers)
Situation	showing an order	time duration & passage, the number of times and items, in counting kinds, etc.	telephone number, time, grade, date, weight, year, etc.
Examples from the corpus of writing	첫 째 chot.jjae first-Suffix "the first"	두 개 tu.kae two piece "two items"	2 월 9 일 yi.wol. ku.il two month nine date "Ninth of February"
Exceptions from the corpus of writing	3 번 째 se. pon jjae third-order-suffix "the third"	2 개 yi.kae two piece	십 여 도 sip.yo.to. 10 about degree "10 or so degree"

Figure 14.3 Three different styles of numeric expressions in Korean.

and 33 in Korean. That 11 of the 14 Arabic number occurrences in this category are made by only three writers, indicates that writers tend to use Korean writing in expressing the second category cases.

Lastly, of the remaining 136 examples, 129 numeric expressions are written in Arabic. Of the exceptional seven Arabic number occurrences, four (two for an amount of money and two for idiomatic expressions) may be disregarded because, although money amounts are usually written in Korean, writers might not bother to use Korean for money amounts in personal letters.

14.3.4   Invented Spellings

Invented spelling refers to spelling words the way that the writer pronounces them. Although Korean writing is highly phonetic, the writing system does not always represent the exact pronunciations of words. For example, a sentential ending suffix, 게, *ke* is often pronounced as a glottal 께 *kke* in:

내가 그곳에 있을께
nae-ka   kukot-e   it-ul-kke
I-nom there-at   exist-will-sentential ending
'I will be there.'

The examples of invented spellings found in the data (167 occurrences) do not seem to present a pattern of class style-markers; rather, they can be seen as individual characteristics in the sense that no apparent differences between men and women, or in terms of age, are found. Although it could be assumed that some other variables, such as use of a dialect or education, could affect the occurrence of invented spellings, the data of this study are not comprehensive enough to determine this.

However, the spelling data do show two significant characteristics with implications for determining possible authorship in Korean. First, when documents are written using a computer-based word processor, some errors of invented spellings are corrected by the computer program. Of the six typed letters, two are e-mails and the other four are computer-generated. The two uncorrected e-mails include eight occurrences of the total 15 invented spellings found in the typed letters. The seven other examples in the typed letters are abbreviated forms of words which are colloquial but sometimes found in formal writing. This indicates that computer typing will reduce invented spellings.

It can also be inferred that, if e-mails are written on a word processor and then cut and pasted, at least some of errors might be removed. Secondly, the two elementary school students with the most errors in writing (20 occurrences of the total 167 errors) received the lowest grades, which suggests the reasonable hypothesis that less educated writers will be more likely to make this kind of error.

14.3.5 Punctuation Marks

In the collected data, the letters of three male writers in particular gave the impression that their writing lacked certain aspects of usual male writing or contained certain features usually found in the writing of Korean women. The analysis of punctuation marks provides a basis for this impression.

A variety of punctuation marks is found in the data. The marks with the highest frequency (573/665) are those that people usually come across in reading: question mark (205), exclamation point (137), and ellipsis mark (231). Of the 573 usual marks, 177 occurrences of the three kinds are found in male writers. Of the 177 examples, 136 are found in the three male writers (46, 39, and 51 occurrences, respectively). Female writers, therefore, have a greater tendency to use the usual punctuation marks than male writers, making the high frequency of quotation marks in male writing a function of individual style.

In addition, one female writer showed a strong tendency to use ellipsis marks (...) — 78 times in her two pages of personal letters. Twelve occurrences of inch-long horizontal lines that possibly replace ellipsis marks are found in another female writer. Thus, this kind of ellipsis use could certainly be characteristic of a writer.

14.4   Word Spacing

14.4.1   Difficulty of Spacing for Korean Writers

Both before and after the establishment of the 1988 KOR, many previous works that deal with the Korean language such as Lee (1983), Kim et al. (1990), and Martin (1992) consistently express the difficulty of spacing for Korean writers, saying, for example, that "spacing is the area in the current orthographic rules in which people are most likely to make mistakes and which they see as the trickiest problem" (Lee, 1983, translated from Korean by the author). It becomes apparent from works published after 1988 that the problem has remained the same since the establishment of the 1988 orthographic rules. Regarding the complexity of spacing, Lee (1988) states that "[o]ne of the most difficult problems in the Korean spelling system is to determine the word boundary in a consistent manner." In plain terms, how difficult spacing is for Korean writers can be understood from a recent newspaper commentary by Y. H. Park on Korean orthography (*The Kukmin Daily*, October 11, 2000). The columnist says that, although he is writing about the Korean orthography, there would be errors galore in the column if KOR were strictly applied to his writing.

14.4.2   The Spacing Rule and Selected Exceptions

The principal rule of spacing in the 1988 *Revised Korean Spelling System* is deceptively simple: every word in a sentence should be spaced from the neighboring words. What presents difficulty regarding spacing is the definition of a *word*. For example, whereas functional suffixes are treated as individual words in school grammar, the definition of word in the context of the spacing rule does not include function words.

Furthermore, the perception of what a word is varies, such that some people do not put a space between the elements of a compound noun, but some do. Also, a number of words can be used as individual words in one context but dependent (unseparated) words in another. To determine how to space them, writers first need to know the rules. Then syntactic and morphological analysis should be done to know how the word in question functions in a particular context, for example, by consulting a dictionary that indicates the possible categories of words.

The wide spectrum of variations of spacing among writers reflects the fact that the 1988 orthographic system (KOR, Chapter 5) allows 10 exceptions to the one principal rule of spacing. Since the discussion of these exceptions in detail is beyond the range of this chapter, only selected exceptions that served as criteria for selecting examples for data sets will be discussed here:

1. Suffixes are attached to their host words. In other words, case markers, postpositions, and so forth should be attached to the preceding host word.
2. Dependent nouns should be spaced from the preceding word. The category of dependent nouns refers to words with so meager a lexical meaning that they could be categorically located between functional and lexical words.
3. Number and unit words should be spaced, but when number and unit words appear in order, they should not be spaced. Although the 1988 rules allow the possibility of not spacing number from unit words in showing an order, in this study, those that are not spaced are put in the incorrectly spaced category.

14.4.3 Spacing Variations in Writing: What Can Occur?

This section shows how spacing variation looks in actual writing from the data. As stated earlier, the data present three spacing variants: incorrectly spaced, incorrectly not spaced, and ambiguously spaced.

The five examples below commonly involve a word, 데 *te*, that can be either a dependent noun that should be spaced from the preceding segmentation, or a suffix that should not be spaced, depending on the context in which it appears. One example involves a dependent noun, 거 *ko*, which is the colloquially abbreviated form of 것 *kot*. This word should be spaced from the preceding word but is ambiguously spaced in Figure 14.4.

14.4.4 Findings

Particles in Korean are theoretically divided into nominal and verbal. Nominal particles are subdivided into postpositions, conjunctives, delimiters, etc., and verbal suffixes into mood, discourse, honorifics, etc. (Sells, 1995; Sohn, 1999). In this study, particles are broadly divided into two kinds: case markers and those that have certain semantic properties such as *pute* (from) and *kkaci* (to). Except for one instance in the writing of an elementary school student, no spacing variation with case markers is found in any of the writers. Hence, a safe generalization is that native speakers of Korean will rarely make spacing errors with case markers.

The area that accounts for the largest portion (n = 111) of the incorrectly not-spaced category (n = 310) is related to dependent nouns. As stated earlier, dependent nouns have very weak semantic properties, so they cannot be independently employed. It is probable that people who made spacing errors in this area perceive dependent nouns as function words that attach to their host words, i.e., they regard the preceding words and dependent nouns as

CORRECT	Examples
Should be spaced, and IS spaced.	
Should not be spaced, and is NOT spaced.	
INCORRECT	**Examples**
Should be spaced, but is NOT spaced.	
Should not be spaced, but IS spaced.	
AMBIGUOUS	**Examples**
Should be spaced, and has $\frac{1}{2}$ space.	
Should not be spaced, and has $\frac{1}{2}$ space.	

Figure 14.4 Spacing variations in writing.

one graphic segment. This assumption would be one possible explanation for the large number of spacing variation related dependent nouns.

Another factor that can cause this difficulty is more complex. Some dependent nouns can, according to the context, be used as particles. To determine the grammatical category of certain words in sentences, careful linguistic analysis is required, which ordinary writers cannot usually do. Therefore, even with explicit awareness of this spacing rule, a writer may still demonstrate considerable spacing variation related to dependent nouns.

Spacing also appears to be associated with a writer's gender. The hand-written letters of women writers (except those written on manuscript sheets) present an interesting tendency of ambiguous spacing. Of 31 writers, 9 writers show the tendency to ambiguously space words that are prone to spacing variation, such as dependent nouns, compound nouns, lexical particles, etc. For example, Figure 14.5 shows how a dependent noun, 것 *kot*, varies in writing among writers. As mentioned above, 거 *ko* shown in Figure 14.5 is the colloquially abbreviated form of 것 *kot*.

Types of Variation	
Clearly Not Spaced	정말 웃긴건 같아
Ambiguously Spaced	더 힘든거 같애
Clearly Spaced	않을 거 같아.

Figure 14.5 Spacing: Nonspaced and spaced vis-à-vis ambiguous.

Of the 18 female writing samples, three are written on manuscript sheets and five are typed. Among the remaining 10 handwritten samples of female writers, seven demonstrate ambiguous spacing. In contrast, only the letters of the two male writers considered previously as not usual male writers present ambiguous spacing examples.

Although the data collected for this study are not sufficient to make a strong generalization about spacing and gender, it appears that the style characteristic of ambiguous spacing may be a class marker of Korean female writers. Given that 31 examples (of the total 84 examples of ambiguous spacing) occur in the nine letters of the two atypical male writers, the appearance of ambiguous spacing in male writers may prove to be a strong individual style-marker.

Korean writers demonstrate less variation in words that should not be spaced but are (n = 86), and more variation in words that should be spaced but are not (n = 310). A common feature in the data for cases of words that should be spaced but are not is related to the dual properties of certain words that can function as different grammatical elements in sentences according to the context in which they appear.

For example, one writer consistently spaces from the preceding word, a suffix, 데 *te*, that can also act as a dependent noun in another context. Only in cases where 데 denotes the meaning of a place, case, or point, can 데 function as a dependent noun. Otherwise, it should be regarded as a suffix, 데, that should be attached to its preceding host word (Examples related to this word are illustrated in Figure 14.4).

The same kind of error with a different dependent noun is found in a different writer. He spaces (five times) a suffix, 지 /ci/, that can be used in a different context as a dependent noun showing a temporal meaning, *since,* depending on the context. For example, 지 in the following excerpted phrase is used as a suffix that comes after the predicate of a clause assigning an interrogative nuance to the clause, but it is incorrectly spaced from the preceding part:

커피 중독증이 내게 전염되었는 지
ko.fi.   cung.tok.cung.i. nae.ke. con.yum.toe.ot.nun.   ci
coffee addiction symptom-Nom   I-to   transmitted   Suffix
'whether your coffee addiction has been transmitted to me'

Another interesting finding concerning incorrectly spaced words involves writers' perceptions of individual words and their semantic properties. Suffixes usually do not have concrete meanings, but some suffixes have relatively strong semantic properties, which would lead some writers to see them as independent words. In this regard, for example, seven occurrences of spacing a postposition, 부터 *pwu.the* 'from', from its host word are found in four writers. And spacing errors of suffixes such as 밖에 *pak.e* (seven occurrences in four writers), 까지 *kka.ci* (three occurrences in three writers) can be understood in the same way. The fact that the word 밖 *pak* in 밖에 *pak.e* can be used as a noun meaning *outside* would be another possible cause of the spacing error.

Comparing the incorrectly nonspaced errors and the incorrectly spaced errors made by the five children reveals a significant implication for spacing as a style-marker of children's writing. The number of incorrectly spaced errors made by the elementary school students is 24, accounting for more than a quarter of the total 86 incorrectly spaced errors. By comparison, the number of incorrectly nonspaced errors made is only 14, a very small portion of the total 310 errors. This difference indicates that children are more likely to make errors by inserting a space where it should not appear than by leaving out a space where it should appear — the opposite of the adult tendency in spacing variation.

Lastly, it should be pointed out that computer word processor programs may reduce especially spacing errors related to dependent nouns and particles, but they are not entirely reliable. HWP, for example, will automatically identify some errors of this kind as correct; MSW will mechanically show as errors possibly correct forms as questionable, suggesting similar forms in the pop-up menu created by the right button of the mouse.

14.5   Conclusions

The reasonably large size of this corpus of Korean writing allows this study to identify a reliable list of style characteristics for Korean. Specifically, Chinese characters for Sino–Korean words in writing are found to be class characteristics of old and/or educated people. Use of Roman alphabetic letters from English is found in the writings of 22 writers, including two children. Words with Roman letters are usually used to express certain English words, such as *good bye, from,* etc., proper names, and unit words. For Arabic numbers in Korean number expressions, an informal survey suggests dividing possible situations where numeric expressions are needed into three, with the use of Arabic numbers varying for each.

Next, the study suggests the possibility that invented spelling functions as an individual rather than class marker of style, with the two caveats that a computer-based word processor would remove invented spelling errors, and less educated writers would be more likely to make this kind of error. With respect to punctuation, the data suggest that female writers have a greater tendency to use certain punctuation marks than male writers.

A principal focus of this research is word spacing, a feature with considerable variation due to its difficulty for Korean writers. The data present three categories of spacing variations: incorrectly not-spaced words, incorrectly spaced words, and ambiguously spaced words. Adult writers demonstrate no spacing variation with suffixes that are case markers. The largest portion of the incorrectly not-spaced category involves dependent nouns. Also, the data suggest a tendency for women to use more ambiguous spacing than men. Adults tend to demonstrate more variation by incorrectly not-spacing, in contrast to children, who demonstrate more variation by incorrectly spacing.

Also with regard to word spacing, certain words have dual properties ultimately specified by their context, and the relatively strong semantic properties that some suffixes have increase spacing variation for those suffixes. Lastly, it is possible that computer word processors might remove some of characteristics related to spacing errors, particularly those involving dependent nouns and particles.

This research demonstrates a need for descriptive research on spacing vis-à-vis Korean morphology and syntax. Further morphosyntactic research on Korean will provide a good basis not only for developing knowledge of spacing as stylistic variation but also for meaningful pedagogical approaches to teaching spacing, thereby lessening the tangible difficulty that Korean writers have with it.

References

Choo, M. and O'Grady, W., *Handbook of Korean Vocabulary: a Resource for Word Recognition and Comprehension,* University of Hawaii Press, Honolulu, 1996.

Hannas, W. C., Korea's attempts to eliminate Chinese characters and the implications for Romanizing Chinese, *Lang. Probl. Lang. Plann.,* 19:3:250–270, 1995.

Hannas, W. C., *Asia's Orthographic Dilemma,* University of Hawaii Press, Honolulu, 1997.

Kim, D. B., Choi, K. S, and Kang, J. W., Morphological analysis of Korean and its dictionary: Hangul spelling and word-spacing checker using the connectivity information, *Lang. Res.*, 26:1:87–116, 1990.

Kim–Renaud, Y. K., The phonological analysis reflected in the Korean writing system, in Kim–Renaud, Y. K., Ed., *The Korean Alphabet: Its History and Structure*, University of Hawaii Press, Honolulu, 1997, 345–357.

Lee, H. B., Revised Korean spelling system, *Korean J.*, 28:4:34–41, 1988.

Lee, S. O. Problem areas in Korean orthography, *Lang. Res.*, 19:1:123–137, 1983.

Martin, S. M., *A Reference Grammar of Korean*, Charles E. Tuttle Company, Rutland, VT, 1992.

McMenamin, G., *Forensic Stylistics*, Elsevier, New York, 1993.

Ministry of Education, *The Korean Spelling System* (한글맞춤법), Seoul, 1988.

Park, Y. H., Correctly using our words and language (translated from the Korean), *The Kukmin Daily*, October 11, 2000, p. 6.

Sampson, G., *Writing Systems: a Linguistic Introduction*, Stanford University Press, Stanford, CA, 1985.

Sells, P., Korean and Japanese morphology from a lexical perspective, *Linguis. Inquiry*, 26:2:1995, 277–325.

Sohn, H. M., *The Korean Language*, Cambridge University Press, Cambridge, 1999.

Taylor, I. and Taylor, M., *Writing and Literacy in Chinese, Korean and Japanese*, John Benjamin Publishing Co., Amsterdam, 1995.

Style and Stylistics of Japanese

15

WAKAKO YASUDA

ABSTRACT

この論文を書くにあたっての私の目標は、今日まで文体学者によって研究されてきた文体（スタイル）の意義に基づき、現存する文体の種類と著者鑑定におけるその重要性を、現代人の手紙を通して探ることにある。ある文章を与えられたとき、その著者を確定するのにどのような言語特徴を彼のスタイルとして重要視すべきか。鑑定者の参考になるような「著者鑑定のためのスタイルのリスト」を試験的ではあるが完成させたい。

使った資料は、１９９６年から２０００年までの４年間に２０歳から２５歳の若者によって書かれた６８通の私的な手紙である。筆者のうち５９人が女性、９人が男性である。

手紙文に使われている様々な表現のうちどれをその手紙のスタイルとして認識するべきか。『法廷文体学』(Forensic Stylistics 1993) という論文の中で、言語学者のマクメナミン氏はスタイルを大きく２種類に分けている。一つは、ある言語の標準文法の範囲内の（「文法上」正しい）表現の変形であり、もう一つはその範囲外、即ち標準文法にかなっていない（「文法上」間違った）表現の変形である。彼の論述を参考にあらゆる言語要素（体裁、句読点、書体、つづり、語形、統語、音韻）について手紙を分析した。

こうして多量に見つかった文法的または非文法的スタイルの特徴性を判断するのに用いたのが、それぞれのスタイルの頻度である。６８通を通して最も頻度の高いスタイルは多くの人が使うという点で重要であり、それが若者全体の特徴文体となる。また頻度の低いスタイルはある特定の人物のみが使うという点で重要であり、その人物個人の特徴文体となる。つまり、頻度の高低の直線のグラフを思い浮かべたときその両極端に属するスタイルが、使用度の多さまたは珍しさで重要ということになる。

さらに個人の特徴文体は、ある表現の反復使用、またはいくつかの
表現の同時使用にも見ることができる。前者はひとつの手紙に同じ
（文法的または非文法的）表現が何度も使われていることであり、そ
れは筆者の癖、つまり彼のスタイルとなる。後者はひとつの手紙に
いくつかの特徴ある表現が使われていることであり、一つ一つはそ
の手紙のスタイルとして不十分でも集合体として見たときには彼の
スタイルとなり得るということである。例えば、私のデータの中に
従来漢字とひらがなで書くものとされている言葉（漢語・大和言葉）
にカタカナを使っている若者が 21 人いる。また間投助詞にカタカナ
を使っている若者が 11 人いる。さらに固有名詞にカタカナを使って
いる若者も 7 人いる。しかし、漢語・大和言葉にも間投助詞にも固
有名詞にもカタカナを使っている者は 1 人しかいない。この筆者は
６８人中唯一「カタカナの三つの異なる使用法」を同時にする者で
あり、この事実は著者鑑定時強力な手がかりとなる。つまり、三つ
の特徴ある表現は「集合体」として初めてその筆者個人のスタイル
となったのである。この論文を書くにあたっての私の目標は、今日
まで文体学者によって研究されてきた文体（スタイル）の意義に基
き、現存する文体の種類と筆跡鑑定におけるその重要性を、現代人
の手紙を通して探ることにある。ある筆跡者不明の文章を与えられ
たとき、その著者を確定するのにどのような文法的特徴を彼のスタ
イルとして重要視すべきか。鑑定者の参考になるような「筆跡鑑定
のためのスタイルのリスト」を試験的ではあるが完成させたい。

分析結果は若者全体の特徴（Class Style）と個人の特徴（Individual Style）
とに分けられ、二つのカテゴリーの中で特徴性の高いものから順に
リストした。ここではその一部を紹介する。

Summary of Marker Categories and Specific Markers

Category	Specific Marker
1．体裁	横書き（全員）
2．句読点	エクスクラメーション　マーク
	まるの不使用
3．漢字	接続詞（て・で）の接尾辞的用法（新解釈）
	漢字の非標準使用 「方行」
4．ひらがな	長音の「ー」を使った表現
	反復語の「×2」を使った表現
	長音の「ー」を使った表現

Category	Specific Marker
5．カタカナ	日本語表現にカタカナ使用
	接尾辞にカタカナ使用
	擬声語・擬態語にカタカナ使用
	固有名詞にカタカナ使用
	日本語表現にカタカナ使用
6．ローマ字	固有名詞にローマ字使用
	外来語の日本略「ＴＥＬ」
	接尾辞にローマ字使用
7．口語表現	「います・いる」の「い」省略
	「けれど」の「れ」省略
	さまざまな語の短縮
8．形態素選択	接続詞（て・で）の接尾辞的用法（新解釈）
	接続詞（けど）の接尾辞的用法（新解釈）
	助動詞（かも）の接尾辞的用法（新解釈）
	女性による男性接尾語使用
	間投助詞（ね）
	従位接続詞 （って）
8．単語選択	英単語の使用
	英単語 letter
9．文章構成	助動詞（です）の不使用
	目的格助詞（を）の不使用
	倒置法（主語・述語の倒置）
	倒置法（副詞節の文末配置）
	言葉の反復（×２を使った）による強調
	体言止

15.1 Introduction

While previous studies on stylistics provide definitions of style and methods of stylistic analysis, e.g., Enkvist (1973) and McMenamin (1993), little work has been done as to exactly what linguistic features to look for in a stylistic study of languages other than English. The purpose of this chapter is to identify an initial set of variable style-markers in contemporary Japanese writing.

This analysis is based on data consisting of personal letters written by native Japanese speakers during the 5-year period of 1996 to 2000. Linguistic style-markers identified in these letters are of two kinds: variations within a norm, i.e., language that varies but still conforms to the normative grammar of the language, and deviations from a norm, which are those variations in language considered ungrammatical within the scope of the prescriptive grammar of a language.

In order to determine the importance of a linguistic variable within or away from a norm, three analytical bases were used: frequency of occurrence, recurrent linguistic habit, and stylistic sets. First, a linguistic variable increases its importance as a style-marker if it occurs frequently in a piece of writing by the same writer or in writings of many different writers. Infrequent or once-occurring markers may also represent important style-markers if they are peculiar to a particular writer. Since such distinguishing features are often present in a piece of writing regardless of external factors, including social context of writing, they serve as the identifiers of authorship.

Second, variation is often found in the habitual use of a particular language form by the same writer. In order for a linguistic feature to be characterized as a recurrent habit of writing, it must appear frequently. It may also occur consistently, but frequency must not be confused with consistency. What may be frequent as well as consistent is the systematic alternation of one form with one or more other forms.

Finally, different style-markers occurring in the same text constitute an aggregate set of stylistic markers, and together they form the style of the writer. For example, a piece of writing may include a choice of *cannot* over *can't* (variation within the norm), misspelling of *receive* as *recieve* (deviation from the norm), indentation of one space instead of five spaces at the beginning of every paragraph (variation), and certain comma splices (deviation). All these variations and deviations in the aggregate serve as a basis for describing the writer's style.

15.2 The Japanese Writing System

An understanding of the basic characteristics of the Japanese language and principles of the Japanese writing system is a necessary background for understanding the corpus analysis that follows. Japanese writing incorporates two writing systems, traditionally called *kanji*, an ideographic system, and *kana*, a syllabic system; they are used in combination in a systematic way. *Kanji* (Chinese characters) is a graphic symbol representing a lexical morpheme. Since a morpheme is a unit of meaning, the writing system is called ideographic. It is not logographic, since the *kanji* does not represent an entire word, unless the morpheme it stands for is a monomorphemic word. *Kana* is a character representing a light syllable or a *mora*; thus, the writing system using *kana* script is called a syllabic system or, more precisely, a moraic system.

Kana scripts are of two kinds: *hiragana* and *katakana*. *Hiragana* is used for Japanese words for which *kanji* cannot be easily provided. While *kanji* represents a lexical morpheme, *hiragana* represents a grammatical morpheme, such as particles and auxiliary verbs. *Katakana* is used for transcribing foreign loan words (other than Chinese) and some onomatopoetic words. *Katakana* is also used for stylistic reasons, for example, to attract special attention from the reader (Maynard, 1990).

A word may be represented in one of the following four ways: as a single *kanji*, as multiple *kanji*, as a combination of a *kanji* with a *hiragana* suffix, and as multiple *kanji* with a *hiragana* suffix. Examples include the earlier mentioned Chinese-derived vocabulary words (*kango*) that are usually two *kanji* character compounds, and the native Japanese vocabulary words (*yamatokotoba*) written either in *hiragana* or *kanji-hiragana* combination.

15.3 Data Collection and Corpus Development

The present corpus consists of 68 personal letters, handwritten by native Japanese speakers ranging in age from 20 to 25 years during the period of 1996 to 2000. The writers include 9 men and 59 women; they are speakers of Tokyo, Osaka, and Nagoya dialects. The lengths of the letters range from one to six pages. The total number of sentences is 8 in the shortest letter, 125 in the longest letter, and 50 on average in all the letters. Some letters are originals and others are photocopies. The letters are organized according to the last names of writers in alphabetical order. Each letter is line-numbered and marked with an identification code identifying the writer number, page number, hand- or typewritten, sex, and geographical dialect of the writer.

15.4 Analysis and Findings

Two well-documented analytical approaches were used in this study: top-down and bottom-up. The analysis of the data is top-down insofar as a broad set of style-marker categories is taken from previous literary or linguistic analyses and used as benchmarks. On the other hand, the analysis is bottom-up because within each of the pre-established broad categories, linguistic subcategories of potential style-markers are established based directly on analysis of these data.

The style-marker categories identified in this study are listed in order of importance as class style-markers and individual style-markers, determined according to interwriter frequency of occurrences. As mentioned earlier, when the same linguistic variable occurs in the writings of many different

MARKER	EXAMPLE
Exclamation Point	バレーは できる!
Exclamation Points	どうしよう!!
Question Mark	ですか?

Figure 15.1 Punctuation.

writers, the variable becomes important as a class style characteristic, i.e., a style-marker of the group of the writers.

When a variable occurs frequently in a piece of writing by just one of the 68 writers, it is considered an important individual (but not necessarily idiosyncratic) characteristic, i.e., a style-marker of the individual writer. Once-occurring markers or infrequent markers are also very important for identifying individual authorship, as they indicate individualized language uses of the particular author. Both ends of the frequency continuum are important. Style-markers are determined by paying attention to the continuum ends, i.e., frequently occurring vis-à-vis once-occurring features.

15.4.1 Format

Although vertical writing is still the norm in Japan, especially for older Japanese, horizontal writing is found to be a class characteristic of modern writing. All letters (64 writers) in the data are written in a horizontal manner.

15.4.2 Punctuation

Traditionally, Japanese has three punctuation marks: *maru* (。) used for indicating sentence endings, *ten* (、) for indicating phrasal and clause breaks, and *kagikakko* (" 「」 ") for indicating direct quotes. However, various other punctuation marks (such as ?, ! and …) are commonly used today. Since written language cannot convey intonation, pitch, and the other voice qualities of the spoken language, use of different punctuation marks helps writers show such phonetic characteristics of the spoken language (Kabashima, 1979). Variation in number and kinds of punctuation marks used in one's writing is considered to be his or her style-marker. Frequently and infrequently occurring style-markers, with examples directly from the corpus appearing in Figure 15.1 are:

Exclamation marks (13 writers/48 occurrences):
    bare- ha dekiru!   "I can play volleyball!"

***ka* (question marker) + question mark** (10/18):
    ogenki desuka?   "How are you?"

Exclamation marks (1/8):
> *attanoni!*
> *komattottanyo!*
> *mitakoto!!!*
> *mitayo!*
> *yokatta!*
> *shimashita!*
> *aitaine!!!*
> *oideoide!!!*

Interrogative sentence without *ka* (question marker) + question mark (1/8):
> *nani??*
> *okashiiyone?*
> *DAY jan?*
> *dou omou??*
> *jootai??*
> *douomou?*
> *abazure??*
> *shiranaihazu??*

Absent period (1/1)
> *kakunin shitemita dake nanda* (∅) *kinishinaide.*
> "I only made sure (∅) please do not care about that."

15.4.3 *Kanji* Spelling

To judge the presence or absence of *kanji*, the national mandatory 1945 *kanji* listed in *wakariyasui jooyookanjireishuu* (Kobayashi, 1982) are used as the norm. Three levels of *kanji* are recognized by the Japanese government: 996 educational *kanji*, 949 "general purpose" *kanji*, and thousands of other *kanji* (Kobayashi, 1982). Educational *kanji* are mandatory for junior-high graduates, and general *kanji* for high-school graduates. They are together called *jooyoo kanji*, and absence of any *jooyoo kanji* is considered a *kanji*-spelling style-marker.

No significant class style-marker is found in *kanji* spelling; however, absence of various *jooyoo kanji* is common in personal letters, as can be seen below, with examples directly from the corpus appearing in Figure 15.2:

Absent Kanji (55 writers/75 occurrences):
> <u>sabishii</u> "lonely"   (1/3)
> <u>gamba</u>(-tte) "do one's best" (1/3)

Nonstandard *Kanji* use (1/1):
> 方行 hoo<u>koo</u> "direction" (normative *kanji*: 方向)

MARKER	EXAMPLE
Absent Kanji	がんばってやって…。もう、バイトも
Absent Kanji	来年は行きたい!!それまで、がんば
Absent Kanji	何事でもがんばろうと思ってるヨ。
Absent Kanji	がんば
Absent Kanji	がんばろ
Absent Kanji	がんば:
Nonstandard Kanji Usage	予行に.

Figure 15.2 *Kanji* spelling.

MARKER	EXAMPLE
Dash for Long Vowel	どうしようかなー
Superscript *x2*: *yes, yes*	そうx2
Superscript *x2* : *every day, every day*	毎日x2
chi + dakuten	飲もーぢゃないか
konnichi *wa*	これにちわ。手紙ありがとう。
Subscript Hear + Dash	なりんだぁ〜っ

Figure 15.3 *Hiragana* spelling.

15.4.4 *Hiragana* Spelling

Many writers apply the writing rules of *katakana* to *hiragana*. Although the two *kana* scripts are used differently (have distinct functions), there are many cases of overlap between the two in how to represent particular sounds. The first characteristic shows how *katakana* writing rules are applied to *hiragana* writing, and examples directly from the corpus appear in Figure 15.3:

Representation of long vowel with a dash in *Hiragana* (16 writers/76 occurrences): (In *katakana* script, a dash "-" represents the second mora in a long vowel. In *hiragana* script, the second mora is normatively written in the appropriate *hiragana* letter.)

どうしようかなー *dooshiyookana-* (instead of *kanaa*) ("what should I do")
いこー *iko-* (instead of *ikoo*) ("let's go")

Reduplication of morpheme represented with superscript "2" (5/8):

そう x2 *sou* x2   "yes, yes, I remember"
毎日 x2 *mainichi* x2   "every day, every day"

MARKER	EXAMPLE
Exclamatory Particle *ne*	気を付けてネ。
Native Japanese Word: *gaman*	ガマンして
Onomatopoetic Adverb	ぺらぺろ
Personal Name	マツ
Nonstandard Transcription	「ビューテフル ライフ」
Native Japanese Word: *easy*	ラク
Native Japanese Word: *difficult*	ムズカシイ

Figure 15.4 *Katakana* spelling.

Representation of long vowel with a dash in Hiragana (1/12):

よー   *saserun dayo—.*   "they made me do it"
さー   *yaritakune—nonisa—.*   "I don't want to do it"
ねー   *ne—sou omou desho*   "don't you think so?"
なー   *sonna toko kana—.*   "that's about it."

[ji] spelled "*chi*+dakuten" (the normative spelling "*shi* +dakuten") (1/2):

のもーぢ ゃないか   *nomo-janaika* "Let's drink."
C' m o n ぢ ゃー   *C'mon ja-* "Come on!"

The topic marker "ha" (pronounced [wa]) spelled "wa" (1/1):

こんにちわ *konnichiwa* "hello"

Subscript hiragana + dash + sokuon (1/1):

ないんだあーっ *nainda$_{a\text{-}tu}$* "no need to"

15.4.5 *Katakana* Spelling

The primary roles of *katakana* script are to transcribe loan words and to spell out onomatopoeic words. In addition, *katakana* also has some stylistic effects such as attracting special attention from the reader (Maynard, 1990). Since writers may differ in their perspective towards the stylistic effects achieved by *katakana,* when and how individual writers make use of the script are indicative of group and individual style-markers. Examples directly from the corpus appear in Figure 15.4.

Use of *katakana* for native Japanese word (21 writers/73 occurrences):

ケンカ   *kenka* "quarrel"
ムズカシイ   *muzukashii* "difficult"
ガンコ   *ganko* "stubborn"

MARKER	EXAMPLE
Loan Word	からTELが
Personal Name	今週のNaoko
Proper Name	来週は KYOTO
Exclamatory Particle	届いたyo。

Figure 15.5 Roman letter spelling.

Use of *katakana* for exclamatory particles (11/29):

気をつけてネ   *kiotuketene*   "Take care."
うれしかったヨ   *ureshikattayo*   "I was glad."

Use of *katakana* for onomatopoetic adverb (9/11):

ベラベラ   *perapera*   "fluently"
ブツブツ   *butubutu*   "grumble"

Use of *Katakana* for personal names/nicknames (7/14):

マツ   *matu*   (Nickname)
ババくん   *babakun*   "Mr. Baba"

Use of *katakana* for native Japanese word (1/13):

ゴメンネ   *gomenne*   "I'm sorry."
ラク   *raku*   "easy"
タダ働き   *tadabataraki*   "work for nothing"

Nonstandard transcription of loan word in *katakana* (1/1):

ビューテ（イ）フル   *byuute(i)furu*

Use of *katakana* for copula (1/1):

してマス   *shitemasu*

15.4.6 Roman Letter Spelling

Roman letters have traditionally been used to spell out English words or to indicate the pronunciation of characters. However, findings in the present study indicate that Roman letters have extended their function and are now used in a way similar to *katakana* scripts; that is, they indicate some stylistic effect. Examples directly from the corpus appear in Figure 15.5.

Use of Roman letters for proper names, personal names, nicknames
(5 writers/13 occurrences):
Naoko
KYOTO

MARKER	EXAMPLE
i- Deletion	はなれてるこ
re- Deletion	見たけど
re- Deletion	暑くなってきたけど
Various Contractions	いろんなとこ 行けるねー

Figure 15.6 Phonological variation.

Abbreviation of loan words using Roman letters (6/10):
TEL "telephone"

Use of Roman letters for exclamatory particles (1/7):
届いた <u>yo</u> *todoitayo* "has arrived"

15.4.7 Phonological Variation

Since *kana* script is a syllabic writing system, the written language corresponds with the way syllables sound in spoken language. That is, Japanese spells words in *kana* scripts according to the pronunciation. Although English does not have such rules for spelling–pronunciation correspondence, modern written texts do show some phonological variation such as dropping the consonant [g] after [n], indicated with an apostrophe, e.g. *kickin'*. Variations in spoken language directly appear in written Japanese and are called "phonological variations." Examples directly from the corpus appear in Figure 15.6.

Contraction: *i*-deletion in *iru/imasu* "be" (11 writers/60 occurrences):
hanarete(i)ru   "be away"
itadaite(i)masu   "I'm getting"

Contraction: *re*-deletion in *ke<u>re</u>do* "but" (7/27):
mitake(re)do   "I saw it, but..."
atuku natte kita kitake(re)do   "became hot, but..."

Various contractions (1/11):
nanka (for *nandaka*)	"somewhat"
dokka (*dokoka*)	"somewhere"
<u>*ironna*</u> *toko ikerune-* (*iroirona*)	"various"
ironna <u>*toko*</u> *ikerune-* (*tokoroni*)	"to places"
ironna toko <u>*ikerune-*</u> (*ikarerune*)	"can go"

Other contractions:
kai<u>teta</u>kedo (*kai<u>teatta</u>kedo*)   "although it was written" (1/1):
reihai <u>tteno</u> o shite (*reihai <u>toiumono</u> o*)   "visited church" (1/1):

MARKER	EXAMPLE
Abbreviation *kamo* for Full Form	買うかも。
Masculine Clause - Final Forms	写真まってるぜ！
Masculine Pronoun	オマエ
Functional Reanalysis	りいけど。
Functional Reanalysis	連絡するけど。
Choice of *tte* for *to*	どうしようかなあ … って
Conjunctive Particle as S-Final Particle	信用できなくて。
Conjunctive Particle as S-Final Particle	って思って。
Conjunctive Particle as S-Final Particle	やって…。
S-Medial/Final *sa*	あってさ、
S-Medial/Final *sa*	会社でさー。
S-Medial/Final *sa*	やりたかねーのにさー。

Figure 15.7 Morpheme choice.

15.4.8 Morpheme Choice

Various instances of functional reanalysis are found in the data, i.e., a new function for a morpheme, usually caused from repeated misuse of the morpheme. Present findings indicate that reanalyses of different function morphemes are the prominent characteristic of young people (Okamoto, 1995). Also, among the writings of female writers, use of different masculine morphemes is found. Examples directly from the corpus appear in Figure 15.7.

**Function reanalysis: conjunctive particle used as S-final particle *-te/de*
"and"** (15 writers/32 occurrences):

dakara heyaga semaku<u>te</u>.   "so the room is small <u>and</u>"
konnaburu—na tegamishika kakenaku<u>te</u>.   "I can only write such a blue letter <u>and</u>"

Function reanalysis: conjunctive particle used as S-final particle *–kedo* **"although"** (17/24):

kakitakattandakedo.	"<u>although</u> I wanted to write"
renrakusurukedo.	"<u>although</u> I'm going to keep in touch"

Choice of *tte* **for** *to* **(a complementizer or quotative marker "that" signaling the end of an embedded clause)** (8/25):

dooshiyookanaa…tte	"<u>that</u> I wonder what I should do"
ittekita tte itteta	"he said <u>that</u> he went"
shitakunai tte omottayo	"I thought <u>that</u> I did not want to do it"

Choice of the abbreviation *kamo* **for the auxiliary** *kamoshirenai* **"may"** (6/6):

sorosorokamo…	"it <u>may</u> be soon"
kaukamo.	"I <u>may</u> buy it"

Function reanalysis: conjunctive particle *-shi* **"and" used as S-final particle** (5/10):

kakkoiishi.	"he's handsome and"
yoru suru mitai dashi.	"it seems we're doing it at night and"

Use of masculine clause-final forms by female writers (6/9):

matteruze	"I'll be waiting"
nijuuhassaidaro	"You're 28!"

Use of *de* **for** *soshite* **"then"** (4/5):

arundayo. de	"there is, <u>then</u>"
naindawa. de	"there is not, <u>then</u>"

Use of masculine pronoun by female writers (4/4):

yatsu	"he"
omae	"you"

Frequent use of tentative suffix *-soo* (1/5):

ogenki-soode	"<u>sounds like</u> you are fine"
nari-soodesu	"<u>seems like</u> it's going to be"
tanoshi-soodane	"<u>sounds like</u> fun"
jootatsushi-soo	"<u>seems like</u> you are going to improve your English"
atsu-soo	"<u>sounds like</u> it's hot"

Frequent use of *tte* **(a complementizer or quotative marker "that" signaling the end of an embedded clause)** (1/12):

oogenkashita tte itta	"I said <u>that</u> I had a big argument"
wakareruno tte kikarete	"I was asked <u>if</u> we are breaking up"
kotodakara tte ittano.	"I said <u>that</u> I had already decided it"
shitakunai tte omotta.	"I thought <u>that</u> I didn't want to do so"

MARKER	EXAMPLE
English Word Choice	Dear ゆかこ。
English Word Choice	From ゲい子。
English Word Choice	P.S. 体

Figure 15.8 Word choice.

Function reanalysis: conjunctive particle used as S-final particle -*te* "and" (1/6):

wakarerutte watashi zutto itte<u>te</u>.   "I was saying that I want to break up, and"

nanka tukarete kichat<u>te</u>.   "I was somewhat getting tired, and"

Function reanalysis: conjunctive particle used as S-final particle -*te* "and" (1/4):

shinyoo deki naku<u>te</u>   "I cannot trust him and"

...tte omot<u>te</u>   "I thought that... and"

15.4.9   Word Choice

In terms of the choices writers make as to what kinds of words to use, one prominent characteristic found is the use of various English words. There are 48 writers (71% of the total) who use more than one English word. Among those words, the most frequently used are words related to personal letters: *dear, from,* and *PS.* Examples directly from the corpus appear in Figure 15.8.

Use of English words (45 writers/185 occurrences)
Use of *Dear* (27/27)
Use of *From* (13/13)
Use of *PS* (12/12)

15.4.10   Word Formation

No prominent class characteristic is found in this style-marker category. However, one individual characteristic, verb formation by omission of *ni,* has been used among young people in spoken language.

Formation of a verb *genki-suru* (health-stay) "stay healthy" by omission of *ni* (adverb marker) (1/1)

元気して   genkishite

15.4.11   Syntax

Since Japanese has subject–object–verb (SOV) word order, all auxiliaries indicating tense, aspect, and mood appear at the end of sentences. Here are comparisons between Japanese sentences (a) and their English counterparts (b):

1a. *boku wa kuruma o untenshi masen.* (negation)
1b. I <u>do not</u> drive a car.

2a. *anatawa [ruutsu] o yomimashita ka.* (question)
2b. <u>Did</u> you read *Roots?*

3a. *hayaku ieni kaeri nasai.* (request; command)
3b. <u>Go</u> home early.

4a. *yooroppa ni iki tainaa.* (desire)
4b. I <u>wish</u> I could go to Europe!

5a. *anootoko niwa nidomo dama sare ta.* (passive)
5b. I <u>was</u> deceiv<u>ed</u> by that man twice.

6a. *bokuwa otoutoni kippuo kaini ikaseta.* (causative)
6b. I <u>had</u> my brother go buy the ticket.   (Makino, 1983)

As grammatical aspects of Japanese are expressed sentence-finally, syntactic style-markers appear at the ends of sentences. For word order, the preferred word order stated by Maynard (1990) is the norm. According to her, although the grammatical word order in Japanese is relatively free, there is a preferred order of elements within the sentence:

Topic + Marker (locative, subject, object, etc.) + Predicate + Copula

The most frequently found deviation from this word order is the stylistic characteristic called *toochihoo* "scrambling," which is a way to show emphasis by placing the phrase to be emphasized before the rest of the items in the sentence — an instance of semantics controlling syntax. Examples directly from the corpus appear in Figure 15.9.

Absent copula (20 writers/67 occurrences):
urayamashii (desu)!	"I (am) jealous!"
kotoshiwa mou 26 (desu).	"I (will be) 26 this year."
eizoo wa muri (desu).	"The vision (is) impossible."

Absent direct object marker (DO) (11/20):
toreenaa(o)*todokete*	"deliver the sweatshirt (obj. marker)"
shashin(o)*mita*	"saw the picture (obj. marker)"
chuugokugo (o) *gambara*	"study Chinese (obj. marker)"

MARKER	EXAMPLE
Absent Copula	もう夏。
Absent Subject Marker	仕事終わ.たんだよね。
Absent Subject Marker	メール届いてて.
Absent Copula	今年は もう 26.
Absent Object Marker	トレーナー 届けて
toochihoo Adverbial	まあ.1年ある.ね. また.
Absent S-Final Verb	安心。
Absent S-Final Verb	の音楽。
Absent S-Final Verb	オレンジ ジュース。
Absent S-Final Verb	や.ぱ. 49ers。
Absent S-Final Verb	NFLの話。
Absent S-Final Verb	バイト。
Absent S-Final Verb	の仕事。
Emphasis by Repetition	うれしくって。^{x2}

Figure 15.9 Syntax.

Absent subject marker (SB) (8/17):

ninzuu (ga) *ooi*	"the number of people (subj. marker) is big"
me-ru (ga) *todoitete*	"the mail (subj. marker) came"
shigoto (ga) *owatta*	"the work (subj. marker) was over."

Toochihoo: placement of predicate before subject phrase and nominative particle (11/15):

ima 25sai da kara <u>watashi-(wa)</u>.	"because am now 25 I-(subj)"
ammari kawattenakatta. <u>gaiken-wa</u>.	"hasn't changed very much. <u>the look-subj.</u>"

Toochihoo: placement of adverbials at the end of sentence (11/15):

onsenniittekitanoyo, izuno shimodamade.	"I went to a hot spring, to Shimoda in Izu"
ba-bon ni hamattane hontoni.	"I'm into barbon, really."
aenakattane, kotchidewa.	"We could not see each other, over here."

Emphasis by repetition (1/4):

ureshikutte^{x2}	"very glad"
mainichi^{x2}	"every day"
hito $^{x\ mugen}$	"many people"
natsukashikutte^{x2}	"very sentimental"

Absent copula - ending with a noun (1/8)

hitomazu anshin (desu).	"(be) relieved for the time being"
NFL no hanashi (desu).	"is a story about NFL"
ryoorino hoono shigoto (desu).	"(is) a job related to cooking"

15.5   Conclusion

It is clear that significant stylistic variation is present in Japanese writing. Although this chapter has been a study of style-markers appearing in a corpus of Japanese writing, observation of individual writers in the corpus indicates that each writer demonstrates a combination of stylistic characteristics comprising a range of variation unique to each writer. Thus, forensic application of such stylistic analysis of Japanese is indicated.

References

Enkvist, N. E., *Linguistic Stylistics,* The Hague, Mouton, 1973.

Kabashima, T., *Nihongo no sutairu bukku,* Tokyo, Taishuukan Shoten, 1979.

Kobayashi, K., *Wakariyasui Jooyookanjireishuu,* Tokyo, Tokyo Hoorei Shuppan, 1982.

Makino, S., "Shoryaku to hanpuku," in Nakamura, A., Ed., *Nihongo no retorikku,* Series Koza Nihongo no hyogen 5, Chikuma shobo, Tokyo, 73–88, 1983.

Maynard, S., *An Introduction to Japanese Grammar, The Japan Times,* Tokyo, 1990.

McMenamin, G., *Forensic Stylistics,* Elsevier Science Publishers, Amsterdam, 1993.

Okamoto, S., Pragmatization of meaning in some sentence-final particles in Japanese, in Shibatani, M. and Thompson, S. A., Eds., *Essays in Semantics and Pragmatics,* John Benjamins, Philadelphia, 1995.

Appendix 1: Possible Questions and Responses for Direct and Cross Examination

A.1 Direct Examination of Linguist (Example)

A.1.1 Qualifications

What is your profession and how are you employed?

Would you review your educational background?

Would you outline where and what you have taught during your academic career?

What is the scope of your forensic work?

How many and what types of cases have you testified in before?

Do you have a record of publications in linguistics?

What professional organizations are you active in?

A.1.2 Language and Linguistics

What exactly is linguistics, and how is it related to language?

In what ways is linguistics a science?

What are some subfields or branches of linguistics?

A.1.3 Forensic Linguistics and Stylistics

What is forensic linguistics and what kinds of problems do forensic linguists solve?

What is stylistics, and what is forensic stylistics?

What is linguistic variation and why is it important?

How do linguists approach cases of questioned authorship?

A.1.4 This Case

What were you asked to do in this case?

What steps did you follow to analyze the writings in this case?

What is your conclusion in this case?

Would you outline the general scope of your findings in this case?

Now, specifically, what formed the basis for your conclusion in this case?

What is your opinion regarding the authorship of the questioned letter?

A.2 Cross Examination of Linguist (Example)

A.2.1 Education

What universities did you attend?
What undergraduate and undergraduate degrees do you hold?
What were your areas of specialization (majors) for each degree?
What subspecialties (minors) do you have?
What is your work history?
What is your present work activity?
What classes have you taught at your university?
Have you taught any courses in linguistics?
Have you taught any courses in linguistic variation?
    Such as sociolinguistics (variation related to social variables)?
    Such as geographical linguistics (variation related to region)?
    Such as historical linguistics (variation related to time)?
    Such as stylistics (variation in written language)?
What is your research and publication history?
What publications do you have on linguistic variation?
What publications do you have on stylistics?
What is the focus of your present research?
To what professional organizations do you belong?
What professional journals do you receive and read?
    Any related to the analysis of style?
    Any related to forensic applications of linguistics?

A.2.2 Experience

Have you done studies of literary authorship?
Have you done authorship studies in any forensic contexts?
Have you ever testified as an expert linguist?
    In what areas of linguistics?
Have you ever testified in the area of authorship identification?
    When, where, who, and outcomes of these cases?

A.2.3 Areas of Expertise

What is your general area of expertise, e.g., linguistics?
Why do you work in an English (not linguistics) department?
What is linguistics?
What does a linguist do?
What are the major subfields of linguistics?
In your opinion, is linguistics a science?
What is the nature of scientific knowledge (both terms)?

A.2.4 Specialization

What are your areas of specialization in linguistics?
Does authorship identification require any particular expertise?
Are you an expert in the particular field known as "stylistics"?
What about in "forensic stylistics"?

A.2.5 Methodology

How would you generally define "style" in human behavior?
How do you define style in language?
What is the field known as "stylistics"?
Is author elimination possible using stylistic analysis?
Is author identification possible using stylistic analysis?
How are literary studies of authorship done?
How are forensic studies of authorship done?
What is your procedure for doing authorship cases?
What are some examples of style-markers in writing?
How do you relate descriptive and quantitative observations?
How do you identify class vs. individual features in writing?
How do you exclude or identify a possible suspect author?

A.2.6 Analysis

Describe how you organize your work in an authorship study.
Do you analyze questioned and known writings independently?
Do you use a computer? In what ways?
  In this case?
Describe your complete involvement in this case.
Did you do your own study?
  Please describe it and how you did it.
Have you read all the questioned and known writing in this case?
How did you decide on the methodology of this case?
Do you have notes that you made during your analysis of the writings?
How did you analyze the questioned and known documents?
What style-markers did you find in the questioned writings?
What style-markers did you find in the known writings?
How did you identify the markers of style in this case?
What was the outcome (conclusion) of your analysis in this case?
Have you formed an opinion regarding the questioned writings of this case?
Have you written a report of your findings and conclusions?
On what basis do you relate your findings to your opinion?
Did you study and evaluate the other expert's work?
Do you have notes that you made for your study of the other expert's report?
Have you formed an opinion regarding the other expert's analysis and opinion?

Appendix 2: Expert Testimony (Susan Morton)

Susan Morton,
Criminalistics Laboratory,
San Francisco Police Department

Expert witnesses are perceived very differently from lay witnesses, both by the law and by the public. It gives you some rights and advantages but imparts added responsibilities. Juries will forgive fear, nervousness, and some confusion in a lay witness, but experts don't impress much if they show those conditions. An expert needs to be knowledgeable, polished, and professional, but not slick or rehearsed.

The rights of the expert are these: 1. you may state an opinion and give the supporting data and reasons for it, 2. you may testify in narrative form rather than question and answer (though some judges won't allow narrative), 3. you may demand to see and examine any published texts being used to cross-examine you, and 4. you may refuse to state your opinion until you have been compensated.

The following are "lessons learned" over the years that will allow the expert to make use of his or her rights and fulfill all responsibilities.

1. Know your mannerisms, e.g., if you fiddle with your hair, wear a headband, or fix hair in place some way. Make sure you are heard. A very soft voice can be perceived as indicative of a lack of confidence. And for sure if they can't hear you, they can't accept what you say. Watch videos of your moot courts to see if you have other habits that may distract a jury.
2. Attire, hair, make-up should be business-like and inconspicuous. Get noticed for your expertise, not your appearance. This is much harder for women than for men, as men can rely on the coat and tie to state their degree of seriousness. Women should study the attire of women executives and politicians and pick one to emulate. Suits are perfect in Federal court, but a bit much for Superior Court. A blazer in a muted color (black, navy, or camel) can dress up an outfit without looking too stiff. Make sure that any accessories such as scarves or jewelry are well secured so that you do not have to fiddle with or adjust them. Think of any potential disaster, e.g., as you are being seated in the witness chair, your large pendant swings forward and collides with the microphone, creating a thunderous clang. And definitely wear "sensible shoes." Sensible shoes bespeak serious intent and terrify attorneys.

3. Be wary of the incompetent or devious attorney, few in number as they may be. He or she will make you look like an idiot by asking idiotic questions and then blame you for looking like an idiot. Be prepared for this.

4. Be very careful not to change your body language when cross-examination starts. I have seen witnesses fold their arms across their chests and look belligerent. Just keep in mind that you are an impartial witness. It also helps to remember the contents of number 3.

5. Listen very carefully to the question. Lawyers will often word a question so that it sounds like a familiar one, but has a very different implication. Or sometimes they get it mixed up and ask one thing when they really mean something else. Answer the question asked. If the question is tricky, you avoid a trap. If the question is mixed up, the lawyer looks foolish. This is equally true of both sides. If the question contains multiple questions, ask that they be separated. If the question is long and convoluted, ask that it be repeated. Even if you understand it, the jury may not. If the lawyer is blowing smoke, he won't be able to repeat the question. If it gets read back by the reporter, it is exposed for the shenanigan that it is.

6. If you don't know the answer to a question, say you don't know. Juries expect you to know your subject, but they don't expect you to be omniscient. Lawyers can dream up some pretty wild things to ask. Be up-front and don't let yourself be made to look defensive about not knowing something. This is a mistake that many experts make. They think that they can't admit that they don't know everything so they spin moonshine. Juries pick right up on that. It makes the expert look pompous and can cast doubt on other points he or she may have made. If an answer is more than a few words, turn to the jury to deliver it. They are the target. Find one or two that seem interested and make eye contact. It is very hard to learn to do this, as it is natural to get into an exchange with the person asking the questions. It feels very awkward at first, but the juries love it and cross-examining lawyers hate it.

7. Don't answer too quickly. It is okay to pause and look thoughtful. This also allows time for an objection. It looks better if you are not cut off by one.

8. It sometimes happens that you will have a legal question during testimony. It may be that you suspect that the answer to a question will bring out inadmissible information or something similar. Lawyers for the other side may be distracted at that moment. Technically it isn't your fault if you answer and cause a mistrial, but everyone will blame you, especially the lawyers. What to do? Consult your designated legal representative — the judge. The judge is any witness's designated legal

representative. Look up and say, "Your Honor, may I consult you on a legal matter?" Then do exactly what he or she says.

9. Remember the court reporter and have mercy on him or her. If you leave the witness stand to make a demonstration, make sure your back is not toward the reporter. The jury and the reporter are your audience; everybody else can rearrange themselves. Spell scientific words for him or her. That slows things down a bit and gives the jury a few more seconds to absorb unfamiliar terms. It also creates an accurate record.

10. Obtain and read a transcript of your testimony early on. Look for wording habits that need to be tuned up. Everyone has little catch phrases they emit by habit while the brain is engaged elsewhere. Some are fine, even charming; others are irritating. Evict the irritating ones.

11. When you are referring to court exhibits, use both the exhibit number and a descriptor. "I am holding People's Exhibit 4, a claw hammer." Describe exactly what you are talking about so that someone reading the written record without the physical evidence can understand what you are saying. You can't say, "This matches that." It has to be "This hole in Exhibit A, the shoe, matches that point on Exhibit B, the awl." It is very hard to train yourself to do this and it seems very stilted and awkward, but you will be creating a much better written record. Fortunately, it doesn't sound as tortured as it seems. There is a real difference between spoken English and written English. Written English sounds okay when read aloud, but spoken English sounds vague and unclear when written down.

12. Use some graphics, if you can. Everybody loves pictures; they make it all more interesting. Before you go to court, run your graphics by a nonexpert to make sure that they are clear to the uninitiated. Experts lose the ability to see the way that lay-people do. Find someone who will see your charts the way that the jury will. Use his or her reaction to prepare your pitch for the jury.

13. If you do use displays, try to get into the courtroom during a recess to see the set-up. Decide how you are going to set up your display, taking into account the sightlines of the jury, what equipment is available, and the location of the court reporter. If you need audio visual equipment, be sure your client has made arrangements to have it there. A bit of fuss as you set up will heighten the suspense; too much looks disorganized. If you are using large poster type displays, wrap them in paper or carry them in some sort of cover. You look prepared, and it covers you if the judge should rule that you can't use them. You haven't given the defense an opening to say that you have "contaminated" the jury. But be sure that the posters will come out easily. Seal paper wrappers with masking tape.

14. Learn to gauge how crucial your testimony is to the case and tailor your testimony and demonstrations accordingly. Sometimes you are the most important witness, and other times you are just there for procedural reasons. You can usually gauge this by how you are treated beforehand. If you are given much deference and consideration, you are a key witness; make a detailed presentation. If no one is much interested in you ahead of time, you are probably not very important to the case; make a bare-bones presentation and be gone. The jury has a lot to absorb; don't clog their input ports.

15. Explain scientific terms and concepts in ordinary English. Don't dumb it down, but do translate it. Don't talk down to the jury, but make sure they understand. Analogies are very helpful. You can talk down to attorneys who are willfully obtuse. It is a ploy that they often use in the usually vain hope that the jury will identify with them. After you have been around with it a few times, you can get away with being sweetly condescending, in the spirit of trying to help. The jury will usually get mildly amused; the lawyer may not figure it out.

16. A common ploy of attorneys is to propose some outlandish scenario that explains the physical evidence, proposing that this constitutes "reasonable doubt." The urge is to pooh-pooh the whole thing, but in fact you can exploit it. Go along with it, but add more unlikely things that would be needed to explain all the evidence. "Well, yes, it could have been a motorcycle gang, but, wait, they would have had to have a key because there was no forced entry...." Keep adding things needed to meet the case until you have an absurd set of conditions. The lawyer may follow you down this path, unable to believe his luck.

17. Another strategy is for the examining attorney to repeat something you said earlier, but using slightly different language. Unless you are paying careful attention, you might miss the shift. Then he or she gets you to agree that you said that. Then it's asked again and again, each time with another slight shift, until it is not what you said at all. Be aware of this and stick to your original wording. You chose it for a reason. Tell them that.

18. Lawyers will often wave around books or articles and ask if you recognize so and so as an authority on the subject. If you do, say yes. If you don't recognize the name, or if you recognize the name, but don't consider the person an authority, say so. In any case, *demand to see the book or article*. You have a right to see it. Be polite but firm. Refuse to answer any questions based on a publication until you have seen it. The "article" may be just a prop.

19. Never rise to being baited. If you lose your cool, you have lost the case. Opposing lawyers will mount venomous personal attacks in hopes of

getting you riled. It isn't pleasant, but just take it. Remember that a lawyer doing that has no gas in his tank. It is a desperate measure. Being a woman is an advantage here because our culture does not like to see women attacked; men can also outwit this tactic by staying cool.

20. A cross-examining lawyer will sometimes try to paint you as a paid hack or a hired gun. Don't get defensive, but work into the exchange that you get paid exactly the same no matter what your findings are. Being a woman in a law enforcement agency is an advantage here, as police agencies are perceived as mostly masculine. It gives us some separation. Men will be okay, however, if they don't get defensive. Private practitioners can point out that they get hired by both sides.

21. Don't get led outside your area of expertise. Usually one lawyer or the other will object to this, but if they don't, refuse to go there. Even if you know the answer, it can open up a can of worms that you will not be able to stuff back into the can.

22. Don't volunteer information. It can get you in trouble with both sides and the judge. Let things unfold. However, if at the end of your testimony, you feel that the court has been misled, ask for one of those conferences with the judge.

23. Know the law as it pertains to your area. Never make any comments about the law in court, but be armed with information for your own protection. You will find it useful in pretrial conferences or in avoiding pitfalls in court. Some busy clients are even grateful that you can save them the work of looking up pertinent citations about getting certain evidence admitted. Knowledge of subpoena law will also be very helpful if you ever have conflicting summonses or other conflicts.

24. If you work for a government agency, don't resist being called as a witness by a defense attorney. It will not lead to any miscarriage of justice, and it will look very good on your resume.

25. Always tell the exact truth. You are an unbiased witness, so don't let yourself be seen as part of the "the team," whether prosecution or defense, plaintiff or defendant. Don't try to conceal warts on a case. This is not only honest, but also useful. Some lawyers are not prepared to deal with this. When you take that oath, really think about it and let your answer ring out, "I SO SWEAR." That will set the tone of your whole testimony.

26. Never talk to anyone you don't know about a case outside a courtroom while you are waiting to testify, or allow him or her to speak to you about it. Observers may initiate or overhear this, prompting later claims of improper discussion of a case. Once the Rule of Exclusion has been invoked, as it almost always is, it is not proper for you to discuss the case with any other potential witness.

27. Politely avoid loose jurors. They wear tags so you can pick them out, but you don't know which case that they are on. Assume it is yours. Don't get in the elevator with them, and wait till they have left the restroom. If you are seen to have any interaction with a juror, there could be a request for a mistrial. Treat jurors as you would nice people who happen to be carriers of highly contagious, incurable diseases.

28. You may discuss your findings with the opposing side if you wish and your client and the rules allow. They know about what you said from discovery and are often genuinely seeking information. I'd rather that they get the word from me than from someone who might give them gratuitous stuff that they might use against me. In civil matters, one might speak to them after notifying the client of their request. Rules and expectations for such discussions may be different in civil and criminal matters.

29. Never enter the courtroom until you are told to do so. When you arrive, get a bailiff or someone else to let the attorney know that you are there, or just wait. If you barge in, you may be in violation of the Rule of Exclusion. Then you will not be allowed to testify.

30. Fight letting your testimony sound routine and rote. It may seem to you to be routine after many times, but try not to let it sound so. It is all new to the jury. They won't be impressed if you sound bored and disinterested. The note you want to strike is, "I do this a lot because it is part of my job, and I am good at it. But I take it very seriously."

31. Never refer to yourself as an expert, and discourage others from doing so. That is a legal definition and it sounds rather pompous. Point out that designation as an expert is for the judge and jury to decide. Seeming cocky or overconfident can lose a jury in a minute.

32. When you have finished testifying, ask the judge if you may be excused. If you are simply told to stand down, you may be expected to hang around until the trial is done and you cannot discuss it with anyone. Getting yourself specifically excused lets you off the hook. When you ask the judge, make it clear you are planning to leave the building, as in "Your Honor, may I be excused to return to the laboratory?" That covers you when the cross-examining attorney remembers all the things that he forgot to ask. Some judges will remember to excuse you, so you don't have to ask.

33. Avoid staying in the courtroom after you have been excused. It makes you look like you have a stake in how the case comes out and may make you look biased. If there is an opposing expert you want to watch, get a colleague unknown to the jury to sit in and report. At times, your client cannot be talked out of having you sit in on opposing testimony, in which case you may have to comply.

34. Learn of any quirks that a particular judge may have before you testify in his or her court. Some judges favor certain phraseology and object to some wording. Knowing ahead of time can make things go more smoothly and save possible embarrassment. Do not make the judge angry. Remember that the judge is the sole arbiter of his or her court-room. If he or she wants to be unreasonable, he or she can. Mostly, though, you will find judges well disposed toward you, and helpful. They like honest, well-organized witnesses, two features that are rare to vanishing in many courtrooms.

35. Check up on lawyers that you will meet. Your colleagues can probably tell you about them. Find out anything that you can about opposing attorneys, and what they may know about your specialty.

36. All these things may sound trivial, but put yourself in the jury's shoes. They are watching a parade of witnesses presenting varying degrees of truthfulness. They have only a short time and limited data from which to decide how much weight to put on your testimony. They are going to use every clue they can find. All these suggestions will add up to make you look polished and professional. In general, juries like scientists and people who have something interesting to say. All that you have to do is not dispel that good will.

37. In dealing with attorneys before and during testimony, it is good to bear in mind that they have a fundamentally different approach to evidence from that of scientists: they are advocates. Scientists try as hard as humanly possible to remove bias from their findings; lawyers embrace it. Scientists collect data and draw a conclusion from them. Lawyers start with a conclusion and muster data to support it. Good lawyers recognize this difference and don't try to get around it. Clueless ones won't be able to understand why you won't tailor your evidence to suit their theory of the case. Stonewalling is the best way to deal with them; don't waste valuable oxygen trying to explain. They will not get it. Just say "no" to perjury.

The other very interesting difference is how lawyers and scientists view authoritative sources. Scientists accept as guiding principle the latest word on a subject that has been verified and vetted; lawyers go by the oldest precedent. You can see the conflict. If physicians were lawyers instead of scientists, we would still be worrying about whether our humors were out of balance and dressing our wounds with cow dung. Hypocrites, not the Surgeon General, would be The Man. Sooner or later, some lawyer is going to produce a moldy tome with the cover falling off and cross-examine you about how many gills of that substance you need for testing. Lead him gently into the 21st Century. Invoke your right to see the book and look at the publication date. Suggest that knowledge on the subject may have advanced since 1899 or whatever.

38.   Those are general things. Here are some specifics: Do not fall headfirst into the jury box. Do not eat something that nauseates you just before court. Try to keep insects out of your underwear. Do not tip over a cup of water so that it flows along the rail of the witness box and dribbles into your lap. Do not torch a piece of evidence on a projector so that all see and are amazed. These may all seem outlandish, but they have all happened to me, and I am still here to tell about it. So when you finish testifying and stride confidently out of the courtroom, only to find the hem of your skirt tucked into the back of the waistband of your pantyhose, it is not the end of the world. There is life after humiliation.

39.   Above all, enjoy yourself. Testifying is a chance to teach some receptive folks about our very interesting work. If the opposing counsel decides to take you on, remember this: 1. you know more about the subject than the lawyer does, 2. juries like scientists more than they like lawyers, and 3. there is no greater sport than getting an attorney all twisted around till he doesn't know whether he is coming or going and wishes that he had taken that job in quality control at the glue factory.

Index